AF782935

Publishers' Rights and Copyright Law

This book assesses the related rights of press publishers in the context of access to information and media pluralism.

Discussing Art. 15 of the Directive (EU) 2019/790 of 17 April 2019, the book looks to create balance between publishers' rights and both the protection of freedom of expression and freedom of information. With the rise of AI and an increasing interest on internet users' right to access information, the book focuses on online platforms and the dissemination of information as well as on the legal challenges posed by the use of AI to produce and disseminate news. Using the French transposition of Art. 15 as a case study and referring to its implementation in numerous Member States, the book discusses the broad picture of publishers' protection across Europe and even further, as international case studies in Australia and Canada are also discussed.

The book will be of interest to researchers in the field of media law, EU law, copyright law and freedom of information.

Michalina Kowala, of the College of Europe in Bruges and of Stanislaw Moniuszko Academy of Music in Gdańsk, defended her PhD thesis, written at the AMU of Poznań and Nantes University in 2024. Her doctoral research focused on the impact of press publishers' related rights on access to information and media pluralism. She conducted her research as a visiting researcher at numerous research centres in Europe. Michalina gained professional experience working at the European Parliament in Brussels, at the Commissioner for Human Right Office in Warsaw and at the Polish Ministry of Economic Development and Technologies during the Polish Presidency of the Council of the EU. Michalina shares her passion for music by giving solo violin concerts and participating in orchestras around Europe.

Routledge Research in Media Law

Available titles in this series include:

Public Service Broadcasting 3.0
Legal Design for the Digital Present
Mira Burri

Mediation & Popular Culture
Jennifer L. Schulz

Journalists, Anonymous Sources and the Law
A Comparative, Theoretical and Critical Analysis
Damian Carney

Public Service Media and the Law
Theory and Practice in Europe
Karen Donders

Photography and the Law
Rights and Restrictions
Michael O'Flanagan

Publishers' Rights and Copyright Law
Safeguarding Access to Information and Media Pluralism
Michalina Kowala

Publishers' Rights and Copyright Law

Safeguarding Access to Information and Media Pluralism

Michalina Kowala

Routledge
Taylor & Francis Group
LONDON AND NEW YORK

First published 2025
by Routledge
4 Park Square, Milton Park, Abingdon, Oxon OX14 4RN

and by Routledge
605 Third Avenue, New York, NY 10158

Routledge is an imprint of the Taylor & Francis Group, an informa business

© 2025 Michalina Kowala

The right of Michalina Kowala to be identified as author of this work has been asserted in accordance with sections 77 and 78 of the Copyright, Designs and Patents Act 1988.

All rights reserved. No part of this book may be reprinted or reproduced or utilised in any form or by any electronic, mechanical, or other means, now known or hereafter invented, including photocopying and recording, or in any information storage or retrieval system, without permission in writing from the publishers.

Trademark notice: Product or corporate names may be trademarks or registered trademarks, and are used only for identification and explanation without intent to infringe.

British Library Cataloguing-in-Publication Data
A catalogue record for this book is available from the British Library

ISBN: 978-1-032-97471-2 (hbk)
ISBN: 978-1-032-98590-9 (pbk)
ISBN: 978-1-003-59949-4 (ebk)

DOI: 10.4324/9781003599494

Typeset in Times New Roman
by Deanta Global Publishing Services, Chennai, India

Dla moich Rodziców

Contents

Preface

The scope of protection of press publishers and its impact on the free flow of information is a fascinating topic. This is because the adoption of publishers' rights affects users' access to information, influences the infrastructure for disseminating information and reshapes the relationship between the press sector and online platforms.

The search for an answer to the question of whether the press sector can really be strengthened by the adoption of the new law led me to interesting findings that are important for legislators, press publishers, platforms, non-governmental organisation, practitioners, researchers, law students and, above all, internet users. Although investigating publishers' rights at the time when successive Member States were adopting their implementation – and in the midst of technological transition, particularly related to the use of AI – could be seen as a challenge, the assessment of publishers' protection proved to be an intellectually exciting adventure. Its result is this monograph, which provides a comprehensive analysis of publishers' rights in the broader context of enabling the free flow of information and guaranteeing media pluralism.

I hope that the subject I am so passionate about will interest readers and that this monograph will be a source of knowledge, topics for discussion and inspiration for further reflection.

January 9, 2025
Michalina Kowala

Acknowledgements

I wish to express my sincere gratitude to my supervisor, professor Katarzyna Klafkowska-Waśniowska, for her guidance and insightful remarks.

Je tiens à remercier Madame Audrey Lebois de Nantes Université pour ses conseils et pour nos discussions passionnantes qui étaient une grande source d'inspiration pour mes recherches.

I spent nearly two of the four years of my doctoral studies abroad, undertaking research stays at numerous research centres in Europe. These experiences shaped me as a researcher. I would like to thank Prof. T. Margoni and Prof. M. C. Janssens from the Center for IT&IP Law, Prof. S. von Lewinski from the Max Planck Institute for Innovation and Competition, Dr. O. Bulayenko who welcomed me at the Center for International Intellectual Property Studies in Strasbourg and B. Brzeziński from the European Parliament for the time and guidance provided.

It would not have been possible without the scholarship of the French Government. Je voudrais remercier l'Ambassade de France en Pologne pour le soutien de mes recherches.

Dziękuję Przyjaciołom. Une pensée particulière à mes amis du Collège d'Europe à Bruges pour les moments inoubliables qu'on a passés ensemble.

Merci à Celui qui m'est cher.

Dziękuję Rodzicom, za wszystko.

List of abbreviations

AG	Advocate General
AI	Artificial Intelligence
Charter	Charter of Fundamental Rights of the European Union
Copyright and Related Rights Commission	CDADV
CJEU	Court of Justice of European Union
CDSM Directive	Directive EU 2019/790 of the European Parliament and of the Council of 17 April 2019 on copyright and related rights in the Digital Single Market and amending Directives 96/9/EC and 2001/29/EC
ECHR	European Convention on Human Rights
ECtHR	European Court of Human Rights
EMFA	Proposal for a regulation establishing a common framework for media services in the internal market, {SEC(2022) 322 final} – {SWD(2022) 286 final} – {SWD(2022) 287 final}
Et al.	Et alia (and others)
Etc.	Etcetera
EU	European Union
InfoSoc Directive	Directive 2001/29/EC of the European Parliament and of the Council of 22 May 2001 on the harmonisation of certain aspects of copyright and related rights in the information society
ISSP	Information Society Service Provider
MFA	Media Freedom Act
P.	Page
Para.	Paragraph
TDM	Text and Data Mining
TEU	Treaty on European Union
TFEU	Treaty on the Functioning of the European Union
TPM	Technological Protection Measures
TRIPS	Agreement on Trade Related Aspects of Intellectual Property Rights
WCT	WIPO Copyright Treaty
WPPT	WIPO Performances and Phonograms Treaty

Introduction

Over the past decades, a new model of information dissemination has become more common. This model is based on information society service providers[1] supplying press publications as part of news aggregation or monitoring services. For instance, Google, through its services such as Google News, provides its users with access to numerous articles from various news websites through hyperlinks, headlines and pictures that, when clicked, allow the user to read all the content on the original page. Press publishers considered such practices as unauthorised, believing they harmed their interests and further weakened the already struggling press sector.[2] In response, the related rights of press publishers have been adopted in the the "Directive (EU) 2019/790 of the European Parliament and of the Council of 17 April 2019 on copyright and related rights in the Digital Single Market"[3] with the objective of strengthening the bargain power of press publishers and rewarding their investments in producing press content.[4] The purpose was also to protect a free and pluralistic press, which is essential for ensuring citizens' access to information. The press plays a fundamental role in public debate and the proper functioning of a democratic society.[5] The new protection was intended to have an important role in ensuring access to information and safeguarding media pluralism. To this end, press publishers were granted exclusive rights to authorise or prohibit the reproduction or making available of press publications by ISSPs.

The main objective of this monograph is to discuss and assess the press publishers' rights within the specific context of access to information and media pluralism, understood as essential elements of freedom of expression and information. Analysing press publishers' rights, their holders, scope and subject matter enables an evaluation of the adopted mechanisms and identification of the missing safeguards from the perspective of achieving the objectives of publishers' protection within this context. A safeguard is understood as the mechanism or

1 Hereinafter: ISSP.

2 European Commission, *Online News Aggregation and Neighbouring Rights for News Publishers*, Ref.Ares(2017)6256585-20/12/2017, (2017), (unreleased), https://www.asktheeu.org/en/request/4776/response/15356/attach/6/Doc1.pdf, accessed: 06.11.2023.

3 Hereinafter: The CDSM Directive.

4 Recitals 54, 55 of the CDSM Directive.

5 Recitals 54, 55 of the CDSM Directive.

solution adopted "in order to protect someone or something from harm or damage"[6] to prevent undesirable effects. For the purpose of this monograph, a safeguard is a measure adopted to protect access to information and media pluralism – the elements of freedom of expression – from undesirable effects.

The choice of this monograph's research subject is justified by its topicality and importance, especially in the context of preserving access to information and media pluralism in an age in which the press and methods of information dissemination are evolving, requiring adjustments to the legal framework. This monograph is important in light of the European Union's (EU) current legislative efforts to regulate the functioning of online platforms and may serve as a guideline on how to regulate the relationship between platforms and other (weaker) entities. It discusses the challenges associated with the use of artificial intelligence (AI) to produce and disseminate news, provides an assessment of the current legal framework and proposes amendments in this context. Moreover, it will help users to better understand how press publishers' rights affect their own rights and freedoms as well as identify the benefits and risks resulting from the new law.

The research conducted holds relevance from the perspective of the current debate about striking balance among the competing interests of encouraging investment, protecting intellectual property, enabling access to information and providing effective legislation regarding online platforms. It allows for the examination of publishers' rights from the perspective of different legislations and within the broader context of access to information and media pluralism.

The research aims to provide an answer to the following main research question:

> Whether, and, if so, which, safeguards should be adopted by Member States while implementing publishers' rights in the context of the objectives of these rights which are the protection of access to information and media pluralism.

Answering the following research questions will help identify key elements that will contribute to formulating an answer to the main research question:

1) What is the scope of protection that fundamental rights provide in regard to access to information and media pluralism? To what extent were press publishers protected before the adoption of Art. 15 of the CDSM Directive? How could the relationship between press publishers and online platforms be described before the adoption of the publishers' rights?
2) What is the subject matter of protection resulting from publishers' rights, and what contribution does the press publisher, as the rights holder, make for a press publication to arise? What is the scope of the exclusive rights granted to press publishers, and what is excluded from the protection?

6 Cambridge Dictionary, "Safeguard," https://dictionary.cambridge.org/dictionary/english/safeguard, accessed: 10.01.2024.

3) What safeguards and risks can be identified based on the assessment of the publishers' rights in the context of access to information and media pluralism?
4) What are the shortcomings of the French implementation, which could potentially impact the regulation's effectiveness, especially in the context of the free flow of information and the safeguard for media pluralism? Whether the implementations of the publishers' rights in Italy, Spain, Belgium, the Czech Republic and, finally, Poland which followed the French implementation, include remedies to its shortcomings?

The research encompasses provisions from Articles 2(4) and 15 of the CDSM Directive, the French implementation of the publishers' rights adopted in 2019, which was the first in the EU, and the Polish implementation, which, adopted in 2024, was the last in the EU. Choosing to discuss these legal regimes allows for in-depth scrutiny of publishers' rights over several years. It also allows for discussion on the technological changes since the adoption of the CDSM Directive, which impacted the way press publications are used, information is disseminated and the effectiveness of publishers' protection. The discussion of the first and the last implementations of publishers' rights in the EU, enriched by many references to the implementations of Art. 15 of the CDSM in Spain, Italy, Belgium, Germany and the Czech Republic, will enable a comprehensive assessment of the said rights in this specific context. This assessment is conducted on the basis of the criteria developed through:

- the analysis of the provisions from the European Convention on Human Rights,[7] the EU Charter of Fundamental Rights[8] and case law of the European Court of Human Rights[9] and the Court of Justice of European Union.[10]
- the analysis of the safeguards resulting from the international, EU and national (Polish and French) copyright laws as well as the case law of the CJEU and national courts.

This monograph is composed of five chapters. Chapter 1, providing introductory remarks, discusses different perspectives of access to information and media pluralism in order to provide insights into the main functions of press publishers' rights. The context of fundamental rights is analysed with a focus on freedom of expression and intellectual property rights and their interconnections. Then, the legal and economic framework of press publishers' activities is examined using the Polish and French examples. Moreover, the press's role in enabling access to information and contributing to the protection of media pluralism is explained. The analysis provided in this chapter also relates to how online platforms provide news

7 Hereinafter: ECHR, Convention.
8 Hereinafter: Charter.
9 Hereinafter: ECtHR.
10 Hereinafter: CJEU.

aggregation services, impact press industry and play a role in enabling access to information and contributing to the protection of media pluralism.

Chapter 2 provides the characteristics of the related rights regime and outlines the *ratio legis* of the adoption of publishers' rights, giving a better understanding of the related rights regime on which the EU legislator based its regulation of press publishers, and sheds more light on the reasons for adopting publishers' rights. Then, it determines what is protected by the press publishers' rights and what is excluded from the protection. The legal status of press publishers as rights holders is presented. The analysis also focuses on the relationship between press publishers and the authors of works as well as other holders of rights to subject matters included in press publications.

Chapter 3 discusses the scope of the exclusive rights granted to press publishers. In addition, it describes ISSPs as the entities against which publishers' rights apply and details regarding how publishers' rights are exercised are examined. Through a case study analysingthe legal situation of press publishers in France after the adoption of related rights, the chapter identifies and assesses the shortcomings of the French implementation that could potentially impact the regulation's effectiveness, especially in the context of the free flow of information and the protection of media pluralism. Moreover, the chapter sheds more light on the mechanisms implemented in the Belgian, Spanish, Italian, German and Czech implementations of Art. 15 of the CDSM Directive designed to prevent the circumvention of the regulation. These considerations are important for the final stage of the analysis, which focuses on determining how the implementation of Art. 15 of the CDSM Directive should be structured to ensure the regulation's effectiveness, especially in preserving media pluralism and the free flow of information. The final stage of the analysis is preceded by an assessment of publishers' rights from the perspective of market realities and fundamental rights framework for access to information.

This is a study in copyright law, which regulates the protection of literary and artistic works and the related rights regime, which regulates their dissemination. It also concerns the broader area of information law. The latter regulates "the production, distribution and use of information goods and services"[11] and comprises "a wide set of legal issues at the crossroads of intellectual property, media law, telecommunications law, freedom of expression and right to privacy."[12] The study is based on an analysis of EU primary law, including the TEU, TFEU and the EU Charter of Fundamental Rights, as well as secondary law, including numerous directives on copyright and related rights. The analysis conducted also concerns national solutions adopted in Poland and France.

11 IViR, *Information Law: Expanding Horizons' IViR Research Program 2012-2016*, (2012),2-3, https://www.ivir.nl/syscontent/pdfs/80.pdf, accessed: 06.11.2023.

12 IViR, *Information*, 2–3.

Answering the research questions required the use of the formal-dogmatic research method, incorporating elements of the comparative legal method.[13] The selection of the legal systems examined (Polish, French, with elements of Spanish, Italian, Belgian, German and Czech) stems, first, from their relevance to the research being carried out and, second, is justified by the author's linguistic skills. Emphasis in the analysis are made by the author.

This book is based on the PhD dissertation defended at the Faculty of Law and Administration of Adam Mickiewicz University in Poznań, Poland on October 17, 2024. The research for this monograph was completed on January 9, 2025. Subsequent developments in relevant law are, therefore, not reflected.

13 See: I. Calboli, "Comparative legal analysis and intellectual property law: A guide for research," in *Handbook of Intellectual Property Research. Lenses, Methods and Perspectives*, ed. I. Calboli, M.L. Montagnani (Oxford University Press, 2021), 48.

1 Access to information and media pluralism in the technological, economic and legal context – introductory remarks

1. Introduction

Media pluralism has been approached from different perspectives[1] and at many layers.[2] For the purpose of the analysis conducted in this monograph, I accept the understanding of the term developed by P. Valcke, according to whom, media pluralism is defined as **plurality and "diversity of media supply, use and distribution**, in relation to 1) ownership and control, 2) media types and genres, 3) political viewpoints, 4) cultural expressions and 5) local and regional interests."[3] The definition of media pluralism is, therefore, based on several factors. The ownership and control of the media should not be concentrated in the hands of a very limited number of actors; the media should be of varying size and of different types to respond to many and diverse needs of the audience. Moreover, the media should represent a plurality of political viewpoints, contribute to cultural enrichment and satisfy global and local information needs.[4] The plurality and diversity of these factors should be ensured at the supply, use and distribution stages of media.

1 See: Council of Europe, *Pluralisme des médias et enjeux de la concurrence* (IRIS spécial, l'Observatoire européen de l'audiovisuel, 2020), 11; B. Klimkiewicz, "Is the clash of rationalities leading nowhere? Media pluralism in European Regulatory Policies," in *Press Freedom and Pluralism in Europe. Concepts and Conditions, Intellect Books*, ed. A. Czepek, M. Hellwig (ECREA, 2009), 45–48; P. Bárd, J. Bayer, *A Comparative Analysis of Media Freedom and Pluralism in the EU Member States* (European Parliament's Committee on Civil Liberties, Justice and Home Affairs, 2016) 34–36, https://www.statewatch.org/media/documents/news/2016/oct/ep-study-media-freedom-in-EU.pdf, accessed: 07.01.2022. K. Jakubowicz, "New media ecology: Reconceptualizing Media Pluralism," in *Media Pluralism and Diversity. Concepts, Risks and Global Trends*, eds. P. Valcke, M. Sükösd, R.G. Picard (Palgrave Global Media Policy and Business Series, 2015), 32.

2 P. Valcke, "Looking for the user in Media –Pluralism regulation: Unraveling the traditional diversity chain and recent trends of user empowerment in European Media Regulation," *Journal of Information Policy* 1 (2011): 287–320; K. Karppinen, "Rethinking media pluralism and communicative abundance," *McGannon Center Research Resources* 5 (2009): 1–27; E. Brogi et al., "EU and media policy: Conceptualising media pluralism in the era of online platforms. The experience of the Media Pluralism Monitor," in *Research Handbook on Media Law and Policy*, ed. P.L. Parcu, E. Brogi (Edward Elgar, 2021), 16–31.

3 P. Valcke et al., *Independent Study on Indicators for Media Pluralism in the Member States – Towards a Risk-Based Approach* (KU Leuven ICRI, 2009), 5.

4 See: Valcke, "Looking," 287–320.

DOI: 10.4324/9781003599494-1

Media pluralism should be understood in both external and internal dimensions. It means that it can be internal, with various information, opinions and interests expressed within one media organisation or one type of media, and external in nature, with an important number of media organisations or types of media.[5] The media should be understood as any means of transmission of information and entertainment,[6] taking various technical forms and being perceived by sight and hearing.[7]

The media ecosystem has evolved over past few years as the result of societal, technological and economic changes. This evolution is reflected in the emergence of new actors such as, for example, social medial platforms or news platforms[8] whose functioning is increasingly based on their algorithms[9] that recommend, prioritise and propose content.[10] D. Tambini observes that, today, everything and everyone is potentially media.[11] Given the significant expansion of means by which information is created, distributed and received, one cannot disagree with his opinion.[12]

K. Karppinen notes that the multiplicity of media and sources of information that are accessible, especially in the age of the internet, is not enough to guarantee media pluralism.[13] What matters is the "democratic distribution of communicative power in the public sphere"[14] to media organisations. In other words, the multiplicity of media should reflect different voices of the society. The internet enables the diffusion of large amounts of information. J. van Hoboken underlines that, from the perspective of media pluralism in the face of digital transformation, it is crucial

5 Council of Europe, *Pluralisme*, 11; Klimkiewicz, "Is the clash," 45–48; Bárd, Bayer, *A Comparative*, 34–36.

6 See: E. Derieux, *Le droit des médias*, 6 (Dalloz, 2019), 2.

7 K. Święcka, J.S. Święcki, "Dyferencjacje prawne pojęcia 'Media'," *Roczniki Nauk Prawnych*, 16 (2006): 458.

8 New actors replaced to some extent the traditional media. Their role has also evolved. Limited at the beginning to the service of host, intermediary or auxiliary, they have become gatekeepers and the active players in mass communication editorial process. See: Committee of Ministers, *Recommendation CM/Rec (2011) 7 of the Committee of Ministers to Member States on a New Notion of Media*, https://search.coe.int/cm/Pages/result_details.aspx?ObjectID=09000016805cc2c0, accessed: 06.01.2022.

9 Council of Europe, *Pluralisme*, 18–20.

10 The use of algorithms by online platforms is increasingly discussed in the context of the impact on media pluralism. See also: E. Brogi, "Cascading risks to media pluralism and a European approach to tackle them, Henrich Böll Stiftung," The Green Political Foundation, October 10, 2022, https://www.boell.de/en/2022/10/10/cascading-risks-media-pluralism-and-european-approach-tackle-them, accessed: 06.01.2022; I. Engelmann, S. M. Luebke, S. H. Kessler, "Effects of news factors on users' news attention and selective exposure on a news aggregator website," *Journalism Studies* 22, no. 6 (2011): 780–798; M. Poiares Maduro, F. de Abreu Duarte, "Regulating Big Tech will take pluralism and institutions," Euronews, October 7, 2021, https://www.euronews.com/2021/10/07/regulating-big-tech-will-take-pluralism-and-institutions-view, accessed: 06.01.2023.

11 D. Tambini, "A theory of Media Freedom," *Journal of Media Law* 13, no. 2 (2021): 135–152.

12 J. Oster proposes that "media" as a legal term should be broadly conceptualized. See: J. Oster, *Media Freedom as Fundamental Rigths* (Cambridge University Press, 2015), 66–67.

13 See also: P. Valcke et al., *Independent*, 42; K. Karppinen, "Rethinking," 23.

14 K. Karppinen, "Rethinking," 23.

that information that is "publicly accessible in theory, is actually visible and likely to be encountered by Internet users."[15] The **visibility and the real accessibility** of information coming from media organisations becomes an important factor in conceptualising media pluralism. The mere existence of media and the act of providing information may mean little if this information is not visible to the public and, consequently, does not reach it. In the age of digital communication and infinite information sources, gaining visibility and being able to reach audiences becomes challenging. Different media are competing to gain visibility, and they have to adapt their business models to this end.[16]

Of interest is the concept of exposure diversity, which relates to the users' dimension of media pluralism. It should be understood as the content that the audience actually chooses as opposed to the content that is available.[17] According to Ofcom, citizens should be able "to access and consume a wide range of viewpoints across a variety of platforms and media owners."[18] Therefore, what really proves that the media are pluralistic is not the amount of information that potentially circulates, but **the amount and variety of information that can actually be accessed and consumed** by the user. P. M. Napoli notes that exposure diversity can be understood "horizontally through the distribution of audiences across all available content options, or vertically through the diversity of content consumption within individual audience members."[19] P. Valcke points out that measuring the exposure diversity, setting the precise policy goals and regulating this issue may, however, be complicated.[20]

The media disseminates information, ideas or opinions. Traditionally, it acts as a public watchdog and provides a forum for public debate.[21] The media plays the role of intermediaries and gatekeepers of communication flow; they are an essential medium for the creation and distribution of information. The more numerous and diverse the media are, the greater the opportunities for society to receive information. The existence of pluralistic media is a prerequisite for ensuring public

15 J. van Hoboken, "Search engines, pluralism and diversity: What is at stake and how to move policy forward," in *Media Pluralism and Diversity. Concepts, Risks and Global Trends*, ed. P. Valcke, M. Sükösd, R.G. Picard (Palgrave Global Media Policy and Business Series, 2015), 343.

16 See: N. Helberger, "Diversity label: Exploring the potential and limits of a transparency approach to media diversity," *Journal of Information Policy 1* (2011): 337–369.

17 See: N. Helberger, K. Karpinen, L. d'Acunto, "Exposure diversity as a design principle for recommender systems," *Information, Communication & Society* 21, no. 2 (2018): 191–207.

18 Ofcom, *Measuring Media Plurality Ofcom's Advice to the Secretary of State for Culture, Olympics, Media and Sport*, https://www.ofcom.org.uk/__data/assets/pdf_file/0031/57694/measuring-media-plurality.pdf, 8, accessed: 01.04.2023.

19 P.M. Napoli, "Deconstructing the diversity principle," *Journal of Communicatio*n 49, no. 4 (1999): 26.

20 P. Valcke, "Looking," 287–320; See also: N. Helberger, "Merely facilitating or actively stimulating diverse media choices? Public service media at the crossroad," *International Journal of Communication* 9, (2015): 1324–1340.

21 See: Committee of Ministers, *Recommendation CM/Rec (2018) of the Committee of Ministers to Member States on Media Pluralism and Transparency of Media Ownership*, https://search.coe.int/cm/Pages/result_details.aspx?ObjectId=0900001680790e13, accessed: 06.01.2023.

access to information, which, for the purpose of this book, is understood as the possibility of receiving information. The possibility means that the information is accessible and visible, and the audience is able[22] to consult it. Information is understood as knowledge about someone or something or facts or details about a subject[23] that can be either communicated as pure reporting of facts or transformed into an element of artistic or literary expression that qualifies as a work under copyright law. Information, in both mentioned forms, reaches its audience through the media as mere facilitators of communication.[24]

The main objective of the first chapter is to provide insights into the functioning of the main areas affected by the related rights of press publishers that were adopted in the CDSM Directive. The analysis conducted in this chapter will serve as a reference and as a starting point for many considerations carried out in the later stages of my research as regards, for example, the reasons for adopting publishers' rights, the way in which it has been done, the objectives of the regulation, the scope and subject matter of protection and its exercise; it will also facilitate an assessment of those aspects from different perspectives already explored here.

2. Fundamental rights

2.1. Media pluralism, access to information and protection of fundamental rights

2.1.1. The European Convention on Human Rights

According to Art. 10 (1) of the ECHR:

> Everyone has the right to freedom of expression. This right shall include freedom to hold opinions and **to receive and impart information** and ideas without interference by public authority and regardless of frontiers. This article shall not prevent States from requiring the licensing of broadcasting, television or cinema enterprises.

Freedom to receive and impart information is explicitly indicated as an element of right to freedom of expression, sometimes called "passive freedom of information."[25]

An important part of the ECtHR's case law regarding this right is devoted to freedom of access to information in the context of access to documents and

22 The issue of availability of technical means to have access to online information is another important problem in the context of media pluralism which will not be further discussed in this dissertation.

23 The Britannica Dictionary, https://www.britannica.com/dictionary/information, accessed: 01.04.2023.

24 See: J. Oster, *Media*, 57.

25 Ch. Grabenwarter, *Article 10: Freedom of Expression. European Convention on Human Rights: Commentary* (Bloomsbury Academic, 2013), 256.

administrative procedures.[26] Access to information expressed through the media is evoked by the ECtHR more occasionally.[27] Nevertheless, it remains a significant element, and this perspective will be examined further.[28]

Everyone who has the right to freedom of expression is understood broadly as natural but also legal persons.[29] Therefore, citizens as well as media service providers and press publishers have a right to access information. The particular emphasis in this research is on the perspective of internet users' access to information, but this perspective is not of an exclusive nature.

The said freedom relates to the media's mission to inform the public.[30] The task of imparting information and ideas should be read in conjunction with the right of the public to receive them.[31] Freedom to receive and impart information protects not only the passive behaviours of receiving information but also the effort to acquiring it,[32] limited, however, to information that is "publicly accessible."[33] As to the latter, S. Eskens, N. Helberger and J. Moeller specify that the right to receive information does not mean "a general subjective right of news consumers to request specific information from the government, let alone from news organisations."[34] **It should be understood as the right to access information that is available to the public.**

The media should be pluralistic to allow all ideas and information to be expressed freely. Although media pluralism is not explicitly mentioned in the provision from Art. 10 of the ECHR, its significant contribution to freedom of expression has been widely recognised.[35] The Council of Europe and its advisory committees considered[36] media pluralism as "the most important tool for freedom of expression in the public sphere, enabling people to exercise their right to seek and receive

26 See for example: ECtHR, Társaság a Szabadságjogokért v. Hungary, 37374/05, April 14, 2009; ECtHR, Kenedi v. Hungary, 31475/05, May 26, 2009.

27 R. Bustos Gisbert, "The right to freedom of expression in a democratic society (Art. 10 ECHR)," in *Europe of Rights: A Compendium on the European Convention of Human Rights*, ed. J. G. Roca, P. Santolaya, Martinus (Nijhoff Publishers, 2012), 386.

28 See: ECtHR, Guerra and others v. Italy, 116/1996/735/932, February 19, 1998, para. 53; ECtHR, Cengiz and others v. Turkey, 48226/10 and 14027/11, December 1, 2015.

29 ECtHR, Autronic AG v. Switzerland, 12726/87, May 22, 1990.

30 S. Eskens, N. Helberger, J. Moeller, "Challenged by news personalisation: Five perspectives on the right to receive information," *Journal of Media Law* 9, no. 2 (2017): 262. See: J. Oster, *Media,* 36–37.

31 ECtHR, Worm v Austria, 83/1996/702/894, August 29, 1997, para. 50; ECtHR, Handyside v United Kingdom, 5493/72, December 7, 1976, para. 52.

32 Ch. Grabenwarter, *Article 10*, 256.

33 See: ECtHR, Guerra and others v. Italy, paras. 52–53.

34 S. Eskens, N. Helberger, J. Moeller, "Challenged", 262. See: A. Strowel, F. Tulkens, "Freedom of expression and copyright under civil law: Of balance, adaptation, and access," in *Copyright and Free Speech* (Oxford University Press, 2005) 291.

35 According to J. van Hoboken: "Diversity and pluralism are among the most fundamental normative starting points for the regulation of the media and the public information environment more generally." See: J van Hoboken, "Search," 341.

36 Recommendations and declarations of the Council of Europe and its advisory committees are of non-binding nature for Member States.

information."[37] Media freedom and pluralism are considered to be central to the functioning of a democratic society, as they help to ensure the availability and accessibility of diverse information and views from which individuals can form and express their opinions and exchange information and ideas.[38]

The ECtHR reaffirmed the essential role of media pluralism in the functioning of a democratic society and considered it as a corollary of the fundamental right to freedom of expression.[39]

The particular importance in disseminating information and ideas on matters of public interests has been attached to the press.[40] The court underlined that the press plays a "vital role of 'public watchdog'"[41] and that freedom of the press "affords the public one of the best means of discovering and forming an opinion of the ideas and attitudes of political leaders and on other matters of general interest."[42] In Társaság a Szabadságjogokért's case, the ECtHR noted that "The function of press includes the creation of forums for public debate."[43] However, according to the court, the realisation of this function should not be limited, for example, only to professional journalists.[44]

In recent cases, the court focused on the legal qualification of "new media." The "advent of new information technology" has necessitated the expansion of freedom of expression protections, originally directed toward traditional media, to encompass "new electronic media."[45] The increasing role of online platforms – new actors in the media ecosystem[46] – in disseminating content and facilitating access to information has been acknowledged[47] as well as the importance of users' participation in the production of content, so-called "citizen journalism."[48]

The fundamental right to freedom of expression is not absolute and can be subject to restrictions according to Art. 2 of the ECHR. National authorities, in specific cases and when all requirements are met, are, therefore, authorised to interfere with the right in question. The legal framework of such an interference will be discussed in detail in Section 2.5. of this chapter.

37 Committee of Ministers, *Recommendation CM/Rec (2011) 7.*
38 Committee of Ministers, *Recommendation CM/Rec (2018) 1.*
39 See: ECtHR, Handyside v. the United Kingdom, para. 49; ECtHR. See also: E. Komorek, *Media Pluralism and European Law* (Wolters Kluwer Law & Business, 2013), 63; E. Barendt, *Freedom of Speech* (Oxford University Press, 2005), 447.
40 See for example: ECtHR, Guerra and others v. Italy, para. 53.
41 ECtHR, Observer and Guardian v. The United Kingdom, 13585/88, November 26, 1991, para. 59.
42 ECtHR, Lingens v. Austria, 9815/82, July 8, 1986, para. 42.
43 ECtHR, Társaság a Szabadságjogokért v. Hungary, para. 27.
44 ECtHR, Társaság a Szabadságjogokért v. Hungary, para. 27.
45 ECtHR, OOO Regnum v. Russia, 22649/08, September 8, 2020, para. 60. See also: ECtHR, Magyar Jeti Zrt v. Hungary, 11257/16, December 4, 2018, para.70; see also: ECtHR, Delfi AS v. Estonia [GC], 64569/09, June 16, 2015.
46 See: S. Eskens, N. Helberger, J. Moeller, "Challenged," 260.
47 ECtHR, Cengiz and Others v. Turkey, para. 52.
48 ECtHR, Cengiz and Others v. Turkey, para. 52.

2.1.2. Charter of Fundamental Rights of the European Union

According to Art. 11 of the Charter:

> 1. Everyone has the right to freedom of expression. This right shall include freedom to hold opinions and to receive and impart information and ideas without interference by public authority and regardless of frontiers.
> 2. The freedom and pluralism of the media shall be respected.

The provision mirrors Art. 10 of the ECHR with one exception: in the second paragraph of Art. 11 of the Charter, there is a direct reference to the freedom and pluralism of the media. The absence of reference to media pluralism in Art. 10 of the ECHR could be explained by the fact that, in the period preceding the adoption of the Convention, no specific threats to media diversity were identified. It is with the authorisation of privately owned television and the danger of the monopolisation of the flow of information that the need to protect media diversity was expressed explicitly and put on the equal footing with free expression and the free flow of information in the Charter.[49]

Provisions from the Charter should be interpreted in accordance with the provision from the ECHR and case law of the ECtHR, as according to Art. 52 (3) of the Charter:

> in so far as this Charter contains rights which correspond to rights guaranteed by the Convention for the Protection of Human Rights and Fundamental Freedoms, the meaning and scope of those rights shall be the same as those laid down by the said Convention. This provision shall not prevent Union law providing more extensive protection.

The CJEU, in 2019, confirmed that Art. 11 of the Charter should be given the "same meaning and the same scope" as Art. 10 of the ECHR and should be interpreted in light of the case law of the ECtHR.[50]

The CJEU, like the ECtHR, delivered a broad interpretation of notions relating to the freedom of expression, in particular, of the media.[51] The Court noted that "whether it be classic in nature, such as paper or radio waves, or electronic, such as the internet, is not determinative"[52] as to whether an activity is solely for journalistic purposes.[53] Every activity with the "object [of] the disclosure to the public of information, opinions or ideas, irrespective of the medium which is used to

49 Commissioner for Human Rights, *Media Pluralism and Human Rights* (Strasbourg, 2011), 7–8, https://rm.coe.int/16806da515, accessed: 01.03.2023.

50 CJEU, Sergejs Buivids v. Datu valsts inspekcija, Case C–345/17, February 14, 2019, para. 65.

51 See: CJEU, Tietosuojavaltuutettu v Satakunnan Markkinapörssi Oy and Satamedia Oy, Case C-73/07, December 16, 2008, para. 56.

52 CJEU, Satamedia, para. 79.

53 European Commission, *Study on Media Plurality* (Publication Office of the European Union, 2022), 12–13, https://op.europa.eu/en/publication-detail/-/publication/475bacb6-34a2-11ed-8b77-01aa75ed71a1/language-en/format-PDF/source-266738523, accessed: 02.03.2023.

transmit them"[54] should be considered as an activity important from the perspective of forming public debate and providing the public with access to information. The particular importance of the press in disseminating information and ideas on matters of public interests resounded also in its judgements. In *Familiapress v. Bauer Verlag*, the CJEU held that "press diversity helps to safeguard freedom of expression."[55]

The rights protected under Art. 11 of the Charter are not absolute and can be limited according to Art. 52(1) of the Charter. Any limitation on the exercise of the rights and freedoms recognised by this Charter must be provided for by law and respect the essence of those rights and freedoms. Subject to the principle of proportionality, limitations may be made only if they are necessary and genuinely meet objectives of general interest recognised by the EU or the need to protect the rights and freedoms of others. Interference with these rights is authorised when the mentioned requirements are met.[56]

To conclude:

- following the analysis of the ECHR, the Charter and the case law of the ECtHR and the CJEU, the core of the right to receive information **is the public's right to be adequately informed**, particularly on matters of public interest, which means that public has the right to access information that is available, and this access cannot be limited in an unjustified manner.
- the right of the public to be adequately informed is linked to the role of the media, which is to impart such information and ideas to the public. The media should be pluralistic to allow all ideas and information to be expressed freely.

2.2. *Intellectual property rights and protection of fundamental rights*

2.2.1. *European Convention on Human Rights*

According to Art. 1 of the Protocol to the Convention for the Protection of Human Rights and Fundamental Freedoms:

> Every natural or legal person is entitled to the peaceful enjoyment of his possessions. No one shall be deprived of his possessions except in the public interest and subject to the conditions provided for by law and by the general principles of international law. The preceding provisions shall not, however, in any way impair the right of a State to enforce such laws as it deems necessary to control the use of property in accordance with the general interest or to secure the payment of taxes or other contributions or penalties.

54 CJEU, Satamedia, para. 80.
55 CJEU Familiapress v. Bauer Verlag, Case C-368/95, June 26, 1997, para. 18.
56 See Section 2.5. of this chapter.

According to the ECtHR:

> the concept of "possessions" referred to in the first part of Article 1 of Protocol No. 1 has an autonomous meaning which is not limited to the ownership of physical goods and is independent from the formal classification in domestic law: certain other rights and interests constituting assets can also be regarded as "property rights", and thus as "possessions" for the purposes of this provision.[57]

This means that intangible goods are protected as property, and this also applies, for example, to copyright.[58] The term *possessions* can refer to either existing possessions or assets, including claims, for which the applicant has at least a legitimate expectation of effectively enjoying property rights.[59]

Scholars expressed different views as to the qualification of intellectual property rights as fundamental rights. C. Geiger considered it as an important development.[60] For P. Yu, "the inclusion in the human rights debate of a relatively trivial item like intellectual property protection would undermine the claim that human rights are of fundamental importance to humanity."[61] Concerns have also been raised that the right in question may have an overly broad reach, bordering on an absolute right.[62] It should be pointed out, however, that the right from Art. 1 of the Protocol to the ECHR is not an absolute right, and this is confirmed by both the wording of the provision and the case law of the ECtHR.[63] There is no hierarchy of

57 ECtHR, Anheuser-Busch Inc. v. Portugal, 73049/01, January 11, 2007, para. 63.

58 ECtHR, Dima v. Romania, 58472/00, May 26, 2005, para. 87. For the historical context of copyright understood within the property perspective see: C. Sganga, "EU copyright law between property and fundamental rights: A proposal to connect the dots," in *Balancing Copyright Law in the Digital Age. Comparative Perspectives*, ed. R. Caso, F. Giovanella (Springer, 2015), 1–24.

59 ECtHR, Kopecký v. Slovakia, 44912/98, September 28, 2004, para. 35.

60 See: Ch. Geiger, E. Izyumenko, "Shaping intellectual property rights through human rights adjudication: The example of the European Court of Human Rights," *Mitchell Hamline Law Review* 46, no. 3 (2020): 527–612; Ch. Geiger, "The constitutional dimension of intellectual property," in *Intellectual Property and Human Rights. Enhanced Edition pf Copyright and Human Rights*, ed. P.L.C. Torremans (Information Law Series, Kluwer Law International, 2008) 114–120; Ch. Geiger, "Constitutionalising intellectual property law? The influence of fundamental rights on intellectual property in the European Union," *II-C International Review of Intellectual Property in the European Union* 37, no. 4 (2006): 268–280.

61 P. Yu, "Ten common questions about intellectual property and human rights," *Texas A&M University School of Law* 23, no. 7 (2007): 713–714, https://scholarship.law.tamu.edu/cgi/viewcontent.cgi?article=1385&context=facscholar, accessed: 24.03.2023. For the critical view see also: J. Griffiths, "L. McDonagh, fundamental rights and european intellectual property law: The case of Art 17(2) of the EU Charter," in *Constructing European Intellectual Property: Achievements and New Perspectives*, ed. Ch. Geiger (Edward Elgar Publishing, 2013), 75.

62 See: P. Yu, "Challenges to the development of a human-rights framework for intellectual property," in *Intellectual Property and Human Rights. Enhanced Edition of Copyright and Human Rights*, ed. P.LC. Torremans (Kluwer Law International, 2008), 80–81.

63 See for example: ECtHR, Ashby Donald and others v. France, 36769/08, January 10, 2013.

the rights and freedoms protected by the Convention,[64] meaning that no right takes precedence over another right.

2.2.2. *Charter of Fundamental Rights of the European Union*

According to Art. 17 of the Charter:

> (1) Everyone has the right to own, use, dispose of and bequeath his or her lawfully acquired possessions. No one may be deprived of his or her possessions, except in the public interest and in the cases and under the conditions provided for by law, subject to fair compensation being paid in good time for their loss. The use of property may be regulated by law in so far as is necessary for the general interest. (2) Intellectual property shall be protected.

Contrary to the provision from Art. 1 of the Protocol to the ECHR, in Art. 17 (2) of the Charter, the explicit protection of intellectual property was recognised because of "its growing importance and Community secondary legislation."[65] Despite this difference in wording, the ECHR, connected to the interpretation of the Charter, set the minimum standard of protection, which "does not prevent the EU from providing more extensive protection."[66] According to the CJEU, intellectual property rights are designated to fulfil certain social goals.[67] Their existence is for economic reasons, namely the necessity to protect the investments,[68] economic interests of authors and other entities disseminating art,[69] justifying the recognition of intellectual property rights within the framework of fundamental rights and principles.

Attention should be paid to the wording of the provision from Art. 17 (2) of the Charter. According to the latter, intellectual property shall be protected. The legislature did not specify who has the rights or their scope. It limited itself to a

64 See: Ch. Geiger, "The constitutional," 115. See: P. Ducoulombier, "Interaction between human rights: Are all human rights equal?," in *Research Handbook on Human Rights and Intellectual Property*, ed. Ch. Geiger (Edward Elgar Publishing, 2016), 39–69.

65 Explanations relating to the Charter of Fundamental Rights, OJ C 303, December 14, 2007, https://eur-lex.europa.eu/legal-content/EN/TXT/?uri=CELEX:32007X1214, (01), accessed: 24.03.2023.

66 T. Mylly, "Regulating with rights proportionality? Copyright, fundamental rights, and internet in the case law of the CJEU," in *Copyright versus (Other) Fundamental Rights in the Digital Age. A Comparative Analysis in Search of a Common Constitutional Ground*, ed. O. Pollicino, G.M. Riccio and M. Bassini (Edward Elgar Publishing, 2020), 57; see also: P.L.C. Torremans, "Copyright as a human right," in *Intellectual Property Law and Human Rights*, ed. P.L.C. Torremans (Kluwer Law International, 2015), 233.

67 CJEU, Martin Luksan v. Petrus van der Let, case C-277/10, 02.02.2012, para. 68. See: A. Peukert, "Intellectual property as an end in itself?," *European Intellectual Property Review* 33 (2011): 67–71.

68 CJEU, Metronome Musik and Music Point Hokamp GmbH, Case C- 200/96, April 28, 1998.

69 CJEU, Phil Collins and Imtrat Handelsgesellschaft mbH, Case C-92/92 and C-326/92, 20 October 1993; see: A. Strowel, "Copyright strengthened by the Court of Justice interpretation of art. 17 (2) of the EU Charter of Fundamental Rights," in *Copyright versus (Other) Fundamental Rights in the Digital Age. A Comparative Analysis in Search of a Common Constitutional Ground*, ed. O. Pollicino, G. M. Riccio and M. Bassini (Edward Elgar Publishing, 2020), 28–53.

general statement. This is a principle of legal protection.[70] In practice, it means that the provision discussed does not confer any rights, does not entitle individuals to establish titles of protection, or provide an independent basis for determining the scope of ownership rights. It does, however, offer the possibility of extending the scope of protection to new entities.

It should be specified that, on the basis of this provision, intellectual property does not enjoy weaker protection compared to the protection granted in Art. 17 (1) of the Charter, as the EU legislature considers intellectual property to be property – subject to the protection under provision from Art. 17(1) of the Charter.[71] Art. 17(2) of the Charter implies an obligation to protect intellectual property, which is addressed to EU bodies and Member States. So far, this obligation does not translate into an obligation for other entities to prevent third parties from infringing the exclusive rights of right holders.[72] Although, in Art. 17 (2) of the Charter, the limitations to which other forms of property are subjected in Art. 17 (1) are not indicated, it should be assumed that they also apply to intellectual property. According to A. Ohly, "all rules and principles that govern the protection of property in tangible subject-matter will apply *mutatis mutandis* to intellectual property as well."[73] In this vein, the provision from Art. 17 (2) of the Charter should be considered as a specification of Art. 17 (1) of the Charter.

In the Charter, as in the ECHR, there is no hierarchy for rights and freedoms. The protection resulting from intellectual property rights is not absolute and may be limited in specific cases to balance different interests at stake.

To conclude:

- the provision from Art. 1 of the Protocol to the Convention does not include an explicit reference to intellectual property rights. It does not follow directly from the provision that intangible goods, such as copyrighted works, fall within the scope of possessions. However, the concept of "possessions," referred to in the first part of Art. 1 of Protocol No. 1, has an autonomous meaning, so intangible goods are protected as property, and this applies to intellectual property.
- the explicit protection of intellectual property has been recognised in Art. 17(2) of the Charter as a principle. In practice, this means that this provision does not confer any rights, entitle individuals to establish titles of protection,

70 D. Miąsik, I. Ziulczyk-Nierubca. „Komentarz do art. 17 Karty Praw Podstawowych UE," *Karta Praw Podstawowych Unii Europejskiej. Komentarz*, ed. A. Wróbel (Legalis, 2020), points 48–62.

71 See: E. Hancox, "The relationship between the charter and general principles: Looking back and looking forward," *Cambridge Yearbook of European Legal Studies* (Cambridge University Press, 2020), https://www.cambridge.org/core/journals/cambridge-yearbook-of-european-legal-studies/article/relationship-between-the-charter-and-general-principles-looking-back-and-looking-forward/A211AA0828910B38002F4B4805410223, accessed: 18.12.2023.

72 See: D. Miąsik, I. Ziulczyk-Nierubca, "Komentarz," points 48–62.

73 A. Ohly, "European fundamental rights and intellectual property," in *The Europeanization of Intellectual Property Law*, A. Ohly, ed. J. Pila (Oxford University Press, 2013), 151.

or provide an independent basis for determining the scope of ownership rights. It does, however, offer the possibility of extending the scope of protection.

2.3 Balancing fundamental rights

Fundamental rights do not exist independently; they interact with each other. They can be compatible, pursuing a common goal. D. Gervais notes that, according to this compatibility model, "both sets of rights strive towards the same fundamental equilibrium"[74] by dealing with different, specific aspects of "multi-facet public interest."[75] This complementarity reinforces the mutual claims, with copyright focusing on the materialisation of creative expression and freedom of expression, ensuring its circulation and accessibility to the public.[76] E. Derclaye explains that the rights aim to "strike the right balance between giving an incentive to create and innovate whilst insuring the public has sufficient access to such creations and inventions."[77] According to H. C. Jehoram, "copyright is one of the oldest means of securing freedom of expression and information,"[78] which could lead to the conclusion that the instruments of copyright law can be used to pursue objectives related to freedom of expression, such as protecting media pluralism and improving access to information.

The interaction between fundamental rights may take also the form of **conflict**. Especially now, in a time of rapid technological development, copyright becomes more economically centred[79] what in consequence may hamper the achievement of the goals set by freedom of expression.[80] According to Ch. Angelopoulos, "this would understand human rights and intellectual property law as mutually incompatible, so that, in every interaction between them, compliance with one would

74 D. Gervais, "Intellectual property and human rights: Learning to live together," in *Intellectual Property and Human Rights*, enhanced edition of *Copyright and Human Rights,* ed. P.L.C. Torremans (Kluwer Law International,2008), 3

75 G. Spina Ali, "Intellectual property and human rights: A taxonomy of their interactions," *International Review of Intellectual Property and Competition Law (IIC)* 51, no. 4 (2020): 435.

76 See: G. Spina Ali, "Intellectual," 411–445.

77 E. Derclaye, "Intellectual property rights and human rights: Coinciding and cooperating," in *Intellectual Property and Human Rights*, enhanced edition of *Copyright and Human Rights,* ed. P.L.C. Torremans (Kluwer Law International, 2008),134.

78 H.C. Jehoram, "Freedom of expression in copyright and media law," *GRUR Int.* (1983): 385; see also: B.J. Jütte, "The beginning of a (happy?) relationship: Copyright and freedom of expression in Europe," *European Intellectual Property Review* 38, no. 1 (2016): 11–22.

79 B.J. Jütte, "The beginning," 11–22.

80 See: S. Dormont, "L'élaboration de la norme en droit d'auteur : les discours sur la légitimité," *Légipresse*, no. 62, (2019): 79–87; A. Peukert, "Intellectual," 67–71; H.G. Ruse-Khan, "Overlaps and conflict norms in human rights law: Approaches of European courts to address intersections with intellectual property rights," in *Research Handbook on Human Rights and Intellectual Property,* ed. Ch. Geiger (Edward Elgar Publishing, 2016), 70–88. Opposing view is presented by E. Derclaye in: E. Derclaye, "Intellectual," 134; G. Spina Ali, "Intellectual," 424–425.

result in the violation of the other."[81] For example, seeking to broaden the scope of the authors ' rights and to strengthen their protection may result in rendering the access of audience to artistic or journalistic expressions more difficult.

A third conceptual framework regarding the relationship between fundamental rights merge the two already discussed.[82] The protection resulting from the intellectual property rights and freedom of expression may both be complementary and conflicting depending on goal pursued.

To conclude:

- legislation on copyright could pursue the objectives specific to the field of freedom of expression, such as protecting media pluralism or improving access to information. However, the interaction between protection resulting from fundamental rights may take also the form of conflict or may both be complementary and conflicting depending on the goal pursued.

2.4. Obligation to respect and to protect fundamental rights

Protection of fundamental rights is enshrined in the ECHR and the Charter. Provisions from the ECHR are addressed to contracting parties – the States[83] – while the provisions of the Charter apply to the institutions, bodies, offices and agencies of the EU with due regard for the principle of subsidiarity. They also apply to the Member States, but only when they are implementing EU law.[84]

The ECHR guarantees protection from unjustified interference by States. According to D. Voorhoof, it provides "a qualified prohibition for the States and public authorities to interfere."[85] However, in some specific cases, interference with fundamental rights is inevitable and does occur. The criteria for such interference will be discussed in detail in Section 2.5. of this chapter.

In addition to the obligation to respect fundamental rights, an obligation to protect fundamental rights can be extracted from the Convention. According to Art. 1 of the ECHR: "The High Contracting Parties shall secure to everyone within their jurisdiction the rights and freedoms defined in Section I of this Convention." The scope of the positive obligation to adopt measures of protection is **limited**. According to ECtHR case law, this role does not extend to guaranteeing "freedom of forum"[86] or access to a particular medium/service.[87] As to the intellectual

81 Ch. Angelopoulos, "European copyright and human rights in the digital sphere," in Human Rights, *Digital Society in the digital sphere*, ed. M. Susi (Routledge, 2019), 243–245.

82 See: Ch. Angelopoulos, "European," 243–245.

83 See Art. 1 of the Convention.

84 See Art. 51.1 of the Charter.

85 D. Voorhoof, *Critical Perspectives on the Scope and Interpretation of Art. 10 of the European Convention on Human Rights* (Strasbourg: Council of Europe Press, 1995), 54.

86 ECtHR, Appleby & Others v. the United Kingdom, 44306/98, May 6, 2002, para. 47.

87 ECtHR, Haider v. Austria, no. 25060/94, October 18, 1995. See also: ECtHR, Melnychuk v. Ukraine, Decision of inadmissibility of the European Court of Human Rights (Second Section) of July 5, 2005.

property rights, P. K. Yu notes that States have an obligation to fully realise the right to the protection of interests in intellectual creations, but he points out that "this ability to fulfil these obligations is often limited by the resources available to them and the competing demands of the core minimum obligations of other human rights."[88]

Amongst the measures that could be undertaken, the adoption of legislation or various policy measures should be indicated. The adopted measures should not interfere with fundamental rights, and if so, this interference should be justified.[89] The State may be held responsible for not fulfilling its obligation to enact domestic legislation if such failure results in unjustified interference with fundamental rights.[90] The effect of the ECHR in conflicts between individuals is indirect, meaning that individuals can enforce human rights provisions against others by relying on the State's positive obligation to protect their rights.[91] In *Özgür Gündem v. Turkey*, the ECtHR held that "Genuine, effective exercise of (the right to freedom of expression) does not depend merely on the State's duty not to interfere, but may require positive measures of protection, even in the sphere of **relations between individuals**."[92] Therefore, in the case of a violation of fundamental rights by private parties, States can be considered as answerable for any violation if they fail to act and do not undertake the preventive measures.[93]

The obligation not to interfere with fundamental rights unless justified also arises from Art. 51(1) of the Charter. The bodies to which the Charter is addressed shall respect the rights, which can be understood as an obligation not to interfere with fundamental rights. According to the same provision, the enumerated bodies shall "observe the principles and promote the application thereof in accordance with their respective powers and respecting the limits of the powers of the Union as conferred on it in the Treaties."

The question arises whether the obligation "to observe the principles and promote the application thereof" could be considered as a positive obligation for EU institutions and Member States to act to protect the fundamental rights. It should be noted that according to Art. 51 of the Charter, read in conjunction with Art. 52, the level of protection granted in the Convention should be the same as in the Charter. It applies also to the jurisprudence of the ECtHR.[94] Therefore, because the positive obligations to protect fundamental rights result from the provisions of Convention, they apply also to the addressees of the provisions included in the

88 P.K. Yu, "Challenges," 81.
89 See Section 2.5 of this chapter.
90 ECtHR, Verein gegen Tierfabriken Schweiz v. Switzerland, 24699/94, June 28, 2001.
91 L. Zwaak, "General survey of the European Convention" in *Theory and practice of the European Convention on Human Rights,* ed. P. van Dijk, F. van Hoof, A. van Rijn, L. Zwaak (Intersentia, 2018), 15.
92 ECtHR, Özgür Gündem v. Turkey, 23144/93, March 16, 2000, para. 43.
93 See also: ECtHR, Remuszko v. Poland, 1562/10, October 16, 2013.
94 CJEU, Sergejs Buivids, para. 65.

Charter. The conclusion is that, although the doctrine of positive obligations could be considered as less developed under the Charter,[95] the scope of its application encompasses both negative and positive obligations. As to the latter, it should be justified by the requirement of effective protection of the EU law, including the rights enshrined in the Charter, which results from Art. 4(3) TUE and 19(1) TUE as well as from the CJEU's interpretation.

In Coty Germany case, the CJEU formulated a requirement that Member States ensure the effective exercise of fundamental rights.[96] The effective protection of fundamental rights needs to be exercised without undue limitation. However, according to the CJEU, a fair balance has to be struck between fundamental rights that must be reconciled.[97] The positive obligation to ensure effective exercise of the fundamental rights under the Charter applies not only to Member States when implementing EU law but also to EU itself when acting as a legislator. This is confirmed by the CJEU's interpretation in the *Kadi I* case, which states that "all Community acts must respect fundamental rights, that respect constituting a condition of their lawfulness which it is for the Court to review in the framework of the complete system of legal remedies established by the Treaty."[98]

The issue of the Charter's horizontal effect remains the subject of ongoing debate. For some scholars, private parties are not enumerated amongst the entities to whom the provisions of this Charter are addressed to and, therefore, the provisions of the Charter cannot be the source of horizontal effects.[99] On the other hand, the Charter has the status of primary EU law, bearing the same legal values as the Treaties,[100] meaning that it should be capable of being invoked horizontally if the necessary conditions are met.[101]

95 A. Kuczerawy, *Private Enforcement of Public Policy: Freedom of Expression in the Era of Online Gatekeeping* (KU Leuven, 2018), 147, https://www.kuleuven.be/doctoraatsverdediging/fiches/3H13/3H130125.htm, accessed: 31.03.2023.

96 M. Husovec, "Intellectual property rights and integration by conflict: The past, present and future," in *Cambridge Yearbook of European Legal Studies* (Cambridge University Press, 2016): 257.

97 CJEU, Coty Germany GmbH v Stadtsparkasse Magdeburg, case C-580/13, July 16, 2015, para. 35.

98 CJEU, Yassin Abdullah Kadi and Al Barakaat International Foundation v Council of the European Union and Commission of the European Communities (Kadi I), Joined cases C-402/05 P and C-415/05 P, September 3, 2008, para. 285.

99 K. Lenaerts, "Exploring the limits of the EU Charter of Fundamental Rights," *European Constitutional Law Review* 8, no. 3 (2012): 377.

100 Art. 6(1) of TEU.

101 See: D. Leczykiewicz, "Horizontal application of the charter of fundamental rights," *European Law Review* 4, (2013), https://papers.ssrn.com/sol3/papers.cfm?abstract_id=2328175, accessed: 31.03.2023; E. Frantziou, "The horizontal effect of the Charter of Fundamental Rights of the EU: Rediscovering the reasons for horizontality," *European Law Journal* 21, no. 5 (2015): 657–679.

To conclude:

- according to the ECHR, there is an obligation to respect fundamental rights and an obligation to protect fundamental rights. The obligation to secure fundamental rights means that States have the obligation to take necessary measures to enable the effective enjoyment of the rights, safeguarding the rights of individuals. The ECtHR considers the State as the ultimate guarantor of the principle of pluralism. However, technological development affecting the media landscape have altered the framework for State engagement in this context. The growing role of private actors, particularly intermediaries such as online platforms, in the flow of information has become increasingly important.
- the obligation not to interfere with fundamental rights unless the interference is justified also from the Charter. The positive obligation to ensure effective exercise of the fundamental rights under the Charter applies to Member States when implementing the EU law and to the EU when undertaking legislative steps. The EU legislature should respect, observe and promote fundamental rights. The issue of the horizontal effect of the Charter is the subject of ongoing debate.

2.5. *Interference with fundamental rights*

Because fundamental rights are not absolute, they may interfer with one another;[102] however, for such interference to be justified, it should be based on specific criteria, which will be thoroughly discussed in this section. The aim of the analysis provided in this section is to determine a check list of factors that EU and national legislators should consider and verify when proposing new legislation – specifically copyright legislation – that could potentially interfere with freedom of expression.

Considering that the Charter should be interpreted in accordance with the provisions of the ECHR and the case law of the ECtHR, the criteria for interference with freedom of expression enshrined in these two acts will be discussed jointly. The focus will be on Art. 52(1) of the Charter read in conjunction with Art. 10(2) of the ECHR. According to Art. 10(2) of the ECHR, any interference with freedom of expression by the State should

a) **be prescribed by law**;
b) **be necessary in a democratic society**;
c) **have a legitimate aim**.

102 The Convention protects the rights and freedoms of everyone from unjustified interference by States what is called the "duty to abstain," obligation to "respect" or "negative obligation." See: D. Voorhoof, *Critical*, 5. However, in some cases the interference with fundamental rights by States is justified. This section discusses in details the legal framework of such an interference.

This corresponds with the areas of interference enumerated in the Art. 10(2).[103] The criteria should be interpreted strictly, as the list provided in the provision is exhaustive.[104] According to Art. 52(1) of the Charter: any limitation on the exercise of the rights and freedoms recognised by this Charter must

a) **be provided for by law and respect the essence of those rights and freedoms**;
b) be subject to the principle of **proportionality, limitations may be made only if they are necessary**;
c) genuinely meet objectives of **general interest** recognised by the EU or **the need to protect the rights and freedoms of others**.

In the following points, the requirements for the **prescription by law, legitimate aim and proportionality** criteria will be discussed.

2.5.1. Prescription by law

Any interference with freedom of expression has to be prescribed by law, meaning it must originate from a national legislature or, in case of the Charter's application, derive from EU law or the implementation of an EU directive by Member States. In *Facebook Ireland and Schrems*, the CJEU emphasised that

> The requirement that any limitation on the exercise of fundamental rights must be provided for by law implies that the act which permits the interference with those rights must itself define the scope of the limitation on the exercise of the right concerned.[105]

According to ECtHR case law, interference should be adequately accessible and foreseeable, meaning that the law should be formulated with sufficient precision to enable individuals to understand how they should behave and the potential consequences of their behaviour.[106] However, the ECtHR noted that:

> Those consequences need not be foreseeable with absolute certainty: experience shows this to be unattainable. Again, whilst certainty is highly desirable, it may bring in its train excessive rigidity and the law must be able to keep pace with changing circumstances. Accordingly, many laws are inevitably

103 In Art. 10(2) of the ECHR the legitimate aim should correspond with: the interests of national security, territorial integrity or public safety, for the prevention of disorder or crime, for the protection of health or morals, for the protection of the reputation or rights of others, for preventing the disclosure of information received in confidence, or for maintaining the authority and impartiality of the judiciary.
104 ECtHR, Sunday Times v. the United Kingdom, April 26, 1979, paras. 194–195.
105 CJEU, Facebook Ireland and Schrems, case C-311/18, July 16, 2020, para. 175.
106 ECtHR, Sunday Times, para. 49.

> couched in terms which, to a greater or lesser extent, are vague and whose interpretation and application are questions of practice.[107]

This difficulty in defining and foreseeing all the consequences that a law may have is particularly relevant today, in an age of rapid technological change when new actors and new business models are emerging, shaping access to information and contributing to the evolution of media landscape.

2.5.2. Legitimate aim

Interference with freedom of expression must, according to the ECHR, be based on at least one of the grounds indicated in Art. 10(2) of the Convention. In the case of copyright legislation, potential interference with freedom of expression can be justified by the need to protect reputation or safeguard the rights of others. According to the Charter, the interference must meet the objectives of general interest recognised by the EU. "It covers both the objectives mentioned in Article 3 of the TEU and other interests protected by specific provisions of the Treaties such as Article 4(1) of the TEU and Articles 35(3), 36 and 346 of the TFEU."[108] According to the CJEU, the restrictions of fundamental rights have to "correspond to objectives of general interest pursued by the measure in question."[109] The concept of general interest under the Charter, in the context of copyright legislation, could be understood as encompassing the protection of copyright and related rights holders, the protection of cultural diversity and the promotion of innovation.

2.5.3. Proportionality

Interference with freedom of expression has to be necessary, which should be understood from the perspective of a pressing social need.[110] It is the legislator's role to assess whether a pressing social need exists and whether the interference is necessary.[111]

107 ECtHR, Sunday Times, para. 49.

108 See: EU Charter of Fundamental Rights, Scope and Interpretation, https://fra.europa.eu/en/eu-charter/article/52-scope-and-interpretation-rights-and-principles, accessed: 29.03.2023.

109 CJEU, Alassini and Others, Joined Cases C-317/08, C-318/08, C-319/08 and C-320/08, March 18, 2010 para. 63.

110 ECtHR, Observer and Guardian v. the United Kingdom, para. 57.

111 Some margin of appreciation is given to legislator, but it should take into account the different interests protected both by the Convention and by the Charter. In case of application of the Convention, the ECtHR has a supervisory role, "limited to reviewing whether or not the particular solution adopted can be regarded as striking a fair balance" (see: ECtHR, Hatton and Others v. the United Kingdom, 36022/97, July 8, 2003, para. 123). In case of the application of the Charter, it is the role of the CJEU (see: CJEU, Kadi, para. 285)

The requirement to justify interference based on necessity should be seen within the broader framework of the principle of proportionality,[112] which lies at the core of human rights protection.[113] Understood as a mean of interpretation, the principle is generally used to "delimit the substantive content of rights."[114] The proportionality test involves assessing three elements: effectiveness (suitability), necessity and proportionality (in narrow sense) of the interfering measures.

2.5.3.1. EFFECTIVENESS/SUITABILITY

The measures adopted should be suitable for achieving the objective pursued. It means that there should be a relationship between the aim of the measure and the implemented means to achieve these aims. In other words, it should be assessed to determine whether the chosen measure can actually contribute to the achievement of the expected result. J. Christoffersen points out that if the measure is ineffective, the restriction would benefit no one.[115] However, it should be noted that achieving and assessing the perfect effectiveness of a chosen measure in pursuing its declared goals can be difficult. Factors such as the unpredictability of human behaviour[116] and technological development may influence its outcomes. Nevertheless, efforts should be made to choose the measure that best achieves the objective among the available options.

2.5.3.2. NECESSITY

The legislator should examine whether a less intrusive measure exists that could achieve the legitimate goal while causing minimal harm to the right being affected by the interference. For example, according to the CJEU, an injunction is not precluded by fundamental rights if the adopted measure does not **unnecessarily deprive** users of lawful access to the information available.[117] The assessment of a measure's necessity should involve identifying and comparing alternative options to determine which is the least intrusive and causes the least harm while still achieving the intended objective.

112 See: R. Markiewicz, *Zasada proporcjonalności w prawie autorskim Unii Europejskiej* (Wolters Kluwer Polska, 2023).

113 See: J. Christoffersen, *Fair Balance: Proportionality, Subsidiarity and Primarity in the European Convention on Human Rights*, 99 (Brill, 2009), 1–30.

114 J. Christoffersen, "Human rights and balancing: The principle of proportionality," in *Research Handbook in Human Rights and Intellectual Property*, ed. Ch. Geiger (Edward Elgar Publishing, 2016), 19.

115 J. Christoffersen, "Human," 28.

116 J. Gerards, "How to improve the necessity test of the European Court of Human Rights," *I•CON* 11, no. 2 (2013): 474.

117 CJEU, UPC Telekabel Wien GmbH v Constantin Film Verleih GmbH, Wega Filmproduktionsgesellschaft mbH, case C-314/12, March 27, 2014, para.63.

2.5.3.3. PROPORTIONALITY (IN THE NARROW SENSE)

Measuring proportionality should be understood as balancing different rights and interests to resolve the conflict. Although in the Convention, the requirement for the proportionality of the interference is not explicitly indicated, according to the ECtHR

> an interference must achieve a "fair balance" between the demands of the general interest of the community and the requirements of the protection of the individual's fundamental rights. …there must be a reasonable relationship of proportionality between the means employed and the aim pursued. In determining whether this requirement is met, the Court recognises that the State enjoys a wide margin of appreciation with regard both to choosing the means of enforcement and to ascertaining whether the consequences of enforcement are justified in the general interest for the purpose of achieving the object of the law in question.[118]

The fact that any limitation on the exercise of rights and freedoms should be subject to the principle of proportionality is recognised explicitly in Art. 52(1) of the Charter. The CJEU attached high importance to striking a fair balance between different fundamental rights. However, in relatively few cases does it provide clear indicators on how to achieve this balance.[119] In *Republic of Poland v European Parliament, Council of the European Union*, which concerned the annulment of two provisions under Art. 17 of the CDSM Directive regarding the liability of online content-sharing service providers for user-uploaded content, the CJEU explained that

> the legislation which entails an interference with fundamental rights must lay down clear and precise rules governing the scope and application of the measure in question and imposing minimum safeguards, so that the persons whose exercise of those rights is limited have sufficient guarantees to protect them effectively against the risk of abuse. That legislation must, in particular, indicate in what circumstances and under which conditions such a measure may be adopted, thereby ensuring that the interference is limited to what is strictly necessary. The need for such safeguards is all the greater where the interference stems from an automated process.[120]

In the *Schmidberger* case, the CJEU highlighted that when conducting a balancing exercise, it is important to examine whether the interference does not impair the very substance of the rights guaranteed. Additionally, all relevant circumstances of the

118 ECtHR, Chassagnou and Others v. France, 25088/94, 28331/95 and 28443/95, April 29, 1999, para. 75.

119 See for example: CJEU, L'Oréal SA and Others v eBay International AG and Others Case C-324/09, July 12, 2011.

120 CJEU, Republic of Poland v European Parliament, Council of the European Union, Case C-401/19, April 26, 2022, para. 67.

case must be considered to determine whether a fair balance was struck.[121] In other words, the core of the fundamental right should be preserved despite the interference.

To conclude:

- interference with fundamental rights must pursue a general interest, which can be understood as the protection of copyright and related rights holders, the preservation of cultural diversity or the promotion of innovation. Additionally, it has to be prescribed by law.
- before adopting new legislation, the legislator should assess whether there is a pressing social need justifying the necessity of its adoption. The adopted measures should be suitable for achieving the pursued objective. Additionally, the legislator must evaluate whether a less intrusive measure could achieve the legitimate goal. The assessment of necessity should involve identifying, comparing and evaluating alternatives to ensure that the chosen method is the least intrusive and causes the least harm while still fulfilling its purpose.
- any interference with fundamental rights should be subject to the test of proportionality, which requires balancing the different interests at stake. A thorough analysis of all elements of the proportionality test in all cases of potential interference with fundamental rights would be ideal. However, a comprehensive assessment of all elements of the proportionality test may not be possible. In some cases, a general balancing of interests is carried out instead of assessing the individual elements.[122] This does not alter the fact that it is the duty of legislator to examine whether the new regulation interferes with fundamental rights. If the result of this test is positive, the regulation should be assessed to determine whether it pursues a legitimate aim; is necessary, proportionate and the least intrusive option; and guarantees the achievement of the set objective. If at least one of these criteria is not met, the legislator should consider another legal solution, as the assessed one can be considered as unjustified interference with fundamental rights.

3. Competence of the European Union to legislate on media pluralism

The value of pluralism constitutes one of the founding principles of the EU expressed in Art. 2 of the TEU and Art. 11 of the Charter. According to Art. 11(2) of the Charter, the freedom and pluralism of the media shall be respected. However, the EU legislature does not provide any definition of media pluralism. According

121 CJEU, Eugen Schmidberger, Internationale Transporte und Planzüge v Republik Österreich, case C-112/00, June 12, 2003, paras.80–81.

122 According to A. Barak, balancing is "an analytical process that place the propoer purpose of the limiting law on one side of the scales and the limited constitutional right on the other, while balancing the benefit gained by the proper purpose with the harm it causes to the right." See: A. Barak, *Proportionality. Constitutional Rights and Their Limitations* (Cambridge University Press, 2012), 343.

to the Council of the EU, "it encompasses all measures that ensure access to a variety of information and content sources and allow diverse actors with different opinions to have equal opportunities to reach the public through the media."[123] According to Recital 64 of Regulation 2024/1083 of 11 April 2024, establishing a common framework for media services in the internal market (hereinafter: EMFA), media pluralism should be understood as the possibility to have access to a variety of media services and media content that reflects diverse opinions, voices and analyses.

The EU should contribute to the flourishing of the cultures of Member States, and its actions should be guided by respect for and the promotion of cultural diversity, in accordance with to Art. 167 (1) and (4) of the TFEU. Its competences are subsidiary in nature and should focus on supporting and supplementing Member States' efforts in the dissemination of culture as well as artistic and literary creation. According to Art. 167(5) of the TFEU, the EU is prohibited from pursuing primarily cultural objectives through the approximation of laws and regulations in the Member States. The scope of the EU's cultural competences is significantly limited and holds only marginal importance.[124]

The EU's legislative actions concerning aspects of media functioning[125] are mainly justified by their reference to the protection of the internal market.[126] The aim of establishing or ensuring the functioning of the internal market, as enshrined in Art. 26 of TFUE, along with the EU's role in harmonising the national laws under Art. 114 of the TFUE, serves as the legal basis for EU action in this field. The legal basis for the establishment and functioning of the internal applies when the subject matter to be harmonised has cross-border relevance.

The EU has the competences to harmonise the national laws in order to prevent, according to the CJEU, "the emergence of future obstacles to trade resulting from

123 See: Council of European Union, *Council Conclusions on Safeguarding a Free and Pluralistic Media System* (2020/C 422/08, 2020) 10.

124 See: K. Irion, P. Valcke, "Cultural diversity in the digital age: EU competences, policies and regulations for diverse audiovisual and online content" in *Cultural Governance and the European Union,* ed. E. Psychogiopoulou (Palgrave Macmillan, 2014) 76.

125 Media law, according to J. Oster, "focuses on media as a means to disseminate information and ideas to a mass audience, and the persons disseminating such information and ideas. Media law is thus intrinsically tied to the concept of communication." Media law understood generally encompasses amongst other the regulations concerning print media (I), TV, radio broadcasting (II), dissemination of information and ideas through internet (III), the issues of advertising and copyright protection. See: J. Oster, *European and International Media Law* (Cambridge University Press, 2017), 24.

126 The EU Media law is based on the EU's focus on the development of the internal market. "Media goods and services, had, in the first place, been perceived as economic commodities" (J. Oster, *European*, 24). It remains an essential justification for legislative interference in this area. However, as observed by J. Oster, it has been recognised that media is a factor of public interest going far beyond the market specificities and touching upon diversity of opinions, cultural diversity, right to information or protection of consumers.

multifarious development of national laws."[127] However, traditionally, media law remained outside the area of harmonisation.[128] To illustrate, during the legislative process for the Television without Frontiers Directive, the majority of Member States argued that cultural and social issues are inherently linked to national sovereignty and constitute a competence exclusive to Member States.[129]

Regarding the adoption of the CDSM Directive in 2019, the EU's competence was based on Art. 114 of the TFUE. Recital 2 of the Directive highlights that

> the protection provided by that legal framework of the CDSM Directive contributes to the Union's objective of respecting and promoting cultural diversity, while at the same time bringing European common cultural heritage to the fore. Article 167(4) of the Treaty on the Functioning of the European Union requires the Union to take cultural aspects into account in its action.

Although the protection of media pluralism is not invoked explicitly, the role of "free and pluralist press" is acknowledged in Recital 54 of the CDSM Directive, and the importance of promoting cultural diversity is emphasized in in Recital 2 of the Directive. According to the EU legislature, the harmonised legal framework contributes to the proper functioning of the internal market. The focus, as specified in Recital 2 of the CDSM Directive, is on stimulation of "innovation, creativity, investment and production of new content, also in the digital environment, in order to avoid the fragmentation of the internal market" but also on "the Union's objective of respecting and promoting cultural diversity." The objective of promoting the development of cultural heritage and its diversity is pursued alongside the primary goal of protecting and developing the internal market, based on the competence provided in Art. 114 of the TFUE.

The adoption of the Digital Services Act[130] in 2022, aimed at modernising the current legal framework for digital services, was also based on the competence enshrined in Art. 114 of the TFUE. One of its objectives was to set clear obligations for digital service providers, such as social media platforms, which play a significant role in distributing information, influencing the media ecosystem and impacting media pluralism. The EU legislature makes reference to media pluralism to shape the new obligations of online platforms and to outline the areas that should be particularly protected in terms of their activities. The objective of the regulation

127 CJEU, British American Tobacco (Investments) and Imperial Tobacco, case C-491/01, December 10, 2002, para. 61.

128 O. Castendyk, E. Dommering, A. Scheuer, *European Media Law* (Kluwer Law International, 2008), 14; J. Oster, *European*, 24. See: European Parliament, *The European Media Freedom Act: Media Freedom, Freedom of Expression and Pluralism*, 17–19, https://www.europarl.europa.eu/RegData/etudes/STUD/2023/747930/IPOL_STU(2023)747930_EN.pdf, accessed: 23.10.2023.

129 P. Papp, "The promotion of European works: An analysis on quotas for European audiovisual works and their effect on culture and industry," *European Union Law Working Papers* no. 50 (2020), https://law.stanford.edu/wp-content/uploads/2020/10/papp_eulawwp50.pdf, accessed: 01.09.2023.

130 The Digital Services Act.

is to safeguard and improve the functioning of the internal market in view of the practices of intermediary service providers. Because this activity touches upon the issues related to media pluralism, the EU legislature acknowledges the necessity of its protection, and this accompanies or results from the primary objective of the regulation.

Numerous doubts have been raised about the EU's competence to regulate the media sector. For this reason, the adoption of the EMFA has been questioned. The potential lack of EU competence in regulating media pluralism has been highlighted, as such regulation is anchored in cultural aspects, which fall within the exclusive competence of Member States. Moreover, some scholars argue that the proposed solutions are not adapted to the cultural and media differences among Member States and tend to introduce unjustified uniformisation.[131]

The EU justifies its competence to adopt the discussed regulation based on Art. 114 of the TFEU. According to the Explanatory Memorandum, "the proposal aims to address the fragmented national regulatory approaches related to media freedom and pluralism and editorial independence."[132] Therefore, despite the significantly limited scope of competence in cultural matters, the EU legislature declares its intention to pursue the objectives in this field. However, it explains that this legislative step "will foster a common approach and coordination at EU level, ensure the optimal functioning of the internal market for media services, and prevent the emergence of future obstacles to the operation of media service providers across the EU."[133] It is highlighted that

> Independent media, and in particular news media, provide access to a plurality of views and are reliable sources of information to citizens and businesses alike. They contribute to shaping public opinion and help people and companies form views and make informed choices.[134]

The EMFA, however, seeks "to tackle a series of problems affecting the functioning of the internal market for media services and the operation of media service providers,"[135] according to the Explanatory Memorandum.

In consequence, cultural objectives, such as those related to the functioning of the media, which are meant to be regulated at the national level, are "smuggled"

131 Talk with D. Flisak by the author, June 2022. The proposal has been criticised by press industry being afraid of limitation of the editorial control of press publishers in case of the adoption of the EMFA. See: C. Goujard, "We're fine as we are, Press tells EU as Brussels plans media freedom law," Politico, 2022, https://www.politico.eu/article/eu-law-to-protect-media-freedom-scares-off-press-publishers/, accessed: 03.03.2023; see also: Press, "Projekt Media Freedom Act w obecnej postaci jest dla wydawców nie do przyjęcia," 2022, https://www.press.pl/tresc/74375,projekt-media-freedom-act-w-obecnej-postaci-jest-dla-wydawcow-nie-do-przyjecia, accessed: 03.03.2023.

132 EMFA, 7.

133 EMFA, 7.

134 EMFA, 1.

135 EMFA, 1.

into regulations addressing issues relating to the functioning of the internal market and the freedom to provide services, which fall within the EU's competence. Based on the analysis provided, it can be concluded that the European Commission, in proposing the EMFA, demonstrates a hyper-proactive approach despite the lack of clear legal grounds for the legal intervention. The EU, when enacting new legislation, should take into account and respect the value of media pluralism. However, the responsibility for safeguarding media pluralism falls under the competence of EU Member States.[136]

To conclude:

- the EU's legislative competences in the field of culture are significantly limited.
- the objectives related to the functioning of media industry and linked to the context of media pluralism are achieved through the legal acts adopted on the basis of the provisions from Art. 26 and Art. 114 of the TFEU.
- the legal justification for the EU's legislative actions concerning culture and the functioning of media is rooted in – or hidden behind – the protection of the internal market. It is framed as addressing the removal of barriers impacting investment conditions at the EU level, arising from different national rules, and as a means to reduce internal market fragmentation.

4. Press publishers and flow of information

4.1. Introductory remarks

At the EU level, the activity of press publishers has been regulated in in Art. 15 of the CDSM Directive, specifically concerning the use of their press publications by information society service providers (hereinafter: ISSPs). As it is of crucial importance to the analysis presented in this book, this provision will be discussed in detail in the following chapters. The EMFA, adopted in 2024, will certainly impact the press media sector, especially concerning editorial independence of news media companies and the transparency of their ownership. However, its final outcomes should be assessed once the regulation is fully applicable (as of August 8, 2025).

Specific regulations regarding the functioning of press publishers are found within national legal frameworks and remain outside the scope of EU harmonisation. In Poland, the Polish press law[137] sets the legal framework for the activity of press publishers. The Polish legislature does not provide a precise definition of the concept of publisher.[138] Instead, in Art. 8(1) of the Polish press law, it enumerates examples, including legal or natural persons and other organisational units, even if they lack legal personality. The conclusion can be drawn that press publishing

136 See: Council of European Union, *Council Conclusions on Safeguarding*, 10.

137 Ustawa z dnia 26 stycznia 1984 r. Prawo prasowe, https://isap.sejm.gov.pl/isap.nsf/download.xsp/WDU19840050024/U/D19840024Lj.pdf, accessed: 08.01.2023.

138 E. Ferenc-Szydełko, *Prawo prasowe. Komentarz, art. 8* (Wolters Kluwer, LEX, 2013).

activity may be undertaken by any entity conducting business.[139] It is accepted in legal doctrine that a publisher is a person/entity who/that establishes the editorial office, creates the technical conditions for preparing periodicals, organises the technical process of production and manages distribution and advertising.[140]

According to Art. 7.2(1) of the Polish press law, the press is defined as periodical publications that appear at least once a year, have a fixed title or name, a running number and a date, including newspapers and periodicals, agency services, bulletins or radio and television programmes. The press also includes all existing and technologically advanced mass media that disseminate periodical publications by means of print, visual, audio or any other dissemination techniques. The legislature acknowledges both the traditional print method of distribution of the press as well as its dissemination through visual, audio or other technological means. Online distribution is not explicitly mentioned; however, it should be interpreted within the category of "any other technique." Both in the legal literature and case law, it is accepted that the definition of the press applies to the distribution of periodicals both offline and their online equivalents as well as to the exclusively online or exclusively offline distribution.[141] Whether the press is distributed offline or online, it retains the same defining characteristics: **periodicity**, **availability in print or on the web**, **a fixed title (name)**, **consecutive issues** and **visible dates**. The concept of periodicity is understood broadly and relates to press that is published at regular intervals of time as well as continually. This interpretation allows news websites to be classified as press, provided that the publication date of the information can be determined.[142]

The Polish legislature defines a **journal** (Art. 7.2(2)) as a general-interest periodical that is published in print or broadcast via sound or audiovisual media and is disseminated more than once a week. It defines a **periodical** (Art. 7.2(3)) as a printed publication or sound or audiovisual transmission that differs from a journal in that it is published less frequently. While journals should be of general interest, the topics of periodicals are not specified. **Press material** (Art. 7.2(4)) refers to any text or image of an informative, journalistic, documentary or other nature that is published or submitted for publication in the press, regardless of the medium, type, form, purpose or authorship. Journals and periodicals consist of press materials.

139 J. Sobczak, *Prawo prasowe. Komentarz, art. 8* (Wolters Kluwer, LEX, 2008). The basic feature of business activity is its making profit nature according to art. 3 of Ustawa z dnia 6 marca 2018r. Prawo przedsiębiorców, Dz. U. 2018 poz. 646 t.j. Dz. U. z 2021 r. poz. 162, 2105, z 2022 r. poz. 24, 974, 1570 (Enterpreneurs law).

140 J. Maślanka, *Encyklopedia wiedzy o prasie* (Ossolineum, 1976), 200–201.

141 See: J. Barta, R. Markiewicz, "Postęp techniczny w mediach," in *Prawo mediów*, ed. J. Barta, R. Markiewicz, A. Matlak (LexisNexis, 2005), 189; Polish Supreme Court, Decision of December 15, 2010, III KK 250/10, OSNKW 2011/3/26; Polish Supreme Court, Decision of July 26, 2007, IV KK 174/07, LEX nr 287505.

142 B. Błońska, "Komentarz do art. 25 Ustawy o prawie autorskim i prawach pokrewnych," in *Prawo autorskie i prawa pokrewne. Komentarz,* ed. W. Machała, R. Sarbiński (Wolters Kluwer Polska, LEX, 2019), point 10.

To give some examples from the Polish press market, Ringier Axel Springer Polska sp. z o.o.[143] is a publisher with the largest circulation of journals, including *Fakt* and *Przegląd Sportowy* and periodicals such as *Newsweek Polska* and *Forbes*.[144] It also publishes the popular news website "onet.pl,"[145] which falls into the information and journalism category. Polska Press[146] is known especially for publishing regional newspapers and journals such as *Dziennik Bałtycki* and *Kurier Lubelski*, both of which have online and print versions.[147] Agora S.A.[148] publishes, among other titles, the journal *Gazeta wyborcza*, which is one of the most popular journals in Poland along with to *Fakt*. The online version of *Gazeta wyborcza* is "wyborcza.pl." Bauer sp. z o. o. sp.k.,[149] part of the German Bauer Media Group, publishes the periodicals such as *Pani* and *Twój styl*, both of which also have online versions. AVT is a much smaller and less recognisable publisher, focusing on specialised topics. It publishes, for example, the periodical *T3*, which as a print run of 34,000 copies.[150] The magazine is also available as an e-edition (PDF), has a tablet version and operates an independent web portal. It should be noted that in Poland, many journals and magazines still do not have an online version.

In France, the legal framework governing the activities of press publishers' is provided in la Loi n° 86-897 du 1 août 1986 portant réforme du régime juridique de

143 According to the data collected between 2013–2021 and published by Chamber of Press Publishers, Ringier Axel Springer Polska sp. z o.o has the largest circulation of journals among Polish publishers. See: Izba Wydawców Prasy, "Rynek wydawców," https://www.iwp.pl/rynek-wydawcow/, accessed: 09.01.2023.

144 All exist in online and offline version with the exception of Przegląd Sportowy, some publications of which are published on the website "onet.pl" also run by Ringier Axel Springer Polska S.A.

145 See: Onet, https://www.onet.pl, accessed: 10.01.2023.

146 In 2021 Polska Press has been acquired by PKN Orlen, Oil & Gas company in which the State has 49% of shares. See: Orlen, "Organy i struktura spółki," https://www.orlen.pl/pl/o-firmie/o-spolce/organy-i-struktura-spolki/struktura-akcjonariatu, accessed: 09.01.2022. This acquisition raised doubts about the independence of the publisher and the potential influence of the state on the content issued, see: Rzecznik Praw Obywatelskich, "Zakup Polska Press przez PKN Orlen. Rzecznik o zagrożeniach dla wolności słowa," 2020, https://bip.brpo.gov.pl/pl/content/rpo-o-zagrozeniach-wolnosci-prasy-po-kupnie-polska-press, accessed: 09.01.2022.

147 According to the data collected between 2013–2021 and published by Chamber of Press Publishers, Polska Press has the second largest circulation of journals among Polish publishers. See: Izba Wydawców Prasy, "Rynek."

148 According to the data collected between 2013–2021 and published by Chamber of Press Publishers, Agora SA has the fourth largest circulation of journals among Polish publishers. See: Izba Wydawców Prasy, "Rynek."

149 According to the data collected between 2013–2021 and published by Chamber of Press Publishers, Bauer sp. z o. o. sp.k. has the first largest circulation of periodicals among Polish publishers. See: Izba Wydawców Prasy, "Rynek."

150 AVT, https://avt.pl, accessed: 01.04.2023. To compare, the print run of Fakt amounted to 138 160 in 2022. See: M. Kurdupski, "Sprzedaż 'Faktu' spadła do 138 tys. egz. w 2022 roku. 'Perspektywa rezygnacji z papieru nieunikniona.'" Wirtualne Media, February 07, 2023, https://www.wirtualnemedia.pl/artykul/wyniki-sprzedazy-dzienniki-2022-rok-koniec-pracy-gazeta-wyborcza-fakt-rzeczpospolita, accessed: 01.04.2023.

la presse.[151] The term press publisher does not appear in the mentioned act. Instead, the French legislature refers to a publishing company being any natural, legal person or collectivity under the law according to Art. 2 of French press law. According to E. Derieux, "publishing company" should be understood as the structure gathering the various financial, material, intellectual and human means necessary for the realisation and the publication of a printed periodical but also of an online press service.[152] It means that a publishing company provides structure and necessary resources for the press publications and online press services to be created. It is not directly involved in the creative process, which is based on the engagement of journalists and the editor-in-chief, but it facilitates and enables this process. The conclusion can be drawn that the understanding of a press publisher in Poland and France is similar, despite some differences in wording of the relevant legal provisions.

According to Art. 1 of the French press law, a press publication is defined as any service that uses a written mode of disseminating of thought, is made available to the public in general or to categories of the public and appears at regular intervals.[153] The term applies only to the written mode of disseminating thought. In this context, the definition is narrower compared to the Polish definition of press, which encompasses all **means of dissemination**. A press publication can be intended for the general public or focus on a specific topic, thereby being targeted at a particular category of the public. Other than requiring press publications to be published at regular intervals, the French legislature does not provide any further distinctions regarding the regularity of publication for press publications, unlike the Polish legislature, which differentiates between journals and periodicals based on their frequency of publication. A publishing company can apply for the recognition of the status of press publications published by them by the Joint Committee on Publications and Press Agencies (*Commission paritaire des publications et agencies de presse*). It results in tax benefits and opportunities for direct aid from the state but is not mandatory neither necessary to carry out the publishing activity.[154] Under French press law, a press publication is considered to be published only in print format. This distinction is justified by the fact that, within the same provision, the French legislature introduced the term "online press service," which refers exclusively to digital publications with online-only reach.[155] The term "online press service" has not been identified and defined in Polish press law.

Online press service, according to Art. 1 of the French press law, means any online public communication service published on a professional basis by a natural or legal person who has editorial control over its content, consisting of the

151 Law n° 86-897 of August 1, 1986 reforming the legal regime of the press, https://www.legifrance.gouv.fr/loda/id/JORFTEXT000000687451, accessed: 09.01.2023, hereinafter: French press law.

152 E. Derieux, *Droit des médias. Droit français, européen et international*, 8 edition (LGDJ, 2018), 77.

153 English translation made by the author.

154 See: CPPAP, http://www.cppap.fr/publications/, accessed: 12.01.2023.

155 See: E. Derieux, *Droit*, 78. See also: E. Dreyer, *Droit de la communication*, 2ème édition (LexisNexis, 2022), 118.

production and provision to the public of the original content of general interest, renewed regularly, composed of information linked to current events and news and having been processed in a journalistic manner, which does not constitute a promotional tool or an accessory to an industrial or commercial activity. For online press services providing political and general information, according to the same provision, this recognition implies the regular employment of at least one professional journalist within the meaning of Article L. 7111-3 of the Labour Code.[156]

An online press service can either serve as a supplement to the printed press or function as an independent service with no print equivalent.[157] It should be edited on a professional basis by a natural or legal person and published by a publishing company. Therefore, blogs published outside of professional activities, e.g., travel blogs, that are published for pleasure without pursuing any economic objectives[158] are excluded from the scope of understanding.

Editorial control over an online press service consists of the production and distribution of original content of general interest to the public. The obligation to have editorial control over an online press service means that platforms relying on user-generated content, in which editorial control is absent (e.g., Facebook, Twitter), are excluded from the scope of the definition.

The content should be original, meaning that the core activity of an online press service should not primarily consist of publishing content originating from other online press services, linking to other websites or republishing content published from other publishing companies. As a result, the activity of news aggregators does not meet the criteria set in the definition of an online press service.

An online press service has to be updated regularly; however, the legislature does not define the exact meaning of regularity. For E. Dreyer, regularity does not mean one-off and partial updates, and every new publication published within an online press service should be dated.[159] The service discussed should be composed of information linked to current events and news. In other words, if a service provides information on a specific topic (e.g., architecture, interior design) and does not provide information related to current events and news, it cannot be considered an online press service. The service should provide content of general interest that has been processed in a journalistic manner. The journalistic processing is perceived as the guarantee of quality of the press content.[160]

The content of an online press service can include not only written forms of expression but also pictures and videos. Online press services can apply for recognition of their status as online press services by *Commission paritaire des*

156 English translation made by the author.

157 See: E. Derieux, *Droit*, 78.

158 See differently: C. Castets – Renard, "Éditeur de contenus ou éditeur de services," *Victoires éditions, LEGICOM* 46, no. 1 (2011): 48–49.

159 E. Dreyer, *Droit*, 386.

160 E. Dreyer, *Droit*, 386.

publications et agencies de presse. This recognition grants tax benefits and opportunities for direct state aid but is not mandatory or necessary to operate such a service.[161]

Le Monde was the most read national newspaper in France between 2021 and 2022, with a circulation of around 458,611.[162] The Le Monde group publishes a print version of the journal, which corresponds to the definition of a press publication, as well as an online format, which meets the criteria for the definition of an online press service. *Le Figaro*, the second most read national newspaper in France between 2021 and 2022,[163] is published by the Société du Figaro, owned by the Figaro group, itself owned by the Dassault group. It is published online and in print. Mediapart is an online press service that has no paper equivalent. It is published by la Société éditrice de Mediapart (SAS). Ouest France[164] and has been the leading French daily newspaper in terms of circulation since 1975, with 624,455[165] copies distributed. It is an example of a regional newspaper published by le groupe Sipa – Ouest-France in online and print versions. These are known and large players in the French press market. However, the latter also consists of small, less well-known publishers, sometimes publishing on topics other than general information and politics, with a much smaller readership. For example, So Press publishes titles such as *So Foot* published monthly with about 40,000 copies distributed through subscription in digital version.[166]

Within the analysis conducted in this monograph the terms "large press publishers" and "small press publishers" are used. For the purpose of this analysis, large press publishers refers to publishers that cover general-interest topics at a regional and national level, in electronic or print format, or in only both. Additionally, their newspaper circulation or number of subscriptions exceeds 100,000. A small press publisher is defined as a publisher that covers either general-interest or specialized topics, at a regional or national level, in electronic or paper format, or in both. Additionally, its newspaper circulation or number of subscriptions is fewer than 100,000.[167]

161 See: CPPAP, "Critères d'admission," http://www.cppap.fr/criteres-dadmission/, http://www.cppap.fr/linscription-sur-les-registres-de-la-cppap-est-elle-une-obligation-pour-faire-paraitre-une-publication-de-presse/, accessed: 12.01.2023.

162 According to data provided by l'Alliance pour les chiffres de la presse et des médias: ACPM, "Classement Diffusion Presse Quotidienne Nationale 2023–2024," https://www.acpm.fr/Les-chiffres/Diffusion-Presse/Presse-Payante/Presse-Quotidienne-Nationale, accessed: 10.01.2023.

163 ACPM, "Classement."

164 Ouest France is the regional journal the coverage of which exceeds the coverage of national journals. Press publishers' strategy is based on the principle of proximity and enjoys great success among French readers. See: K. Gajlewicz-Korab, "Wpływ preferencji czytelników na rozwój francuskiego rynku współczesnej prasy codziennej," *Studia Medioznawcze 3*, no. 66 (2016): 70.

165 See: ACPM, "Classement."

166 ACPM, "Classement."

167 This distinction has been made for the purpose of the analysis conducted in this monograph It is based on the current data on print circulation and subscription figures, and represents some averaging that takes into account differences in the Polish and French publishing markets.

To conclude:

- in Polish law, there is no formal definition of press publishers, but the legislature provides numerous examples. A distinction between a journal, a periodical and press material. The concept of the press is interpreted broadly, with notable tendency in doctrine and case law toward expanding its scope.
- in French press law, a distinction is made between press publications, which exist in print form, and online press services, which involve the production and dissemination of original content of general interest. This content must be regularly updated, linked to current events and news and processed in a journalistic manner. The French legislature, therefore, explicitly differentiates between online and offline publications.

4.2. Business models

The press publishing industry is in a "transition phase."[168] Circulation of print newspapers is marked by a constant decline.[169] The ongoing digital transformation has offered new tools for the dissemination of news and allowed publishers to reach a wider audience. However, it is also seen as a cause of financial losses for publishers[170] and a source of increased market competition. New actors, such as social media platforms and news aggregators, have emerged and now play an important role in the distribution of information. All these factors challenge existing business models, forcing publishers to adapt and innovate the way they operate.

Technological changes have introduced a new differentiation among press publishers; in addition to the traditional divisions into small and large or local and national, publishers are now categorized into those operating exclusively online,

168 K. Panagiotidis, A. Veglis, "Transitions in journalism—toward a semantic-oriented technological framework," *Journal.Media* 1, no. 1 (2020), https://www.mdpi.com/2673-5172/1/1/1, accessed: 06.09.2023. See also: A. Leurdijk, O. Nieuwenhuis, M. Slot, "Statistical, ecosystems and competitiveness analysis of the media and content industries: The newspaper publishing industry," *JRC Technical Reports* (2012): 10.

169 According to data provided in Impact Assessment accompanying the document Proposal for the CDSM Directive, print circulation of daily newspapers has been constantly declining for years by 17% in the period 2010–2014 in 8 EU MS a trend that is expected to continue. See: European Commission, *Impact Assessment on the Modernisation of EU Copyright Rules Accompanying the Document Proposal for a Directive of the European Parliament and of the Council on Copyright in the Digital Single Market Print* (SWD (2016) 301 final, 2016), 156, https://eur-lex.europa.eu/legal-content/EN/TXT/?uri=celex:52016SC0301, accessed: 27.10.2022, hereinafter: *Impact Assessment*. The recent studies showed that the number of Europeans who read print newspaper dropped from 37% in 2012 to 21% in 2022. See: Statista, "Share of respondents who read the written press every day or almost every day in the European Union from 2011 to 2022," April 2022, https://www.statista.com/statistics/452430/europe-daily-newspaper-consumption/, accessed: 18.01.2023; see also: Standard Eurobarometer 96, "Public opinion in the European Union," January–February 2022, T196, https://europa.eu/eurobarometer/api/deliverable/download/file?deliverableId=81059, accessed: 18.01.2023.

170 See: European Commission, *Impact Assessment*, 156.

those maintaining both an online and offline presence and those yet to transition into the digital environment. Publishers operating online either begin their activities exclusively in the digital sphere without ever having a printed equivalent, as seen with the French online press service *Mediapart*, or transition to an online-only model due to declining print revenues and raising production costs, as in the case of the Polish weekly *Wprost*, which stopped print publication copies in 2020.[171] Small and local publishers are particularly reluctant to move their services online, and even when they do, they face greater difficulties than larger industry players[172] because of a lack of sufficient resources and technological infrastructure or expertise as well as difficulties in adapting to market demands or a general fear and reluctance to change. It should be noted that some newspapers have an audience primarily composed of older people who, being accustomed to print editions and less inclined to use electronic devices, are reluctant to purchase digital subscriptions. For this reason, unless a publisher can attract a new audience, investing in a digital version of their newspaper may not be profitable. However, given that 88% of Europeans get at least some of their news online via their smartphones or laptops,[173] those who choose not to transition to digital will face difficulties in the future.[174]

Although for print press, the form of communication remains rather traditional, publishers introduce supplemental magazines, free newspapers and special or weekend editions to boost revenue and circulation.[175] The objective of publishers of print and digital press is to offer the content that "adds value as compared to free information."[176] The development of the press sector is increasingly linked to the

171 Polityka, "Wprost już tylko online," March 31, 2020, https://www.polityka.pl/opolityce/1950926,1,wprost-juz-tylko-online.read, accessed: 18.01.2023.

172 A. Cornia, A. Karogelopulos, R.K. Nielsen, *Challenges and Opportunities for News Media and Journalism in Increasingly Digital, Mobile, and Social Media Environment* (Council of Europe report, DGI 2016, 18, Reuters Institute for the Study of Journalism, 2016), 28; N. Rashidian, et al., *Friend & Foe: The Platform Press at the Heart of Journalism* (Tow Center for Digital Journalism A Tow/Knight Report, 2018), 7.

173 European Union, *Flash Eurobarometer: News & Media Survey 2022*, July 2022, https://europa.eu/eurobarometer/surveys/detail/2832, accessed: 18.01.2023.

174 N. Newman et al., *Journalism, Media and Technology Trends and Predictions 2022* (Digital News Project, Reuters Institute for the Study of Journalism, University of Oxford, 2022), 8, https://reutersinstitute.politics.ox.ac.uk/sites/default/files/2022-01/Newman%20-%20Trends%20and%20Predictions%202022%20FINAL.pdf, accessed: 18.01.2023.

175 Deloitte, *The Impact of Web Traffic on Revenues of Traditional Newspaper Publishers. A Study for France, Germany, Spain, and the UK* (2016), 9, https://www2.deloitte.com/content/dam/Deloitte/uk/Documents/technology-media-telecommunications/deloitte-uk-impact-of-web-traffic-on-newspaper-revenues-2016.pdf, accessed: 18.01.2023.

176 M. Buiten, K. Heine M. Kerk, M. Senftleben, "New rights or new business models? An inquiry into the future of publishing in the digital era," *International Review of Intellectual Property and Competition Law* 48, no. 10 (2017): 539; P.J. Boczkowski, E. Mitchelstein, "The news gap: When the information preferences of the media and the public diverge," *The MIT Press* (2013): 23–48; A. Cornia, R.K. Nielsen, A. Sehl, *Digital News Project. Private Sector Media and Digital News* (Reuters Institute for Study of Journalism, 2016), 27.

growing use of artificial intelligence (AI) in the preparation, distribution and consumption of content.[177] AI is widely used to filter information published on social media, tag content, alert journalists[178] and collect and process data.[179] According to a survey conducted by N. Newman, 40% of respondents reported that AI is used to automatically write or complete stories.[180] Robo-journalism or automated journalism relies on clear algorithmic rules, human input and well-organised data sources.[181] All these factors contribute to AI being used primarily in areas such as sports reporting, weather forecasting, press summaries[182] and finance analysis.[183]

Currently, the primary focus is on using AI to recommend and personalise news content.[184] News personalisation is an "interface to news, ...which selects, highlights and filters individual news items, and compiles and aggregates them into news packages in a different manner for each individual newsreader."[185] It enables publishers to provide users with content that meets their needs and interests while also competing with online platforms that heavily integrate AI into their operating models.[186] It should be noted that personalisation is often viewed negatively, as it can contribute to the formation of filter bubbles and echo chambers.[187] However,

177 N. Diakopoulos, *Automating the News: How Algorithms Are Rewriting the Media* (Harvard University Press, 2019), 96–144, 177–203.

178 See: R. Fletcher, S. Schifferes, N. Thurman, "Building the 'truthmeter': Training algorithms to help journalists assess the credibility of social media sources," *Convergence* 26, no. 1 (2020), 19–34, https://journals.sagepub.com/doi/epub/10.1177/1354856517714955, accessed: 20.01.2023.

179 N. Thurman et al., "Giving computers a nose for news: Exploring the limits of story detection and verification," Digital Journalism 4, no. 7 (2016): 838–848, https://eprints.qut.edu.au/221748/1/cardiff-2015-v26%2Bfor%2Bopen%2Baccess%2Bcity.pdf, accessed: 19.01.2023.

180 N. Newman, *Journalism*, 35.

181 J. Diaz-Noci, "Authors' rights and the media," in *Interaction in Digital News Media. From Principles to Practice*, ed. M. Pérez-Montoro (Palgrave Macmillan, 2018), 162.

182 P. Fray, E. McKewon, S. Molitorisz, D. Wilding, *The Impact of Digital Platforms on News and Journalistic Content* (University of Technology Sydney, 2018), 66.

183 See: M. Kowala, "Algorytmiczne dziennikarstwo w świetle prawa autorskiego," *Zeszyt Studencki Kół Naukowych Wydziału Prawa i Administracji UAM* no. 10, (2020); See also: P. Farhi, "A news site used AI to write articles. It was a journalistic disaster," The Washington Post, January 17, 2023, https://www.washingtonpost.com/media/2023/01/17/cnet-ai-articles-journalism-corrections/, accessed: 19.01.2023.

184 According to the survey conducted by N. Newman: "More than eight-in-ten of our sample say these technologies will be important for better content recommendations (85%) and newsroom automation (81%). More than two-thirds (69%) see AI as critical on the business side in helping to attract and retain customers." See: N. Newman, *Journalism*, 35.

185 B. Bodó, "Selling news to audiences – a qualitative inquiry into the emerging logics of algorithmic news personalization in European quality news media," *Digital Journalism* 7, no. 8 (2019): 1054.

186 The NZZ Companion App is an example of application, used by press publishers which is a digital companion that personalises through-the-day news delivery, creating tailored news based on each user's profile, location and situation. See: Google News Initiative, "Companion App," https://newsinitiative.withgoogle.com/dnifund/dni-projects/nzz-companion-app/, accessed: 23.01.2023.

187 Marijn Sax, "Algorithmic news diversity and democratic theory: Adding agonism to the mix," *Digital Journalism* (2022); M. Bastian et al., "Explanations of news personalisation across countries and media types," *Internet Policy Review Journal on Internet Regulation* 9, no. 4 (2020); C.

according to B. Bodó,[188] unlike online platforms, which rely on large amounts user data to maximise engagement and sell user attention to advertisers,[189] press publishers primarily use personalisation to "cultivate interest in quality information, including hard news, and to promote journalistic authority and reliability."[190]

Technological development and investment in AI in the press sector should be regarded as essential for the continuation and sustainability of the industry. The example of *Globe & Mail*, a Canadian news organisation, perfectly illustrates this trend. The company developed a software program called Sophi, which determines whether an article should be freely accessible or placed behind a paywall based on article content and user data. The results have been impressive, as the use of this software has accelerated the growth of digital subscribers to 170,000.[191] This also demonstrates that the nature of investments in the press sector has evolved, with a growing emphasis in AI-driven solutions.

The traditional press industry is characterised by high sunk costs associated with investments in printing presses, ink and paper.[192] The total costs, including distribution, account for up to 50% of all newspaper publishing expenses[193] and remain costly to sustain, even for large publishing companies.[194] However, given the decline in print press circulation, there has been a notable shift in investment, with a growing focus on digital strategies. C. Joly, General Secretary of the Le Monde Group, in an interview with A. Cornia, argues that "organisations such as her own need to continually rationalise legacy operations and cut printing, distribution, and production costs to remain sustainable and be able to invest in digital opportunities."[195] This reflects the growing trend of gradually shifting investments away from print media in favour of digital development.

A key aspect of digital transformation is "the shift from a linear business model in offline news publishing to a multi-sided market or platform business model in online news publishing"[196] with a strong focus on demand-side factors. Therefore, significant investments today are focused on the development of digital platforms

Monzer et al., "User perspectives on the news personalisation process: Agency, trust and utility as building blocks," *Digital Journalism* 8, no. 9 (2020): 1142–1162.

188 B. Bodó, "Selling," 1071.

189 B. Bodó, "Selling," 1054.

190 J. Kunert, S.C. Lewis, N. Thurman, "Algorithms, automation, and news," *Digital Journalism* 7, no. 8 (2019): 983.

191 James Breiner: Entrepreneurial Journalism, "How AI and data boost journalism sustainability," https://jamesbreiner.com/how-ai-and-data-boost-journalism-sustainability/, accessed: 25.12.2024.

192 A. Leurdijk, O. Nieuwenhuis, M. Slot, "Statistical," 25.

193 B. Martens et al., *The Digital Transformation of News Media and the Rise of Disinformation and Fake News*, JRC Digital Economy Working Paper 2018-02 (2018), 15–17.

194 Deloitte, *The Impact* 10. See also: R. Xalabarder, "Google News and copyright," in *Empirical Approaches to Legal Aspects of Knowledge-Economy Business Models,* ed. A. Lopez-Taruella (Springer, 2012), 116.

195 A. Cornia, R.K.Nielsen, A. Sehl, *Digital News*, 15.

196 B. Martens et al., *The Digital*, 15.

and their ongoing modernisation.[197] Press publishers need to acknowledge the changing news consumption habits of their readers and adapt their business models to the growing popularity of mobile apps, which also requires significant investment. According to N. Wakim, director of editorial innovation at *Le Monde*, traffic on their mobile apps "is growing between 5% and 10% per year and, on their mobile website, at a rate that can vary from 50% to 100% per year."[198] The digital environment is distinguished by high initial technological investments in platform development and operational capacity; However, these upfront investments result in lower investment costs for publishers in the following years.[199]

Amongst the planned technological investments highlighted by press publishers, 90% focus on data analytics and AI; 83% on video, audio and podcasts; 80% on customer management; and 72% on automation.[200] It is difficult to estimate the exact size of these investments, as they depend on a variety of factors and vary from publisher to publisher. However, digital transformation in the press sector should be viewed, first, as leading to a change in the type of investments made by publishers, and second, leading to a reduction in overall investment costs over time.[201] Adapting to the pace of change and its technical complexity can be particularly challenging for small and local publishers.

Traditionally, the main revenue sources for press publishers came from print sales, subscriptions and advertising.[202] Digital transformation and the declining demand for printed press have made it necessary for publishers to seek new sources of funding and adjust their business models.[203] Publishers' current revenues come primary from subscriptions (particularly digital subscriptions), advertising and state aid as well as, to a lesser extent, from philanthropy, press development funds provided by platforms such as Facebook or Google and other revenue streams, such as brand exploitation and diversification strategies.[204]

4.2.1. Subscriptions revenue

For a significant number of publishers (76%) interviewed for the Digital News Project report, driving digital subscriptions is considered an important or very important source revenue.[205] In 2022, 79% of publishers declared that driving digi-

197 M. Buiten, K. Heine M. Kerk, M. Senftleben, "New rights," 543.
198 A. Cornia, R.K.Nielsen, A. Sehl, *Digital News*, 43.
199 M. Buiten, K. Heine M. Kerk, M. Senftleben, "New rights," 543.
200 World Association of News Publishers, "World Press Trends preview: Publishers brace for a period marked by uncertainty," September 29, 2022, https://wan-ifra.org/2022/09/world-press-trends-preview-publishers-brace-for-a-period-marked-by-uncertainty/, accessed: 20.01.2023.
201 See: R.G. Picard, *Mapping Digital Media. Digitalisation and Media Business Models* (Open Society Foundations, no. 5, 2011), 9.
202 See: B. Martens et al., *The Digital*, 15; A. Cornia, R.K. Nielsen, A. Sehl, *Digital News*, 11.
203 D. Bossio, *Journalism and Social Media. Practitioners, Organisations and Institutions* (Palgrave Macmillan, 2017), 72.
204 See: A. Cornia, A. Karogelopulos, R.K. Nielsen, *Challenges*, 26–27.
205 N. Newman, *Journalism*, 10.

tal subscriptions would be one of their most important revenue priorities, ranking above both display and native advertising.[206] Revenue from subscriptions is seen as an important element to reduce reliance on advertising revenue, which is increasingly being captured by large platforms.[207] According to a Reuters Institute publication, 66% of newspapers and 71% of magazines in Europe offer some type of subscription model. The highest subscription rates are found in France (95%), Poland (90%) and Finland (87%).[208]

The subscription models are based on a paywall system, which prevents web users from accessing certain content without a paid subscription. A paywall is a method of monetising content, which can, however, lead to a decrease in page views and advertising revenue because fewer readers have access to the content.[209] A **hard paywall** provides access to publishers' content only to users with a paid subscription.[210] **Soft paywalls**, or metered models, allow free access to a limited number of articles with a specified amount of time. Once the limit is reached, the user must purchase a subscription to continue reading.[211] The **freemium model** allows users to access most content for free, while certain premium articles are reserved exclusively for subscribers.[212] *Gazeta Wyborcza* has a metered paywall with elements of a hard paywall. *Le Figaro* opted for a freemium system in which for some articles, only the short introductory passages are visible to readers without a subscription, while others can be read in their entirety.

The long-standing availability of news for free on publishers' websites, combined with the ability to access it via news aggregators and social media, has led to a situation in which readers not fully willing to accept the need to pay for online press content.[213] Publishers have, to some extent, accustomed their readers to free access to content. As a result, the subsequent introduction of paid access has led some readers to look for free alternatives elsewhere. Moreover, the digital transformation has significantly changed reading habits. Today, it has become popular to read selected articles from different newspapers.[214] As a result, the requirement to subscribe to an entire newspaper – often the only option offered by press publishers – may be unappealing and discourage readers, especially if they are only

206 N. Newman, *Journalism*, 6.

207 N. Newman et al., *Reuters Institute Digital News Report 2022* (Reuters Institute, University of Oxford, 2022), 18; Deloitte, *The Impact*, 12.

208 A. Cornia et al., *Pay Models in European News* (Reuters Institute for Study of Journalism, 2017), 1–2, https://reutersinstitute.politics.ox.ac.uk/sites/default/files/2017-07/Pay%20Models%20in%20European%20News%20Factsheet.pdf, accessed: 20.01.2023.

209 Deloitte, *The Impact*, 12.

210 Deloitte, *The Impact*, 12.

211 Deloitte, *The Impact*, 12.

212 A. Cornia, A. Karogelopulos, R.K. Nielsen, *Challenges*, 24. See also: A. Szynol, "Czy paywall to być albo nie być wydawców prasy codziennej?" *Zeszyty prasoznawcze* 64, no. 4 (2019).

213 See: A. Cornia, A. Karogelopulos, R.K. Nielsen, *Challenges*, 26–27. In relation to the discussed problem, the term subscription fatigue is also used. See: N. Newman, *Journalism*, 20.

214 J. Rutt, *Aggregators and the News Industry: Charging for Access to Content* (NET Institute, Working Paper 11-19, 2011), 2.

interested in a single article. According to a survey conducted by Ipsos European Public Affairs, 70% of online news consumers only use free news content or services.[215] Meanwhile, 11% of the population in France and 14% in Poland pay for online news.[216]

However, there is a noticeable upward trend in the number of subscribers to digital press. For example, the number of active paid digital subscriptions to *Gazeta Wyborcza* at the end of December 2021 was more than 286,100.[217] In comparison, in 2017, the average total sales of *Gazeta Wyborcza*'s digital editions amounted to 124,000 copies. In France, *Le Figaro* had 250,000 online subscribers between 2021 and 2022,[218] compared to 80,000 in 2017.[219] "The paper-only readership is losing ground to the digital readership. Between the first quarter of 2014 and the third quarter of 2018, the paper-only readership of the newspaper *l'Equipe* fell from 48% to 21% of the total readership."[220]

Mediapart is an undeniable success story in terms of its business model. Unlike other publishers that introduced paid subscriptions after several years of providing news for free, resulting in a loss of readers, *Mediapart* has consistently operated as a paid service from its inception.[221] The readers got used to this operating mode, and their numbers gradually grew.

It should be also noted that some titles, primarily large press publishers, managed to attract a significant number of readers willing to pay for content and continue to see growth.[222] Local and small press publishers face greater challenges in adapting to technological change, investing in new technologies and developing a subscription model that is both effective and well-received by readers. Moreover, their readers are particularly reluctant to pay for online news, which results in declining print revenues. As a consequence, they lack a clear,

215 European Union, *Flash, 3.*

216 N. Newman et al., *Reuters*, 79, 95.

217 Grupa Kapitałowa Agora S.A., *Sprawozdanie niezależnego biegłego rewidenta z badania roku obrotowego kończącego się 31 grudnia 2022r.*, 37.

218 MindMedia, "Abonnements numériques (1/2) : la croissance des médias d'information en ligne payants se stabilise en 2021," 2022, https://www.mindmedia.fr/medias-audiovisuel/abonnements-en-ligne/abonnements-numeriques-1-2-la-croissance-des-medias-dinformations-en-ligne-payants-se-stabilise-en-2021/, accessed: 12.02.2023.

219 E. Renault, "Le groupe Figaro a terminé l'année 2017 sur de bons résultats," February 15, 2018, Le Figaro, 2018, https://www.lefigaro.fr/medias/2018/02/15/20004-20180215ARTFIG00017-le-groupe-figaro-a-termine-l-annee-2017-sur-de-bons-resultats.php, accessed: 12.01.2023.

220 Decision 20-MC-01 of April 9, 2020 on requests for interim measures by the Syndicat des éditeurs de la presse magazine, the Alliance de la presse d'information générale and others and Agence France-Presse, 17, https://www.autoritedelaconcurrence.fr/sites/default/files/integral_texts/2020-06/20-mc-01_en.pdf, accessed: 12.01.2024, hereinafter: FCA Decision of April 9, 2020 on interim measures.

221 M. Rubio, "Mediapart : les clés du succès d'un média d'enquête indépendant," Global Investigate Journalism Network, March 16, 2022, https://gijn.org/2022/03/16/francais-mediapart-independance/, accessed: 20.01.2023.

222 A. Cornia, A. Karogelopulos, R.K. Nielsen, *Challenges*, 26.

ready-to-implement alternative for sustaining their business.[223] Due to their size, local and small publishers lack bargaining power when negotiating with platforms regarding the use of their content.[224] On the other hand, Facebook's initiative aimed at helping local publishers enhance their digital subscription business serves as an example of how large platforms support small and local publishers.[225] Moreover, the concentration of digital subscriptions among a few major press publishers leads to their dominance and the consolidation of power in the media landscape.[226] This reinforces the "winner takes most dynamics"[227] and contributes to the declining diversity in news production.[228]

4.2.2. Advertising revenue

In addition to revenue from newspaper sales, whether in print or digital form, publishers also generate income by monetising readers' attention through advertising.[229] With the growth of the online space, the traditional business model of press publishers has been affected. Online platforms, such as search engines, news aggregators and social media, attract far more users than individual newspaper websites and can, therefore, reach a much wider audience. As a result, advertisers increasingly prefer these digital platforms, often to the detriment of press publishers.[230] The decline in print revenue, coupled with sometimes unsuccessful attempts to launch subscription models[231] and a decrease in online advertising revenue, poses a serious threat to the survival of some press publishers.[232]

223 M. Shapiro, "The false promise of paywalls for local news," E&P, April 3, 2020, https://www.editorandpublisher.com/stories/shoptalk-the-false-promise-of-paywalls-for-local-news,1303, accessed: 21.01.2023.

224 N. Rashidian et al., *Friend*, 45–46.

225 Meta, "Facebook helps local news publishers build digital subscriptions," February 27, 2018, https://www.facebook.com/formedia/blog/facebook-local-news-digital-subscriptions, accessed: 21.01.2023.

226 A. Cornia, A. Karogelopulos, R.K. Nielsen, *Challenges*, 9.

227 N. Newman et al., *Reuters*, 11–13.

228 R.K. Nielsen, A. Cornia, A. Karogelopulos, *Challenges*, 9.

229 A. Leurdijk, O. Nieuwenhuis, M. Slot, *Statistical*, 26.

230 B. Martens et al., *The Digital*, 26.

231 The publisher of Polish Gazeta Radomszczańska describes the process of the implementation of the subscription model as difficult and fraught with failures. Ultimately, however, it is proving increasingly popular. See: Wirtualnemedia.pl, "Subskrypcje 'Gazety Radomszczańskiej': 90 proc. czytelników odnawia abonament," January 21, 2022, https://www.wirtualnemedia.pl/artykul/subskrypcje-gazety-radomszczanskiej-przekroczyly-polowe-papierowego-nakladu-90-procent-czytelnikow-odnawia-abonament, accessed: 24.01.2023.

232 European Parliament, *Strengthening the Position of Press Publishers and Authors and Performers in the Copyright Directive* (Policy Department for Citizens' Rights and Constitutional Affairs Directorate General for Internal Policies of the Union, Study for the JURI Committee, 2017), 15.

The trend in advertising revenue is declining. For example, newspaper ad revenues in Europe fell from €22 billion in 2009 to around €12 billion in 2018.[233] Similarly, the advertising revenue of *Gazeta Wyborcza* decreased from 68.5 million PLN in 2017[234] to 64.7 million PLN in 2021.[235]

However, advertising is still an important source of revenue for press publishers.[236] According to a 2022 survey on publishers' expectations for 2023, 41% of surveyed publishers said that most of their revenue would come from advertising, and some publishers declared that advertising still accounts for up to 80% of revenue. By comparison, reader-generated revenue is expected to account for 33% of revenue.[237] It should be noted that some press publishers, still offer digital news for free and rely on advertising as their main business model.[238] This is the case for *Fakt*. Nevertheless, the number of press publishers operating in this way is decreasing.

For online news, the amount of advertising revenue depends on factors such as number of visitors and the time they spent on the website.[239] Larger publishers have a greater ability to generate advertising revenue and are better positioned to compete or cooperate with online platforms in the advertising market.[240] This sheds light on two problems. First, press publishers have to look for other sources of revenue due to the dominance of large platforms in the online advertising market, the decline in print circulation and subscription systems that are just gaining popularity. Second, local and small publishers are the most affected by this phenomenon, as they are less attractive to advertisers and unable to compete with online platforms and larger publishers in terms of audience reach. When considering these factors as well as their difficulties in implementing subscription models, their overall situation can be described as difficult.[241]

233 J.G. Navarro, "Newspaper advertising expenditure in the European Union (EU 28) from 2009 to 2018," Statista, November 9, 2024, https://www.statista.com/statistics/434708/newspaper-advertising-expenditure-in-the-eu/, accessed: 23.01.2025.

234 Grupa Kapitałowa Agora S.A., *Sprawozdanie niezależnego biegłego rewidenta z badania roku obrotowego kończącego się 31 grudnia 2017r.*(2017), 40.

235 Grupa Kapitałowa Agora S.A., *Sprawozdanie niezależnego biegłego rewidenta z badania roku obrotowego kończącego się 31 grudnia 2021r. (2021),* 6.

236 Deloitte, *The Impact*, 14.

237 WNIP, "News publishers expect revenues to more than double this year," World Press Trends 2022–23 Preview, 2022, https://whatsnewinpublishing.com/news-publishers-expect-revenues-to-more-than-double-this-year-world-press-trends-2022-23-preview/, accessed: 23.01.2023.

238 See: A. Cornia, A. Karogelopulos, R.K. Nielsen, *Challenges*, 25.

239 Deloitte, *The Impact*.

240 N. Rashidian et al., *Friend*, 10.

241 See: Press Gazette, "Next challenge for publishers is restoring revenue back to print levels," December 12, 2022, https://pressgazette.co.uk/publishing-services-content/next-challenge-for-publishers-is-restoring-revenue-back-to-print-levels/, accessed: 23.01.2023.

4.2.3. State aid revenue

In some countries, direct or indirect subsidies are provided to some or all newspapers.[242] In France, financial support from the state plays an important role.[243] It is seen as a commitment to guarantee freedom of press and to strengthen media pluralism. To illustrate, in France, "In order to mitigate the consequences of the crisis, on 27 August 2020 the government announced a support plan for the press industry comprising, on the one hand, of emergency measures to guarantee the continuity of press distribution, amounting to €106 million, and, on the other hand, an envelope of €377 million to finance recovery measures over the period 2020–2022."[244]

In France, there are two types of aid:[245] a) indirect aid, which includes measure such as preferential tariffs for the distribution of newspapers via postal service and tax relief, and b) direct aid, which is intended to support certain categories of publications, particularly those covering political and general topics.

The objectives of these types of aid include supporting the distribution of publications, assisting financially vulnerable general and political information outlets to preserve pluralism and promoting the modernisation and development of press companies. In 2021, 431 publications received direct and indirect aid.[246] For example, in 2021, the Le Monde Group received €2.6 million in direct aid, which accounted for 0.8% of its total turnover.[247]

However, the aid system and the methods of allocation are often subject to criticism. According to the French Court of auditors, the aid system remains fragmented and consists of multiple mechanisms, most of which do not align with the new digital publishing landscape and its specific requirements. Moreover, it has been noted that the aid allocation process lacks transparency, is rather discretionary and produces unpredictable outcomes.[248]

242 A. Cornia, A. Karogelopulos, R.K. Nielsen, *Challenges*, 31.

243 France has a long tradition of subsidising press, dating back to the period after the French Revolution. The model of aid to press has been developed after the end of the second World War. Initially, it was intended to restore the press' honour and credibility, which had been damaged during the occupation and more precisely, during the collaboration of the popular press with the occupying forces. See: K. Gajlewicz-Korab, "Wpływ preferencji," 71.

244 FCA Decision 21-D-17 of July 12, 2021 on non-compliance with the injunctions issued against Google in Decision 20-MC-01 of April 9, 2020, 82, https://www.autoritedelaconcurrence.fr/sites/default/files/attachments/2022-02/21-d-17_en.pdf, accessed: 08.12.2024, hereinafter: FCA Decision of July 12, 2021 on non-compliance with the interim measures of April 9, 2020.

245 See: B. Beignier, E. Deyer, B. de Lamy, *Traité de droit de la presse et des médias* (Lexis Nexis Lites, 2009), 328–364.

246 See: République Française, "Aides à la presse, Tableaux des titres de presse aidés en 2021," September 2, 2022, https://www.culture.gouv.fr/Thematiques/presse-ecrite/Tableaux-des-titres-et-groupes-de-presse-aides-par-le-ministere-de-la-Culture/Tableau-des-titres-de-presse-aides-en-2021, accessed: 26.12.2024.

247 Le Monde, "Les revenus du 'Monde', des sources diversifiées," January 26, 2022, https://www.lemonde.fr/le-monde-et-vous/article/2021/01/26/les-revenus-du-monde-des-sources-diversifiees_6067680_6065879.html, accessed: 21.01.2023.

248 Cour des comptes, *Les aides à la presse écrite : des choix nécessaires*, Rapport public annuel (2018), https://www.ccomptes.fr/sites/default/files/2018-01/12-aides-presse-ecrite-Tome-2.pdf, accessed: 12.02.2023.

In Poland, the system of state aid for press publishers is less developed than in France and is provided directly in the form of subsidies only in very specific cases. The Ministry of Culture and National Heritage grants subsidies to certain journals covering cultural or historical topics, recognizing their role in preserving national heritage and enhancing public awareness. In 2022, nearly 3.6 million PLN in funding was allocated to 45 projects.[249] However, it should be noted that the selection of subsidised journals and the allocation of funds have been criticised in the press for being discretionary.[250] Some forms of indirect support, such as tax incentives, are also provided.[251] The current initiative by local press publishers, who have called on the Polish Prime Minister and the Minister of Culture and National Heritage to introduce direct financial support, deserves attention.[252] Unfortunately, no solution has been implemented to address this request so far.

4.2.4. *Other sources of revenue*

Philanthropy in Europe plays only a marginal role as an alternative source of press revenue.[253] The technological transition of press is, in some cases, financially supported by digital platforms.[254] According to a 2020 report published by Google, the €150 million Google Digital News Innovation Fund supported 662 digital news projects across Europe. Of those funds, 27% were directed to regional and national publishers, 14.5% to news startups and 11% to local publishers.[255] Additionally, 12% of the funds were intended to boost digital revenue, while 52% was dedicated to exploring new technologies.[256] Meta introduced the Meta News Accelerator

249 See: Ministerstwo Kultury i Dziedzictwa Narodowego, "Czasopisma," https://www.gov.pl/web/kultura/czasopisma4, accessed: 21.01.2023.

250 WirtualneMedia.pl, "64 projekty wspierające czasopisma kulturalne otrzymają dotację MKiDN," February 12, 2021, https://www.wirtualnemedia.pl/artykul/64-projekty-wspierajace-czasopisma-kulturalne-otrzymaja-dotacje-mkidn, accessed: 21.01.2023; oko.press, "Minister Gliński i czasopisma. Dotacje tylko dla swoich. Dostała nawet kościelna gazetka dla dzieci," February 13, 2020, https://oko.press/minister-glinski-i-czasopisma-dotacje-tylko-dla-swoich, accessed: 21.01.2023.

251 Indirect support through tax benefits is provided for specialised print periodicals or regional press. See: Ustawa z dnia 11 marca 2004 o podatku od towarów i usług Dz. U. 2004 Nr 54 poz. 535, t.j. Dz. U. z 2022 r. poz. 931, 974, 1137, 1301, 1488, 1561, 2180 (Act of 11 March 2004 on tax on goods and services), Art. 41 ust.2a.

252 See: M. Zdzieborska, Rząd milczy w sprawie dotacji dla prasy lokalnej, Press, June 24, 2022, https://www.press.pl/tresc/71406,rzad-milczy-w-sprawie-dotacji-dla-prasy-lokalnej, accessed: 11.01.2023.

253 See: M. Borger, "Journalism funding in Europe. Reflections and key lessons from the Journalism Funders Forum," Philantropy Europe Assosiation, June 26, 2019, https://philea.eu/journalism-funding-in-europe/, accessed: 23.01.2023.

254 29% of publishers surveyed by N. Newman for the purpose of the Digital News Report, declared to expect to get significant revenue from tech platforms for content licensing or innovation. See: N. Newman et al., *Journalism*, 6.

255 See: Google, "Digital News Innovation Fund Impact Report," 2021, https://newsinitiative.withgoogle.com/impact/, accessed: 23.01.2023.

256 See: Google, "Digital."

programs, which helped European publishers generate more than $18 million in value for their companies.[257]

Some press publishers have adopted diversification strategies by expanding into sectors outside of their core market. This includes entering into e-commerce, engaging in offline activities such as events and merchandising[258] and by exploiting their brand name.[259] Crowdfunding is another alternative funding model for journalism;[260] however, it is currently not expected to become a primary source of revenue but, rather, as "an add-on or something extra."[261]

To conclude:

- the digital transition has proven to be highly challenging for press publishers. The decline in print circulation has necessitated the adoption of new business models and the search for new sources of revenue. However, according to current data, the overall situation for press publishers in Europe is promising: 59% of surveyed publishers report that their overall revenue, including subscriptions and advertising, has increased.[262] Moreover, investments in new revenue streams are starting to pay off, with a significant rise in digital reader revenue.[263]
- large press publishers have been more successful in adapting to the digital landscape, while small and local publishers face significant challenges. Dominated by large platforms and major press publishers in the advertising market, they struggle to develop a sustainable business model and convince their readers to adopt it, putting their survival at risk. In many cases, they lack the financial capacity to make substantial investments that are especially crucial at the early stages of digital transformation.
- the systems of state aid for publishers in Poland and France differ, yet both provide significant support to the industry. However, more resources should be allocated to support local and small publishers, and the aid distribution process should be conducted in a more transparent manner.

257 See: Meta, "European news publishers build big business through Meta Accelerators," October 03, 2022, https://www.facebook.com/formedia/blog/european-publishers-accelerator-program, accessed: 23.01.2023.

258 A. Cornia, A. Karogelopulos, R.K. Nielsen, *Challenges*, 26–27.

259 A. Leurdijk, O. Nieuwenhuis, M. Slot, *Statistical*, 9.

260 See: M. Pérez-Montoro, *Interaction* ..., 123.

261 A. Majid, "Alternative ways of funding journalism: Crowdfunding has raised $20m+ and seeded some major titles," Press Gazette. Future of Media, 2021, https://pressgazette.co.uk/media-audience-and-business-data/alternative-funding-journalism-crowdfunding/, accessed: 23.01.2023

262 N. Newman et al., *Journalism*, 8.

263 T. Henriksson, "World Press Trends preview: Publishers brace for a period marked by uncertainty," World Association of News Publishers, September 29, 2022, https://wan-ifra.org/2022/09/world-press-trends-preview-publishers-brace-for-a-period-marked-by-uncertainty/, accessed: 23.01.2023.

4.3. Press publishers, access to information and media pluralism

The press plays an essential role in a democratic society.[264] As an indispensable tool for the transmission and reception of ideas and thoughts, it contributes to the exercise of freedom of expression. The crucial task of ensuring citizens' access to information is entrusted to journalists[265] but also to press publishers, who participate in the exercise of freedom of expression by supporting authors[266] and disseminating news content to readers. Freedom of press, according to the ECtHR, affords the public one of the most effective means of discovering, forming opinions and participating in public debate.[267]

According to the definition of media pluralism outlined in the introduction to this chapter, the plurality and diversity of ownership and control should be ensured. In this context, it is important to note that an increasing number of large press publishers are becoming part of multinational media companies that produce a variety of media content. The business activities of Axel Springer serve as an example of this trend. Moreover, a single press publisher often publishes multiple titles, consolidating control over various publications. For example, the Le Monde Group, which publishes *Le Monde*, also publishes *L'OBS*, *Télérama*, *Courrier International* and *Le Monde Diplomatique*. As a result, the publication of several journals and magazines is concentrated within a single entity.

The authors of the report "The Newspaper Publishing Industry," prepared for the European Commission, point out that

> Compared to other media markets, the level of concentration in the newspaper market is relatively low, with a few large publishers which are part of multimedia companies and many medium-sized and small publishers, especially at regional and local levels. Nevertheless, the concentration of newspaper publishers is ongoing, especially as newspaper publishers are increasingly having trouble in sustaining their business as stand-alone, individual businesses.[268]

The increasing concentration in the press sector and its impact on media pluralism are becoming significant legal concerns.

As to the other factors that contribute to media pluralism, the press should reflect **diverse and plural viewpoints as well as cultural expressions**. Moreover,

264 ECtHR, Thoma v. Luxembourg, 38432/97, March 29, 2001, para. 45.

265 CDSM Directive, recital 54.

266 ECtHR, Editions Plon v. France, 58148/00, May 18, 2004, para. 22.

267 ECtHR, *Guide on Article 10 of the European Convention on Human Rights* (2022), 16, https://rm.coe.int/guide-on-article-10-freedom-of-expression-eng/native/1680ad61d6, accessed: 26.12.2024.

268 A. Leurdijk, O. Nieuwenhuis, M. Slot, *Statistical*, 5. See also: J. Skrzypczak, "Media ownership regulation in Europe – a threat or opportunity for freedom of speech?" *Przegląd Polityczny* no. 4 (2017): 109–118; B. Klimkiewicz, "Krajobraz medialny w Polsce: Struktura własności i pluralizm mediów," in *Własność medialna i jej wpływ na pluralizm oraz niezależność mediów*, ed. B. Klimkiewicz (Wydawnictwo Uniwersytetu Jagiellońskiego, 2005).

the press sector should be diverse in terms of **both types and genres of content it offers as well as the actors involved in its creation and distribution**. Finally, the press sector should address both **national and local interests**. This means that, for the press industry to comply with the presented definition of media pluralism, it should be characterised by the presence of various types of press publishers, both small and large, operating at both local and national levels, and covering both general and specific topics.

The plurality and diversity of the media landscape should be guaranteed at all stages, including supply, consumption and distribution of media content. The mere existence of multiple and diverse press publishers producing varied content is not enough to ensure media pluralism. This content must be distributed and reach the audience. The increasing importance of visibility in ensuring media pluralism should also be emphasised. Press distribution takes place more and more at the global level[269] in the digital era. The internet has significantly expanded publishers' reach. On the other hand, access to content has become more restricted, as readers are unable to see and access all available content. Although readers potentially have access to content from numerous press publishers, only a small portion of it will be visible to them. R. Baduard using the example of LeMonde.fr points out that while the internet enables a greater diversity of voices, it does not equal visibility for all. Instead, historical media actors continue to dominate the public sphere and remain the most widely heard.[270] The issue of attention allocation is a significant challenge, particularly for local and small press publishers. To ensure their visibility, they must invest in promotional campaigns, partnerships or collaborations with social media platforms and news aggregators, as visibility is essential for their existence.

The issue of visibility and attention allocation is closely linked to another threat to media pluralism – the growing dominance of the press market by a small number of very large press publishers. This can lead to a significant concentration of power in both the production and distribution the content, placing control in the hands of a few dominant players.[271] The "winners take all/most" pattern[272] contradicts the principle of media pluralism, which emphasises the need for a diverse range of publishers of different sizes and types, producing varied content. P. L. Parcu considers the increasing concentration of media and platforms as a deteriorating factor for democratic debate, posing a significant risk of manipulation, particularly in electoral processes.[273] On the other hand, market fragmentation and the artificial proliferation of press publishers are not advisable, as they do not necessarily lead to higher quality content. Neither excessive fragmentation nor market dominance by a few press publishers is desirable from the perspective of media pluralism and

269 Understood as the opposite to local level.

270 R. Badouard, "Pluralisme, indépendance, diversité : peut-on encore 'sauver les médias' ?," *Participations* 2, no. 15 (2016), 8.

271 A. Cornia, A. Karogelopulos,R.K. Nielsen, *Challenges*, 28.

272 M. Hindman, *The Myth of Digital Democracy* (Princeton University Press, 2008), 93.

273 P.L. Parcu, "New digital threats to media pluralism in the information age," *Robert Schuman Centre for Advanced Studies Centre for Media Pluralism and Media Freedom*, no. 19 (2019): 106.

freedom of expression. Instead, what is needed is the optimisation[274] of the number of publishers to ensure both diversity and quality.

To conclude:

- for the press industry to align with the definition of media pluralism, it should be characterised by the presence of diverse press publishers, both small and large, operating at both local and national levels, and covering general and specialized topics. However, the mere existence of multiple press publishers producing diverse content is not enough to ensure media pluralism. This content must also be effectively distributed and reach the audience. In this regard, the visibility factor is of becoming increasingly important.
- the problem of attention allocation in the press industry is becoming increasingly important. Press publishers, particularly local and small ones, must work to ensure their visibility, as it is essential for their existence. At the same time, the increasing dominance of the press market by a small number of very large publishers corresponds with the "winners take all" principle, which has a negative impact on media pluralism.

5. News aggregators and flow of information

5.1. Introductory remarks

More than 50% of respondents interviewed by N. Newman for the Reuters Institute Digital News Report 2019[275] prefer to access news through search engines, social media or news aggregators.[276] Because these platforms are listed among the most frequently used sources of information, it is worth examining how they are defined, how they operate, how they affect the activity of press publishers and how they impact media pluralism. The main objective of this section is to provide answers to these questions.

News aggregators emerged as a reaction to the overload of information in the digital environment.[277] They are defined as websites that take information from multiple sources, organise it in a specific manner and display it in a single place.[278] They aggregate and consolidate content, which reduces transaction costs for

274 A. Lebois during the discussion at Institut de recherche en droit privé, Nantes University, 25.01.2023.

275 The choice of the report from 2019 to quote the data is justified by the fact that the same year the press publishers' rights were adopted.

276 N. Newman et al., *Reuters Institute Digital News Report 2019* (Reuters Institute for the Study of Journalism, University of Oxford, 2019), 13.

277 See: A. Mohamed et al., "News aggregator and efficient summarization system," *International Journal of Advanced Computer Science and Applications* 11, no. 6 (2020): 636–641.

278 K.A. Isbell, "The rise of the news aggregator: Legal implications and best practices," *Berkman Center Research Publication*, no. 10 (2010), 2; W.A. Hanff, "News aggregator," Britannica, https://www.britannica.com/topic/news-aggregator, accessed: 31.01.2023.

obtaining information[279] and allows users access selected and categorised news from different sources. News aggregators are seen "as prototypes for digital newspaper kiosks,"[280] relying on content published by press publishers on their newspapers' websites.

They are mostly based on the RSS format,[281] a software protocol that

> allows applications and their users to access automatic website or content updates. RSS feeds rely on simple text files, extracting important information from XML (extensible markup language). Simplified, streamlined content is then input into an RSS reader, which converts text files into digital updates. Through this process, an RSS feed makes it possible to turn simple information, like a site name or a content's title description, into a steady stream of news articles and new content pieces. This helps readers stay up to date with the latest online developments.[282]

The analysis conducted in this monograph focuses significantly, but not exclusively, on the feed aggregator Google News, a computer-generated news service, launched in 2006, that collects articles from more than 20,000 publishers worldwide.[283] Described as the world's largest news aggregator,[284] Google News had 329.2 million visits in September 2024.[285] It is available in more than 125 countries and in 40 languages.[286]

279 L. Chiou, C. Tucker, "Content aggregation by platforms: The case of the news media," MIT Sloan Research Paper no. 6925-23 (2015): 2.

280 G. Priora, "News aggregation and the reform of EU copyright law," *CEU Democracy Institute, Center for Media, Data and Society* (2018), https://cmds.ceu.edu/article/2018-07-03/news-aggregation-and-reform-eu-copyright-law, accessed: 31.01.2023.

281 RSS stands for "really simple syndication" or "rich site summary"; see: A. Mohamed et al., "News," 636–641.

282 S. Robles, "What is an RSS Feed: Beginners guide on how RSS feeds work," RIVERSIDE, December 28, 2023, https://riverside.fm/blog/what-is-an-rss-feed, accessed: 31.01.2023. See: A. Mohamed et al., "News," 636–641.

283 J. Cohen, "Same protocol, more options for news publishers," Google News Blog, December 2, 2009, https://news.googleblog.com/2009/12/same-protocol-more-options-for-news.html, accessed: 31.01.2023.

284 Q. Wang, "Normalization and differentiation in Google News: A multi-method analysis of the world's largest news aggregator," *Rutgers University* (2020), https://rucore.libraries.rutgers.edu/rutgers-lib/62647/, accessed: 31.01.2023.

285 PressGazette, "Future of media, top 50 news websites in the world: Half grow traffic year on year," December 19, 2024 https://pressgazette.co.uk/media-audience-and-business-data/media_metrics/most-popular-websites-news-world-monthly-2/, accessed: 26.12.2024.

286 B. Bender, O. Ma, "Read all about it: A new look for Google News," June 22, 2022, https://blog.google/products/news/google-news-anniversary-local-reporting-funding/, accessed: 31.01.2023.

5.2. Business model

Google News relies on the use of third-party content.[287] Users can view headlines, which are either identical to or a shortened version of the original headlines displayed on various newspaper websites. By clicking on a news item, the user is redirected to the original source's web page.[288] Consumers also see images, the name of the news source, the time of publication and an indication of whether the news item is local. The current design[289] of the Google News website presents a list of news items grouped according to different categories, including country, world, local news, business, science, technology, entertainment or sports. News items no longer include the full of the news items; instead, they typically display only the headline.[290] The design of the website differs slightly when a user logs in, affecting the displayed content due to personalisation features. However, users can partially[291] deactivate this option.[292] They also have the ability to subscribe to an alert service, receiving regular notifications on their favourite topics and latest updates.

From a technical perspective, press publishers must ensure that their articles comply with the Accelerated Mobile Pages ("AMP") – a system optimised for mobile web browsing – in order to appear on the Google News homepage.[293] This adaptation aligns with changing reader habits, as research conducted for Ofcom shows that online news is accessed primarily via smartphones.[294] The main purpose of the AMP format is to help web pages load more quickly.[295]

D. Geradin notes that "because unlike traditional mobile pages AMP pages are loaded on and served from Google servers, Google can maintain readers in

287 C. F. Mela, J. M.T. Roos, R. Shachar, "The effect of links and excerpts on internet news consumption," *Journal of Marketing Research* 57, no. 3, (2020): 398.

288 The link is not displayed on the Google News' page separately but in the form of headline.

289 Previous design of Google News included snippets defined as a small and often interesting piece of news, information, or conversation (see: Cambridge Dictionary, https://dictionary.cambridge.org/dictionary/english/snippet, accessed: 09.11.2022.)

290 S. Engelmann, S., S. H. Kessler, S. M. Luebke, "Effects," 794.

291 Previously activity and purchases within other Google services are the factors taken into account in provision of the content and this cannot be switched off by the user.

292 Google Official Blog, "Personalized search for everyone," December 04, 2009, https://googleblog.blogspot.com/2009/12/personalized-search-for-everyone.html, accessed: 07.02.2023.

293 In response to the adoption of the related right of press publishers in France Google implemented new display policy. "Google has implemented new 'tags', which are code fragments, that publishers and news agencies can insert into the source code of their web pages to allow Google to take excerpts from their editorial content in the form of text, images and video. (…) These tags, which take the form of a piece of computer code exploitable by Google's robots." FCA Decision of April 9, 2020 on interim measures, 27.

294 Ofcom, *Scrolling News: The Changing Face of Online News Consumption*, A report for Ofcom (2018), 20, https://www.ofcom.org.uk/__data/assets/pdf_file/0022/115915/Scrolling-News.pdf, accessed: 06.02.2023.

295 Google Ads Help, "About Accelerated Mobile Pages (AMP)," https://support.google.com/google-ads/answer/7496737?hl=en, accessed: 01.02.2023.

its environment, as well as collect all the data generated on such pages."[296] This reflects a form of platform dependency, as Google gains a degree of control over the content that appears on Google News. Consequently, this can impact the visibility and recognition of a press publisher's brand as well as limit its monetisation and advertising opportunities.[297] Press publishers, as well as anyone managing a news-related website that meets the specified technical requirements, can share their content on Google News by submitting it through the Google Publisher Centre. This interface helps publishers publish, manage and monetise their content within Google News.[298]

In theory, to prevent content from being displayed on Google News,[299] it would be enough to change the content format or include a notice explicitly stating that the use of press materials is not permitted. In practice, however, this scenario seems highly unlikely. Given the benefits of being featured on news aggregators, particularly in terms of increased visibility, publishers are rather reluctant to opt out from being displayed on news aggregators.

Regarding the copyright framework for the use of third-party content by news aggregators, there was no specific regulation at the EU level to address this practice until the adoption of the CDSM Directive in 2019. In France, la loi 2019-1063 of 18 October 2019, on the status of groupage and distribution companies for newspapers and periodicals,[300] introduced a provision related to the transparency of data processing by news aggregators. According to Art. 15§2, news aggregators must provide users with fair, clear and transparent information regarding the use of their personal data in the classification or referencing of content. Each year, news aggregators must compile and publish statistics on the titles, publishers and number of consultations of the content they display. This measure can be seen as an important step toward increasing the transparency of news aggregators' practices, which will likely lead to greater awareness regarding the use of their data.[301] In Poland, however, no specific provisions regulating the functioning of news aggregators have been adopted.

296 D. Geradin, "Complements or substitutes: The competitive dynamics between news publishers and digital platforms and what it means for competition policy," *Antitrust & Public Policies*, no. 0 (2019): 10–11.

297 D. Geradin, "Complements," 10–11. See also: S.A. Ganter, R.K. Nielsen, "Dealing with digital intermediaries: A case study of the relations between publishers and platforms," *New Media and Society* 20, no. 4 (2018), 1601.

298 Google, Publisher Center Help, "Show up in Google News," https://support.google.com/news/publisher-center/answer/9607025?hl=en, accessed: 04.02.2023. This interface is rather dedicated to small and unknow to wider public publishers.

299 According to Google: "Until the end of last year (2019), publishers had to fill out a form to be displayed in Google News. Now, editors can opt out of Google News by giving an instruction to the robots," see: FCA Decision of April 9, 2020 on interim measures, 18.

300 Loi n° 47-585 du 2 avril 1947 relative au statut des entreprises de groupage et de distribution des journaux et publications périodiques.

301 See: E. Dreyer, *Droit*, 387–388.

It could be presumed that news aggregators should use press publishers' content on a license-based model; however, in practice, this approach remains relatively uncommon.[302] In the vast majority of cases, platforms use the excerpts from press publications without acquiring legal rights to these elements and without paying the publishers for their use. They justify their practice by referring to copyright exceptions. For example, Art. 5(3)(c) of the InfoSoc Directive allows Member States to establish exceptions or limitations to the right of reproduction and the right of communication to the public, including making content available in cases in which press publications **reproduce, communicate or make available published articles on current economic, political or religious topics as well as broadcast works or similar subject matter; when such use is not expressly reserved by the rights holder; and the source, including the author's name, is indicated, unless it is impossible to do so**. The limitation covers articles that have already been published, broadcast works and other subject matters of the same character. This limitation is subject to a topic restriction, meaning that press articles must relate to current economic, political or religious topics, while other works or subject matter must have a similar character. According to A. Lazarova "the permitted use encompasses reproduction – by the press – and communication to the public or making available – by everyone." However, some academics argue that this broad interpretation extends beyond the scope of the exception outlined in Art. 5(3)(c) of the InfoSoc Directive.[303] J. Barta and R. Markiewicz suggest interpreting this provision as applying specifically to the making available of such content by press, radio, television and other entities whose primary purpose is the dissemination of information.[304] Following this interpretation, news aggregators could be included in the category of entities covered by the discussed provision,[305] as they contribute to the dissemination of information. Key in assessing whether the exception applies to the activities of news aggregators is the three-step test. Based on this assessment, it is my opinion that the exception would not be justified.

Another exception that platforms reference to justify their activity is the quotation exception. According to Art. 5(3)(d) of the InfoSoc Directive, Member States may establish exceptions or limitations to the reproduction and making available rights for quotations, provided they serve purposes such as criticism or review. The quotation exception applies only to a work or other subject matter that has already been lawfully made available to the public. Unless this turns out to be impossible, the source, including the author's name, must be indicated, and the use must be in accordance with fair practice and be limited to what is necessary

302 Google News licenses the use of the entire articles of some press publishers within the Google News Showcase section. Launched in 2020 it allows readers to access for free the selected articles originating from the websites of newspapers thanks to the licensing program established between Google and some press publishers.

303 See: E. Laskowska-Litak, J. Marcinkowska, J. Preussner-Zamorska, "Dozwolony użytek chronionych utworów," in *System Prawa Prywatnego*, ed. J. Barta (C.H. Beck, Legalis, 2017), 632–636.

304 J. Barta, R. Markiewicz, *Prawo autorskie* (Wolters Kluwer, 2016), 478.

305 J. Barta, R. Markiewicz, *Prawo*, 478.

for the specific purpose. In the *Pelham* case, the CJEU observed that, as part of the conditions for quotation, the content should be "unaltered and distinguishable" from the original.[306] Quotation cannot be "so extensive as to conflict with a normal exploitation of the work of another subject matter or prejudices unreasonably the legitimate interests of the rightholder"[307] and is required to be in accordance with fair practice and be aligned with a specific purpose. The essence of a quotation, according to both EU law and national laws (e.g., French and Polish), is the incorporation of an unaltered fragment of someone else's work[308] into a new work. J. Barta, R. Markiewicz describe quotation as having an ancillary role in relation to the work as whole.[309] The extent of the quotation should not exceed what is justified by the purpose of explanation, polemics, critical or scientific analysis or teaching or by the rights inherent to a particular artistic genre. Quotation needs to be accompanied by the comments of a critical, comparative or analytical nature.[310] This disqualifies the justification for the operation of news aggregators based on the quotation exception, as reflected in the court decisions[311] issued in the context of disputes between press publishers and aggregators.[312]

306 CJEU, Pelham, paras. 72–73. J. Parkin criticizes the requirement of recognizability or identifiability of the quoted work by the audience See: J. Parkin, "The copyright quotation exception: Not fair use by another name," *Oxford University Commonwealth Law Journal* 19, no. 1 (2019): 4.

307 CJEU, Spiegel Online, para. 79.

308 J. Barta, R. Markiewicz, *Prawo autorskie*, 236.

309 J. Barta, R. Markiewicz, *Prawo autorskie,* 236.

310 In France the issue had been controversial due to the case Microfor v. Le Monde. Microfor included in its database and published in its France-actualités index the titles of French newspapers, in particular Le Monde and Le Monde diplomatique, accompanied by an indexation, as well as, under the name of "Résumés signalétiques", sentences extracted from the articles from these newspapers, which it claimed to report on. Microfor's work thus consisted of the collection and arrangement of various extracts from the French daily press, enriched with an index. One of the questions that arose was whether the quotation exception applies to a collection of short quotes from a single daily newspaper without any commentary added. According to the Court of Cassation, due to the information context, such a collection devoid of critical remarks can be considered as meeting the requirement of the quotation exception. It should be however noted that the judgement has been highly criticized as contradicting the basic premises of the citation exception and considered by some scholars as being contra legem to Art. 122-5 of French Intellectual Property Law. See: Judgement of the Court of Cassation, Civil Chamber, November 9, 1983, 82-10.005, https://www.legifrance.gouv.fr/juri/id/JURITEXT000007012957/, accessed: 03.05.2023. See: F. Pollaud-Dulian, *Propriété intellectuelle. Le droit d'auteur* (Economica, 2014), 859–860; Ch. Caron, *Droit d'auteur et droits voisins* (Lexis Nexis, 2017), 367–368.

311 See for example: The Court Appel of Brussels, Google Inc vs. Copiepresse, 2011, http://www.copiepresse.be/pdf/Copiepresse%20-%20ruling%20appeal%20Google_5May2011.pdf, accessed: 02.02.2023.

312 List of legal disputes between Google News and newspaper publishers before the adoption of the CDSM Directive is long. To mention some conflicts: News Agency Agence France - Presse sued Google claiming the search engine breached its copyright by reproducing its pictures and articles. To close litigation, the licensing agreements between these two actors have been signed. In 2012, the agreement has been reached between Google and Belgian newspaper publishers' group, Copiepresse that accused Google of copyright infringement. In 2013, a fund of 60 million euros has been created by Google to put an end to disputes that arose with French press publishers. In 2014,

According to the Brussels Court of Appeal, the role of Google News is not limited to a "passive mediator.[313] Instead, it actively selects and classifies information according to its own methods, chooses one article over another, highlights certain text in bold and sometimes duplicates sections.[314] The news pieces published on Google News are selected[315] and ranked automatically as the result of the use of the algorithms.[316] In some cases, human judgement is involved,[317] but it should not be understood as a traditional publishing process that entails editorial responsibility.[318]

The news are selected according to criteria[319] such as frequency of appearance across different websites,[320] recency of the articles,[321] relevancy of the topic, credibility of the source,[322] originality, freshness, localness[323] and the position of the articles on other websites.[324] Two tendencies should be identified in this context. First, Google News promotes content that is covered by a large number of sources, reflecting the phenomenon of the circular flow of information, which has been observed in traditional media.[325] Second, content from local publishers is being

the Google News Spain closed down due to the conflicts that arose around the reformed Spanish intellectual property law obliging Google to pay press publishers for the use of their content and reopened in 2022.

313 The Court Appel of Brussels, Google Inc vs. Copiepresse, 2011, para. 55.

314 The Court Appel of Brussels, Google Inc vs. Copiepresse, 2011, para. 55. See also: A. Lebois, "La légitimité du nouveau droit voisin de l'éditeur et de l'agence de presse." *Légipresse* (2019): 3.

315 However, in case of Google News Shawcase the partnership with selected publishers has been established and according to Google News, they "have direct control of their presentation and branding, which provides a way to form deeper relationships with their audiences." Google, "What's Google News Showcase," https://support.google.com/news/publisher-center/answer/10018888?hl=en, accessed: 31.01.2023.

316 I. Engelmann, S.H. Kessler, "Why do we click? Investigating reasons for user selection on a news aggregator website," *Communications* (2018), 5. See: F. Pasquale, *The Black Box Society: The Secret Algorithms That Control Money and Information* (Harvard University Press, 2015), 59–100.

317 Google News Help, "How Google News stories are selected," https://support.google.com/googlenews/answer/9005749?hl=en, accessed: 02.02.2023.

318 The role of human in the distrubtion of news on Goolge News consists mostly in rating the content, see: The Cairncross Review, *A Sustainable Future for Journalism*, (2019), 28, https://assets.publishing.service.gov.uk/media/5c6bfcd4e5274a72b933311d/021919_DCMS_Cairncross_Review_.pdf, accessed: 30.12.2024. See also: J.N. Jeanneney, A. Strowel, *Quand Google défie le droit* (De Boeck& Larcier, 2011): 62.

319 See: F. Rebillard, N. Smyrnaios, "L'actualité selon Google. L'emprise du principal moteur de recherche sur l'information en ligne," *Communication & Langages* no. 16 (2009): 96.

320 I. Engelmann, S.H. Kessler, S.M. Luebke, "Effects," 786.

321 I. Engelmann, S.H. Kessler, "Why," 6.

322 I. Engelmann, S.H. Kessler, S.M. Luebke, "Effects," 786.

323 S. Machlis, "Inside the Google News algorithm, Computer World," October 5, 2009, https://www.computerworld.com/article/2467854/inside-the-google-news-algorithm.html, accessed: 02.02.2023.

324 I. Engelmann, S. H. Kessler, S. M. Luebke, "Effects," 786.

325 F. Rebillard, N. Smyrnaios, "L'actualité," 105.

increasingly promoted, with Google News offering new services and providing special funds for this purpose.[326]

As to the users' perception of the content, there is a relationship between the amount of information displayed by news aggregators and the probability that readers will click on the link to read the article in its entirety. It should be acknowledged that the content displayed on news aggregators allows users to quickly assess whether the article corresponds to their interests. For some users, news aggregators already serve as an important and, in many cases, sufficient source of information, which leads to a decrease in click-through rates. It has been proven that the longer the snippet, the lower is the click-through rate tends to be.[327] However, when users have a choice between several publications, they are more likely to click on a headline or snippet that is longer.[328]

Platforms such as Google, Facebook and Twitter are called "attention brokers" because their business model is based on attracting users by providing them with content for free and then on reselling their attention and their personal data to advertisers.[329] The users do not see the advertisements directly on the Google News website, but these ads are visible on other Google services pages. According to the T. L. Cobos, the profits of aggregators are derived from "the information they collect about the audience's behaviours and digital consumption."[330] They monetise the readers' attention and data by displaying the targeted advertising within its services.[331] This practice contributes to the reinforcement of the "winner takes all" or "winner takes most"[332] dynamics, as one branch of the Google's business drives the other. This results in an increasingly dominant position for Google in the market, leading to a weaker position and greater dependence for other media outlets, including press publishers. This is even more relevant given that there is no charge for using news aggregators, and one of the most important criteria for readers when choosing a service to access news online is whether the service is free.

326 D. Goodwin, "Google gives more visibility to local news publishers," February 9, 2022, https://searchengineland.com/google-news-local-visibility-showcase-panels-380139, accessed: 02.02.2023.

327 M. Calin et al., "Attention allocation in information rich environments: The case of news aggregators," *Boston University School of Management Research Paper Series* no. 4 (2013): 4.

328 B. Martens et al., "The digital," 19.

329 D. Geradin, "Complements," 7.

330 T.L. Cobos, "New scenarios in news distribution: The impact of news aggregators like Google News in the media outlets on the web," in *Present Scenarios of Media Production and Engagement*, ed. S. Tosoni et al. (Lumière Bremen, 2017), 98.

331 European Publishers Council, *Online Platforms and Digital Advertising Market Study Observations of the European Publishers Council (EPC) on the Statement of Scope*, (2019), 3–5, https://assets.publishing.service.gov.uk/media/5d6906e9e5274a17125628c2/European_Publishers_Council__-_Response_to_SoS.pdf, accessed: 30.12.2024.

332 P.L. Parcu, "New digital," 94.

To conclude:

- Google is an important actor in the news media ecosystem, especially in the context of digital transformation, which determines the new modes of distributing and receiving information. Its increasingly strong position in the market leads to the weaker position and greater dependence of press publishers. The important imbalances between these two actors should be highlighted.
- news aggregators provide readers with access to a wide variety of content, saving them time and reducing costs, as selected materials are gathered in one place. They serve as a basic source of information that can always be further explored by visiting the press publishers' websites.[333] Moreover, they are adapted to changing readers' habits and offers the compilation of selected articles that match readers' interests, sourced from different outlets.[334]
- there is a relationship between the amount of information displayed by news aggregators and the likelihood that readers will click on the link to read the article in its entirety. When users are presented with a choice between several publications, they are more likely to click on a longer headline or snippet.

5.3. Relationship between Google and press publishers from a market perspective

Considering the previous discussion, it is important to focus on the impact of Google on the interests and functioning of press publishers. Based on existing empirical studies and analyses, four key characteristics of the relationship between these two actors can be identified: **competition**, **substitution**, **dependence** and **complementarity**.

In regard to **competition**, major online platforms, including Google, possess "the unique data economies of scale and scope."[335] This means they have a larger user base, which provides them with a rich set of data that is highly valuable to advertisers, along with a large audience for advertisements. The digital advertising market is highly concentrated and dominated by the large players. In 2021, Google generated $147 billion in advertising revenue, accounting for approximately 42% of global ad revenue.[336] Furthermore, the advertisers tend to favour user-oriented over context-oriented advertising displays.[337] Press publishers are unable to collect as much and as accurate information about users as online platforms. Moreover, they have smaller audiences, which makes them less attractive to advertisers. As a result, both actors compete for audience attention and advertising revenue, but, as noted earlier, press publishers are in a weaker position.

333 L. Chiou, C. Tucker, "Content," 1.
334 J. Rutt, *Aggregators*, 2.
335 European Publishers Council, *Online Platforms*, 3.
336 Statista, "Advertising revenue generated by Google from 2017 to 2026," August 2023, https://www.statista.com/statistics/539447/google-global-net-advertising-revenues/, accessed: 03.02.2023.
337 D. Geradin, "Complements," 14.

As the press sector becomes increasingly less reliant on advertising-based models, publishers are forced to look for other sources of revenue.[338] The dominance of Google News is even more difficult for press publishers to accept, especially considering its business model, which is based on the use of the press publishers' content. Publishers accuse aggregators of free riding and claim that Google News generates advertising revenues by exploiting their content without sharing the profits.[339]

Of consumers browsing and reading news extracts on social media websites, news aggregators and search engines, 47% do not click on links to access the full article on the publisher's page.[340] The "scanning effect" occurs when news aggregators substitute press publishers' content,[341] which means the reader does not click through to the publisher's website, does not read other publications and does not contribute to the advertising revenue. The decrease in traffic to newspaper home pages is described as the "business stealing effect,"[342] leading to financial losses for press publishers.

News aggregators **substitute** newspapers' websites, making the reader less aware of the source of the press material. As a result, the press publisher's brand is less reinforced in the reader's' memory and becomes less recognisable, which may lead to fewer users willing to subscribe to the newspaper. This is primarily because news aggregators bypass the press publishers' homepage and replace it with their own index page.[343]

The relationship between these two actors is complex and contradictory. In some cases, they are not only substitutes or competitors but also **vertically complementary**.[344] While news aggregators use content produced by press publishers, they

338 D.S. Jeon, "News aggregators and competition among newspapers on the internet," *American Economic Journal: Microeconomics* 8, no.4, (2016) 107; E. Bell et al., *The Platform Press. How Silicon Valley Reengineered Journalism* (Tow Center for Digital Journalism, Columbia Journalism School, 2017), 43.

339 The European Publishers Council points out that the content used by news aggregators is professionally produced under the editorial responsibility and legal liability of press publishers and is of vital importance for the attractivity and the mere existence of such a platform. (European Publishers Council, Online Platforms, 6).

340 European Commission, *Flash Eurobarometer 437: Report, Internet Users' Preferences for Accessing Content Online*, September 14, 2016, 437, https://digital-strategy.ec.europa.eu/en/library/eurobarometer-internet-users-preferences-accessing-content-online, accessed: 30.12.2024. The reference to this data has been also made in the Impact Assessment on the modernisation of EU copyright rules Accompanying the document Proposal for a CDSM Directive.

341 L. Chiou, C. Tucker, "Content aggregation," 4.

342 D.-S. Jeon, N. Nasr, "News aggregators," 93.

343 Google News is considered as a complement to overall news reading and articles but a substitute for landing pages since it directly links to publishers' articles and not to their home pages. See: S. Athey, M. Mobius, J.Pal, "The impact of news aggregators on internet news consumption: The case of localization," *National Bureau of Economic Research*, NBER Working Paper No. 28746 (2021), 14, 18,https://www.nber.org/system/files/working_papers/w28746/w28746.pdf, accessed: 03.02.2023.

344 See: D. Geradin, "Complements," 2.

enhance their online visibility, which, in turn, generates traffic to the publishers' websites.[345] Consumers can discover the number of outlets, find new ones and identify those that best match with their interests. This is particularly relevant for small, niche and local publishers, who may be less well-known to readers. Thanks to news aggregators, newspapers are able to reach audiences that they may not have been able to reach otherwise.[346]

Increased visibility for press publishers leads to more traffic to their websites. Google claims that

> each month, people click through from Google Search and Google News results to publishers' websites more than 24 billion times – that's over 9,000 clicks per second. By sending free traffic to news sites, we generate significant monetary value for publishers.[347]

According to data provided by some French press publishers, search engines such as Google search account for, "depending on the publisher, between 26% and 90% of redirected traffic, and two-thirds of this traffic on average. For more than three-quarters of SEPM [Le Syndicat des Éditeurs de la Presse Magazine] respondents (and 80% of APIG [Alliance de la Presse d'Information Générale]respondents), this percentage is greater than 50%."[348] Multiplying the number of clicks by the value per click generates a significant monetary value for press publishers.

An important source of data regarding the relationship between these two actors comes from research assessing the effects of conflicts between them. When Google News stopped to host Associated Press content in France in 2009, 28% fewer users visited news websites where Associated Press articles were featured.[349] Additionally, users were less likely to visit other news websites as well.[350] After the shutdown of Google News in Spain in 2014, Spanish news outlets observed an overall decrease in daily visits ranging from 8% to 14%, with a larger reduction in visits for smaller and less well-known outlets.[351] NERA Economic Consulting reported 30% traffic decreases for some websites,[352] highlighting how strongly connected these two actors are and how dependent they are on each other.

345 L. Chiou, C. Tucker, "Content aggregation," 1.

346 D. Geradin, "Complements," 11.

347 Google, "How Google supports journalism and the news industry," https://blog.google/supporting-news/#overview, accessed: 04.02.2023.

348 FCA Decision of April 9, 2020 on interim measures, 51.

349 L. Chiou, C. Tucker, "Content aggregation," 783.

350 L. Chiou, C. Tucker, "Content aggregation," 85.

351 J. Calzada, R. Gil, "What do news aggregators do? Evidence from Google News in Spain and Germany," *Marketing Science* 39, no. 1 (2020): 135.

352 P. Posada de la Concha, A. Gutiérrez García, H. Hernández Cobos, *Impacto del Nuevo Artículo 32.2 de la Ley de Propiedad Intelectual Informe para la Asociación Española de Editoriales de Publicaciones Periódicas (AEEPP)* (2015), 6, https://clabe.org/pdf/InformeNera.pdf, accessed: 04.02.2023.

News aggregators are particularly influential in increasing traffic to small and local press publishers. According to S. Athey, M. Mobius and J. Pal, who examined the effects of Google's adoption of the "local news" feature in France in 2009, local outlets saw a 26.3% increase in traffic and a 44.6% rise in article views due to their presence on Google News.[353] The previously discussed conflicts significantly affected small publishers, leading to reduced traffic to their websites and, as a result, financial losses.[354]

The relationship between the two actors is characterized by a peculiar dependency. Google News and online platforms, in general, rely on the content produced by press publishers. For press publishers, particularly small and local ones, visibility on online platforms and the traffic generated traffic are crucial, often being a matter of survival. The fear of missing out and the challenges of[355] managing website traffic without intermediaries make some publishers reluctant to risk damaging relationships with Google. The asymmetries and significant imbalances in bargaining power between platforms and publishers of small and local newspapers should be emphasised. For many small and local publishers, the risk of no longer being displayed on platforms such as Google can mean the end of their business.[356] **They are vulnerable to the conditions dictated by platforms**. Moreover, it should be noted that it is not in the interest of every press publisher, especially small and local ones, to engage in disputes with Google, as this could lead to reduced visibility on the platform's services or even result in the removal of their content.[357]

To conclude:

- it is not possible to draw an entirely positive or absolutely negative conclusion regarding the impact of news aggregators on press publishers. Their relationship is nuanced.
- in the areas of advertising revenue, brand recognition and contributing to the scanning effect, news aggregators have a negative impact on the interests of press publishers. However, in terms of increasing visibility and driving traffic to their websites, the impact is positive, which is especially important for small and local publishers, for whom visitibility on news aggregators is of vital for their survival.[358]

353 S. Athey, M. Mobius, J. Pal, "The impact," 5.
354 See: J. Calzada, R. Gil, "What do," 135.
355 S.A. Ganter, R.K. Nielsen, "Dealing," 1602.
356 See: D. Geradin, "Complements," 22.
357 See: SudOuest, "Bataille entre Google et la presse française : qu'est-ce que 'le droit voisin' et quels sont les enjeux ?," SudOuest, October 5, 2020, https://www.sudouest.fr/international/europe/bataille-entre-google-et-la-presse-francaise-qu-est-ce-que-le-droit-voisin-et-quels-sont-les-enjeux-1716961.php, accessed: 07.02.2023.
358 See: S. Athey, M. Mobius, J. Pal, "The impact."

5.4. News aggregators, access to information and media pluralism

To define the role of news aggregators in the context of media pluralism, their functioning should be analysed, particularly from the perspective of plurality and diversity in media distribution. Their activity primarily consists in enabling access to information. It is a well-established view in academic literature that news aggregators contribute to the increase in diversity and the amount of information accessible in the online environment.[359] They serve as gatekeepers, involved in the process of selecting, organising, scheduling, prioritising and distributing news.[360] They constitute a kind of "access industry" by organising and providing access for the general public to the content produced by media outlets.[361] They act as intermediaries,[362] connecting publishers with a large number of consumers.

Access to information provided by news aggregators and platforms, in general, is broad. First, it allows users to confront different political, social, economic views, which contrasts with newspapers, typically considered to present a particular line of views, often from either a more liberal or more conservative perspective.[363] Second, the information distributed through news aggregators are available for free, which encourages users to use such platforms and increases their exposure to news. Lastly, by ensuring the visibility of diverse press materials, including content produced by the less well-known, small, local or niche press publishers, news aggregators enable a wider audience to access content they might would not have encountered if they had not visited the aggregator's website.[364]

> Google is able to make a profit from any Internet user accessing news content on the Internet, whether this access takes place through a news-related search on (Google) Search and results in the display of protected content, or via any other means. In the case of an Internet user that uses the general search

359 R. Fletcher, N. Newman, "Platform reliance, information intermediaries, and News Diversity. A look at the evidence," in *The power of Google, Amazon, Facebook and people*, ed. M. Moore, D. Tambini (Oxford University Press, 2018), 133; see also: S.C. Lewis, E. Nechushtai, "What kind of news gatekeepers do we want machines to be? Filter bubbles, fragmentation, and the normative dimensions of algorithmic recommendations," *Computers in Human Behavior* 90 (2019): 298–307.

360 See: S. C. Lewis, E. Nechushtai, "What kind," 299.

361 F. Rebillard, N. Smyrnaios, "L'actualité," 96.

362 See: A. Del Águila, A. Padilla, C. Serarols, "Value creation and news intermediaries on Internet: An exploratory analysis of the online news industry and the web content aggregators," *International Journal of Information Management* 27, no. 3 (2007): 187–199.

363 Results of the study conducted by R. Fletcher, R.K. Nielsen show that "those who find news via search engines (i) on average use more sources of online news, (ii) are more likely to use both left-leaning and right-leaning online news sources, and (iii) have more balanced news repertoires in terms of using similar numbers of left-leaning and right-leaning sources." See: R. Fletcher, R. K. Nielsen, "Automated serendipity. The effect of using search engines on news repertoire balance and diversity," *Digital Journalism* 6, no. 8 (2018): 986.

364 R. Fletcher, A. Kalogeropoulos, R. K. Nielsen, "More diverse, more politically varied: How social media, search engines and aggregators shape news repertoires in the United Kingdom," *New Media & Society* 0, no. 0 (2021): 2–3.

> engine Search, Google is in fact able to collect revenues, whether or not the Internet user clicks on a link displaying protected content and redirecting it to a press publisher's website. In the case of an Internet user that accesses a press publisher's website by a means other than Search, Google can still take advantage of its role as an intermediary in online advertising. Thus, unlike publishers, which are still dependent for their advertising revenue solely on the traffic directed to them, Google derives a benefit from any Internet user search for news, even though it does not produce news content.[365]

Research shows that distributed access is the primary way of accessing news online for a significant number of readers.[366] It is partially governed by self-selection but, mostly, by algorithmic selection, which leads to content recommendation.[367] The latter is often perceived as a threat to media pluralism. According to the Committee of Ministers to Member States, the control that online intermediaries have over the flow, availability, findability and accessibility of information and other content online

> may affect the variety of media sources that individuals are exposed to and result in their selecting or being exposed to information that confirms their existing views and opinions, which is further reinforced by exchange with other like-minded individuals (this phenomenon is sometimes referred to as a "filter bubble" or "echo chamber"). Selective exposure to media content and the resulting limitations on its use can generate fragmentation and result in a more polarised society.[368]

The phenomenon of filter bubbles and echo chambers is considered to have a negative impact on media diversity and, in broader sense, on media pluralism.[369] However, according to recent studies, there is no evidence to suggest that news aggregators prioritise the distribution of like-minded content or content that aligns with users' existing preferences, which could lead to societal fragmentation.[370] It has not been proven that the information displayed on Google News differs significantly based on user profiles.[371] Additionally, studies indicate that aggregation

365 FCA Decision of April 9, 2020 on interim measures, 50.

366 According to the Reuters Institute Digital News Report around 65% surveyed people prefer to get to news though side door. See: N. Newman et al., *Reuters Institute Digital News Report 2018* (Reuters Institute for the Study of Journalism, University of Oxford, 2018), 13.

367 See: F. J. Zuiderveen Borgesius et al., "Should we worry about filter bubbles?," *Internet Policy Review* 5, no. 1 (2016).

368 Committee of Ministers, *Recommendation CM/Rec* (2018).

369 Council of Europe, *Pluralisme*, 6–7.

370 N. Helberger, J. Moeller, "Beyond the filter bubble: Concepts, myths, evidence and issues for future debates," *University of Amsterdam* (2018), https://www.ivir.nl/publicaties/download/Beyond_the_filter_bubble__concepts_myths_evidence_and_issues_for_future_debates.pdf, accessed: 06.02.2023.

371 See the results of the study conducted by H.B., Brosius, A, Graefe, M. Haim, "Burst of the Filter Bubble? Effects of personalization on the diversity of Google News," *Digital Journalism* 6, no. 3 (2018): 334–335.

can actually increase the diversity of sources consulted.[372] J. Calzada and R. Gil point out that "aggregators offer content of a higher quality and variety than traditional news outlets, which induce consumers to read more news stories."[373] It is worth noting that Google News, as part of its 2018 redesign, offered users the option to opt out of content personalisation.[374] Therefore, as M. Haim, A, Graefe and H.-B. Brosius suggest, the filter bubble phenomenon in the case of algorithmic personalisation within Google News may be overestimated.[375] N. Helberger and J. Moeller interestingly point out that concerns about filter bubbles may discourage media companies in Europe from investing in new technologies to explore better ways of distributing content, offering better services and competing with other platforms.[376]

In this context, I have identified another problem that has not been discussed in academic literature in detail yet and has not been the subject of much research so far. I see a risk of Google News and platforms, in general, leading to the over-representation of some media outlets and the under-representation of others. Because Google News decides what information from which publishers it distributes, press publishers, in this aspect, dependent on the aggregator. It is possible that many articles from one press publisher will be displayed on the news aggregator's website, while none from another press publisher may appear for a certain period of time. There are two possible justifications for such practices. The first relates to the technical aspects of Google News, in that the algorithms may highly favour up-to-date information or content that include popular keywords. The second justification concerns the relationship between the platform and the press publishers. Because some of press publishers have engaged in legal disputes with Google, it can be assumed that the platform, in an attempt to penalize them, may partially exclude their content.[377] However, it should be emphasised that this issue still requires further examination through empirical studies. In addition, it is important to highlight that platforms have the freedom to provide services and, unless otherwise agreed, are not obligated to display content from all publishers. Nevertheless, users should be aware that such practices may occur, particularly when news aggregators serve as their primary source of information.

To conclude:

- news aggregators contribute to the increase in diversity of information in the online environment. Their role in enabling access to information involves selecting, organising, scheduling, prioritising and distributing news, as well as

372 L.M. George, Ch. Hogendorn, "Local news online: aggregators, geo-targeting and the market for local news," *The Journal of Industrial Economics* 68, no. 4 (2020).
373 J. Calzada, R. Gil, "What do," 139.
374 See: E. Nechushtai, S.C. Lewis, "What kind," 301.
375 H.B., Brosius, A, Graefe, M. Haim, "Burst," 339.
376 N. Helberger, J. Moeller, "Beyond," 24–25.
377 See: H.B., Brosius, A, Graefe, M. Haim, "Burst," 339.

organising and providing access for the general public to the content produced by media outlets and connecting publishers with a large number of consumers.
- the filter bubble phenomenon, in the case of algorithmic personalisation within Google News, does not pose a significant threat to the safeguarding of media pluralism.
- I see a risk of Google News favouring content from certain publishers, leading to the over-representation of some media outlets and the under-representation of others. This could have negative consequences for media pluralism.

6. Conclusion

Legislative interference in areas of rights and freedoms protected by the Charter must be justified. The legislature's role is to assess whether the proposed law does not interfere with fundamental rights, and if it does, whether it meets the criteria justify such interference. This assessment is often complex. Not all factors can always be considered due to technological development or unpredictable human behaviour. Only a thorough evaluation of the proposed legal solution, conducted according to the discussed criteria, can minimise its potential negative impact on other fundamental rights.

The provided analysis also discussed the ongoing transformation and technological development of press sector. This transformation is linked to the need to reconstruct business models and seek new sources of revenue, especially when compared to the past era of printed press. Adapting to the pace of change and its technical complexity can be particularly challenging for small and local publishers. They are the victims of the winner-take-all dynamic, both in their competition with larger press publishers and with online platforms. They are also the ones most likely to enter into partnerships with larger platforms, gaining the online visibility they need to survive. The difficult situation of small and local press publishers, many of whom are going out of business, can be seen as a threat to media pluralism.

Given the emerging asymmetries within the press sector and the discussed difficult economic situation of small and local publishers, I believe that States should act as the guarantors of media pluralism. Therefore, first, state aid for publishers should be strengthened, with a particular focus on small and local publishers, especially in terms of supporting their technological transition. Second, and this is a recommendation that merely reiterates what has already been said, during the legislative process for enacting laws directly or indirectly affecting press publishers, the legislature should take into account all factors that may potentially conflict and interfere with the public's interest, impacting the right to receive information and the safeguard of media pluralism. In this context, the complex landscape of the press sector, along with the differences between the situations of large and small publishers, should be carefully considered.

An important role in enabling access to information and contributing to the protection of media pluralism is played by online platforms providing various services, such as news aggregation. It is not possible to draw an entirely positive or negative conclusion about the impact of news aggregators on press publishers' interests. Their relationship is nuanced. In the area of advertising revenue, brand recognition or in terms of contributing to the scanning effect, news aggregators have a negative impact on the interests of press publishers. However, in terms of increasing the visibility of press publishers and driving traffic to their websites, the impact is positive. This is particularly important for small and local publishers, for whom visibility on news aggregators is vital. The legislature should take this into account when regulating the relationship between press publishers and news aggregators.

2 Related rights to press publication in light of the CDSM Directive and national laws

1. Introduction

This chapter begins with an analysis of the main features of the related rights regime. Next, it examines the *ratio legis* of publishers' rights to clarify the rationale behind their adoption. The discussion then shifts to the subject matter of protection, aiming to determine what is and is not protected by publishers' rights. Following this, the characteristics of press publishers as rights holders are outlined. Finally, the legal relationship between press publishers and the authors of the works included in press publications is scrutinised.

The analysis of publishers' rights covers the provisions from Articles 15 and 2(4) of the CDSM Directive as well their implementation in French and Polish law. France was the first Member State (hereinafter: MS) to implement press publishers' rights on July 23, 2019, by incorporating them into the *Code de la propriété intellectuelle* (hereinafter: French Intellectual Property Code).[1] Poland was the last MS to do so, implementing the rights on September 20, 2024, through amendments to the *Ustawa o prawie autorskim i prawach pokrewnych* (hereinafter: Polish Copyright Act).[2] These jurisdictions were chosen for analysis to identify and examine how the approach to implementing publishers' rights evolved over five years, how legislators have addressed ongoing technological advancements and, ultimately, to assess whether the introduced protection can actually achieve its objectives. For the sake of comparison and to complete and enrich the analysis, certain solutions adopted in the implementation of Art. 15 of the CDSM Directive in Belgium, Spain, Germany, Italy and the Czech Republic will also be discussed. In Germany, the legislation was adopted on May 20, 2021, as part of the *Urheberrechtsgesetz*.[3] In Italy, it was implemented on November 8, 2021, in

1 LOI n° 2019-775 du 24 juillet 2019 tendant à créer un droit voisin au profit des agences de presse et des éditeurs de presse, https://www.legifrance.gouv.fr/jorf/id/JORFTEXT000038821358, accessed: 23.11.2022. See in particular Articles L218-1-L.218-5, L.211-3-1, L.211-1,L.211-4 V, L.211-3.

2 Ustawa o prawie autorskim i prawach pokrewnych, https://isap.sejm.gov.pl/isap.nsf/download.xsp/WDU19940240083/U/D19940083Lj.pdf, accessed: 17.11.2024. See Articles 99^7–99^{17}.

3 Urheberrechtsgesetz https://dejure.org/gesetze/UrhG/87f.html, accessed: 15.08.2023. See Articles 87f–87k,127b.

DOI: 10.4324/9781003599494-2

the *Legge sul diritto d'autore*.[4] In Spain, it was adopted on November 2, 2021, in the *Real Decreto Legislativo 1/1996, de 12 de abril, por el que se aprueba el texto refundido de la Ley de Propiedad Intelectual*.[5] In Belgium, the related rights of press publishers were incorporated into the Code of Economic Law on June 19, 2022.[6] In the Czech Republic, an amendment to the *Autorský zákon* (Copyright Law) was adopted on October 14, 2022.[7]

2. Related rights regime – introductory remarks

Related rights constitute a heterogeneous subgroup of intellectual property rights[8] granted to persons involved in the dissemination of works. The objective of these rights is to prevent specific acts of unfair appropriation of others' efforts.[9] What distinguishes related rights from copyright is *inter alia* the fact that they protect the exploitation or performance of intellectual creations in literary, scientific or artistic domains rather than the intellectual creations themselves.

2.1. Rationale for the related rights regime

2.1.1. Protection of the dissemination of preexisting literary or artistic works

The main and common objective of related rights holders is to disseminate the works to a wider public.[10] J. P. Quintais and J. Poort state that the creation of the related rights regime may be justified by the added value generated in connection with works.[11] The common recipient of the activities of both authors and related rights holders is the audience. Thus, the aim of related rights is to reward the effort

4 Legge sul diritto d'autore, https://www.altalex.com/documents/codici-altalex/2014/06/26/legge-sul-diritto-d-autore#titolo1, aceessed: 15.08.2023. See Art. 43 bis.

5 Real Decreto Legislativo 1/1996, de 12 de abril, por el que se aprueba el texto refundido de la Ley de Propiedad Intelectual, hereinafter: Ley de Propiedad Intelectual, https://www.boe.es/buscar/act.php?id=BOE-A-1996-8930#:~:text=La%20propiedad%20intelectual%20est%C3%A1%20integrada,las%20establecidas%20en%20la%20Ley, accessed: 15.08.2023. See Art. 129 bis.

6 Code de droit économique, https://www.ejustice.just.fgov.be/eli/loi/2013/02/28/2013A11134/justel, accessed: 15.08.2023. See Art. IX 216/1, IX 216/2, IX 216/3.

7 Autorsky Zákon, https://www.zakonyprolidi.cz/cs/2000-121, accessed: 09.12.2024. See Articles 87b, 105b.

8 A. Peukert, "Related rights" in *Encyclopedia of European Private Law*, ed. J. Basedow, K. J. Hopt, R. Zimmermann (Oxford University Press, 2011), https://papers.ssrn.com/sol3/papers.cfm?abstract_id=1550103, accessed: 15.10.2022.

9 S. Ricketson and J.C. Ginsburg, *International Copyright and Neighbouring Rights. The Berne Convention and Beyond*, vol. 2 (Oxford University Press, 2006), 1213.

10 See: K. Kurosz, *Artystyczne wykonanie utworu. Prawa osobiste i majątkowe aktorów, muzyków i innych wykonawców* (Wolters Kluwer Polska, 2014), 55–56.

11 J. P. Quintais, J. Poort, "A brief history of value gaps: Pre-internet copyright protection and exploitation models, copyright reconstructed rethinking copyright's economic rights," in *Time of Highly Dynamic Technological and Economic Change*, ed. P. B, Hugenholtz (Wolters Kluwer, 2018), 57.

involved in disseminating works and making them known and available on the widest possible scale.[12]

The legal status of related rights holders is, to some extent, shaped similarly to that of authors. It is worth examining whether these two categories of rights are interdependent and, if so, how these interdependencies are shaped. Numerous concerns have been raised regarding the possibility that granting related rights could diminish authors' revenues.[13] According to Art. 1 of the Rome Convention, the "Protection granted under this Convention shall leave intact and shall in no way affect the protection of copyright in literary and artistic works. Consequently, no provision of this Convention may be interpreted as prejudicing such protection." This provision has also been incorporated into subsequent legal acts at international[14] and EU level.[15] The question of whether this clause establishes a hierarchy between the two categories of rights has been widely discussed in the literature. T. Azzi notes that there is a clear hierarchy between copyright and related rights to the detriment of the latter, which must neither infringe upon nor limit the exercise of the former.[16] This hierarchy can be explained by the relationship of interests, as performers, phonogram producers and broadcasters base their contributions on original authorial creations.[17] Consequently, the derivative nature of these contributions results in a more limited scope of protection for related rights compared copyright.[18] S. Ricketson adds that the notion of hierarchy serves to explain the "chain of production that starts at one point and moves outwards."[19] He clarifies that these contributions are interconnected and interdependent,[20] but there is no question of copyright's superiority. Some scholars view this relationship in terms of subsidiarity of related rights in relation to copyright. Producers of phonograms, first fixations of films, broadcasting organisations and performers contribute to the large-scale distribution of works and make them accessible to a

12 T. Azzi, *Recherche sur la loi applicable aux droits voisins du droit d'auteur en droit international privé* (L.G.D.J, 2005), 38–39.

13 J.C. Ginsburg, S. Ricketson, *International* (2006) 1221.

14 See: Art. 1 of the WIPO Performances and Phonograms Treaty (WPPT).

15 See: Art. 12 of the Directive 2006/115/EC of 12 December 2006 on rental right and lending right and on certain rights related to copyright in the field of intellectual property (hereinafter: Rental and Lending Rights Directive), Art. 1 of the Directive 2001/29/EC of 22 May 2001 on the harmonisation of certain aspects of copyright and related rights in the information society (hereinafter: InfoSoc Directive).

16 T. Azzi, *Recherche*, 45.

17 S. Ricketson, "Rights on the border: The Berne Convention and neighbouring rights," *Copyright Law in an Age of Limitations and Exceptions*, ed. R. L. Okediji, (Cambridge University Press, 2017), 373.

18 T. Azzi, *Recherche*, 2.

19 S. Ricketson, "Rights," 373.

20 S. Ricketson, "Rights," 373.

wide audience, ultimately benefiting the authors.[21] Therefore, copyright holders and related rights holders are not antagonists; they have common interests.[22]

2.1.2. *Protection of investment*

The purpose of granting related rights is to reward investments.[23] However, the threshold of investment in recording or broadcasting technology that merits legal protection has not been established.[24] However, P. B. Hugenholtz indicates that the related rights adopted in the Rome Convention were based on the principle that the technical costs of recording or broadcasting inherently implied an investment threshold.[25]

Scholars analysing the related rights regime often refer to the incentive paradigm. "Related rights allow…to recoup both the initial investment and the marginal production costs, and thereby create incentives to invest and produce."[26] To illustrate, Recital 4 of Directive 2001/29/EC of 22 May 2001 on the harmonisation of certain aspects of copyright and related rights in the information society (hereinafter: InfoSoc Directive) acknowledges that increased legal certainty and a high level of intellectual property protection encourage substantial investment in creativity and innovation, which leads to growth and increased competitiveness.

In the context of digital transformation, the necessity of investment for fixing, distributing or reproducing works is questioned.[27] The way the phonogram industry operated several decades ago was based on fixing the sounds of performances or

21 T. Azzi, "Recherche," 16.

22 A. Kerever, "Est-ce qu'il est nécessaire de réviser la Convention de Rome et, dans l'affirmative, est-ce le moment opportun pour le faire?", *Bulletin du droit d'auteur* 25, no. 4 (1991): 15–16.

23 Doubts may arise as to the link between the protection of performers in the same category of related rights with protection of producers of phonograms and broadcasting organisations. The adoption of related rights was dictated by the need to stop the unfair appropriation of their work. Moreover, their common objective is to disseminate the works protected by copyright. I consider these two main reasons as sufficient to regulate the interests of performers as well as producers, or broadcasting organisations within the same category of rights. As for the importance of the investment and the industrial character of the engagement of these actors, it should be considered as a sub-criterion and one of the characteristics of the related rights which does not apply to performers.

24 Some scholars argue that the investment required for the production of subject matters of related rights should be identifiable in order to trigger the protection. See: N. Ghazal, *Prawo do fonogramu w świetle ustawy o prawie autorskim i prawach pokrewnych* (Wolters Kluwer Polska, 2016), 121–127.

25 P.B. Hugenholtz, "Neighbouring rights are obsolete," *International Review of Intellectual Property and Competition Law (IIC)* 50, no. 8: 1009, https://link.springer.com/article/10.1007/s40319-019-00864-3, accessed: 18.10.2022; A. Kopff considered that the act of making phonogram or videogram is costly and involves the use of new technologies and engagement of highly qualified team. See: A. Kopff, "Prawa pokrewne i sąsiednie," *Zeszyty Naukowe Uniwersytetu Jagiellońskiego, Prace z Wynalazczości i Ochrony Własności Intelektualnej* 61 (1993): 16–17.

26 M.van Eechoud, S.van Gompel P.B. Hugenholtz et al., *Harmonizing European Copyright Law. The Challenges of Better Lawmaking* (Kluwer Law International, 2009), 198.

27 See: K. Grzybczyk, "Komentarz do art. 94," in *Ustawa o prawie autorskim i prawach pokrewnych. Komentarz,* ed. P. Ślęzak (C.H. BECK, 2017), 641.

of other sounds in large recording studios, which necessitated the employment of sound mastering specialists and the use of an expensive equipment. Now, physical sound carriers are no longer in demand. The large and expensive recording studios are no longer needed to record performances.[28] Artists – and, more broadly, anyone – can now record and produce sound on their own using simple equipment. This is also the case with broadcasting. In the past, operating a radio or television station entailed enormous costs. Today, anyone can be a broadcaster or a webcaster with just a smartphone and internet access.

According to B. P. Hugenholtz, the value chain and business model of the recording industry have changed,[29] making the concept of related rights based on technological investment outdated.[30] The role of contemporary record labels has shifted from phonogram production to artist management and promotion.[31] Social media platforms and applications such as podcasts have called into question the foundations of the broadcasting sector. However, it is important to note that an industry driven by low costs does not always guarantee high-quality outcomes. Also, despite advancements in digital technologies, some level of investment is still necessary to promote works to a broad audience.[32] To illustrate, in the press publishing sector, investments in AI-based tools and online platforms utilising subscription models are essential and will continue to be necessary in the future. Moreover, given the challenges posed by new technologies, such as the spread of disinformation, the importance of investing in tools designed to fight against this phenomenon should be emphasised. In addition, as the dissemination of information becomes easier and more accessible, competition intensifies, further increasing the need for innovation and investment.[33] Therefore, the conclusion is that despite digital advancements, investment remains an important factor in areas protected by related rights.

28 See: S. Tomczyk, "Komentarz do art. 94," in *Ustawa o prawie autorskim i prawach pokrewnych. Komentarz*, ed. E. Ferenc-Szydełko (C.H. Beck, 2016), 875–876.

29 P. Bernt Hugenholtz, "Neighbouring," 1007–1008.

30 P. Bernt Hugenholtz, "Neighbouring," 1007–1008.

31 K. Bowrey, *Copyright, Creativity, Big Media and Cultural Value. Incorporating the Author* (Routledge, 2021), 141–170.

32 For example, French Press Agency produces around 5,000 dispatches and 3,000 photographs every day, thanks to 2,400 employees in 151 countries around the world and is the only press agency to be represented in Afghanistan what requires significant financial investment. See: V. Duby-Muller, L. Garcia, *Rapport d'information sur l'application du droit voisin au bénéfice des agences, des éditeurs et professionnels du secteur de la presse*, Assemblée Nationale (2022), 23, https://www.assemblee-nationale.fr/dyn/15/rapports/dv/l15b4902_rapport-information.pdf, accessed: 18.07.2023.

33 For the further analysis of the current investment needs in press publishing sector see: M. Estivalèzes, L. Franceschini, *Rapport sur l'objet et le champ d'application du droit voisin des éditeurs de publication de presse*, Ministère de la Culture, Conseil Supérieur de la propriété littéraire et artistique (2018), 13, https://www.culture.gouv.fr/content/download/182559/file/Rapport%20droit%20voisin%20des%20éditeurs%20de%20presse%20vdef.pdf?inLanguage=fre-FR&version=1, accessed: 30.12.2024.

2.1.3. *Answer to the development of new technologies*

The development of new technologies has led to the emergence of new forms of creation and dissemination of works. While these advancements offer clear benefits, they may also have some negative consequences for the interests of authors and related rights holders. J. P. Quintais and J. Poort point out that proposals to extend existing rights or create new ones must be analysed from larger perspective[34] – one that seeks to balance the facilitation of communication with the protection of the legal interests of authors and related rights holders. New technologies often create the need to extend or modify existing rights or introduce ones. However, such changes should be implemented with careful consideration of the balance between individual rights and the broader interests of society as a whole.

Technological advancements have not only created new possibilities for cultural creation, dissemination audience expansion but also new dangers, one of which is piracy. For example, C. Masouyé mentions the case of phonogram producers, noting that hundreds of millions of discs have been placed on the market "without the consent of those who made the original sound recordings which those discs contained and without the consent required by law of authors and composers of the works and the artists who performed them,"[35] which has resulted in significant financial losses not only for phonogram producers but also for performers and authors.[36] J. Ginsburg and S. Ricketson observe that while authors, composers and performers were protected by national laws and international conventions,[37] phonogram producers, who were the most affected group, did not receive sufficient protection under the Rome Convention, as it did not extend to the importation and unauthorised distribution of phonograms. Therefore, strengthening the protection of this group in response to the described challenges was necessary and led to the adoption of the Phonogram Convention. This convention granted phonogram producers the legal means to oppose not only unauthorised reproduction but also the importation and commercial distribution of duplicates made without their consent.

2.2. *Related rights in the EU law*[38]

Under EU law, **performers** are granted reproduction and making available rights (Articles 2(b) and 3(2)(a) of the InfoSoc Directive). They are also granted rental and lending rights, distribution rights and the right to authorise or prohibit the fixation of their performances (Articles 3 and 9 and Art. 7(1) of the rental and lending rights

34 P. Quintais and J. Poort, "A Brief," 55.

35 C. Masouyé, *Guide to the Rome Convention and to the Phonograms Convention*, WIPO, no. 617 (E) (1981), 91.

36 C. Masouyé, *Guide to the Rome Convention*, 91–92.

37 J.C. Ginsburg, S. Ricketson, *International* (2006), 1233.

38 Since the objective of this point is to provide a general overview of holders of related rights to better understand who is already protected within this legal regime the analysis is limited and does not delve into the study of national legislations.

directive). Performers are entitled to receive a single equitable remuneration under the conditions set out in Art. 8 of the InfoSoc Directive.[39]

Phonogram producers are granted reproduction and making available rights. They also have rental and lending rights as well as distribution rights. The single equitable remuneration obtained by performers, in accordance with the conditions set out in Art. 8 of the rental and lending rights directive, must be shared with phonogram producers.

Under EU law, **broadcasting organisations** are granted reproduction and making available rights. They also have distribution rights, fixation rights and the rights to public rebroadcasting and communication.

Producers of the first fixation of a film are granted reproduction and making available rights. They also have rental and lending rights as well as distribution rights.

According to Art. 4 of the Term Directive,[40] **any person who, after the expiry of the copyright protection, for the first time lawfully publishes or lawfully communicates to the public a previously unpublished work**, shall benefit from a protection equivalent to the economic rights of the author.[41] The term of protection for such rights is 25 years from the date the work was first lawfully published or lawfully communicated to the public. Moreover, according to Art. 5 of the Term Directive, MS may grant protection to[42] critical and scientific publications of works that have entered the public domain.

To conclude:

- the purpose of the protection granted through related rights is to reward the effort involved in the performance or dissemination of works, ensuring they are made known and accessible. The need to prevent the unfair appropriation of the results of activity related rights holders' activities justifies their legal protection. The adoption of related rights serves as a response to technological advancements and aims to recognise and compensate the investments made in the creation and distribution of works.
- there is no hierarchy between authors and holders of related rights. The provisions of the Rome Convention, which safeguard author's interests, ensure that the protection granted to related rights holders does not undermine authors' rights. In fact, the activities of related rights holders can be seen as contributing to authors' financial gains, as the dissemination of their works can, ultimately, lead to increased revenue for authors.

39 EU harmonisation of copyright concerns only the economic rights.

40 Directive 2006/116/EC of 12 December 2006 on the term of protection of copyright and certain related rights, hereinafter: Term Directive.

41 See: J. Barta, "Prawa pokrewne," in *Prawo autorskie, System Prawa Prywatnego*, ed. J. Barta, 13 (2017): 143–144.

42 The implementation of the provision is not mandatory.

3. *Ratio legis* of publishers' rights from the CDSM Directive

This section analyses the *ratio legis* of publishers' rights to provide a basis for discussion.

The study, which aims to explain the reasons behind the adoption of publishers' protection, will be divided in four points. The first point will focus on arguments related to the activities of press publishers. The second point will focus on arguments related to the activities of news aggregators and the media monitoring services. The third point will discuss the legislative steps taken in Germany and Spain to regulate the press publishers' rights and the inspiration drawn from these approaches. Finally, the issue of media pluralism, as emphasised the EU legislature, will be explored in detail. All four of these threads intertwine with each other. Their separation in this analysis is solely for the purpose of thoroughly examining each element of the justification for introducing the new rights. To this end, the main documents related to the CDSM Directive will be analysed, including the Communication "Promoting a fair, efficient and competitive European copyright-based economy in the Digital Single Market,"[43] the Impact Assessment,[44] the Explanatory Memorandum to the Proposal of the CDSM[45] and the selected recitals from the CDSM Directive.

3.1. Press publishers

The primary reason for the adoption of the publishers' rights was the digital transformation of the press publishing sector. The shift toward online platforms resulted in a decline in revenues for traditional print media. The decline is also linked to changing advertising practices. As advertisers increasingly opted for online marketplaces, such as search engines, news aggregators or social media,[46] a reduction in spending on traditional print media became inevitable.[47]

43 European Commission, *Communication from the Commission to the European Parliament, The Council, the European Economic and Social Committee and the Committee of the Regions Promoting a Fair, Efficient and Competitive European Copyright-Based Economy in the Digital Single Market*, COM/2016/0592 final (2016), https://eur-lex.europa.eu/legal-content/EN/TXT/?uri=CELEX%3A52016DC0592, accessed: 27.10.2022.

44 European Commission, *Impact Assessment*.

45 European Commission, Proposal for a Directive of the European Parliament and of the Council on copyright in the Digital Single Market – COM(2016)593, https://digital-strategy.ec.europa.eu/en/library/proposal-directive-european-parliament-and-council-copyright-digital-single-market, accessed:27.10.2022.

46 See: M.M. van Eechoud, "A publisher's intellectual property right. Implications for freedom of expression, authors and open content policies" (University of Amsterdam, 2017), 14, https://www.openforumeurope.org/wp-content/uploads/2017/01/OFE-Academic-Paper-Implications-of-publishers-right_FINAL.pdf, accessed: 27.10.2022.

47 See: European Parliament, *Strengthening the Position of Press Publishers and Authors and Performers in the Copyright Directive*, Policy Department for Citizens' Rights and Constitutional Affairs Directorate General for Internal Policies of the Union, Study for the JURI Committee (2017), 13.

Although newspapers have experienced noticeable growth in their online audience,[48] the European Commission notes that publishers increased digital revenues have not compensated for the decline in print revenues.[49] The decline in publisher's revenues underscores the necessity of adopting a protection. Although the free flow of information is crucial, safeguarding publishers' investment and the long-term sustainability of journalism also benefits the public interest.[50] However, it should be noted that the official documents accompanying the CDSM Directive provide only limited data on the expected increase in publishers' revenues resulting from the introduction of the new rights.[51] According to the Impact Assessment, "the introduction of a new related right could lead to a 10% increase in revenues or between 10-15% in publishers' operating profit margin."[52] The Commission neither provides detailed data nor explains how the anticipated results were calculated. This lack of transparency represents a significant deficiency in the justification for establishing these new rights, as their primary intended outcome – an increase in publishers' revenues – is difficult to estimate.

According to Recital 54 of the CDSM Directive, the licensing and enforcement of rights in press publications for online use by ISSPs are often complex and inefficient. The European Commission explains that, prior to the adoption of related rights, in cases of alleged infringement, publishers, as the licensee or transferee, were asked by the Court to prove their ownership of the allegedly infringed works included in the press publication.[53] Given the number of individual works included in press publications – and thus, a large number of legal titles – demonstrating ownership for all of them was an arduous task. The issue has also been voiced in the literature. According to some scholars, in cases of mass exploitation, requiring publishers to demonstrate either the transfer of rights from authors or the granting of an exclusive license poses significant difficulties.[54] As for the expected result of the adoption of the new rights, the European Commission states that press publishers would be recognised as original rights holders rather than licensees,

48 The European Commission underlined that for 42% of users in the EU, newspaper and magazine's websites and apps are the main services used to access news. See: Annex 13 A of the *Impact Assessment*.

49 The European Commission provides a comprehensive data regarding the shift form print to digital in the press publishing industry, the trend of print circulation of daily newspapers, proportion of consumers who indicated that the Internet was their main source to access news or the decline in publishers' print revenues. See: European Commission, *Impact Assessment*, 156.

50 Recital 54 of the CDSM Directive.

51 European Commission, *Impact assessment*, 167. See: O. Bulayenko, G. Frosio, Ch.Geiger, "Opinion of the CEIPI on the European Commission's copyright reform proposal with a focus on the introduction of neighbouring rights for press publishers in EU law," *CEIPI Research Paper* (2016): 14–15, https://papers.ssrn.com/sol3/papers.cfm?abstract_id=2921334, accessed: 27.10.2022.

52 European Commission, *Impact Assessment*, 167.

53 European Commission, *Impact Assessment*, 166.

54 T. Höppner, "EU copyright reform: The case for a publisher's right," *Intellectual Property Quarterly* 1 (2018): 13, https://papers.ssrn.com/sol3/papers.cfm?abstract_id=3081733, accessed: 27.10.2022; a different opinion is presented in O. Bulayenko, G. Frosio, Ch.Geiger, "Opinion."

making it easier for them to get injunctive relief or initiate infringement proceedings in court.[55] Consequently, the adoption of these new rights is expected to increase legal certainty and simplify the enforcement process for press publishers seeking to protect their interests.

Recital 55 of the CDSM Directive expresses the need to recognise and encourage the organisational and financial contribution of publishers in producing press publications. The objective is to ensure the sustainability of the publishing industry and to foster the availability of reliable information. Press publishers are considered to be insufficiently protected compared to film producers, phonogram producers and broadcasting organisations, all of whom benefit from related rights protection.[56] The Impact Assessment highlights that, despite the important role in assembling and editing press content[57] as well as their comparable level of investment, press publishers have not been granted protection under the related rights regime. What is missing in the argumentation provided in the Impact Assessment is an analysis of how the legal situation of related rights holders has improved following the introduction of their rights. Consequently, there is a lack of evaluation of how the adoption of new rights could specifically impact press publishers.[58]

3.2. News aggregators and media monitoring services

According to Recital 54 of the CDSM Directive,

> the wide availability of press publications online has given rise to the emergence of new online services, such as news-aggregators or media monitoring services, for which the reuse of press publications constitutes an important part of their business models and a source of revenue.

In 2016, social media, news aggregators and search engines collectively served as the primary source of online news for 57% of users.[59] Press publishers accused these online platforms of free riding, as they used the press publishers' content mostly

55 European Commission, *Impact Assessment*, 166.

56 See: M. Estivalèzes, L. Franceschini, *Rapport*.

57 European Commission, Impact Assessment,159. See critically: S. Dusollier, Ch. Geiger, P.B. Hugenholtz, M. Kretschmer, "The European Commission's public consultation on the role of publishers in the copyright value chain: A response by the European Copyright Society," *CREATe Working Paper* (2016): 5–6.

58 L. Bently made an interesting parallel with the situation of broadcasters and pointed out the fact that their legal situation has not improved significantly as the result of the protection within the related rights regime. The author does not specify which stage in the development of related rights protection he is referring to. See: L. Bently in *Copyright, Related Rights and the News in the EU: Assessing Potential New Laws*, Transcript of Conference (University of Amsterdam, 2016), 52, https://resources.law.cam.ac.uk/cipil/documents/potential_legal_responses_complete_transcript.pdf, accessed: 27.10.2022.

59 European Commission, *Impact Assessment*, 157.

without seeking permission.[60] Moreover, press publishers and online services were seen as competitors for advertising revenues.[61] The European Commission recognised the complex role of news aggregators and media monitoring services. On the one hand, they "increase the visibility of press content and bring new traffic and thus advertising revenues to newspaper websites,"[62] while, on the other hand, they provide enough information to satisfy readers and, consequently, do not encourage them to click on the link to go to the website from which the press material originated, which, in turn, has the effect of reducing publishers' revenues.[63]

The aim was also to strengthen publishers' bargaining position, as they faced significant challenges in negotiating on equal footing with large online service providers. Attempts to negotiate licenses with platforms for the use of publishers' content were not very successful.[64] Even though some agreements were reached,[65] it has not contributed to a significant and general improvement of press publishers' situation. According to the Impact Assessment, the adoption of the publishers' rights and, consequently, "the clear identification of press publishers as rightholders is likely to prompt more online service providers to conclude agreements with publishers for the use of their content online, thus accelerating the cooperation which is starting to emerge between larger online service providers and the publishing sector."[66]

In the legal framework of some MS, such as Poland or France, there exists a concept of a collective work. Scholars often cite newspapers as an example when discussing the concept of a collective work,[67] as they consist of numerous contributions from different authors who have no control over the final version.

60 See F. Pollaud- Dulian, "Droit d'auteur et droit voisins dans le marché numérique," *Revue trimestrielle de droit commercial et de droit économique* no. 3, (2019): 661; T. Pihlajarinne, J. Vesala, "Proposed right of press publishers: a workable solution?" (2018), 1, https://helda.helsinki.fi/bitstream/handle/10138/312548/Pihlajarinne_Vesala_2018_proposed_right_of_press_publishers.pdf?sequence=1, accessed: 27.10.2022.

61 See: T. Höppner, "EU," 11.

62 European Commission, *Impact Assessment*, 157.

63 According to the Impact Assessment, 47% of consumers browse and read news extracts on these websites without clicking on links to access the whole article in the newspaper page which erodes advertising revenues from the newspaper webpages. See: European Commission, *Impact Assessment*, 157. (data provided for 2015, 2016).

64 European Commission, *Impact Assessment*, 157.

65 The private agreement between press publishers and Google was reached for example in France in 2013 in order to support digital transition, investments and innovations to the benefit of the press. See: France24, "Google and France reach landmark agreement," February 02, 2013, https://www.france24.com/en/20130201-google-france-reach-landmark-agreement, accessed: 28.10.2022. See: O. Bulayenko, G. Frosio, Ch. Geiger, "The introduction of a neighbouring right for press publisher at EU level: The unneeded (and unwanted) reform," *European Intellectual Property Review* 39, no. 4, (2017): 203–204.

66 European Commission, *Impact Assessment*, 168.

67 See for example: A. Nowicka, "Podmiot prawa autorskiego, Utwory zbiorowe," in *System Prawa Prywatnego Prawo autorskie,* ed. J. Barta, vol. 13 (2017), §12; A. Niewęgłowski, "Komentarz do art.11," in *Prawo autorskie. Komentarz*, ed. A. Niewęgłowski (Wolters Kluwer Polska, LEX, 2021), points 14–15.

Each independent part of a collective work must align with the concept proposed by the publisher. As the result of the publisher's role, these individual contributions are combined into a unified whole. Polish scholars hold differing opinions as to whether each contribution to a collective work should be considered a - work under copyright law. For many scholars, it is not necessary for all components of a collective work to qualify as copyright-protectable works. According to Polish doctrine, a collective work must contain at least two copyright-protectable works.[68] However, it may be technically impossible for a collective work to consist solely of such works. It may also include unprotected elements that are necessary for the creation of a collective work, such as those used to connect, label or categorise its individual components.

Under Polish law, the protection granted to a collective work extends to its publishers or producers.[69] The *ratio legis* of this provision is to reward the publisher's multi-faceted involvement in the creation of the collective work and to address the potential problems in identifying its authors. Art. 11 of the Polish Copyright Act introduces an exception to the principle expressed in Art. 8, which states that copyright belongs to the author. Under French law, a collective work can be created by either a "'natural or legal person." French scholars use interchangeable terms such as *initiator*, *producer* or publisher[70] to describe the entity responsible for its creation.[71] Under Polish law, the moral and economic rights belong to the authors of contributions included in a collective work. The publisher acquires economic rights to these individual contributions through contracts negotiated with the authors.[72] In this way, the publisher acquires the rights to each individual component of the collective work. Moreover, the publisher holds the rights to the collective work as a whole.[73] In France, copyright protection extends to the publisher of a collective work and, in the case of conclusion of the relevant agreements, the economic rights to individual parts are transferred to the publisher, while the authors retain the moral rights to their respective works.[74]

From a practical perspective, the legal framework surrounding the concept of a collective work can be seen as complex. Publishers point to the difficulties involved in negotiating and finalising agreements with the authors of each individual contribution that will be included in the collective work.[75] This framework enables publishers to hold legal title to each individual component,

68 B. Błońska, "Komentarz do art.11 Ustawy o prawie autorskim i prawach pokrewnych," in *Prawo autorskie i prawa pokrewne. Komentarz,* ed. W. Machała, R. Sarbiński (Wolters Kluwer Polska, LEX, 2019).

69 Taking into account the perspective of this study, in further considerations, the term "publisher" will be exclusively used.

70 A.R., Bertrand, *Droit d'auteur* (Paris Dalloz action, 2010), 206.

71 For the purpose of the following analysis reference to term "publisher" will be made.

72 Appellate Court in Warsaw: Judgement of 18 November 1999, I ACa 792/99, LEX no. 535049.

73 B. Błońska, "Komentarz do art.11."

74 The Court of Cassation, Civil Chamber 1, Judgement of 15 April 1986, Ref. No. 84-12.008, published in bulletin.

75 M. van Eechoud, "A publisher's," 27.

which is essential in cases copyright infringement. However, when a collective work consists of hundreds of individual parts, proving rights to each can be both difficult and time-consuming.[76] In the case of a collective work, press publishers hold exclusive rights to the "surplus" created through the selection and arrangement of its components. For instance, the publisher's name may appear on the cover of an encyclopaedia, signifying their role in organising and presenting the work as a whole. However, the publisher is not the original rights holder of the individual components of a collective work. Therefore, to get injunctive relief or initiate infringement proceedings in court, they may be required to prove ownership of all the allegedly infringed rights as a licensee or transferee. This requirement can make the legal process complicated. Moreover, the concept of a collective work is not recognised in every EU MS. While provisions regarding collective works exist in legal systems such as those of Poland, France, Germany and Italy, the lack of uniform recognition across the EU results in varying layers of protection for press publishers. This legal fragmentation makes claiming protection complex and time-consuming. According to the EU legislature, this disparity justifies the introduction of Art. 15 of the CDSM Directive.[77]

3.3. German and Spanish experiences

The Impact Assessment explains that intervention at the EU level will strengthen the bargaining power of press publishers more effectively than the national measures previously adopted in Germany and Spain.[78] In 2013, Germany introduced a one-year related right for press publishers, covering the commercial use of press publications and their fragments (except for individual words or very short text excerpts).[79] This exclusive right applied to commercial operators of search engines that made press content or parts thereof available to the public.[80]

This legislative measure faced criticism from scholars for failing to adequately address publishers' financial interests, as they sought to negotiate paid licensing agreements.[81] In response, Google refused to negotiate with press publishers.

76 M. van Eechoud, "A publisher's," 27.

77 European Commission, *Impact Assessment*, 168.

78 European Commission, *Impact Assessment*, 167.

79 Sections 87f to 87h of Urheberrechtsgesetz, as amended by Law of 1 October 2013, Bundesgesetzblatt (Federal Official Journal) Vol. I, 3728. German version: https://www.bgbl.de/xaver/bgbl/start.xav?startbk=Bundesanzeiger_BGBl&start=//*%5B@attr_id=%27bgbl113s1161.pdf%27%5D#__bgbl__%2F%2F*%5B%40attr_id%3D%27bgbl113s1161.pdf%27%5D__1667226734379, accessed: 31.10.2022. For English version see: European Parliament, *Strengthening*, 14.

80 The right has been declared inapplicable with retroactive effect by the CJEU by default of notification to the Commission in accordance with Directive 98/34/EC laying down a procedure for the provision of information in the field of technical standards and regulations and of rules on Information Society services.

81 See: S. Dworschak, Ch. Kersting, "Leistungsschutzrecht für Presseverlage: Müsste Google wirklich zahlen? – eine kartellrechtliche Analyse," *NZKart – Neue Zeitschrift für Kartellrecht* 46 (2013); See also: Max-Planck-Institut für Immaterialgüter- und Wettbewerbsrecht, "Stellungnahme zum

As a result, publishers were left with two choices: either allow their content to be displayed for free or have it removed or significantly reduced on the news aggregator. The latter option risked reducing their profits due to decreased traffic to their websites.[82] The VG Media Group, representing numerous press publishers in Germany, emphasised Google's significant market power and the weak bargaining position of publishers.[83] R. M. Herty and V. Moscon argued that the right introduced in Germany had only negative effects. They particularly highlighted its detrimental effect on startups and small businesses, as it restricted "innovative services from offering new forms of providing online access to information." [84] M. Kretschmer, S. Dusollier, P. B. Hugenholtz and C. Geiger highlight the negative impact of this right on the freedom of information.[85] An analysis of the German case revealed that the publishers that chose not to opt into Google's policies experienced an 8% decrease in daily visits to their news outlets.[86] This demonstrates, first, the negative impact of the right on the publishers' interests, and second, the strong interdependencies between press publishers and online platforms.

In 2014, Spain amended its quotation exception. According to Art. 32(2) of the *Ley de Propiedad Intelectual*, the making available to the public of non-significant fragments of content by internet service providers and content aggregators was authorised, but only in exchange for unwaivable equitable compensation, which was to be managed by collecting societies.[87] R. Xalabarder criticised this legislative measure for its lack of clarity.[88] Additionally, scholars have highlighted its

Gesetzesentwurf für eine Ergänzung des Urheberrechtsgesetzes durch ein Leistungsschutzrecht für Verleger, Max-Planck-Institut für Immaterialgüter- und Wettbewerbsrecht,"https://www.ip.mpg.de /fileadmin/ipmpg/content/stellungnahmen/leistungsschutzrecht_fuer_verleger_01.pdf, accessed: 31.10.2022.

82 See: H.T. Wolde, E. Auchard, "Germany's top publisher bows to Google in news licensing row," Reuters, November 5, 2014, https://www.reuters.com/article/us-google-axel-sprngr-idUSKBN0IP1 YT20141105, accessed: 31.10.2022.

83 See: Corint Media, "First Decision on Ancillary Copyrights for Press Publishers," September 24, 2015, https://www.corint-media.com/en/first-decision-on-ancillary-copyright-for-press-publishers -google-is-obliged-to-pay/, accessed: 31.10.2022.

84 R.M. Hilty, V. Moscon, *Modernisation of the EU Copyright Rules Position Statement of the Max Planck Institute for Innovation and Competition* (Max Planck Institute for Innovation and Competition, 2017), 84.

85 Dusollier, S., Ch. Geiger, P.B. Hugenholtz, M.Kretschmer, "The European," 5.

86 J. Calzada, R. Gil, What Do News Aggregators Do? ..., https://papers.ssrn.com/sol3/papers.cfm ?abstract_id=2837553, accessed: 31.10.2022, p.4.

87 Art. 32.2 Ley de Propiedad Intelectual, November 5, 2014; version of the article from 2014, Spanish version: https://www.boe.es/buscar/act.php?id=BOE-A-1996-8930&b=52&tn=1&p=20190302#a, 32, accessed: 23.11.2022. For English version see: European Parliament, *Strengthening*, 14–15.

88 R. Xalabarder criticizes for example the use of the term "non-significant fragments of contents" considering the language as insufficiently clear. Scholar points also to the fact, that according to the Spanish regulation, the reproduction is not included in the statutory license without further explanation from Spanish legislator of the reasons of such an approach. See: R. Xalabarder, "The remunerated statutory limitations for news aggregation and search engines proposed by the Spanish Governement: Its compliance with international and EU law," *IN3 Working Paper Series (*2014), https://papers.ssrn.com/sol3/papers.cfm?abstract_id=2504596, accessed: 01.11.2022.

negative and discriminatory impact on new entrants in the news aggregator market as well as its discouraging effects on press publishers seeking to develop new business models.[89] Unlike the German legislation, the Spanish publishers' right to compensation was unwaivable. In response, Google News and several smaller news aggregators withdrew from the Spanish market.[90] As a result, online traffic to publishers' websites decreased by an average of 6.1%, with small publishers experiencing an even greater decline of up to 13.5%.[91]

In the Impact Assessment, the European Commission acknowledged the shortcomings of the two national legislations discussed. It expected the positive effect from the related rights proposed in the CDSM Directive, however, and asserted that the EU-wide approach would be more effective than isolated national measures. The Commission indicated that the German right could only be enforced against specific categories of online service providers, while the Spanish solution was not an exclusive right but, rather, an unwaivable right to a compensation. Therefore,

> the related right at EU level would leave press publishers a greater margin of manoeuvre to negotiate different types of agreements with service providers than it has been the case in Germany and in Spain and is therefore expected to be more effective for them in the long run.[92]

T. Höppner recognises that the rights proposed in the CDSM Directive represent a different approach and argues that it is incorrect to claim that the legislative measures in Germany and Spain were complete failures.[93] However, there is little support for such an argument. S. Dusollier claims that the EU has not learned from the legislative failures in Spain and Germany.[94] A. Peukert challenges the Commission's argument on the effectiveness of press publishers' rights at the EU level by asserting that the competitive conditions in the EU online news market are similar to those in Germany and Spain, so "there is no reason to believe that the mere size of the EU Digital Single Market will make a difference."[95] The conclusion is that if the press publishers' protection at the national level has proven ineffective, the likelihood of successfully implementing an effective solution at EU level remains low.

89 S. Scalzini, "Is there free-riding? A comparative analysis of the problem of protecting publishing materials online in Europe," *Journal of Intellectual Property Law & Practice* 10, no. 6, (2015): 463.

90 O. Williams, "Google News Spain to be shut down: what does it mean?," The Guardian, December 12, 2014, https://www.theguardian.com/media-network/2014/dec/12/google-news-spain-tax-withdraws, accessed: 01.11.2022.

91 P. Posada de la Concha, A. Gutiérrez García, H. Hernández Cobos, *Impacto*, 53–55.

92 European Commission, *Impact Assessment*, 160.

93 T. Höppner, M. Kretschmer, R. Xalabarder, "CREATe public lectures on the proposed EU right for press publishers," *European Intellectual Property Review* 39, no.10, (2015): 607–622.

94 S. Dusollier, "The 2019 Directive on Copyright in the Digital Single Market: Some progress, a few bad choices, and an overall failed ambition," *Common Market Law Review* 57, no.4, (2020): 1005.

95 A. Peukert, "An EU related right for press publishers concerning digital uses. A legal analysis," Research Paper, no. 22 (Goethe Universitat, 2016), 12.

3.4. Media pluralism

It has been argued that the weak legal position of press publishers negatively impacts media pluralism, democratic debate, quality of information and cultural diversity within European society.[96] Recital 54 of the CDSM Directive emphasises the role of a free and pluralist press in ensuring quality journalism and guaranteeing citizens' access to information. The new right is seen as making a fundamental contribution to public debate and supporting the proper functioning of a democratic society. Moreover, according to the Impact Assessment, "better market conditions for the press publishing industry could give rise to the development of innovative offers for the digital distribution of press content, with larger catalogues and more choice."[97]

The Impact Assessment acknowledges consumer concerns that the new rights could lead to online service providers restricting access to press content and imposing additional burdens on users.[98] However, the Commission addressed these concerns by asserting that the problems encountered in Spain are unlikely to arise under the proposed EU-level solution, as it differs from the measures previously implemented in Spain.[99]

To conclude:

- the decline in press publishers' revenue and the need to adapt to the challenges posed by digital information dissemination are the primary justifications for adopting the new rights. Additionally, the introduction of related rights was justified by the need to strengthen the legal position of press publishers. Their important role in assembling and editing press content as well as their level of investment comparable to that of other related rights holders has been emphasised. Furthermore, the potential positive impact of these related rights on the right to access information and media pluralism has been mentioned repeatedly.
- the complex relationship between news aggregators and press publishers, along with the weak bargaining position of the latter, served as a justification for the adoption of the new rights. However, it has not been clearly specified whether these rights will equally improve the negotiating position of all publishers, regardless of their size.
- the Impact Assessment acknowledges that news aggregators have a positive impact (to some extent) on press publishers. However, the legislature has not conducted a thorough balancing analysis to assess the potential limiting effects that the new rights may have on this positive aspect.

96 European Commission, *Impact Assessment*, 160.
97 European Commission, *Impact Assessment*, 169.
98 European Commission, *Impact Assessment*, 163.
99 European Commission, *Impact Assessment*, 169–170.

- the EU legislature acknowledged the shortcomings of the German and Spanish legislations but anticipated a positive impact and greater effectiveness of the new rights, partly due to their adoption at a broader, EU-wide level.

4. Press publication – subject matter of press publishers' rights

4.1. The CDSM Directive

According to Art. 2(4) of the CDSM Directive "press publication means a **collection** composed mainly of literary works of a **journalistic nature**, but which can also include other works or other subject matter, and which:

(a) constitutes an individual item within a **periodical or regularly updated publication** under a single title, such as a newspaper or a general or special interest magazine;
(b) has the purpose of providing the general public with information related **to news or other topics**; and
(c) is published in any media under **the initiative, editorial responsibility and control of a service provider**. Periodicals that are published for scientific or academic purposes, such as scientific journals, are not press publications for the purposes of this Directive."

A press publication is a collection. According to the Cambridge Dictionary, a collection is "a group of objects of one type that have been collected by one person or in one place."[100] A press publication includes different elements of one type, namely, journalistic content. The latter should be understood as an autonomous concept of EU law. It follows from the CJEU's case law that "journalistic activities" are those which aim to disclose to the public of information, opinions or ideas, regardless of the medium used to transmit them.[101] The term "journalistic type" should be understood in the same way. It does not imply that the elements included in a press publication must necessarily be written or created by journalists. In most cases, authors will be the ones producing the content, but introducing such a limitation in the text of the provision would not align with the current developments in the press sector, such as deprofessionalisation[102] or the use of AI.

Art. 2(4) of the CDSM Directive does not specify the minimum number of elements a press publication should contain to be qualified as a collection. In order to establish it, inspiration could be drawn from the Database Directive,[103] in which

100 Cambridge Dictionary, "Collection," https://dictionary.cambridge.org/dictionary/english/collection, accessed: 14.06.2023.

101 CJEU, Satamedia, para. 61.

102 R.K. Nielsen, A. Cornia, A. Kalogeropoulos points to the raise in popularity of non–profit media, volunteer media or "citizen journalism" See: R. K. Nielsen, A. Cornia, A. Kalogeropoulos, *Challenges*.

103 Directive 96/9 of March 1996 on the legal protection of databases, hereinafter: Database Directive.

the term "collection" is used. According to Art. 1(2) of the Directive, a database is defined as a collection of independent works, data or other materials arranged in a systematic or methodical way and individually accessible by electronic or other means. There is, however, no formulated threshold for how many elements a collection should consist of, or from how many elements a given combination qualifies as a collection. In the literature, it has been pointed out that, for a collection to be considered a database, there must be a sufficient number of data, materials or other elements that allows them to be structured. Although there is no statutory requirement as to the size of the collection, the amount of information included in the database may affect the granting of protection. A single piece of information, even if particularly valuable, will never be granted database status.[104] Therefore, the elements of database, in order to constitute a collection, should be numerous and form a certain structure.

Adapting this to the definition of press publication and considering the particularity of database protection, it could be argued that a press publication should consist of a number of elements that will form a structure based on a thematic link, the same journalistic type or common aim, which is the dissemination of information. In regard to the minimum number of elements, M. van Eechoud emphasises that a press publication should contain "at least several 'literary works of a journalistic nature.'"[105] According to E. Czarny-Drożdżejko, "two or three elements are enough, or maybe it is necessary to combine more elements."[106] E. Rosati proposes that the "assessment shall be conducted on a case-by-case basis."[107] In my view, the collection from Art. 2(4) should contain at least two literary works of a journalistic nature, as the collection must primarily consist of them and at least one another element.

The elements of a press publication are **mainly** literary works. This means that a press publication containing only videos will not meet the requirement set in Art.2(4) of the CDSM Directive. Term "mainly" used in relation to literary works indicates that they should be dominant within the collection. A collection will be considered a press publication if it will include literary works of a journalistic nature. Because the EU legislature uses the plural, it can be concluded that a collection must include at least two such works.

A press publication, in addition to literary works, can include **other works**, such as photographs, videos and **other subject matter**.[108] According to the French version of Art. 2(4) of the CDSM Directive "publication de presse est une collection composée principalement d'œuvres littéraires de nature journalistique, mais qui

104 Z. Zawadzka, "Sui Generis Ochrona Baz Danych," in *Prawo własności intelektualnej. Teoria i praktyka*, ed. J. Sieńczyło-Chlabicz (Wolters Kluwer Polska, 2021, LEX).

105 M.M. van Eechoud, "A publisher's," 33.

106 E. Czarny-Drożdżejko, "The subject-matter of press publishers' related rights under directive 2019/790 on copyright and related rights in the Digital Single Market," *International Review of Intellectual Property and Competition Law* (IIC) 51, no. 51, (2020): 627.

107 E. Rosati, *Copyright in the Digital Single Market: article-by-article commentary to the provisions of directive 2019/790* (Oxford University Press,2021), 262.

108 See recital 56 of the CDSM Directive.

peut également comprendre d'autres œuvres ou objets **protégés.**" This means, accordign to the French text, that a press publication can include literary works as well as other works or protected subject matters. The same is reflected in the Polish version of the provision, in which the term "**objęte ochroną**" (protected) is used. The difference lies in the fact that the adjective "**protected**" does not appear in the English version of the provision from Art. 15 of the CDSM Directive in relation to other subject matters. This raises the question of how to understand term "subject matter" and whether it is protected, for example, under the related rights regime or if it constitutes a non-protected element.

The analysis of the English text of the CDSM Directive in its entirety shows that both terms, namely, "subject matter" and "protected subject matter," are used. The latter is used, for example, in Recital 2 of the Directive, according to which,

> The directives that have been adopted in the area of copyright and related rights contribute to the functioning of the internal market, provide for a high level of protection for rightholders, facilitate the clearance of rights, and create a framework in which the exploitation of works and **other protected subject matter** [emphasis added] can take place.

According to the definition of online content-sharing provider from Art. 2 of the CDSM Directive,

> online content-sharing service provider means a provider of an information society service of which the main or one of the main purposes is to store and give the public access to a large amount of copyright-protected works or **other protected subject matter** [emphasis added] uploaded by its users, which it organises and promotes for profit-making purposes."

Finally, according to Art. 17(1) of the CDSM Directive,

> Member States shall provide that an online content-sharing service provider performs an act of communication to the public or an act of making available to the public for the purposes of this Directive when it gives the public access to copyright-protected works or **other protected subject matter** [emphasis added] uploaded by its users.

All these examples, except the first one, relate to the situation of the provision of access to content by an online content-sharing service provider, which encompasses works and other protected subject matters. The latter is understood as subject matter protected, for example, under the related rights regime. Based on the provided examples, we can observe that the EU legislature uses term "copyright-protected works." In this context, the lack of consistency should be noted, as, for instance, in Art. 2(4) of the CDSM Directive, the term "work" (without the term copyright-protected) is used. However, the meaning of both terms is the same.

The EU legislature uses the term "other subject matter" much more frequently in the CDSM Directive than the term "protected subject matter." An example of such usage is found in Recital 3 of the DSM Directive, which states: "Rapid technological developments continue to transform the way works and **other subject matter** [emphasis added] are created, produced, distributed and exploited." According to Recital 6:

> The exceptions and limitations provided for in this Directive seek to achieve a fair balance between the rights and interests of authors and other rightholders, on the one hand, and of users on the other. They can be applied only in certain special cases that do not conflict with the normal exploitation of the works or **other subject matter** [emphasis added] and do not unreasonably prejudice the legitimate interests of the rightholders.

According to Art. 4(1) of the CDSM Directive,

> Member States shall provide for an exception or limitation to the rights provided for in Article 5(a) and Article 7(1) of Directive 96/9/EC, Article 2 of Directive 2001/29/EC, Article 4(1)(a) and (b) of Directive 2009/24/EC and Article 15(1) of this Directive for reproductions and extractions of lawfully accessible **works and other subject matter** [emphasis added] for the purposes of text and data mining.

The provision from Art. 1(1) of the CDSM Directive is of great importance for the analysis conducted. According to it:

> This Directive lays down rules which aim to harmonise further Union law applicable to **copyright and related rights** [emphasis added] in the framework of the internal market, taking into account, in particular, digital and cross-border uses of protected content. It also lays down rules on exceptions and limitations to copyright and related rights, on the facilitation of licences, as well as rules which aim to ensure a well-functioning marketplace for the exploitation of works and **other subject matter** [emphasis added].

The scrutiny of this provision leads to the conclusion that EU law harmonisation applies to copyright and related rights and, consequently, concerns works and other subject matter protected under the related rights regime. The examples mentioned above show that each time the term "subject matter" was used, the legislature referred, although not explicitly, to **protected** subject matter.

In the context of the understanding subject matter included in a press publication, it, first, means that the English text of the CDSM Directive is not consistent regarding the use of terms such "work," "copyright protected work," "subject matter" and "protected subject matter." It is difficult, if not impossible, to find a rational justification for such a differentiation. Additionally, it should be noted that, for example, in the Italian version of the CDSM Directive, a press publication consists mainly of literary works of a journalistic character but may also include other works or **materials**, and the latter should be understood as non-protected materials.[109] This can lead to many interpretative doubts.

Second, in light of the examples provided from the English version of the CDSM Directive, the conclusion can be drawn that the term "subject matter" is understood as a protected subject matter, primarily on the basis of the related rights regime or, as pointed out by R. Markiewicz, on the basis of the *sui generis* regime.[110] The opposite interpretation, which would conclude that only works and (unprotected) subject matters are included in a press publication, would lead to the conclusion that subject matters protected under related rights could not be a part of press publication at all. Such an interpretation must, therefore, be considered erroneous.

The established interpretation of the elements of a press publication has important implications for the protection of press publishers. First, from a purely practical perspective, it seems difficult to ensure that every press publication contains only protected elements. Non-protected elements may include technical components for linking the collection's parts, or even brief items containing information on weather or sports. This raises the question of whether a collection that includes non-protected elements could still be considered a press publication according to Art. 2(4) of the CDSM Directive.

Second, as noted earlier in this chapter in the study of the related rights regime, the protection resulting from related rights had not previously been conditioned by the requirements of already granted protection to the subject matters included under copyright or related rights regime. The understanding of press publication that conditions its protection on the protection of its elements creates an unprecedented requirement for publishers in the context of the related rights regime. Moreover, partial protection under the related rights regime, in this case, depends on the creative nature of the elements of press publication, as it should include both literary and other works.

I propose understanding a press publication as a collection composed mainly of literary works of journalistic nature but that can also include other works or other subject matter. Therefore, we should focus on what must be included in a press publication. If literary works are included, along with potentially other works or subject matter, then, in my opinion, the presence of unprotected elements in the collection should not prevent it from being granted protection under the new law. However, if a non-protected element is included in a press publication and is then used by ISSPs, there will be no encroachment on the publishers' exclusive rights.[111] The opposite assertion would be contrary to the provision from Art. 15 of the CDSM Directive, according to which a press publication is a collection composed mainly of literary works of a journalistic nature but that can also include other

109 English version by the author. According to Art. 2(4) of the Italian version of the DSM Directive: "'pubblicazione di carattere giornalistico': un insieme composto principalmente da opere letterarie di carattere giornalistico ma che può includere anche altre opere o altri materiali, e che (…)."

110 R. Markiewicz, "Prawo pokrewne wydawców prasy," *Zeszyty Naukowe Uniwersytetu Jagiellońskiego* no.4 (2019): 7.

111 See differently: R. Markiewicz, "Prawo,"14.

works or subject matter. The inclusion of a non-protected element, in my view, cannot exclude the qualification of the entire collection as a press publication. If this were the case, the use of a protected element from the collection would not trigger the press publishers' protection because the collection could not be considered a press publication due to the presence of unprotected elements. Nevertheless, it would be going too far to conclude that the use of an element from public domain included in a press publication leads to an encroachment on the publisher's rights in that publication. To illustrate this reasoning, a picture generated by AI without human creative input is not protected by copyright. The inclusion of such a picture in a collection of literary works, other works and subject matter will not make the collection ineligible as a press publication. However, the use of such a picture by an ISSP will not require the authorisation of the press publisher.

It is worth noting that AI is increasingly used in the press sector. For example, Bloomberg uses a program called Cyborg, which transforms financial reports into news stories.[112] Agence France-Presse experimented with automatic writing for sports event announcements as early as 2014.[113] In 2023, Polish *Gazeta Wyborcza* published an article written by ChatGPT.[114] AI is primarily used to report on topics such as sports, weather of finance,[115] but it is also increasingly used to write the entire articles, although the quality remains somewhat contested.[116] AI is used in the press industry to help journalists increase the pace of work, broaden coverage and improve data verification.

Generative technologies, defined as "capable of creating media content largely autonomously and with very little human intervention,"[117] are considered the most

112 Washington Post, "The Washington Post to Debut AI-Powered Audio Updates for 2020 Election Results," October 13, 2020, https://www.washingtonpost.com/pr/2020/10/13/washington-post-debut-ai-powered-audio-updates-2020-election-results/, accessed: 22.05.2023. See: N. Martin, "Did A Robot Write This? How AI Is Impacting Journalism," Forbes, February 8, 2019, https://www.forbes.com/sites/nicolemartin1/2019/02/08/did-a-robot-write-this-how-ai-is-impacting-journalism/?sh=f6ff72a77957, accessed: 22.05.2023.

113 A., Lebois, "Oeuvre de presse – Quelle protection juridique pour les créations des robots journalistes?," *Communication Commerce électronique* no. 1 (2015): 14–20.

114 Wirtualne Media, "Sztuczna inteligencja napisała artykuł w 'Gazecie Wyborczej'. 'Nikt się nie zorientował, tekst był słaby'," April 18, 2023, https://www.wirtualnemedia.pl/artykul/sztuczna-inteligencja-tekst-gazeta-wyborcza-boleslaw-breczko, accessed: 22.05.2023. See: B. Breczko, "Czy dziennikarze są jeszcze potrzebni? Mój ostatni artykuł napisał ChatGPT," Gazeta Wyborcza, April 17, 2023, https://wyborcza.biz/biznes/7,177150,29639137,czy-dziennikarze-sa-jeszcze-potrzebni-moj-ostatni-artykul-napisal.html, accessed: 22.05.2023.

115 See: S.P., "How the Bundesliga Is Using AI to Increase Brand Reach," March 03, 2020, https://www.sportspromedia.com/opinions/bundesliga-ai-dfl-deltatre/?zephr_sso_ott=exInKO, accessed: 22.05.2023; A. Gani, L. Haddou, "Could robots be the journalists of the future?," The Guardian, March 16, 2014, https://www.theguardian.com/media/shortcuts/2014/mar/16/could-robots-be-journalist-of-future, accessed: 22.05.2023.

116 P. Farhi, "A news."

117 P.B. Hugenholtz et al., *Trends and Developments in Artificial Intelligence. Challenges to the Intellectual Property Rights Framework, Final Report* (2020) 57, https://www.ivir.nl/publicaties/download/Trends_and_Developments_in_Artificial_Intelligence-1.pdf, accessed: 22.05.2023.

problematic from the perspective of copyright protection for the products created by AI.[118] As the analysis conducted reveals, AI cannot be granted authorship for the outputs of its activity. Therefore, the question arises whether such products should be protected, and if so, who should be granted exclusive rights.[119] As observed by J. P. Quintais and P. B. Hugenholtz, the process of creation carried out by AI always involves varying degrees of human intervention.[120] Its result should meet criteria such as being a production in literary, scientific or artistic domain; being original; involving creative choices; and constituting an expression[121] in order to be qualified as a work. Moreover, A. Trapova and P. Mezei highlight that news publishers, regarding the use of AI in the press sector, are "strongly in control of the output they communicate,"[122] which means that AI still should be considered as a tool to create news items and not as a creator itself.

As for the question who should be granted copyright protection for such works, potential claims from the developer or programmer of the AI system and the users of the system are discussed.[123] This question is highly important from the perspective of the press industry, as the answer will determine from whom press publishers will acquire press materials created by AI, and who should be asked for authorisation to use for press publishing purposes. I agree with A. Trapova, who points out that "the heavy reliance on AI stretches the causation bond between the human author and the final creative output to breaking point."[124] As AI becomes increasingly autonomous, the scope of human engagement will be limited to a minimum, and this minimum may not necessarily involve created input. This means that such AI-generated outputs are not protected under current copyright law; they enter the public domain and can be used freely. The arising question is whether the

118 P. Mezei, A. Trapova, "*Robojournalism* – A copyright study on the use of artificial intelligence in the European news industry," *GRUR International* 71, no. 7 (2022): 589–602.

119 See: D. Gervais, "Humans as a matter of law. How Courts can define humanness in the age of AI," *Vanderbilt Law Research Paper, No. 22-3 (*2022),https://papers.ssrn.com/sol3/papers.cfm?abstract_id=4213543, accessed: 14.09.2022. J.V. Grubow, "O.K. computer: The devolution of human creativity and granting musical copyrights to artificially intelligent joint authors," *Cardozo Law Review* 40, no. 1 (2018): 404–405; S. Yanisky-Ravid, L.A. Velez-Hernandez, "Copyrightability of artworks produced by creative robots and originality: The formality-objective model," *The Minnesota Journal of Law, Science & Technology* 19, no. 1 (2018): 9.

120 P.B. Hugenholtz, J. P. Quintais, "Copyright and artificial creation: Does EU copyright law protect AI-assisted output?," *International Review of Intellectual Property and Competition Law* (IIC) 52 (2021): 1201.

121 P.B. Hugenholtz, J. P. Quintais, "Copyright," 1200.

122 P. Mezei, A. Trapova, "Robojournalism," 589–602.

123 E. Bonadio, L. McDonagh, "Artificial intelligence as producer and consumer of copyright works: Evaluating the consequences of algorithmic creativity," *Intellectual Property Quarterly* 2 (2020): 112–137; T. Pihlajarinne et al., "European copyright system as a suitable incentive for AI based journalism?," *Legal Studies Research Paper Series* no. 67 (2021). P.B. Hugenholtz, J. P. Quintais, "Copyright,": 208.

124 A. Trapova, "Copyright for AI-generated works: A task for the internal market?," Kluwer Copyright Blog, February 8, 2023, https://copyrightblog.kluweriplaw.com/2023/02/08/copyright-for-ai-generated-works-a-task-for-the-internal-market/, accessed: 02.12.2023.

content created by AI without creative human involvement should be protected, for example, to foster innovation and, if so, on which basis. Nevertheless, under current law, the products generated by AI without human involvement of creative nature are not protected by copyright law, but they can still be included in a press publication, and the publication itself will not be deprived of protection.

According to Art. 15(2) of the CDSM Directive, the rights provided for in Paragraph 1 shall not be invoked to prohibit the use of works or other subject matter for which protection has expired. This, first, implies that a press publication may include elements that are not protected and, second, that press publishers' protection does not apply to the uses of such unprotected elements.

Works and subject matter incorporated in a press publication can originate from one or many authors or other holders of rights.[125] They must be acquired legally.[126] The press publisher must have the legal titles to each of these works, even though the protection resulting from Art. 15 of the CDSM Directive is not conditional on the demonstration of these legal titles.[127]

It is worth pointing out that the EU legislature uses the term "publication" twice in the provision discussed. First, by referring to "**press publication**," meaning a collection composed mainly of literary works of a journalistic nature but that can also include other works or other subject matter. Second, by stating that a press publication must constitute an individual item within a periodical or regularly updated **publication** under a single title. A press publication can, for example, be an issue of a daily, weekly or monthly newspaper.

A press publication can also contain elements such as a table of contents, photos, video, graphics and podcasts. A layout may also be considered an element of a press publication. However, with regard to the latter, in my opinion, if the exploitation concerns only the layout without the text, the protection of press publishers would not apply. This view is shared in the literature by V. Moscon[128] and E. Laskowska-Litak.[129] It is reflected also in practice, as ISSPs using services such as news aggregators typically extract text and photos from press publications rather than the layout.

A press publication constitutes an individual item within a periodical or regularly updated publication under a single title. The list of examples of single titles provided in the provision is not exhaustive. According to the EU legislature,

125 E. Rosati notes that whether the authors of the works and/or other subject matters incorporated in a press publication must be different (each element comes from different author) should be assessed on a case-by-case basis. See: E. Rosati, *Copyright*, 261–262.

126 See: R. Markiewicz, *Prawo autorskie na jednolitym rynku cyfrowym. Dyrektywa Parlamentu Europejskiego i Rady (UE) 2019/790* (Wolters Kluwer, 2021), 185.

127 See: O. Bulayenko, G. Frosio, Ch.Geiger, "Opinion," 16.

128 V. Moscon, "Neighbouring rights: In search of a dogmatic foundation. The press publishers' case," *Max Planck Institute for Innovation and Competition Research Paper*, no. 18–17, (2018), 9, https://papers.ssrn.com/sol3/papers.cfm?abstract_id=3208601, accessed: 22.01.2024.

129 E. Laskowska-Litak, "Sprawa upadłej dyrektywy prawnoautorskiej i (nie)jednolitego rynku cyfrowego," *Europejski Przegląd Sądowy* no. 9 (2018), 8.

a publication can be, for example, a newspaper, a general-interest magazine or special-interest magazine.

A single title can also be understood as the name of an online news service or news website, not just a newspaper or magazine. When comparing publications from *Le Figaro*, onet.pl and France 24, not many differences will be noticed, and any that do exist are more likely to stem from the style of the respective websites. Google News publishes excerpts from both news websites and online versions of newspapers or magazines, which is a significant argument in favour of this broad interpretation. Moreover, it should be noted that, in Recital 56, the EU legislature explicitly indicates that press publications can also be published on news websites.

The question arises whether the requirement to update the publication regularly should be understood in such a way that all the elements included in a press publication should be published regularly on the press publisher's website at specific intervals, several times a day or a week. The latter is becoming increasingly popular in the business models adopted by press publishers, as more and more often they update the press content on their websites several times per day. In my opinion, in both cases, the requirement of updating the publication regularly is met.[130]

It has been already specified that a press publication should have the purpose of providing the general public with information related to news or other topics. E. Rosati points out that such other topics "should in any case relate to current affairs."[131] I do not agree with the latter, as, based on the purposive interpretation of the provision, the aim of the EU legislature was to adopt a protection that applies to all press publishers, not only those who publish on current affairs issues.

Periodicals published for scientific or academic purposes, such as scientific journals, do not constitute a press publication according to Art. 2(4)(b) of the CDSM Directive. A press publication can be published in any media. In Recital 56 of the CDSM Directive, the EU legislature specified that media also includes also paper. The rationale behind this specification seems to be to emphasise that not only network media but also traditional media should be considered. However, as demonstrated in Chapter 1, the prevalence of paper press is decreasing.

The initiative, editorial responsibility and control of a service provider,[132] such as news publisher, are important factors in determining whether a press publication published by a service provider qualifies for protection under the CDSM Directive. Therefore, in Recital 56, the EU legislature excludes websites such as blogs from the protection granted to press publications when they provide information as part of activities that are not carried out under the initiative, editorial responsibility and control of a service provider. However, if the involvement of the person publishing the blog meets these criteria, the protection will apply. According to T. Höppner,

130 See: R. Danbury, "The DSM Copyright Directive: Article 15: What? – Part II, 2021," Kluwer Copyright Blog, April 9, 2021, https://copyrightblog.kluweriplaw.com/2021/04/29/the-dsm-copyright-directive-article-15-what-part-ii/, accessed: 02.01.2025.

131 See: E. Rosati, *Copyright*, 261.

132 See Chapter 3, Section 3.1, for the definition of a service provider.

editorial responsibility should be understood as consisting of distinguishing "reliable information from unreliable sources. Consequently, this responsibility requires significant investments in the verification of information and the editing articles. The corresponding legal liability for any false information ensures the maintenance of the necessary high standards."[133] The concept of editorial responsibility appears in the Audiovisual Media Services Directive in the context of audiovisual media services provided by a media service provider.[134] Striving for consistency in the interpretation of the EU law, its definition could serve to elucidate the scope of the engagement of press publishers.

According to Art. 1(c) of the Audiovisual Media Services Directive of 2010:

> "editorial responsibility" means the exercise of effective control both over the selection of the programmes and over their organisation either in a chronological schedule, in the case of television broadcasts, or in a catalogue, in the case of on-demand audiovisual media services. Editorial responsibility does not necessarily imply any legal liability under national law for the content or the services provided.

According to the literature, effective control encompasses both actual and legal control and consists of the possibility of making final decisions.[135] Such a final decision concerns, first, whether content will be included (criterion of selection) and, second, how it will be structured (criterion of organisation). The selection and organisation of the content follow the professional guidelines on ethics.[136]

When adapting these considerations to the definition of editorial responsibility in the press publishing sector, it could be understood as the exercise of effective control, meaning the possibility of making final decisions both over the selection of materials included in a press publication and over their organisation, which follows professional ethics and does not necessarily imply legal liability under national law for the content provided. Initiative could be understood as the act of initiating the publishing process, while control involves conducting supervision over the process of publishing, overlapping with or concerning other fields controlled within the framework of editorial responsibility.

All the conditions listed in Art. 2(4) of the CDSM Directive must be met cumulatively. The definition of a press publication does not contain any requirement regarding the investment necessary for protection to arise. This could lead to the

133 T. Höppner, *The Proposed Directive on Copyright in the Digital Single Market (Articles 11, 14 and 16). Strengthening the Press through Copyright*, European Parliament (2017), https://www.europarl.europa.eu/RegData/etudes/BRIE/2017/596835/IPOL_BRI(2017)596835_EN.pdf, accessed: 22.10.2024.

134 See: Art. 1(c) of the Audiovisual Media Services Directive.

135 S. Heilmann, W. Schulz, *Editorial Responsibility* (IRIS Special, European Audiovisual Observatory, 2008), 16, https://rm.coe.int/1680783c0e, accessed: 24.01.2024.

136 S. Heilmann, W. Schulz, *Editorial,* 18. See also: H. Aguinis, S.J. Vaschetto, "Editorial responsibility: Managing the publishing process to do good and do well," *Management and Organization Review* 7, no. 3 (2011): 407–422.

conclusion that the protection will extend to every collection composed mainly of literary works and other subject matter that meets the criteria from Art. 2(4) of the CDSM Directive, regardless the substance of investment. This, in turn, will contribute to the widening of its scope.

This point is echoed in the literature.[137] P. B. Hugenholtz argues that the absence of a threshold test "will lead to overprotection and create uncertainty regarding the scope of the press publisher's right."[138] However, the analysis of the related rights regime conducted earlier in this chapter showed that no related right contains a specific investment threshold. As discussed earlier in this chapter, the costs incurred for the first fixation of a film, the fixation of a phonogram or a broadcast already constitute an investment. Of course, the size of these investments varies, but it may be debatable how such a threshold should be formulated if the legislature were to adopt one. The adoption of vague concepts, which are difficult to define, may raise significant interpretative problems, but it allows for flexibility. On the other hand, the adoption of a clear threshold would be arbitrary and rapidly outdated in the age of technological change. Another possibility would be to follow the path of Databases Directive and introduce the requirement of a substantial investment.[139] However, it should be noted that large investments do not always equate to a high-quality press publication. Therefore, it cannot be excluded that the lack of an investment threshold could lead to the overprotection of press publishers due to the extensive formulation of the press publication's definition. Nevertheless, its introduction does not correspond to the construction of the related rights regime, in general, and there is no certainty as to its positive impact on the quality of press publications and their protection. Press publication constitutes an autonomous notion of EU law, which means that "it should be given a uniform application throughout the European Union."[140]

To conclude:

- the use of term "subject matter" in the English text of the CDSM Directive lacks consistency. The analysis conducted on this point showed that the term should be understood as a subject matter protected under the related rights regime or the *sui generis* regime.

137 CH. Geiger, O. Bulayenko and G. Frosio point to the fact that lack of threshold of investment means that "making available on a 'news website' trivial information would attract the same protection as the publication of an article resulting from months of investigative journalism." See: O. Bulayenko, G. Frosio, Ch. Geiger, "Opinion," 16; S. Scalzini observes that the lack of an investment threshold "renders the extent of the subject-matter encompassed by the provision vague, with a risk of overprotection of press publications with little or no underlying investment to recoup." See: S. Scalzini, "The new related right for press publishers: What way forward?," in: *Routledge Handbook of EU Copyright Law*, ed. E. Rosati (Routledge, 2021), 108.

138 P.B. Hugenholtz, "Neighbouring," 1010–1011.

139 See: art. 7 of the Databases Directive.

140 E. Rosati, *Copyright*, 261.

- a press publication should be understood as a collection composed mainly of literary works of a journalistic nature but that can also include other works or other subject matter. If the literary works are included, along with other works or subject matters, then, in my opinion, the fact that the collection in question contains unprotected elements should not prevent it from being under the publishers' rights. If a non-protected element is included in a press publication and is then used by ISSPs to the extent indicated in the CDSM Directive, there will not be an encroachment on the publishers' exclusive rights.
- a press publication as a collection should consist of a number of elements that form a structure resulting, for example, from thematic link or common aim, such as the dissemination of information.
- the regularity with which a press publication updates its content should be understood broadly, encompassing the update of press walls, news websites or websites published by press publishers as well, taking place several times per day or per week.
- a press publication should be published under the initiative, editorial responsibility and control of a service provider. Editorial responsibility should be understood as the exercise of effective control both over the selection of materials included in a press publication and over their organisation, which does not necessarily imply any legal liability under national law for the content provided.
- all the conditions listed in Art. 2(4) of the CDSM Directive must be met cumulatively. Press publication constitutes an autonomous notion of EU law.

4.2. French and Polish law

The French and Polish definitions of press publication follow the wording of the provision from Art. 2(4) of the CDSM Directive as demonstrated in Table 2.1. However, some interesting differences should be highlighted.

First, the French legislature decided to add the examples of other works or subject matter that can be included in a press publication by mentioning the photographs or videograms.[141] These two subject matters are protected by two different regimes, namely by copyright and related rights. The rationale behind it could be to show that the term "protected" does not exclusively refer to copyright protection. These two examples do not constitute an exhaustive list, as the legislature uses the term "in particular."

Second, it should be noted that a press publication, according to the French and Polish provisions, can include literary works of journalistic nature and other **protected** works or **protected** subject matter. Therefore, it could be said that *a contrario*, subject matter that is not protected should not be elements of a press

141 In recital 56 of the CDSM Directive the photographs and videos as examples of works and other subject matters are mentioned.

Table 2.1 Definition of press publication

*Art. L.218-1 of the French Intellectual Property Code**	*Art. 99⁷(1) of the Polish Copyright Act***
A press publication within the meaning of this chapter is a collection composed mainly of literary works of a journalistic nature, which may also include other protected works or protected subject matter, in particular, photographs or videograms, and which constitutes a distinct whole within a periodical or regularly updated publication bearing a single title, with the aim of providing the public with information on current events or other topics, in any medium, on the initiative, under the editorial responsibility and control of the press publishers or a press agency. Periodicals that are published for scientific or academic purposes, such as scientific journals, are not covered by this definition.	A press publication is a collection of works or subject matter protected on the basis of related rights, composed mainly of works comprised of words, of a journalistic nature, constituting a distinct whole within a periodical or regularly updated publication under a single title, such as a daily newspaper, magazine, news agency service or online news service, distributed for information purposes in any form and by any means within the scope of its economic or statutory activities and under the responsibility of the entity that exercises actual and legal control over it. Periodical publications distributed for scientific or academic purposes are not press publications.

Note: *English version by the author. French version of art. L.218-1 (I) of French Intellectual Property Code: https://www.legifrance.gouv.fr/codes/article_lc/LEGIARTI000038826730, accessed: 10.07.2023. **English version by the author. Polish version of art. Art. 99^7: https://isap.sejm.gov.pl/isap.nsf/download.xsp/WDU19940240083/U/D19940083Lj.pdf, accessed: 21.11.2024.

publication. However, I suggest following the interpretation of press publication proposed in the previous point.

Third, in Poland, online news services are indicated as examples of publications. Because the publishers of online news services are just as affected by the activities of news aggregators as the publishers of press *stricto sensu,* the rationale behind the Polish legislature's decision could be to explicitly highlight that online news services are also covered by the definition of publication. Interestingly, Polish legislature refers to "literary works" as "works comprised of words," which broadens the scope of press publication, as, for example, podcasts may be understood as works comprised of words that could not have been protected if the legislature had, instead, opted to use the term "written works." However, due to technological development and the fact that the press now uses various methods to communicate information, I consider the Polish legislature's choice to be appropriate, as it represents an attempt to ensure effective protection of press publishers.

To conclude:

- although the Polish and French implementations of the definition of press publication follow the definition from Art. 2(4) of the CDSM Directive, the Polish implementation is enriched with examples of publications. Moreover, the Polish legislature implements the term "literary works" included in a press publication as "works comprised of words," which broadens the scope of definition.

4.3. Individual words or very short extracts of press publication

4.3.1. The CDSM Directive

According to Art. 15(1) of the CDSM Directive, publishers' rights do not apply to individual words of very short extracts of press publications. Nothing prevents the use of several short extracts from a single press publication on condition that these short extracts do not replace the press publication. In Recital 58 of the CDSM Directive, the EU legislature specified that:

> Taking into account the massive aggregation and use of press publications by information society service providers, it is important that the exclusion of very short extracts be interpreted in such a way as not to affect the effectiveness of the rights provided for in this Directive.[142]

The exclusion of individual words and very short extracts from the publishers' protection limits its scope. However, the EU legislature does not provide any definition of this concept. Intuitively, we would say that a short extract consists of a sequence of words. Examples of such a sequence could be a headline from the press publication or a snippet, defined as a small and often interesting piece of news, information or conversation.[143] The simplification and general classification that all headlines and snippets are subject to exclusion or, conversely, that all of them constitute an element of press publication within of Art. 2(4) of the CDSM Directive is contrary to the provision's wording.

The devil is in detail, and, in this context, it lies in the understanding of what constitutes very short extracts. In Recital 58, the EU legislature explains that the use of individual words or very short extracts of press publications by ISSPs **should not negatively impact** the investments made by publishers of press publications in their production. Immediately following this, it is explained that it is important to interpret the exclusion of very short extracts in such a way as to not affect **the effectiveness of the rights** provided for in the CDSM Directive.

The study of Recital 58 leads to the conclusion that the term should be understood restrictively,[144] meaning that only these very short extracts that, evidently, lack independent value could be "freely appropriable."[145] However, an overly restrictive

142 Recital 58 of the CDSM Directive.

143 Cambridge Dictionary, "Snippet," https://dictionary.cambridge.org/dictionary/english/snippet, accessed: 09.11.2022.

144 See: R. Markiewicz, *Prawo*, 160.

145 F. Banterle, G. Ghidini, "Copyright, news, and 'information products' under the new CDSM Directive," ResearchGate, 2020, 6, https://www.researchgate.net/publication/342707640_Copyright_news_and_information_products_under_the_new_DSM_Copyright_Directive, accessed: 09.11.2022.

approach may negatively impact the free flow of information, interfering with both the content and manner of communication to the public and, consequently, affecting users' freedom to receive information.

It is interesting to consider whether pictures could be regarded as short extracts to which protection does not apply. According to the linguistic interpretation of the exclusion in Art. 15, the use of individual words or very short extracts from a press publication is not protected, as these extracts can be understood as a sequence of individual words combined. Under this interpretation, pictures would not fall within this exclusion.

The question arises as to whether the quantitative approach would more adequately clarify the term under discussion. In this context, reference could be made to the *Infopaq* case, in which the CJEU was asked whether the text extract from an article, consisting of a search word along with the five preceding and five subsequent words, could be considered a work and, thus, be subject to reproduction under Art. 2(a) of the InfoSoc Directive.[146] There is a similarity between the issue of interpreting "very short extracts" in Art. 15 of the CDSM Directive and the problem assessed in the *Infopaq* case. Both involve determining how long a piece must be, despite its brevity, to qualify for protection. However, there are some differences between these two cases. In *Infopaq*, the analysis focused on whether a sequence of 11 words could be considered as a work – an original artistic or literary expression constituting the author's own intellectual creation and, thus, protected by copyright. In contrast, for a press publication protected under the related rights regime, originality is not in question. A press publication does not need to be assessed as a whole to determine whether it qualifies as a copyrighted work. Instead, the issue is how short a "very short extract" of a press publication must be to avoid undermining the effectiveness of publishers' rights. Despite some structural similarities between these cases, they address entirely different legal questions, making direct comparison potentially misleading.

A quantitative approach could provide a concrete answer, determining, for example, that ten words or seven words constitute a "very short extract" of press publication exempt from protection. However, this arbitrary solution was not adopted by the EU legislature. Nevertheless, it could still be implemented at the national level as part of the Directive's transposition.

Key in determining what constitutes a very short extract of a press publication is assessing whether this extract allows the reader to bypass reading the full publication. The definition of "very short extracts" should depend on their economic impact.[147] This interpretation could help resolve ambiguity and uncertainty regarding the term's meaning. When assessing a case in this context, national courts should consider two key factors. Firstly, they should evaluate the impact of

146 CJEU, Infopaq, para. 27, question 1.

147 See: J.C. Ginsburg, "Floors and ceilings in international copyright treaties Berne, TRIPS, WCT minima and maxima," in *Intellectual Property Ordering beyond Borders*, ed. H. G. Ruse-Khan, A. Metzger (Oxford University Press, 2022), 298.

the extract on the reader. A crucial indicator is whether a reader familiar with the publication would recognise the passage as an excerpt from a specific source. If the short excerpt lacks autonomous meaning, this is unlikely. Second, the court should examine the economic consequences of using short extracts of press publications. If an excerpt provides enough information for the reader to forgo clicking on the full article on the publishers' website, it can result in significant financial losses for press publishers. Consequently, such short extracts should not be considered short enough to be excluded from protection.

The criteria discussed offer great flexibility. However, in my opinion, this flexibility, along with the high degree of discretion involved, may be problematic given the impact of technological developments on the flow of information. Platforms operate in a highly automated manner, so the ability to parameterise which extracts qualify as "very short extracts" would enhance predictability for both platforms and publishers, potentially preventing numerous legal disputes. Therefore, the concept should be clarified during the implementation stage.

To conclude:

- to ensure the effectiveness of publishers' rights, "very short extracts" should be interpreted restrictively, meaning that only extracts that clearly lack independent value should be freely appropriable. However, this restrictive approach may negatively impact the free flow of information, interfering both the content and manner in which information is communicated to the public.
- because the EU legislature does not define the concept of "very short extracts" of press publication, the assessment of an excerpt's brevity should consider two key factors – its impact on the reader's willingness to click and read the full publication and the economic consequences of its use on the interests of press publishers.

4.3.2. French and Polish law

According to Art. L211-3-1(2) of the French Intellectual Property Code, as demonstrated in Table 2.2, press publishers cannot prohibit the use of individual words or very short extracts from a press publication. However, it has been specified that such use must not undermine **the effectiveness** of their rights. This means that very short extracts should not serve as a substitute for the full press publication eliminate the need for the reader to engage with the original content. The rationale behind this specification is to define and delimit the boundaries of the exclusion. The French legislature achieves this in two ways: first, by stating that the effectiveness of the right should not be compromised by the use of individual words or very short extracts from a press publication; second, by clarifying that such extracts cannot serve as a substitute for the full publication or discourage the reader from engaging with it.[148] This

148 See: T. Azzi, "Commentaire de la loi du 24 juillet 2019 tendant à créer un droit voisin au profit des agences de presse et des éditeurs de presse," *Dalloz IP/IT* (2020), 63.

Table 2.2 Exclusion of individual words or very short extracts of press publication from the publishers' protection

*Art. L211-3-1 of the French Intellectual Property Code**	*Art. 97⁷(3)(3) of the Polish Copyright Act***
The beneficiaries of the rights provided for in Article L. 218-2 cannot prohibit: 2° The use of individual words or very short extracts from a press publication. This exception should not affect the effectiveness of the rights provided for in the same article L. 218-2. This effectiveness is notably affected when the use of very short extracts replaces the press publication itself or dispenses the reader from reading it.	The provision of Paragraph (2) shall not apply to: 3) individual words or very short extracts from a press publication.

Note: *English version by the author. French version: https://www.legifrance.gouv.fr/codes/article_lc/LEGIARTI000038826394, accessed: 11.07.2023. **English version by the author. Polish version: https://isap.sejm.gov.pl/isap.nsf/download.xsp/WDU19940240083/U/D19940083Lj.pdf, accessed: 21.11.2024.

addition enhances the text of the Directive by offering guidance on the interpretation of the concept, even though it does not provide a precise definition.

The Polish legislature adopted the wording of Art. 15(1) without adding any further specifications. In the explanatory memorandum accompanying the legislative proposal, it noted that any attempt to define this vague the term of "very short extracts of press publication" by setting a word or character limits could raise legitimate doubts about compliance with the CDSM Directive.[149] According to the Polish legislature, it is important to consider that the European Commission does not encourage the clarification of general concepts used in the CDSM Directive, as this could lead to inconsistencies in the application of EU law across MS.[150] This is an example of a passive approach to the undefined and somewhat vague concepts introduced in the CDSM Directive. While this approach has the advantage of maintaining consistency across MS by avoiding discrepancies in implementation, it also means accepting the incorporation of legal provisions that inherently raise interpretative questions.

To conclude:

- the French legislature specified that the use of very short extracts from a press publication is excluded from protection only when it does not undermine the effectiveness of the publishers' rights. The effectiveness of these rights may

149 Ministerstwo Kultury i Dziedzictwa Narodowego, *Uzasadnienie do projektu ustawy o zmianie ustawy o prawie autorskim i prawach pokrewnych oraz niektórych innych ustaw* (2020), 46–47, https://bip.mkidn.gov.pl/media/pu_prawo_autorskie_20220620/Uzasadnienie_do_ustawy.pdf, accessed: 19.11.2022.

150 Ministerstwo Kultury i Dziedzictwa Narodowego, *Uzasadnienie*, 46–47.

be compromised if such use replaces the press publication itself or discourages the reader from engaging with it. While this clarification does not eliminate all uncertainty, it helps define the term and provides guidance for its interpretation.

4.4. *Term of protection of press publication*

4.4.1. *The CDSM Directive*

According to Art. 15(4) of the CDSM Directive,

> publishers' rights shall expire two years after the press publication is published. That term shall be calculated from 1 January of the year following the date on which that press publication is published. Publishers' rights shall not apply to press publications first published before 6 June 2019.

The act of publishing a press publication triggers the protection of press publishers. Some scholars note that, under the related rights regime, protection typically arises from the first fixation of the subject matter, as seen with phonograms or videograms.[151] However, in case of the publishers' rights, it is important to recognise that the works included in press publication have, in most of the cases, already been fixed by their authors.

The act of publishing a press publication occurs when an issue of a newspaper or magazine is published. If a newspaper is published daily, then a new press publication is issued each day. The same principle applies to online versions of such newspapers if they are updated daily as well as to weekly magazines if they are updated every week and so on. The matter becomes more complex when the elements of a press publication are not published simultaneously but are, instead, continuously updated on a website. In other words, if new articles are added hourly to an online press service, determining the precise moment of publication for the press publication as a whole becomes challenging. In my opinion, in such cases, protection should arise at the moment when the elements included in the press publication are first published within the framework of that publication. To illustrate, if a news website adds a new article every hour, protection arises at the moment of its publication within the framework of a press publication, and this protection applies to the whole press publication, including the newly added article. Because the elements of the press publication may change hourly in this scenario, protection will be granted from the moment each element is first published as part of the press publication.[152]

151 A. Lebois, "La légitimité," 133; S. Dusollier, Ch. Geiger, P.B. Hugenholtz, M.Kretschmer, "The European Commission's public consultation on the role of publishers in the copyright value chain: A response by the European Copyright Society," *European Intellectual Property Review* 38, no.10 (2016): 593.

152 See: R. Markiewicz, *Prawo*, 149.

According to the Term Directive, the rights of performers, producers of phonograms and producers of the first fixation of a film, as well as broadcasting organisations, expire 50 years after the act that first triggers protection. For publishers of previously unpublished works, the protection lasts 25 years. In the case of the optional right protecting the publication of critical and scientific editions of works that have entered the public domain, the maximum of protection is 30 years. The two-year protection period for press publications appears relatively short compared to longer terms granted to other related rights. The initial proposal for the Directive suggested a 20-year protection period,[153] but this was deemed too long and unsuitable given the nature of news and its rapid obsolescence. Widely criticised,[154] the initial term was reduced to two years.[155] However, one may still question whether this shorter period remains excessive.

4.4.2. French and Polish law

French and Polish implementations mirror the provisions from Art. 15(4) of the CDSM Directive as can be seen in Table 2.3. Therefore, the observations made in the preceding analysis remain applicable.

Table 2.3 Term of protection

*Art. L. 211-4 V of the French Intellectual Property Code**	*Art. 99^{8} of the Polish Copyright Act***
The duration of the economic rights of press publishers and press agencies shall be two years from January 1 of the calendar year following that of the first publication of a press publication.	The right referred to in Article 99^{7}(2) shall expire at the end of two years following the year in which the press publication was first published.

Note: *English version by the author. French version: https://www.legifrance.gouv.fr/codes/article_lc/LEGIARTI000043499688, accessed: 11.07.2023. **English version by the author. Polish version: https://isap.sejm.gov.pl/isap.nsf/download.xsp/WDU19940240083/U/D19940083Lj.pdf, accessed: 21.11.2024.

153 See Art. 11(4) of the Proposal of the CDSM Directive, https://digital-strategy.ec.europa.eu/en/library/proposal-directive-european-parliament-and-council-copyright-digital-single-market, accessed: 08.11.2022

154 See for example: O. Bulayenko, G. Frosio, Ch. Geiger, "Opinion".

155 Interestingly, P.B. Hugenholtz gives the examples of attempts to regulate the protection of news industry in United States that could last 24 or 48 hours, see: P.B. Hugenholtz, *Copyright, Related Rights and the News in the EU: Assessing Potential New Laws, Transcript of Conference* (University of Amsterdam, 2016), 80, https://resources.law.cam.ac.uk/cipil/documents/potential_legal_responses_complete_transcript.pdf, accessed: 12.11.2022.

To conclude:

- protection arises at the moment a press publication is published. If the elements of a press publication are not released simultaneously but are continuously updated on a news website, protection begins when each element is first published within the framework of the press publication. The duration of protection is calculated from the moment each element is initially included as part of the press publication.
- the two-year protection term is considerably shorter than the protection granted to holders of other related rights. This shorter duration reflects the nature of news and its rapid obsolescence.

5. Publishers of press publications

5.1. The CDSM Directive

The protection provided under Art. 15 of the CDSM Directive applies to **publishers of press publication established in an MS.** According to Recital 55 of the CDSM Directive, the term "publisher of a press publication" includes service providers such as **news publishers** or **news agencies** that have their **registered office, central administration or principal place of business** within the EU and publish press publications as defined by the Directive.

The Directive does not provide explicit definitions for the terms "news publisher" and "news agency." However, the legislature identifies news publishers as an example of press publication publishers, suggesting that the term also encompasses providers of news services, such as France.24, or news websites, such as onet.pl. An example of a news publisher is Ringier Axel Springer Polska, while an example of a news agency is the French Press Agency.

As to the scope of a publisher's involvement, a press publication is published under the publisher's initiative, editorial responsibility and control. The press publisher oversees the production and distribution of the publication. It is important to clarify that, for protection under the related rights regime to apply, the publisher's engagement does not need to have a creative character, nor is it assessed from that perspective.

According to Recital 56 of the CDSM Directive, a press publisher must publish a press publication as part of an economic activity that qualifies as a provision of services under EU law. Art. 57 of the TFEU provides a non-exhaustive list of activities that qualify as services, activities of an industrial character, activities of a commercial character, activities of craftsmen and activities of the professions.

A publisher must be established in an MS. According to Art. 49 of the TFEU, the freedom of establishment allows natural persons or companies to establish themselves in other MS on a permanent basis. This raises the question of whether protection could be extended to publishers based in non-EU MS at the implementation stage. S. Dusollier claims that such an extension might be possible but does not provide details or discuss its potential consequences.[156] R. Markiewicz highlights the possible negative effects such an extension could have on competition rules within the European Single Market.[157] Moreover, according to the CJEU, the notion of establishment entails a "permanent presence in the host Member State."[158] Despite the absence of an explicit prohibition, it does not seem to be the legislature's intention to extend this protection beyond the European MS at the implementation stage. The wording of the provision clearly specifies that the publisher of press publication must be established in a Member State. Given that the objective of the CDSM Directive is to adapt the European copyright framework to technological developments, extending the provision to publishers based in non-EU MS does not seem justified.

The provision in question does not specify whether a publisher of a press publication must be a natural or legal person. However, according to Recital 55, the term encompasses service providers, such as news publishers or news agencies.[159] As derived from Articles 49 and 56 of the TFEU, nationals of EU MS, including natural persons, have the freedom to provide services and establish themselves in another MS. Therefore, if they engage in activities that meet the requirements from Art. 15 of the CDSM Directive – namely, publishing a press publication as defined in Art.2(4) of the Directive – they could qualify as publishers of press publications.

The provision in question does not differentiate between types of press publishers based on the content they publish. Consequently, national legislation should not introduce such distinctions by favouring certain press publishers based on their subject matter, size or level of experience.

To conclude:

- a publisher of a press publication must be established in an MS. Any interpretation that extends the definition of press publishers to those based outside the EU should be excluded.
- a press publisher must publish a press publication as part of an economic activity that qualifies as a provision of services under EU law.
- the provision in question does not differentiate between types of press publishers based on the content they publish. The EU legislature treats press publishers as a homogeneous group.

5.2. French and Polish law

In the French implementation of Art. 15 of the CDSM Directive, as can be seen in Table 2.4, the right of reproduction and communication to the public is granted to press publishers or press agencies. According to Art. L218-1 (III) of the French

156 S. Dusollier, "The 2019," 1007.
157 R. Markiewicz, *Prawo*, 139.
158 CJEU, Centro di Musicologia Walter Stauffer v Finanzamt München für Körperschaften, Case C-386/04, 14 September 2006, para.19.
159 See:T. Höppner, M. Kretschmer, R. Xalabarder, "CREATe," 611.

Table 2.4 Press publisher

*Art. L. 218-1 of the French Intellectual Property Code**	*Articles 99[7], 99[10] of the Polish Copyright Act***
I A press publication … constitutes a distinct whole within a periodical or regularly updated publication bearing a single title, with the aim of providing the public with information on current events or other topics, in any medium, on the initiative, under the editorial responsibility and control of the press publishers or a press agency. Periodicals that are published for scientific or academic purposes, such as scientific journals, are not covered by this definition. II A press agency within the meaning of this Chapter shall mean any undertaking mentioned in Article 1 of Order No 45-2646 of 2 November 1945 regulating press agencies whose main activity is the collection, processing and editing, under its own responsibility, of journalistic content. III A press publisher within the meaning of this chapter shall be understood to be a natural or legal person who publishes a press publication or an online press service within the meaning of Law No. 86-897 of 1 August 1986 on the reform of the legal regime of the press. IV This Chapter shall apply to press publishers and press agencies established in the territory of a Member State of the European Union	Article 99[7] 1) A press publication is … distributed for information purposes in any form and by any means within the scope of the economic activity of the entity which exercises actual and legal control over the selection of the content disseminated. Periodical publications published for scientific or academic purposes are not press publications. Article 99[10] The provisions of the Act shall apply to press publications by: a publisher who has a place of residence or a seat in the territory of the Republic of Poland or a publisher who has a place of residence or a seat in the territory of a European Union Member State or a Member State of the European Free Trade Association (EFTA) – a party to the Agreement on the European Economic Area.

Note: *English version by the author. French version:https://www.legifrance.gouv.fr/codes/article_lc/LEGIARTI000038826730, accessed: 11.07.2023. **English version by the author. Polish version: https://isap.sejm.gov.pl/isap.nsf/download.xsp/WDU19940240083/U/D19940083Lj.pdf, accessed: 21.11.2024.

Intellectual Property Code, a press publisher is defined as a natural or legal person who publishes a press publication or online press service within the meaning of the French Press Law.[160]

Under French law, the role of a press publisher involves having the initiative, editorial responsibility and control, reflecting the provisions from Art. 2(4) of the CDSM Directive. According to the French implementation, a press publisher is responsible for publishing a press publication or an online press service as defined

160 Loi n° 86-897 du 1 août 1986 portant réforme du régime juridique de la presse (Law n° 86-897 of 1 August 1986 reforming the legal regime of the press), https://www.legifrance.gouv.fr/loda/id/JORFTEXT000000687451, accessed: 16.11.2024. See Chapter 1, Section 4, for the further analysis of the terms press publication and online press services in the French Press Law.

by Law No. 86-897 of 1 August 1986 on the reform of the legal regime of the press. However, the scope of the definition of "press publication" under the French implementation of the CDSM Directive does not fully align with the definitions of "press publication" and "online press service" under French Press law.[161] Therefore, Art. L.218-1 of the French Intellectual Property Code specifies that a press publication (as introduced in the CDSM Directive) is also published by a press publisher. As a result, a press publisher now publishes press publications (in the traditional written and printed sense), online press services and press publications as defined by the CDSM Directive.

According to Art. L218-1(II) of the French Intellectual Property Code, a press agency defined in reference to Art. 1 of *Ordonnance n° 45-2646 du 2 novembre 1945 portant réglementation des agences de presse*,[162] which regulates press agencies. Under this definition, a press agency is a commercial entity that collects, processes, formats and supplies information that has undergone journalistic processing under its own responsibility. Additionally, at least half of its turnover must come from supplying such information to press publishers that publish press publications, as defined by French press law; to publishers of electronic communication services to the public; and to other press agencies.[163] The role of a press agency is, therefore, to provide an information product that, subsequently, will be used by press publishers or other press agencies.

According to the French implementation, press publishers and press agencies eligible for publishers' rights must be established within an EU MS. Consequently, the protection has not been extended to publishers from outside of the EU. However, the French legislature did not specify whether the targeted audience of press publishers and press agencies should be primarily, or exclusively within the EU.

The Polish law does not provide an explicit definition of the term "press publisher." According to Art. 99^7(1), a press publication must be distributed for informational purposes as part of the economic activity of an entity that exercises actual and legal control over the selection of the disseminated content. However, there is no reference to the definition of press publisher found in Art. 8 of the Polish press law.[164]

A press publisher must publish a press publication as part of their economic activity. Their role involves exercising actual and legal control over the selection of the disseminated content. However, the term "actual and legal control" is not used in the CDSM Directive or in the French implementation. Additionally, the Polish legislature has not provided further clarification on its meaning.

161 See Chapter 1, Section 4.

162 Ordonnance n° 45-2646 du 2 novembre 1945 portant réglementation des agences de presse (Ordonnance No 45-2646 of 2 November 1945 regulating press agencies whose main activity is the collection, processing and editing, under its own responsibility, of journalistic content), https://www.legifrance.gouv.fr/loda/article_lc/LEGIARTI000025576985, accessed: 16.11.2022.

163 English version by author.

164 See: Chapter 1, Section 4.

"Actual control" could be understood, in line with the conclusions reached in Section 4 of this chapter, as the exercise of effective control, meaning the ability to make final decisions regarding both the selection of materials included in a press publication and their organisation, in accordance with professional ethics. "Legal control" could refer to having a legal basis for the production and dissemination of a press publication, including acquiring the necessary legal rights to the works contained within it.

According to Art. 99[10], a publisher must have their residence or headquarters in the Republic of Poland, an EU MS or an MS of the EFTA that is a party to the Agreement on the European Economic Area. However, the legislature has not clarified whether this refers to the statutory or registered seat or to the actual seat where the entity's activities are conducted. It is difficult to accept that publishers' rights could be acquired by an entity operating outside of the EU or EFTA but merely registered in an MS for protection purposes. On the other hand, the statutory registered office provides more certainty, as it can be easily verified through publicly available registers. Given the objective of ensuring the most effective protection to press publishers, the lack of specificity in this context should be interpreted as allowing a broad understanding of the publishers' seat.

To conclude:

- the French legislature defines terms "press publisher" and "press agency" by referring to existing concepts in press law. In Polish law, the role of a press publisher is outlined through the notion of legal and actual control over the production and dissemination of content. I propose understanding these terms as the exercise of effective control, meaning the ability to make final decisions on both the selection of materials included in a press publication and their organisation in accordance with professional ethics. Additionally, it involves overseeing the legal basis for the production and dissemination of the press publication, which could for include acquiring the necessary legal rights to the works contained within it.

6. Authors and other rights holders of the works and other subject matters incorporated in a press publication

6.1. The CDSM Directive

According to Art. 15(2) of the CDSM Directive

> the rights provided for in paragraph 1 shall leave intact and shall in no way affect any rights provided for in Union law to authors and other rightholders, in respect of the works and other subject matters incorporated in a press publication. The rights provided for in paragraph 1 shall not be invoked against these authors and other rightholders and, in particular, shall not deprive them of their right to exploit their works and other subject matter independently from the press publication in which they are incorporated. When a work or other subject matter is incorporated in a press publication on

> the basis of a non-exclusive licence, the rights provided for in paragraph 1 shall not be invoked to prohibit its use by other authorised users.

Because a press publication is a collection that includes works and other subject matter, it was necessary to regulate the relationship between authors, other rightholders and press publishers. Authors and other rightholders must not be deprived of their right to exploit their works and other subject matter independently of the press publication in which they are incorporated. This provision safeguards the interests of authors and related rights holders against the introduction of an additional layer of protection for another group of entities. The creation of a new protected subject matter must not restrict rightholders from exploiting their works and other subject matter or diminish the protection to which they are entitled.

To illustrate, an author of a photograph protected under copyright law and included in a press publication should retain the right to exploit their work independently. For example, if the photograph is included in a press publication under a non-exclusive licence, the author should still be able to authorise its use under a separate license. In such cases, the press publisher cannot invoke their rights over the press publication to prevent the author from exercising their rights to the photograph.

The regulation aligns with provisions established in both international and EU law.[165] Its purpose is to secure the rights of authors in light of the introduction of protection for a new category of entities. This approach reflects legislative consistency.

Interestingly, the EU legislature opted for a strong safeguard. First, "press publishers' rights shall leave intact and shall in no way affect any rights provided for in Union law to authors and other rightholders, in respect of the works and other subject matters incorporated in press publications." Second, the press publishers' rights "shall not be invoked against these authors and other rightholders and, in particular, shall not deprive them of their right to exploit their works and other subject matter independently from the press publication in which they are incorporated."[166]

To conclude:

- the adoption of safeguards for authors and other rightholders with rights to works and subject matter included in a press publication is justified by the need to protect their interests amid the introduction of a new category of rightholders. This solution limits the publisher's monopoly over the use of elements within a press publication. If the rights to a specific element have not been transferred or licensed exlusively to the publisher, it may still be used independently, allowing for its exploitation elsewhere,for example, in another press publication.

165 In the Rome Convention, the WPPT, the Rental and Lending Rights Directive, the InfoSoc Directive.

166 T. Höppner, M. Kretschmer, R. Xalabarder, "CREATe," 607–622.

Table 2.5 Authors and other rightholders of the works and other subject matter incorporated in a press publication

*Art. L.211-1 of the French Intellectual Property Code**	*Art. 99^{7}(2) of the Polish Copyright Act***
Related rights shall not infringe the rights of authors. Consequently, no provision of this Title shall be interpreted in such a way as to limit the exercise of copyright by its holders.	Without prejudice to the rights of the authors and other right holders, the publisher of a press publication shall have the exclusive right to dispose of and use the press publication to the extent of: 1) reproducing press publication for the purpose of using it in the field of exploitation referred to in point 2; 2) making press publication available to the public by the service provider in such a way that everyone may access it at a time and place of their own choosing.

Note: *English version by the author. French version: https://www.legifrance.gouv.fr/codes/article_lc/LEGIARTI000006279025, accessed: 12.07.2023. **English version by the author. Polish version: https://isap.sejm.gov.pl/isap.nsf/download.xsp/WDU19940240083/U/D19940083Lj.pdf, accessed: 25.11.2024.

6.2. French and Polish law

According to Art. L. 211-1 of the French Intellectual Property Code, as demonstarted in Table 2.5, related rights shall not infringe the rights of authors. They should not be interpreted in such a way that restricts their exercise. Interestingly, despite Art. 15(2) of the CDSM Directive explicitly applying to all copyright and related rights holders, France has not adopted a clause preventing press publishers from limiting the protection of holders of other related rights.[167] It is difficult to justify such an exclusionary approach. To instance, if a press publication includes a phonogram, the French implementation does not explicitly safeguard the rights of phonogram producers from potential limitations imposed by press publishers when exercising the rights granted under the CDSM Directive. This contrasts with the Polish implementation, which explicitly states that press publishers' exclusive rights to reproduction and making available rights must be exercised without prejudice to the rights of authors and other rightholders.

To conclude:

- the French implementation does not include a safeguard protecting the rights of related rights holders concerning subject matter included in a press publication. This omission is unjustified, as it contradicts the provisions from Art. 15 of the CDSM Directive.

167 See: T. Azzi, "Commentaire," 65; E. Derieux, "Droits voisins des éditeurs de presse: mesures conservatoires à l'encontre de Google," *Revue Lamy Droit de l'Immatériel* no. 170 (2020): 8–12.

7. Appropriate share of revenue for authors of works incorporated in a press publication

7.1. The CDSM Directive

According to the last paragraph of Art. 15 of the CDSM Directive, MS must ensure that authors of works incorporated in a press publication receive an appropriate share of the revenues that press publishers receive for the use of their press publications by ISSPs. Recital 59 of the CDSM Directive clarifies that "this should be without prejudice to national laws on ownership or exercise of rights in context of employment contracts, provided that such laws are in compliance with the Union law."

As to the rationale of this solution, M. van Eechoud highlights the difficult situation of journalists, who often have weak bargaining power when negotiating exploitation agreements.[168] This solution addresses concerns that the introduction of new rights for press publishers could result in a reduction of authors' revenue share.

Authors have a right to claim an appropriate share of the revenues, but the EU legislature has not provided a precise definition of the term "appropriate" in the context of Art. 15 of the CDSM Directive. E. Rosati suggests interpreting it as proportionate[169] however, this raises the question: to what should this share be proportionate? Should the share be determined based on the author's contribution to the press publication as a whole, the extent to which ISSPs use that contribution or the frequency its use?

To address these questions, it is important to note that the EU legislature also uses the term "appropriate" in Art.18 of the CDSM Directive, which establishes the principle of appropriate and proportionate remuneration for authors and performers. Recital 73 of the CDSM Directive specifies that such remuneration should be appropriate and proportionate to the actual or potential economic value of the licensed or transferred rights. This assessment should consider the author's or performer's contribution to the overall work or subject matter as well as other relevant factors, such as market practices and the actual exploitation of the work.

While adapting these explanations to the situation of authors whose works are included in a press publication, the appropriateness of their share could be determined based on several factors, including **the scope of their contribution to the overall press publication, market practices and the extent to which the press publication, and specifically their contribution, is exploited**. A. Lucas-Schloetter, referring to German law, explains that:

> A remuneration is deemed appropriate if it conforms to what is regarded as customary and fair in business relations, having regard to the nature and scope of the rights granted, in particular the duration, frequency, extent and

168 M. M. van Eechoud, "A publisher's," 26–37.
169 E. Rosati, *Copyright*, 293.

moment. If the rights granted are unlimited in time and scope, a lump sum payment will usually not be sufficient.[170]

I acknowledge that the interpretation of "appropriate" will vary across different MS, **depending on factors such as market realities of the press sector and existing legal provisions regulating revenue sharing between authors and holders of other related rights.** This perspective is shared by R. Xalabarder, who states that "'Appropriate' would also require that the remuneration is adjusted to cultural and economic circumstances of each country and market, and to the different markets and means of exploitation."[171] In conclusion, further clarification of this concept within more specific provisions at the national level will be necessary.

The right to an appropriate share for authors of works incorporated in a press publication has a distinct nature. First, press publishers must acquire the legal title to the elements of a press publication, either through the transfer of exclusive rights or a licensing agreement. This transaction typically involves remuneration paid to the authors of these elements. Second, authors are entitled to claim a share of the remuneration that press publishers receive for the use of press publications by ISSPs. Therefore, Art. 15(5) of the CDSM Directive does not concern the initial stage of transferring or licensing exclusive rights to the components of a press publication. Instead, it applies to the subsequent stage, in which ISSPs exploit the press publication, generating revenue that should be shared between press publishers and the authors of the incorporated works.

A key distinction between Art. 15(5) and Art. 18 of the CDSM Directive should be noted. Under Art. 18, authors and performers are entitled to receive appropriate and proportionate remuneration when they license or transfer their exclusive rights for the exploitation of their works or other subject matter. In this case, remuneration is directly linked to the initial transfer or license of exclusive rights rather than any subsequent transfer or license, although such subsequent transactions may influence the amount of the remuneration. Under Art. 15(5), authors are entitled to a share of the remuneration that press publishers receive when ISSPs reproduce and make available press publications containing their works, provided that these acts are carried out in exchange for remuneration. However, the EU legislature did not prohibit press publishers from waiving their rights. This means that if a press publisher decides not to enforce its rights or does not generate revenue from ISSPs, the authors will not receive any share.

The issue arises as to whether authors of works incorporated in a press publication would effectively be remunerated twice for the same contribution. Because related rights are designed to compensate for investment rather than creation, the obligation to share revenues derived from the investment in the creation and distribution of a

170 A. Lucas-Schloetter, "European copyright contract law: A plea for harmonisation," *International Review of Intellectual Property and Competition Law* (IIC) 48 (2017): 898.

171 R. Xalabarder, "The principle of appropriate and proportionate remuneration for authors and performers in Art.18 copyright in the digital single market directive," *InDret* 4 (2020): 15, https://indret.com/wp-content/uploads/2020/10/1591.pdf, accessed: 24.01.2024.

press publication with the authors of its elements may seem surprising.[172] A. Lebois questions the logic of this approach, arguing that it blurs the distinction between the protection afforded to journalists under copyright and the new related rights granted to press publishers.[173] However, this revenue-sharing obligation should be viewed as complementary to the overarching objective of press publishers' rights, which is to support and strengthen the sustainability of the press sector.

National legislatures, when implementing the Directive, have the freedom to determine the method for calculating the remuneration and specifying the amount of remuneration, provided it meets the appropriateness criterion. However, the EU legislature did not clarify whether the right to a share is transferable or how it should be collected and distributed. These aspects must be addressed at the implementation stage.

It should be noted that only authors, not holders of rights to other subject matter included in a press publication, are entitled to receive an appropriate share of the revenues. This approach can be seen as a response to concerns from authors that the adoption of Art. 15 could negatively impact their interests. However, this raises the question of why other groups protected by the related right regime are excluded.

To conclude:

- the obligation to share the press publishers' revenues with authors is justified by the challenging financial situation of journalists and their weak bargaining position. However, given that the rationale behind the related rights regime is to compensate for investments made rather than creative contributions, the requirement for press publishers to share their remuneration with authors may be difficult to justify from a purely legal and economic standpoint.
- the term "appropriate" in relation to the authors' share of revenues that press publishers receive for the use of their press publications by ISSPs should be determined by MS based on factors such as the scope of the authors' contribution to the overall press publication, market practices and the extent of the exploitation of both the press publication and the authors' contributions. The interpretation of "appropriate" will vary across MS, depending on market realities, the structure of the press sector and existing legal provisions regulating the distribution of revenues between authors and holders of related rights.
- the principle of "appropriate share" for authors of works incorporated in a press publication does not apply to the initial transfer of rights or licensing of those works. Instead, it applies to the subsequent use of the press publication by ISSPs, which unless otherwise agreed, entails payment of remuneration to press publishers, which should then be shared with the authors.
- when implementing Art. 15 of the CDSM Directive, should clarify the term "appropriate" by defining a method for calculating remuneration or

172 See: S. Dusollier, "The 2019," 1008.
173 A. Lebois, "La légitimité," 133.

establishing a threshold. Moreover, it should be specified whether the right to a share is transferable or how it should be collected and distributed. The EU legislature, recognising market differences and the legislative traditions of the MS, guarantees a large degree of flexibility in this area.

7.2. French and Polish law

According to Art. L218-5 of the French Intellectual Property Code, as demonstrated in Table 2.6, professional journalists, (1) or those treated as such, (2) and other authors of works included in the press publications (3) are entitled to **an appropriate and equitable** share of the remuneration that press publishers receive under agreements with ISSPs.

Professional journalists, as defined in Art. L7111-5 of the French Labour Code, are those who practice their profession in one or more companies that communicate to the public via electronic means.[174] In addition to professional journalists and those treated as such, such as freelancers, other authors of works included in a press publication are also entitled to a share. The French legislature introduces a distinction that is not included in the CDSM Directive. This distinction appears unnecessary, as journalists must already be authors of works included in a press publication to receive the share of remuneration. However, this provision introduces a distinction among negotiating actors, as it establishes different negotiation routes for them. It also suggests a potential implication that the amount of the share may vary depending on which of these categories an individual falls into.

The French legislature refrained from introducing quantitative measures to specify the amount of remuneration and relied, instead, on abstract and subjective terms as "appropriate" and "equitable." While this approach allows for flexibility, it also increases the rise of discretion and significant variations in the authors' compensation. Remuneration should be collectively negotiated and established through company agreements or other collective agreements. It has been specified that the remuneration for other authors should also be negotiated between representative professional organisations of press enterprises and press agencies on one side and professional organisations of authors or collective management bodies on the other.

The negotiated remuneration has an additional nature and cannot be classified as a salary. Therefore, journalists employed by a press publisher who are the authors of works included in a press publication should receive, in addition to their regular salary, a share of the remuneration that press publishers obtain under their related rights.

If an agreement is not reached within six months of the adoption of press publishers' rights in France, either negotiating party may refer the matter to the Copyright

174 English version by the author. French version, https://www.legifrance.gouv.fr/codes/article_lc/LEGIARTI000006904513, accessed: 13.07.2023.

Table 2.6 Share of publishers' remuneration

*Art. L. 218-5 V the French Intellectual Property Code**	*Art. 99^9 of the Polish Copyright Act***
I Professional journalists or those treated as such, within the meaning of Articles L. 7111-3 to L. 7111-5 of the Labour Code, and other authors of works included in the press publications mentioned in Article L. 218-1 of this Code shall be entitled to an appropriate and equitable share of the remuneration mentioned in Article L. 218-4. This share as well as the modalities of its distribution among the authors concerned shall be fixed under conditions determined by a company agreement or, failing that, by any other collective agreement within the meaning of Article L. 2222-1 of the Labour Code. For other authors, this share shall be determined by a specific agreement negotiated between, on the one hand, the representative professional organisations of press enterprises and press agencies and, on the other hand, the professional organisations of authors or the collective management bodies mentioned in Title II of Book III of this Part. In all cases, this additional remuneration shall not have the character of a salary.	1. Authors of works incorporated in a press publication shall be entitled to 50% of the remuneration due to the publisher for the exercise of the rights referred to in Article $99^7(2)$. 2. The remuneration referred to in subsection 1 shall be paid by the publisher to the author no later than 30 days after the publisher has received that remuneration.
II In the absence of an agreement within six months of the publication of law n° 2019-775 of 24 July 2019 tending to create a related right for the benefit of press agencies and publishers and in the absence of any other applicable agreement, one of the parties to the negotiation of the company agreement or specific agreement mentioned in I of this article can refer the matter to the commission provided for in III. The committee shall seek a compromise solution with the parties in order to reach an agreement. In case of persistent disagreement, it shall determine the appropriate share provided for in I as well as the modalities of its distribution between the authors concerned.	
III For the implementation of II, a commission is created, chaired by a representative of the State and composed, in addition, for half of representatives of professional organisations of press companies and press agencies and for half of representatives of organisations representing journalists and other authors mentioned in I. The State representative shall be appointed from among the members of the Court of Cassation, the Council of State or the Court of Auditors, by order of the Minister responsible for communication.	
In the absence of a compromise solution found between the parties, the commission shall render its decision within four months from the date of referral.The intervention of the commission's decision does not prevent new collective bargaining from taking place in the companies concerned. The collective agreement resulting from this negotiation shall replace the decision of the commission, after it has been filed by the most diligent party with the administrative authority, in accordance with Article L. 2231-6 of the Labour Code.	
IV Professional journalists or similar and other authors mentioned in I of this article shall receive at least once a year, if necessary by an electronic communication process, updated, relevant and complete information on the methods of calculating the appropriate and equitable share of remuneration due to them in application of the same I.	
V A decree in the Council of State shall lay down the conditions for the application of this article, in particular the composition and procedures for referral to and operation of the commission, the means of judicial appeal against its decisions and the procedures for publicising them.	

Note: *English version by the author. French version: https://www.legifrance.gouv.fr/codes/article_lc/LEGIARTI000038826736, accessed: 12.07.2023. **English version by the author. Polish version: https://isap.sejm.gov.pl/isap.nsf/download.xsp/WDU19940240083/U/D19940083Lj.pdf, accessed: 25.11.2024.

and Related Rights Commission (hereinafter: CDADV)[175] to seek a compromise solution. If disagreements persist, the CDADV has the authority to determine the appropriate share and establish the modalities of its distribution among the authors concerned. However, there is no obligation to refer disputes to this body.

An example of such an agreement in France is the collective agreement signed in 2022 between the National Union of Journalists (SNJ) and the French Press Agency.[176] However, many negotiations have not been successful. The first intervention of CDADV took place in January 2023, following a referral by from the SNJ concerning a minority agreement on the distribution of revenues from press publishers' related rights paid by the EBRA group[177]to journalists. Due to a persistent disagreement between the negotiating parties, the SNJ escalated the matter to the CDADV. The CDADV ruled in favour of a proportional payment with a rate of 18% and a fixed ceiling of around 680 euros from the total sums from the EBRA group.[178]

According to Art. 99^9 of the Polish Copyright Act, the authors of works included in a press publication are entitled to 50% of the remuneration that the publisher receives for exercising its rights. In comparison, France provides for an appropriate and equitable share, while Spain adopts the term "appropriate share."[179] Germany mandates that authors receive at least one-third of the press publishers' remuneration,[180] whereas Italy specifies that the share should be between 2% and 5% of the remuneration press publishers receive for exercising their reproduction and making available rights.[181]

Among these legislatures, the Polish example is the only one that establishes a fixed threshold of a remuneration. This raises doubts about whether imposing such a fixed threshold is justified and whether it could limit the freedom of contract between press publishers and authors. Conversely, the absence of a threshold, as

175 Ministère de la culture, "Commission droits d'auteur et droits voisins (CDADV)," December 05, 2024, https://www.culture.gouv.fr/Thematiques/Presse-ecrite/Commissions/Commission-droits-d-auteur-et-droits-voisins-CDADV, accessed: 03.01.2025.

176 La Correspondance de la Presse, "Droits voisins: sur la base de l'accord conclu entre l'AgenceFrance-Presse (AFP) et Google, le SNJ de l'AFP a signé un accord collectif relatif à la réversion de la "part appropriée et équitable" des journalistes de l'agence de presse," May 04, 2022, https://www.lacorrespondancedelapresse.fr/2022-05-04, accessed: 13.07.2023.

177 A French regional daily press group operating in eastern France. It claims to be France's largest press group as regards the press circulation. See: Ebra, https://www.ebra.fr, accessed: 13.07.2023.

178 SNJ, "Droits voisins dans le groupe Ebra: chronique d'un échec annoncé," July 08, 2022, https://www.snj.fr/droits-voisins-dans-le-groupe-ebra-chronique-dun-echec-annonce/1589, accessed: 03.01.2025.

179 See: Art. 129 bis of Real Decreto Legislativo 1/1996, de 12 de abril, por el que se aprueba el texto refundido de la Ley de Propiedad Intelectual, regularizando, aclarando y armonizando las disposiciones legales vigentes sobre la materia, https://www.boe.es/buscar/act.php?id=BOE-A-1996-8930, accessed: 11.07.2023.

180 See: §87k of Urheberrechtsgesetz – UrhG, https://www.gesetze-im-internet.de/englisch_urhg/englisch_urhg.html, accessed: 13.07.2023.

181 See: Art. 43 bis of legge 22 aprile 1941, n. 633, https://www.gazzettaufficiale.it/eli/id/2021/11/27/21G00192/sg, accessed: 13.07.2023.

seen in France, allows for broad discretion. Therefore, the best solution seems to be specifying a minimum or flexible threshold, as adopted in Italy and Germany.

During the legislative process in Poland, it was argued that the proposed 50% share fairly reflects the contributions of authors to the creation of a press publication. This approach was supported during the public consultations by organisations such as ZAiKS, the Polish authors' association, and REPROPOL, the Polish Association of Journalists and Publishers.[182] Moreover, the 50% share was formulated by analogy to an existing provision in Polish copyright law. According to Art. 20(2)(1) of the Polish copyright law, producers are required to share with authors 50% of their revenues from the sale of tape recorders, similar devices and blank carriers. This precedent in Polish law likely influenced the decision to adopt a similar revenue-sharing model for press publications. However, consistency within the legislative framework is not always advisable and justifiable. In the case of press publishers, the 50% share could represent a significant financial burden for press publishers, potentially leading to a large and not entirely justified income for authors who have already received remuneration through the transfer or licensing of their exclusive rights. Moreover, the European legislature guarantees authors an "appropriate" share of remuneration, ensuring a degree of flexibility in determining it. The Polish legislature, by imposing a fixed and high percentage split, appears to limit this flexibility. This leads to far-reaching, though not impossible, conclusion that for press publishers, who are already in a weaker position against digital platforms and struggle to negotiate fair compensation, the mandatory 50% share could become an additional financial strain.

The Polish legislature did not specify whether the right to a share of remuneration is transferable. However, based on the legislative technique used in the Polish Copyright Act, when a right is **not** transferable, it is explicitly stated.[183] Because no such restriction is mentioned, the right to a share of remuneration is transferable. The intermediation of collective management organisations is not mandatory. However, the relationship between the implementation of providing authors with a share of the remuneration and their employment status has not been defined in Poland. This lack of clarity may create uncertainty whether remuneration received under an employment contract excludes authors from receiving a share of the press publishers' revenues. To ensure a smooth payment process, the Polish legislature has stipulated that publishers must distribute the authors' share within 30 days of receiving the remuneration.

To conclude:

- the French legislature did not specify a fixed threshold for the share of remuneration obtained by press publishers. Instead, it determined that the share should be appropriate and equitable. While the absence of a threshold provides flexibility, it may also lead to discretionary decisions and significant

182 Ministerstwo Kultury i Dziedzictwa Narodowego, *Uzasadnienie,* 47.
183 See for example Art. 18(3) of the Polish Copyright Act.

disparities in remuneration among authors. A key solution to these concerns lies in the negotiation mechanism established in France, along with the role of the CDADV, which serves as both a supportive and, in cases of disagreement, a substitutive body to ensure a fair and balanced distribution of revenues.

- the 50% share of press publishers' remuneration mandated under Poland's implementation of the CDSM Directive imposes a significant financial burden on press publishers. It also restricts the flexibility envisioned by the EU legislature, which is evident in other national implementations that allow for more adaptable approaches.

8. Conclusion

The purpose of adopting related rights is to reward the effort involved in the dissemination of works and the investments made, regardless of their size. Additionally, these rights aim to adapt the legal framework to the challenges posed by the evolving digital landscape and the use of new technologies in content distribution.

The EU legislature, in justifying the adoption of related rights for press publishers, considered the digital transformation of the press sector and the shift from printed newspapers to online media, which has contributed to a decline in newspaper revenues. However, the fact that this decline is, in many cases, also linked to press publishers' business models not being adequately adapted to the technological challenges was not considered. The need to reinforce the legal position of press publishers was justified by their role in the dissemination of information and the protection of media pluralism. Additionally, the complex relationship between news aggregators and press publishers was acknowledged by the EU legislature, though the focus was placed exclusively on its negative impact on the publishers' interests.

I understand a press publication as a collection composed mainly of literary works of a journalistic nature, which can also include other works or other subject matter. The inclusion of unprotected elements within such a collection should not prevent the press publication from being granted protection under publishers' rights, as long as it meets the necessary criteria. However, if an unprotected element is used independently by ISSPs , it would not constitute an infringement of the press publishers' exclusive rights.

A press publication, as a collection, should consist of multiple elements that form a cohesive structure, which may result from a thematic link or a common objective, such as the dissemination of information. To qualify as a press publication, it should contain at least three elements. The regularity of updates to a press publication should be interpreted broadly, encompassing not only traditional periodic updates (e.g., daily or weekly issues) but also frequent updates to press walls on news websites or digital platforms operated by press publishers. A press publication should be published under the initiative, editorial responsibility and control of a service provider. Editorial responsibility should be understood as the exercise of the effective control over both the selection of materials included in the press publication and their organisation. However, this does not necessarily imply legal liability under national law for the content provided. Moreover, all the conditions listed in Art. 2(4) of the CDSM Directive must be met cumulatively for a publication to qualify as a press publication.

Press publishers' rights do not extend to the use of individual words or very short extracts of a press publication. Because the EU legislature does not define the concept of "very short extracts," their assessment should consider factors such as the impact of the extract on the reader, the reader's willingness to click the link to access the full press publication and the economic consequences of using such extracts on press publishers' interests. Although the CDSM Directive does not provide a specific definition at the EU level, this does not prevent MS from introducing a quantitative threshold or a clear definition of very short extracts in their national implementations.

The French legislature introduced a specification stating that the use of a very short extract from a press publication is excluded from protection only if it does not affect the effectiveness of press publishers' related rights. The effectiveness of these rights may be compromised if the use of very short extracts substitutes the press publication itself or eliminates the need for the reader to engage with the full content. This clarification helps to define the concept of very short extract of press publications, although it still leaves some degree of uncertainty. In contrast, the Polish legislature did not introduce any additional specifications regarding the interpretation of very short extracts. In this context, guidance from the CJEU would be particularly significant.

A press publisher is a natural or legal person established in an MS who publishes in the context of an economic activity that qualifies as a provision of services under EU law. Notably, the EU legislature did not introduce any distinction between different types of press publishers based on the content they publish, as long as they meet the definition of press publication under Art. 2(4) of the CDSM Directive. This is an important consideration at both the implementation and application stages of the law, ensuring that no additional differentiation is introduced.

Press publishers are obliged to share the revenues they receive from ISSPs for the use of press publications with the authors of works incorporated into those publications. This obligation has been criticised as being incompatible with the nature and purpose of related rights, which are traditionally designed to reward investment rather than creative contributions. However, in my opinion, this obligation aligns with the broader objective of press publishers' related rights, which is to support the press sector as a whole. The EU legislature, by using the term "appropriate" to describe the share of remuneration due to authors, intended to allow for a degree flexibility in determining this threshold. However, this flexibility was not reflected in the Polish implementation, in which a fixed 50% share was introduced. This rigid approach could place a significant burden on press publishers. Moreover, neither the EU legislature nor the French or Polish legislatures have introduced a mechanism to safeguard authors' interests in cases in which press publishers choose to waive their rights, which is not prohibited under the CDSM Directive.

3 Exclusive rights of press publishers in light of the CDSM Directive and national laws

1. Introduction

The analysis conducted in this chapter primarily aims to determine the scope of the exclusive rights granted to press publishers. To this end, it examines the provisions of Arts. 2 and 3 of the InfoSoc Directive as they apply to press publishers, alongside the Polish and the French implementations of publishers' rights. Particular attention is given to the interpretation of exclusions from the scope of protection. Additionally, the chapter characterises ISSPs as the entities against whom publishers' rights apply.

Second, the exercise of the publishers' rights will be examined with a particular focus on the role of collective management organisations in facilitating their enforcement.

Third, through a case study of the legal situation of French press publishers following the adoption of related rights, this chapter will examine how they have sought to ensure the effectiveness of their protection by invoking competition law. The analysis will identify the deficiencies, inaccuracies and grey areas in the text of the French implementation. While it is too early to assess the effectiveness of the protection granted to press publishers, it is not too late to identify the shortcomings that have emerged in practice. These gaps could potentially undermine the effectiveness of the regulation, especially in relation to the free flow of information and the safeguarding of media pluralism. Recognising these issues early on is crucial for improving the implementation of the Directive and ensuring the application of publishers' rights.

Finally, this chapter will examine selected aspects of the Belgian, Spanish, Italian and Czech implementations of Art. 15 of the CDSM Directive. These Member States adopted press publishers' rights later than France and incorporated mechanisms aimed at strengthening the effectiveness of publishers' protection, drawing from the lessons learned from the French implementation. The analysis will focus on identifying which legal shortcomings in the French implementation should have been addressed or improved and how the later implementations of Art. 15 of the CDSM Directive in other Member States have introduced legislative solutions to mitigate these deficiencies. Understanding these corrective measures is crucial to assess how different legal approaches can enhance the effectiveness of

DOI: 10.4324/9781003599494-3

the regulation, particularly concerning access to information and the safeguarding of media pluralism.

2. Exclusive rights of press publishers

Since the adoption of the CDSM Directive, reproduction and making available rights extend to publishers of press publications. They have the exclusive right to:

1) authorise or prohibit direct or indirect, temporary or permanent reproduction by any means and in any form, in whole or in part of press publications by ISSPs,

   and to:

2) authorise or prohibit the making available to the public of press publication by ISSPs, by wire or wireless means in such a way that members of the public may access them from a place and at a time individually chosen.

This is an example of maximum harmonisation, meaning that the protection granted to press publishers following the Directive's implementation cannot be more or less extensive than what is prescribed. Press publishers are granted two distinct rights: the right to authorise or prohibit reproduction and the right to authorise or prohibit the making available of press publications. These rights are independent of each other.The rights of authorising or prohibiting the reproduction and making available of a press publication can be waived.

The scope of the right is limited to the **online** use of press publications. As noted by some scholars, this reflects the Directive's focus on regulating the activities of "big commercial re-users of journalistic content."[1]

The protection applies specifically to publishers of press publications in cases in which their press publications are used online by ISSPs. This means that the provision targets a specific category of actors rather than applying universally to all users, as would normally result from the *erga omnes* nature of exclusive rights.[2] Notably, in Art. 11 of the initial proposal of the CDSM Directive, which first introduced the protection of press publications, it was not specified that press publishers' rights would apply only against ISSPs. This limitation was added later in the legislative process.[3] The final wording of Art. 15, with its restriction to ISSPs, reflects a deliberate choice to limit the scope of protection.

1 A. Lazarova, "Re-use the news: Between the EU press publishers' right's addressees and the informatory exceptions' beneficiaries," *Journal of Intellectual Property Law & Practice* 16, no. 3 (2021): 239.

2 See: R. Markiewicz, "Prawo," 146.

3 The original proposal of Art. 11(1) of the DSM Directive see: European Commission, Proposal. The specification that the use of the press publication should be done by information society service providers has been added during the legislative works at the EP and appears in the EP text, council text doc.9134/18, and in the compromise text as it results from the Political Agreement reached with

Such a legal construction is complex and difficult to assess from a legal perspective. The *erga omnes* nature, by definition, pertains to the institution of property rights.[4] R. Markiewicz explains that the correlate of rights effective *erga omnes* is an obligation imposed on an unlimited number of persons to remain passive, i.e. to refrain from preventing the right holder from exercising their right and not to interfere with it.[5] The *erga omnes* nature implies that the right or obligation is enforceable against **everyone**, whereas *inter partes* nature means that a right is enforceable only against specific entities. The latter is characteristic of contract law,[6] in which the obligation applies to individually identified parties, and this identification must occur no later than the fulfilment of the contract. For these reasons, the related rights of press publishers cannot be considered as having an *inter partes* nature. They do not originate from contract law, nor do they concern specifically identified entities. Instead, they apply to ISSPs as a category, which does not constitute individual identification in the legal sense.

It is, however, difficult to state with certainty that publishers' related rights have an *erga omnes* character, as they apply only against specific entities. The legal challenge, therefore, lies in determining their precise nature.[7] First, it can be concluded that publishers of press publications are granted exclusive rights. As previously noted, exclusive rights generally have an *erga omnes* nature, meaning they are enforceable against everyone. Second, the exclusive rights granted to press publishers apply only in specific circumstances, namely, when a press publication or its part is used online by ISSPs. This means the law only defines the group of entities against whom the rights apply but also limits their scope to a specific place of use – the digital environment. As a result, press publishers are granted exclusive rights of an *erga omnes* nature, but their practical scope restricted, allowing claims to be directed against a specific group of entities using press publications in a specific online context.[8]

---

the EP at the trilogue on 13 February 2019 see: CREATe, EU Copyright Reform, Evidence on the Copyright in the Digital Single Market Directive, March 26, 2019, 59, https://www.create.ac.uk/policy-responses/eu-copyright-reform/#table, accessed: 08.11.2022.

4 See the judgement of Court of Appeal in Gdańsk, 3.01.2019 r., V AGa 129/18, LEX nr 2763417; A. Olejniczak, Z. Radwański, *Prawo cywilne – część ogólna* (C.H. Beck, 2015), 90; M. Pyziak-Szafnicka, "Prawo cywilne– część ogólna," in *System prawa prywatnego,* ed. M. Safjan, vol. 1 (Warszawa, 2012), 838.

5 R. Markiewicz, *Ilustrowane prawo autorskie* (Wolters Kluwer Polska, LEX, 2018), point 6.3.

6 See: P.B. Hugenholtz, "Data property: Unwelcome guest in the house of IP," in *Better Regulation for Copyright. Academics Meet Policy Makers*, (2017), 59–63, https://felixreda.eu/wp-content/uploads/2017/09/2017-09-06_Better-Regulation-for-Copyright-Academics-meet-Policy-Makers_Proceedings.pdf, accessed: 08.11.2022.

7 See: G. Sartor, "Fundamental legal concepts: A formal and teleological characterisation," *Artificial Intelligence and Law* 14 (2006): 101–142.

8 For simplicity of further analysis, I will consider the nature of the related right as having practical non *erga omnes* nature.

2.1. EU law

2.1.1. Reproduction rights

The act of reproduction of a press publication by ISSPs occurs, for example, when press clippings are provided on request. This process requires the prior reproduction of all selected newspapers or magazines from a given period by news monitoring organisations. Reproduction also occurs in services that index, scan and store press publications, as these require prior reproduction of the content. Additionally, the algorithmisation of the press sector has led to an increasing reliance on the reproduction of press publications to generate learning materials for artificial intelligence (AI), even when these publications are not made available to the public.[9] However, scholars are divided on whether an act of reproduction actually occurs during the AI training phase. Some argue that because no direct copying takes place but, rather, the affixing of tags or labels to generate patterns, the act of reproduction does not occur; therefore, the right of reproduction does not apply.[10] AI companies also present this argument.[11] Others contend that, "the training stage of the AI tools requires the scraping and extraction of relevant information from underlying datasets, which often contain copyright protected works.''[12] If this interpretation is correct, then the act of copying does take place, making the right of reproduction applicable.[13] Moreover, deep learning models tend to memorise the content they are trained on, which suggests that, in such cases, they do, indeed, perform an act of reproduction.[14] Recital 105 of the AI Act explicitly states that text and data mining on copyright-protected content involves reproduction, which helps to resolve some of the doubts surrounding this issue.[15] Additionally, AI is used to

9 W. Ceron, M.F. de Lima Santos, "Artificial intelligence in news media: Current perceptions and future outlook," *Journalism and Media* (2022), https://www.mdpi.com/2673-5172/3/1/2, accessed: 23.06.2023.

10 J.M., Bruguière, J. M. Deltorn, "Intelligences artificielles génératives. Y a-t-il exploitation des oeuvres, au sens du droit d'auteur ? N'y aurait-il pas d'autres modèles à considérer?," *Recueil Dalloz* (2023): 167.

11 A. Susarla, "Generative AI could leave users holding the bag for copyright violations," The Conversation, March 22, 2024, https://theconversation.com/generative-ai-could-leave-users-holding-the-bag-forcopyright-violations-225760, accessed: 03.01.2025.

12 J.P. Quintais, "Generative AI, copyright and the AI Act," Kluwer Copyright Blog, May 09, 2023, https://copyrightblog.kluweriplaw.com/2023/05/09/generative-ai-copyright-and-the-ai-act/, accessed: 03.01.2025.

13 Reuters, "Apple explores AI deals with news publishers," New York Times, December 22, 2023, https://www.reuters.com/technology/apple-explores-ai-deals-with-news-publishers-new-york-times-2023-12-22/, accessed: 03.01.2025.

14 I. Emanuilov, T. Margoni, "Memorisation in generative models and EU copyright law: An interdisciplinary view," Kluwer Copyright Blog, March 26, 2024, https://copyrightblog.kluweriplaw.com/2024/03/26/memorisation-in-generative-models-and-eu-copyright-law-an-interdisciplinary-view/, accessed 03.01.2025.

15 For an in-depth analysis of the topic see: M. Kowala, "Protection of press publishers in the age of generative AI – in search of legal remedies to adapt to the pace of technology," *International Review of Intellectual Property and Competition Law (IIC)*, 55, no. 10 (2024).

extract the facts and news from existing press publications to generate new news items based on that content. In this case as well, the act of reproduction of a press publication, or at least parts of it, takes place.[16]

The act of reproduction is exempted from the reproduction right, according to Art. 5(1) of the InfoSoc Directive only if it fulfils the following conditions: it must be temporary, transient or incidental, and it must form an integral and essential part of a technological process. Moreover, the act must not have independent economic significance.[17] These conditions must all be fulfiled[18] and should be understood strictly.[19] If these criteria are met, authorisation for the reproduction is not required.

In the case of the exception under discussion, the act of reproduction does not directly facilitate the enjoyment and access to works but, rather, serves as an internal phase within a larger technological process that enables the provision of services. However, assessing whether a reproduction act meets the requirements of Art. 5(1) of the InfoSoc Directive is complex and allows for considerable discretion in interpretation. The CJEU has clarified that an act can be held to be "transient" if its duration is "limited to what is necessary for the proper completion of the technological process in question."[20] According to the CJEU, an act of reproduction qualifies as transient if it is automated and its results are automatically deleted without human intervention once the process is completed. However, in *Meltwater* case, which concerned a dispute between the publisher NLA and Meltwater, a provider of online monitoring press reports, the Court examined whether the creation of "cached" copies, automatically saved on a computer while browsing the web, fell within the exemption under Art. 5(1) of the InfoSoc Directive. The Court clarified that

> the requirement of automatic deletion does not preclude such a deletion from being preceded by human intervention directed at terminating the use of the technological process. It is permissible for the technological process at issue in the main proceedings to be activated and completed manually.[21]

Therefore, the transient character of an act of reproduction cannot be denied simply because technological process is terminated by the end-user.

The incidental character of an act of reproduction should be understood as being dependent on the technological process it contributes to. The limitation under Art. 5(1) applies only to reproductions that occur due to technical necessity and

16 See: J. Diaz- Noci, "Artificial intelligence systems-aided news and copyright: Assessing legal implications for journalism practices," *Future internet* (2020), https://www.mdpi.com/1999-5903/12/5/85, accessed: 23.06.2023.

17 CJEU, Infopaq, para. 54.

18 CJEU, Infopaq, para. 55.

19 CJEU, Infopaq, para. 56.

20 CJEU, Infopaq, para. 64.

21 CJEU, Public Relations Consultants Association Ltd v Newspaper Licensing Agency Ltd and Others, Case C-360/13, June 5, 2014, para. 42.

have no independent economic significance.[22] For some scholars, this distinction creates uncertainty, making the line between infringing and non-infringing acts unpredictable,[23] raising concerns about legal certainty.[24] The CJEU has clarified that technical copies may create economic value by facilitating the use of a subject matter.[25] However, the economic advantage derived from temporary reproduction must be neither distinct nor separable from the economic benefit derived from the lawful use of the work in question.[26]

To apply these considerations to the use of press publications, the reproduction of a press publication will not have additional economic significance if it does not generate a distinct or separable profit. Therefore, if the act of reproduction is conducted solely to populate AI training databases, enabling AI to later generate news items, it will not be considered economically significant, provided that no direct profit is derived from making the database available to users for commercial purposes. However, a counterargument is that such reproduction may still contribute to economic gain by enhancing the value of the final output. A richer AI database leads to higher quality outputs, which, in turn, enhances the value of the final product.

2.3. Making available right

Media monitoring services and news aggregators do not merely reproduce press publications for their own activities but also enable public access to them from a place and at time individually chosen by the user. The right of making available to the public is part of the broader right of communication to the public and should be interpreted consistently[27] with it. According to Art. 3(1) of the InfoSoc Directive, the right of making available is granted to the authors, while Art. 3(2) extends the protection to holders of related rights.

S. Bechtold explains that the right covers "the act of providing a work to the public."[28] Protection is triggered as long as there is **a possibility of access,**[29]

22 S. Bechtold, "Information society directive," in *Concise European Copyright Law*, ed. T. Dreier, B. Hugenholtz (Kluwer Law International, 2006), 45.

23 M.van Echoud et al., *Harmonizing*, 112.

24 See: L. Guibault et al., *Study on the Implementation and Effect in Member States' Laws of Directive 2001/29/EC on the Harmonisation of Certain Aspects of Copyright and Related Rights in the Information Society*, Institute for Information Law (2012), 35.

25 CJEU, Murphy, paras. 174–175.

26 CJEU, Murphy, para. 175.

27 F. Chönherr, Ch. Geiger, "The information society directive," in *EU Copyright Law. A Commentary*, ed. I. Stamatoudi, P. Torremans (Edward Elgar Publishing, 2014), 11.24.

28 T. Dreier, B. Hugenholtz (ed.), *Concise European Copyright Law* (Kluwer Law International, 2006), 361.

29 See: J. Koo, *The Right of Communication to the Public in EU Copyright Law* (Hart Publishing, 2019), 73–77.

meaning that the work is made available as a result of transmission.[30] This right requires that the public be able to access the work "on demand," meaning from a place and at a time individually chosen by the public. It is linked to services that operate on "user-initiated modes of communication, such as offers to download a work from a public website or online streaming services that allow the consumer to 'pull' content at his/her convenience."[31] Because the right of making available must be interpreted consistently with the right of communication to the public under Art. 3(1) of the InfoSoc Directive, the use of press publications by an online platform acting as an ISSP will be subject to authorisation or prohibition:

- if the activity involves deliberately and intentionally providing access to a press publication or at least facilitating access to it.[32] Given that news aggregators operate by providing access to press publication, this criterion of deliberate and intentional intervention will be satisfied.
- if access is provided to a press publication that was published without the authorisation of the rights holder, and the news aggregator knew or could have known about this lack of authorisation.[33] However, this situation is unlikely to arise in cases in which news aggregators "republish" entire press publications or parts of them from newspaper and magazine websites, assuming that they were legally made available on their original sources.

30 T. Rendas, *Exceptions in EU Copyright Law. In Search of a Balance Between Flexibility and Legal Certainty* (Wolters Kluwers Law International, 2021), 52.

31 C. Angelopoulos, "On online platforms and the commission's new proposal for a directive on copyright in the digital single market," *SSRN* (Centre for Intellectual Property and Information Law (CIPIL) University of Cambridge, 2017), 18, https://papers.ssrn.com/sol3/papers.cfm?abstract_id=2947800, accessed: 16.08.2022.

32 CJEU, SGAE v Hoteles SA, Case C-306/05, December 7, 2006, hereinafter: Rafael Hoteles SA. In the later judgements, the approach of the CJEU towards this requirement has changed. The notion of what amounts to an 'indispensable intervention' for the the right of communication to the public to apply was relaxed by the Court. Instead of indispensable intervention, *mere facilitation* should be enough.

33 In GS Media case, a new sub-criterion of knowledge was introduced. According to the test of knowledge, if a link provides access to a work published online without the authorisation of the rightholder and the person providing the access knew or ought to have known about it, the act of hyperlinking constitutes an infringement of the right of communication to the public. (CJEU, GS Media B V Sanoma Media Netherlands BV, Playboy Enterprises International Inc.,Britt Geertruida Dekker, Case C-160/15, September 8, 2016, hereinafter: GS Media.) The criterion of knowledge has been nuanced in YouTube/Cyando (CJEU, Frank Peterson v Google LLC, YouTube Inc., YouTube LLC, Google Germany GmbH (C-682/18), and Elsevier Inc. v Cyando AG (C-683/18), June 22, 2021) as regards the entities providing the access to work and their knowledge about the legality of the availability of the work on the Internet. The Court drew a distinction between the individual user and video-sharing platform or a file-hosting and - sharing platform. In the case of the latter group of actors, due to the nature of their activity, in addition to knowledge that protected content is available illegally, for the act of communication to occur, the said entities should refrain from deleting the illegally available work or blocking access to it, or from putting in place the appropriate technological measures that can be expected from a reasonably diligent operator.

- if the activity is profit-making in nature. However, it should be noted that, according to the CJEU's interpretation, while the profit-making nature of the activity is an important factor, it is not indispensable for determining whether an act of communication to the public has occurred.[34]
- if the engagement of news aggregators does not consist exclusively of providing physical facilities that enable the act of communication to the public. This will not be the case, as news aggregators provide access to press publications, not the physical facilities enabling this access.[35]
- if the use of a press publication is directed toward a new public. This will be the case (except in cases of linking) whenever a whole press publication or its part is republished on a news aggregator's website because the press publisher, when initially publishing the content on its own website, did not anticipate this new audience.[36]

2.3.1. French and Polish law

According to Art. L.218-2 of the French Intellectual Property Code, as demonstarted in Table 3.1, the authorisation of the press publisher or press agency is required before **any reproduction or communication to the public** of its press publications, whether in whole or in part, in digital form by ISSP. The harmonisation of this provision should be maximum, meaning that the level of protection must be neither weaker nor stronger than that the one provided in Art. 15 of the CDSM Directive. The French implementation grants press publishers both the right of reproduction and the right of communication to the public. This results in a broader scope of protection, as the Directive itself only explicitly grants the right of making available, which is included in the broader right of communication to the public. T. Azzi explains that approach aligns with the French tradition, in which all holders of related rights are granted the right of communication to the public rather than the right of making available.[37] Because the right of making available right is

34 CJEU, ITV Broadcasting Ltd and others v TVCatchup Ltd, Case C-607/11, March 7, 2013, hereinafter: TV Catchup.

35 CJEU, Rafael Hoteles SA, para. 46.

36 Linking, according to the CJEU (CJEU, Nils Svensson and others v Retriever Sverige AB, February 13, 2014, C-466/12, para. 18, hereinafter: Svensson) makes the works available to the users and allows direct access to them. All potential website visitors being able to access the link published there are the targeted public taken into account by rightholder while authorising the original communication. Therefore, they do not constitute a new public and in consequence, the communication to the public does not occur. What should be seen differently according to the CJEU's interpretation provided in Svensson case is when the access to the work is restricted and the act of linking intends to circumvent the restrictions in order to enable recipients to access the work. It would constitute an intervention directed towards a new public.

37 See: T. Azzi, "Commentaire," 62; see the provisions from Art. L. 218-2, Arts. L. 212-3, L. 213-1, L. 215-1, L. 216-1 of the Code de la propriété intellectuelle.

Table 3.1 Exclusive rights

*Art. L218 – 2 of the French Intellectual Property Code**	*Art. 99[7](2) of the Polish Copyright Act***
The authorisation of the press publisher or press agency shall be required before any reproduction or communication to the public of his/its press publications in entirety or in part in digital form by information society service provider.	Publishers shall, without prejudice to the rights of authors and other right holders, have the exclusive right to use and manage the use of their press publications to the extent enabling information society service providers to: 1) reproduce press publications online; 2) make press publications available to the public in such a way that anyone can access them at a time and place individually chosen.

Note: *English version by the author. French version of Art. L218-2 of French Intellectual Property Code: https://www.legifrance.gouv.fr/loda/article_lc/LEGIARTI000038826732/2020-10-13, accessed: 12.07.2023. **English version by the author. Polish version of Art. 99[7]: https://isap.sejm.gov.pl/isap.nsf/download.xsp/WDU19940240083/U/D19940083Lj.pdf, accessed: 21.11.2024.

included in the right of communication to the public, the modification introduced by France should be considered in conformity with EU law.[38]

The Polish legislature defines the legal position of press publishers by specifying particular fields of exploitation, namely the reproduction and making available of press publications.

The wording of the Polish provision differs from both Art. 15 of the CDSM Directive and the French implementation. According to Art. 99[7], publishers are granted the exclusive right to use **and manage the use of** their press publications to the extent necessary for ISSPs to reproduce and make them available. The Polish legislature chose to preserve consistency in the legal framework for holders of related rights, as they are also granted exclusive rights to **use and manage the use of** their protected subject matter within the specified scope. It was not necessary to specify that the making available of a press publication must occur in such a way that anyone can access it at a time and place individually chosen, as this characteristic is inherent to the very nature of the act of making available. By definition, making available enables access to a work or other subject matter at a time and place individually chosen by the user.

To conclude:

- the French legislature grants press publishers the right of reproduction and communication to the public instead of the right of making available, despite the principle of maximum harmonisation. This approach aligns with

38 T. Azzi, "Commentaire," 62–63.

France's tradition, in which all holders of related rights are granted the right of communication to the public, which has a broader scope than the right of making available. The Polish legislature, while implementing the publishers' rights, maintains legislative consistency by adhering to the formulation of exclusive rights already applied to other holders of related rights.

2.4. Acts of hyperlinking

2.4.1. The CDSM Directive

The protection granted under Art. 15 of the CDSM Directive does not apply to acts of hyperlinking, as explicitly stated in Art. 15(1) of the CDSM Directive. Hyperlinks can be displayed in various forms, including text, images or URLs.[39] They include deep links, frame links and embedded links.[40] Embedded links differ from standard hyperlinks in that, instead of displaying a clickable link, they directly show the content that originally appears on another website.[41] The key distinction between providing a URL address and embedding[42] is that, in the case of the latter, the user does not need to click on a link but can view the content directly on the website they are visiting, without being redirected.[43] M. Leistner identifies a subcategory of embedded links known as hidden embedded links, which prevent users from recognising whether the content from a third-party website has been incorporated into the website posting the link or whether it remains on the original website while being displayed through an embedded link.[44] Framing involves linking external content on a website within so-called frames, which are enclosed separate spaces in which the linked content is displayed. Websites using this technique often contain multiple frames, allowing users to navigate their contents separately, such as when another website is displayed within the frame.[45] Deep links are a type of link that

39 M. Rouse, "Hyperlink," Technopedia, September 20,2023, https://www.techopedia.com/definition/5175/hyperlink, accessed: 10.11.2022.

40 M. Leistner, "Copyright law on the internet in need of reform: Hyperlinks, online platforms and aggregators," *Journal of Intellectual Property Law & Practice* 12, no. 2 (2017): 136–149.

41 See: CJEU, BestWater International GmbH v. Michael Mebes, Stefan Potsch, Case C-348/13, October 21, 2014, paras. 17–18, hereinafter: BestWater; B.Schuetze, "Bestwater: CJEU embeds decision on framed content in order," Kluwer Copyright Blog, November 3, 2014, http://copyrightblog.kluweriplaw.com/2014/11/03/bestwater-cjeu-embeds-decision-on-framed-content-in-order/, accessed: 10.11.2022.

42 See: E. Rosati, "DSM Directive Series #6: 'hyperlinking' in the press publishers' right," IPKat, June 16, 2019, https://ipkitten.blogspot.com/2019/06/dsm-directive-series-6-hyperlinking-in.html, accessed:10.11.2022.

43 See: Nowe media, "Embeding," February 13, 2019, https://www.nowemedia.org.pl/glossary/embedding/, accessed: 10.11.2022.

44 M. Leistner, "Copyright," 136–149.

45 P. Wasilewski, "Dopuszczalność embedowania w świetle ewolucji orzecznictwa Trybunału Sprawiedliwości Unii Europejskiej w zakresie linkowania," in *Experientia docet. Księga jubileuszowa ofiarowana Pani Profesor Elżbiecie Traple*, ed. P. Podrecki, T. Targosz (Wolters Kluwer Polska, 2017, LEX).

redirect users to a specific location within an app[46] rather than a general webpage. They link to a specific, searchable or indexed piece of web content on a website rather directing users to the website's home page.

In both the English and French versions of Art. 15 of the CDSM Directive, the term "act of hyperlinking' is used, whereas the Polish version refers to the "act of linking." The CJEU, in cases concerning the scope of the right of communication to the public, primarily mentions "clickable links."[47] Despite these linguistic differences, all these terms should be understood as having the same meaning.

The exclusion of the act of hyperlinking from the scope of publishers' protection, without any specification or distinction between various types of hyperlinks, can lead to varied consequences. S. Dusollier explains that

> technically speaking, what Google and similar services do is to refer to media articles by different techniques of hyperlinking, either via a simple underlined and clickable blue text, or via a so-called deep link where the text or image referred to are absorbed by the search engine page, while staying technically hosted by the original webpage.[48]

Advocate General Maciej Szpunar proposed to

> draw a distinction between 'clickable' links, to which the Court's case-law refers, and automatic links, which automatically display the resource to which the link leads on the webpage containing that link, without the need for the user to take any action.[49]

This distinction illustrates that hyperlinks can impact the effectiveness of protection to varying degrees of intensity.[50]

As to the legal basis of linking, early CJEU case law on hyperlinking within the right of communication to the public established that linking to a work that is freely accessible without any access restrictions on the linked website[51] does not constitute communication to the public. The CJEU clarified that all potential visitors to the linked website are already considered part of public envisaged by right holder when authorising the original communication. Therefore, linking does not create a new communication to the public, as it does not introduce a new public. Moreover, this interpretation applies to different forms of linking, such as embedding. [52]

46 Adjust, "What is deep linking," https://www.adjust.com/glossary/deep-linking/, accessed: 11.11.2022.
47 See: CJEU, Svensson; CJEU, BestWater; CJEU, GS Media, CJEU, FIlmspeler.
48 S. Dusollier, The 2019," 1007.
49 Opinion of Advocate General Szpunar delivered on September 10, 2020, Case C-392/19, Case VG Bild-Kunst v Stiftung Preußischer Kulturbesitz, para. 105.
50 See chapter 4.
51 CJEU, Svensson, paras. 29–30.
52 CJEU, BestWater. See: P. Wasilewski, "Dopuszczalność."

However, the CJEU has determined that linking through framing constitutes an act of communication to the public, as this technique makes the framed content available to all potential users of the website embedding the link.[53] Nevertheless, the Court specified that this assessment depends on many other criteria. According to the CJEU case law, linking to qualify as a new act of communication to the public, it must use technical means different from those initially used to make the protected work available on the original website.[54] In the case of online news media services, the same technical means, namely, the internet,[55] are typically used to disseminate content. This suggests that, under normal circumstances, communication to the public does not occur.

Generally, linking to a work that has been made available with the right holder's consent and is freely accessible on a source page does not constitute an act of communication to the public within the meaning of Art. 3 of the InfoSoc Directive. In the absence of restrictive measures to access the protected content, and by making it freely accessible to the public or authorising such access, the right holder is deemed to have envisaged all internet users as the public from the outset. Consequently, this implies that the right holder consented to third parties undertaking acts of communication of that work without requiring additional authorisation.[56]

According to the opinion of A. G. Wathelet, posting hyperlinks by users is both systematic and necessary to the current internet architecture.

> If users were at risk of proceedings for infringement of copyright under Article 3(1) of Directive 2001/29 whenever they post a hyperlink to works freely accessible on another website, they would be much more reticent to post them, which would be to the detriment of the proper functioning and the very architecture of the internet, and to the development of the information society.[57]

The exclusion of acts of hyperlinking from the scope of press publishers' protection represents an attempt to address the complex and evolving legal interpretation of linking provided by the CJEU as well as the factors to be considered in its assessment. This exclusion can be seen as a response to public concerns that hyperlinking by individual users could become prohibited and as a reaction to political criticism of the initial proposal of the provision.[58]

53 CJEU, VG Bild-Kunst, para. 35.

54 CJEU, VG Bild-Kunst, para. 36.

55 CJEU, Svensson, paras. 24–30.

56 CJEU, Soulier and Doke, Case C-301/15, November 16, 2016, para. 36, hereinafter: Soulier and Doke.

57 Opinion of Advocate General Wathelet delivered on April 7, 2016 Case C-160/15 GS Media, paras. 78–79.

58 See: F. Reda, "Last-minute attempt to sneak 'snippet tax' into copyright report," July 06, 2015, https://felixreda.eu/2015/07/last-minute-snippet-tax/, accessed: 10.11.2022; EDRi, "Join the coordinated calls against EU's Censorship Machine," May 30, 2018, https://edri.org/our-work/coordinated-action-censorship-machine-call/, accessed: 27.06.2023.

Table 3.2 Exclusion of hyperlinks from publishers' protection

*Art. L211-3-1 of the French Intellectual Property Code**	*Art. 99^7(3)(2) of the Polish Copyright Act***
The beneficiaries of the rights provided for in article L. 218-2 cannot prohibit: 1° Acts of hyperlinking	The provision of paragraph (2) shall not apply to the acts of making available of a link to a press publication

Note: *English version by the author. French version of Art. L211-3-1 of French Intellectual Property Code: https://www.legifrance.gouv.fr/codes/article_lc/LEGIARTI000038826394, accessed: 12.07.2023. **English version by the author. Polish version of Art. 99^7: https://isap.sejm.gov.pl/isap.nsf/download.xsp/WDU19940240083/U/D19940083Lj.pdf, accessed: 21.11.2024.

To conclude:

- the act of linking to a work or subject matter that has been made available with the right holder's consent and is freely accessible on a source page does not constitute an act of making available within the meaning of Art. 3 of the InfoSoc Directive. Its explicit exclusion from the scope of the publishers' protection reflects the EU legislature's intent to address public concerns that linking by individual users could become prohibited. Additionally, this exclusion underscores the importance of linking in ensuring the free flow of information.

2.4.2. French and Polish law

According to Art. L211-3-1(1) of the French Intellectual Property Code, as demonstrated in Table 3.2, press publishers cannot prohibit the acts of hyperlinking. Similarly, the Polish legislature specifies that publishers' rights do not apply to the making available of a link to a press publication. Despite the slightly different wording, the provision effectively reproduces the exclusion from the CDSM Directive and aligns with the French provision.

3. Information society service providers

3.1. The CDSM Directive

According to Art. 15(1) of the CDSM Directive, Member States must grant publishers of press publications established in a Member State the rights of reproduction and making available for the online use of their press publications by **ISSPs**.

According to Art. 2(b) of the Directive 2000/31/EC on electronic commerce, a service provider is any natural or legal person providing an information society service.[59] Furthermore, Art. 2(5) of the CDSM Directive defines an information

59 Directive 2000/31/EC of the European Parliament and of the Council of 8 June 2000 on certain legal aspects of information society services, in particular electronic commerce, in the Internal Market hereinafter: Directive on electronic commerce.

society service in accordance with Point B of Art. 1(1) of Directive 2015/1535, meaning any service normally provided for remuneration, at a distance, by electronic means and at the individual request of a recipient of services. For the purposes of this definition, "at a distance" means that the service is provided without the parties being simultaneously present; "by electronic means" refers to a service is sent initially and received using electronic equipment for processing (including digital compression) and storage of data and is entirely transmitted, conveyed and received by wire, radio, optical or other electromagnetic means; and "at the individual request of a recipient of services" means that the service is provided through the transmission of data in response to an individual request.[60] Examples of information society service include online sales on platforms such as Allegro.p l, auction services such as eBay, booking services such as Booking.com, digital music streaming services such as Spotify or video-on-demand streaming services such as Netflix.

For many, Google has been the main target of the new rights and the principal actor affected.[61] However, the term ISSP also applies to social media platforms such as Meta, which has also faced conflicts with press publishers over the use of press publications.[62] Interestingly, X (formerly Twitter) has claimed that is a "microblogging platform[63] and, therefore, not subject to press publishers' rights. However, the EU legislature has not restricted the definition of ISSPs to specific activities. Instead, all actors meeting the criteria of an ISSP, regardless of their particular function, fall within the scope of the regulation.

ISSP services must be provided for remuneration. However, news aggregation services are typically offered free of charge to users, as their business model is primarily based on advertising revenues.[64] According to Recital 18 of the Directive on electronic commerce, the economic activity of ISSPs "extends to services which are not remunerated by those who receive them, such as those offering on-line information or commercial communications, or those providing tools allowing for search, access and retrieval of data." The CJEU, in *Papasavvas* case, confirmed that information society services include online information services, even when the service provider is not remunerated by the recipient but, instead, earns revenue

60 Point (b) of Art. 1(1) of Directive 2015/1535 of the European Parliament and of the Council of 9 September 2015 laying down a procedure for the provision of information in the field of technical regulations and of rules on Information Society services (codification).

61 A. Lazarova, "Re-use," 236.

62 S. Ray, "Twitter sued for allegedly ignoring french law that requires it to pay news publishers," Forbes, August 03, 2023, https://www.forbes.com/sites/siladityaray/2023/08/03/twitter-gets-sued-for-allegedly-not-complying-with-french-law-that-requires-it-to-pay-news-publishers/?sh=28dcf-c8f320c, accessed: 15.08.2023.

63 Microblogging is the creation and distribution of short content, generally on social networks. See: Brevo, "Le Microblogging, qu'est-ce que c'est et comment en faire profiter votre entreprise," August 31, 2021, https://www.brevo.com/fr/blog/microblogging/, accessed: 31.08.2023.

64 See Chapter 1.

through advertisements posted on the website.[65] Therefore, the remuneration does not have to be paid by the end-user.[66]

In the context of news media business models, particularly for news aggregators, a second source of remuneration, in addition to advertisements, is the collection and use of personal data or other types of data. User information holds monetary value and can be leveraged to provide personalised news, local content, targeted advertisements and customised services. Recital 16 of the Directive 2018/1972, which establishes the European Electronic Communications Code, notes that remuneration for services

> should also encompass situations where the end-user allows access to information without actively supplying it, such as personal data, including the IP address, or other automatically generated information, such as information collected and transmitted by a cookie. ...The concept of remuneration should therefore also encompass situations in which the end-user is exposed to advertisements as a condition for gaining access to the service, or situations in which the service provider monetises personal data it has collected in accordance with Regulation (EU) 2016/679.[67]

The services discussed fall within the scope of business activities. This raises an interesting question: could OpenAI, the developer of ChatGPT, be considered an ISSP? The classification of OpenAI's activities is complex, as the company describes itself as "an AI research and deployment company,"[68] suggesting that some of its activities may fall outside the traditional business framework. However, OpenAI also operates a for-profit subsidiary, OpenAI Global, LLC, which, according to the company's disclosures, is fully controlled by the OpenAI Nonprofit.[69] This dual structure complicates the classification of OpenAI's services under the ISSP definition, as it blends nonprofit research objectives with commercial activities. The complexity of this situation makes it difficult to assess, but if ChatGPT is considered to be provided within the framework of a business activity and if remuneration is understood to include the collection and use of users' data, then OpenAI could be classified as an ISSP. This classification is particularly significant in the

65 CJEU, Sotiris Papasavvas v O Fileleftheros Dimosia Etairia Ltd, Takis Kounnafi, Giorgos Sertis, September 11, 2014, Case C-291/13, para. 30.

66 See also the opinion of Advocate General Saugmandsgaard Øe in YouTube/Cyando case. The Advocate General puts the revenues from advertising gained by operators like YouTube, "YouTube model" in the same range with remuneration from subscriptions "the Cyando model" when subscriptions constitute also the main source of remuneration for commercial journalism, https://curia.europa.eu/juris/document/document.jsf?text=&docid=228712&pageIndex=0&doclang=EN&mode=lst&dir=&occ=first&part=1&cid=222587, accessed: 07.11.2022, para. 47.

67 Directive 2018/1972 of the European Parliament and of the Council of December 11, 2018 establishing the European Electronic Communications Code.

68 OpenAI, https://openai.com/about, accessed: 06.02.2024.

69 OpenAI, https://openai.com/our-structure, accessed: 06.02.2024.

context of press publishers' rights, as it could impact the extent to which ChatGPT is permitted to use press publications under the CDSM Directive.

There is no requirement for ISSPs to be established in a Member State. However, protection applies when a press publication is used by an ISSP and the press publisher is established in a Member State. This creates a legal connection with EU Member States.

The use of press publication by ISSPs has not been restricted by the legislature to a single service operated by a provider.[70] Similarly, no distinctions were made between ISSPs based on their market relevance, the degree of press publishers' dependence or their influence on information dissemination. Unlike in the common law system,[71] in which similar rights have been limited to dominant market players, the scope of publishers' rights applies broadly to all ISSPs, regardless of the market dominance or impact on the press industry.

To conclude:

- a service provider is any natural or legal person offering an information society service, which refers to any service normally provided for remuneration, at a distance, by electronic means and at the individual request of a recipient of services. Remuneration is understood broadly, encompassing not only direct payments but also income generated through advertisements or the collection of personal data. Additionally, publishers' rights apply to all ISSPs, regardless of the specific nature of their activities.

3.2. French and Polish law

Neither the French nor the Polish implementation of the CDSM Directive includes a definition of ISSPs. To define this term, it is necessary to refer to the provisions implementing Directive 2000/31/EC on electronic commerce within national laws.[72]

According to Art. 14 of French law no. 2004-575 of June 21, 2004 on confidence in the digital economy,[73] electronic commerce refers to economic activities in which a person offers or provides goods or services remotely and by electronic means. Electronic commerce also includes services such as the provision of online information; commercial communications; tools for searching, accessing and

70 For example, Google provides many services such as Google Search, Google News etc.

71 See Section 8.

72 English version by the author, Polish version of Art. 2 (6) of Act of July 18, 2002 on the provision of services by electronic means (Ustawa z dnia 18 lipca 2002 r. o świadczeniu usług drogą elektroniczną, Dz. U. z 2020 r. poz. 344), https://isap.sejm.gov.pl/isap.nsf/download.xsp/WDU20021441204/U/D20021204Lj.pdf, accessed: 11.07.2023.

73 English version by the author, French version of Art. 14 of law no. 2004-575 of June 21, 2004 on confidence in the digital economy (LOI n° 2004-575 du 21 juin 2004 pour la confiance dans l'économie numérique), https://www.legifrance.gouv.fr/jorf/id/JORFTEXT000000801164, accessed: 12.07.2023.

retrieving data; access to a communications network; and hosting information, even when these services are not remunerated by those who receive them. A person is deemed to be established in France when they have set up their activity in a stable and lasting manner to effectively carry it out, regardless of the location of their registered office in the case of a legal entity. Interestingly, French law explicitly states that remuneration can also be provided by entities that do not receive the service.

According to Art. 2(6) of the Polish Act of July 18, 2002 on the provision of services by electronic means, a service provider is a natural person, legal person or an organisational unit without legal personality that provides services electronically, even if only incidentally, in the course of its commercial or professional activity.

To conclude:

- the definitions provided in national laws allow the reconstruction of the ISSP definition from the Directive on electronic commerce. The French definition is more comprehensive, as it contains examples of services and explicitly states that remuneration does not have to be paid directly by the recipient of the services.

3.3. Private or non-commercial uses of press publications by individual users

3.3.1. The CDSM Directive

Art. 15 of the CDSM Directive specifies that the protection of press publishers shall not apply to private or non-commercial uses of press publications by individual users.

Individual users are those who use press publications for their own non-commercial purposes, without engaging in activities that could be classified as the ISSPs activities. A question arises regarding how to classify the activities of non-profit organisations such as Wikipedia or non-governmental organisations (NGOs) such as Panoptykon.[74] The use of press publications by these organisations would infringe the new rights only if they were to engage in ISSP activities by using press publication online. This is because only ISSPs can interfere with the press publishers' rights under Art. 15 of the CDSM Directive. Interestingly, under the German publishers' rights adopted before the CDSM Directive, the exclusion applied to everyone except commercial operators of search engines or commercial operators of services that edit content subject to publishers' rights.[75] Therefore, there were no

74 Fundacja Panoptykon,"Co to jest Panoptykon," https://panoptykon.org/organizacja, accessed: 22.06.2023.

75 Sections 87g of Urheberrechtsgesetz, as amended by Law of 1 October 2013, Bundesgesetzblatt (Federal Official Journal) Vol. I, 3728. German version, https://www.bgbl.de/xaver/bgbl/start.xav?startbk=Bundesanzeiger_BGBl&start=//*%5B@attr_id=%27bgbl113s1161.pdf%27%5D#__bgbl__%2F%2F*%5B%40attr_id%3D%27bgbl113s1161.pdf%27%5D__1667226734379, accessed: 31.10.2022, English version from: European Parliament, *Strengthening*, 14.

doubts regarding the legitimacy of the use of press publications by entities such as non-profit organisations.

Considering the role of non-profit organisations and their contribution to the free flow of information, I propose a **broad** interpretation of individual users, one that includes non-profit organisations. It should be recognised that the primary threat to publishers' interests, which led to the adoption of publishers' rights, was the unrestricted use of press publications by online platforms such as Google. Therefore, in my opinion, including non-profit organisations within the category of individual users, when they use press publications for non-commercial purposes, should not impose a significant burden on press publishers.

It could be said that because the provision applies exclusively to the use of press publication by ISSPs, the clarification that it does not extend to private or non-commercial uses by individual users is unnecessary. On the other hand, this clarification can be seen as a confirmation that only the use of press publications by ISSPs falls under the protection from Art. 15 of the CDSM Directive, ensuring that individual users remain free to use press publications without restriction.

In the English version of the CDSM Directive, the private **or** non-commercial use of press publications is excluded from protection, with "or" indicating that the conditions are alternative. The French version uses "or" in the same way.[76] Interestingly, in the Polish version of the Directive, "**and**"[77] appears instead of "or," which would suggest that the two conditions must be met cumulatively for the exclusion to apply. Considering that the wording of the provision generally treats private and non-commercial uses as alternative conditions, I suggest adhering to this interpretation. This approach better preserves users' interests, protects their fundamental right to receive information and enhances to the free flow of information.

To conclude:

- individual users should be understood broadly, including legal persons, such as non-profit organisations. In such cases, the alternative nature of the exclusion should be favoured, as the use of a press publication would not be private but would still qualify as non-commercial.
- press publishers' protection does not apply when the press publication is used by individual users for non-commercial or private purposes.
- the freedom to use a press publication applies to individual users who use the publication for private or non-commercial purposes and are not ISSPs.

76 French version of Art. 15 (1) second subparagraph of the CDSM Directive, https://eur-lex.europa.eu/legal-content/FR/TXT/PDF/?uri=CELEX:32019L0790&from=EN, accessed: 09.11.2022.

77 Polish version of Art. 15 (1) second subparagraph of the CDSM Directive, https://eur-lex.europa.eu/legal-content/PL/TXT/PDF/?uri=CELEX:32019L0790&from=EN, accessed: 09.11.2022.

Table 3.3 Private or non-commercial use of press publication

The French Intellectual Property Code	*Art. 99[7] of the Polish Copyright Act**
–	3. The provision of paragraph (2) shall not apply to: own personal use, not related to the commercial purposes

Note: *English version by the author. Polish version of Art. 99[7]: https://isap.sejm.gov.pl/isap.nsf/download.xsp/WDU19940240083/U/D19940083Lj.pdf, accessed: 21.11.2024.

3.3.2. French and Polish law

The private or non-commercial use of press publications by individual users is not expressly excluded from the scope of publishers' protection in French law. However, this should not be considered an omission, as the protection granted to press publishers applies only in cases in which the press publications are used by ISSPs. The French legislature's rationale for not transposing this exclusion was that it could be inferred directly from the scope of protection granted to press publishers. This is a legitimate approach.

According to Art. 99[7](3) of the Polish law quoted in Table 3.3, publishers' rights do not apply to personal use that is not related to commercial purposes. The term "personal use" implies that the use of a press publication must be by a natural person, thereby excluding the broader interpretation of individual users proposed in the previous section, which was based on a purposive and systemic interpretation of the provision.

It is difficult to attribute a personal activity to an NGO or similar entity. Consequently, the Polish legislature, by referring to "personal use," mixed "private uses" with "individual users" from the CDSM Directive. This simplification is not fully aligned with the purposes of the regulation, as it limits the scope of the exclusion and may negatively impact the flow of information online. In this interpretation, the activities of non-profit organisations are explicitly excluded from the exemption. While one argument in favour of this approach is that an infringement only occurs when an ISSP uses a press publication without authorisation, the legal classification of press publications use by non-profit organisations, which often contribute to the free flow of information, remains unresolved.[78]

To conclude:

- the wording of the Polish exclusion prevents a broad interpretation of the concept of individual users. This approach contradicts the purposive and systemic interpretation of individual users derived from Art. 15(1) of the CDSM Directive.

78 See Chapter 4.

- the legal qualification of the use of press publications by legal persons who do not engage in business activity remains problematic in the draft of the Polish implementation of Art. 15 of the CDSM Directive.

4. Exceptions and limitations

4.1. The CDSM Directive

According to Art. 15(3) of the CDSM Directive, Arts. 5 to 8 of the InfoSoc Directive, Directive 2012/28/EU on certain permitted uses of orphan works and Directive (EU) 2017/1564 on certain permitted uses of protected works for the benefit of persons who are blind, visually impaired or otherwise print-disabled shall apply ***mutatis mutandis*** to the publishers' rights established under Art. 15(1) of the CDSM Directive. According to Recital 57 of the CDSM Directive,

> the rights granted to publishers of press publications under the CDSM Directive should also be subject to the same provisions on exceptions and limitations as those applicable to the rights provided for in the Infosoc Directive, including the exception in the case of quotations for purposes such as criticism or review provided for in Article 5(3)(d) of that Directive.

Additionally, the CDSM Directive introduces exceptions in Arts. 4 to 6, covering text and data mining(TDM), digital and cross-border teaching activities and the preservation of cultural heritage, all of which should also be applied to publishers' rights.

The application of exceptions and limitations already introduced in the three mentioned directives, *mutatis mutandis,* to publishers' rights means that MS must adopt the mandatory exceptions and limitations, including the exception permitting temporary acts of reproduction under Art. 5(1) of the InfoSoc Directive as well as the exceptions in Arts. 4 to 6 of the CDSM Directive. In addition to these mandatory provisions, MS may choose to implement optional exceptions and limitations, which do not necessarily have to align with those applied to works or other subject matters. As with other exceptions and limitations, those applied to press publishers' rights must comply with the three-step test. MS should not adopt a broader catalogue of exceptions and limitations beyond what is provided in the Directives.

To conclude:

- the exceptions and limitations already established in EU law should be applied *mutatis mutandis* to the rights granted to press publishers. This means that MS must first adopt the mandatory exceptions and limitations. Second, they may choose to implement optional exceptions and limitations. Third, as with other cases involving exceptions and limitations, those applied to press publishers' rights must comply with the three-step test.

4.2. French and Polish law

In the French implementation, regarding the exceptions and limitations applicable to the rights of press publishers, there is no provision explicitly referring to another section of the French Intellectual Property Code. Instead, press publishers' rights have been directly incorporated into the scope of Art. L.211-3 of the French Intellectual Property Code, ensuring that the same exceptions and limitations applicable to authors and other related rights holders also apply to press publishers' rights.[79]

The same approach is reflected in Polish law. According to Art. 100 of the Polish Copyright Act,[80] the exercise of related rights, including press publishers' rights, is subject to the existing provisions on exceptions and limitations.[81] Therefore, both French and Polish legislatures apply the preexisting system of exceptions and limitations from their respective copyright codes to press publishers' rights, without making any adaptations or changes specific to these newly introduced rights.

5. Remuneration for the use of a press publication and information claims

Neither the Polish nor the French legislature excludes the possibility of waiving of the publishers' rights as can be seen in Table 3.4. According to Art. L.218-3 of the French Intellectual Property Code, the rights of press publishers and press agencies under Art. L. 218-2 can be assigned or licensed. In Polish law, the possibility of assigning or licensing these rights can be inferred from Art. 99,[7] which grants publishers the exclusive right to **manage the use** of their press publications. Because economic rights are generally transferable, the Polish Copyright Act explicitly specifies cases when rights **cannot** be transferred, such as the right to additional remuneration for performers under Art. 95^3 of the Polish Copyright Law. However, this restriction does not apply to press publishers.

A press publisher can transfer all or part of their rights through a contract, either by assignment or licensing. The contract should specify the fields of exploitation and define the modalities and conditions of the transfer, such as the geographical scope and duration of the transfer. A contract can establish a framework for the use of multiple press publications rather than just a single publication from a particular press publisher. Given the specific nature of this subject of protection, this will most often be the case.[82] The transfer of rights logically entails the payment of remuneration,[83] which, in legal literature, is considered as "one of the most

79 English version by the author. French version of Art. L211-3 of French Intellectual Property Code, https://www.legifrance.gouv.fr/codes/article_lc/LEGIARTI000044365633/2021-11-26/, accessed: 12.07.2023.

80 English version by the author. Polish version of Art. 100, https://isap.sejm.gov.pl/isap.nsf/download.xsp/WDU19940240083/U/D19940083Lj.pdf, accessed: 21.11.2024.

81 Arts. 23–35 from Polish Copyright Act, https://isap.sejm.gov.pl/isap.nsf/download.xsp/WDU19940240083/U/D19940083Lj.pdf, accessed: 23.11.2022.

82 A. Franque, "Droits voisins: Google signe un accord-cadre avec les éditeurs de presse," Libération, January 21, 2021, https://www.liberation.fr/france/2021/01/21/droits-voisins-google-signe-un-accord-cadre-avec-les-editeurs-de-presse_1818139/, accessed: 24.01.2024.

83 See: P. Ślęzak, *Umowy w zakresie współczesnych sztuk wizualnych* (Wolters Kluwer Polska, 2012), 242–260.

Table 3.4 Remuneration for the use of a press publication and information claims

*Art. L218-3–L218-4 of the French Intellectual Property Code**	*Art. 99^{11}–99^{17} of the Polish Copyright Act***
Art. L218-3 The rights of press publishers and press agencies resulting from Art. L. 218-2 can be assigned or licensed. Such right holders can entrust the management of their rights to one or more collective management bodies governed by Title II of Book III of this Part.	Art. 99^{11}1. The publisher shall have the right to: 1) receive up-to-date information from the service provider; 2) have access to the service provider's documentation to the extent necessary to determine the amount of remuneration due to the publisher for the exercise of the right referred to in paragraph 2 of Art. 99^{7}(2) 2. The information and data obtained by the publisher pursuant to paragraph 1 shall be processed only to determine the amount of remuneration due to the publisher.
Art. L218-4 The remuneration due in respect of related rights for the reproduction and communication to the public of press publications in digital form is based on the revenue from exploitation of any kind, whether direct or indirect or, failing that, assessed on a flat-rate basis, particularly in the cases provided for in Art. L. 131-4 The fixing of the amount of this remuneration shall take into account elements such as the human, material and financial investments made by publishers and press agencies, the contribution of press publications to political and general information and the extent to which press publications are used by online public communication services. The online public communication services shall be required to provide press publishers and press agencies with all the information relating to the use of press publications by their users as well as all the other information necessary for a transparent evaluation of the remuneration mentioned in the first paragraph of this article and its distribution.	Art. 99^{12}1. The parties, in determining the amount of remuneration for the use of press publications by the ISSPs, shall take into account all relevant circumstances, in particular the following information and data: 1) revenues derived directly or indirectly by the service provider from the reproduction or making available to the public of the publisher's press publications, in particular revenues derived from advertising, in the last two full financial years preceding the date of submission of the offer by one of the parties, and if this period is shorter - in this period; 2) the type of press publications reproduced or made available to the public; 3) the period of the service provider's use of the right referred to in Art. 99^{7}(2). 2. If, within 3 months from the date of submission by one of the parties of an offer to conclude an agreement on the use of the right referred to in Art. 99^{7}(2), the parties do not reach an agreement, either party may apply to the President of the Office of Electronic Communications, hereinafter referred to as the 'President of UKE', for mediation on the determination of remuneration.

Art. 99^{13} 1. The President of UKE shall, within 14 days of the date of submission of a request for mediation, notify the parties of the commencement of mediation, setting a date for the commencement of mediation and the place of mediation, provided that the date of commencement of mediation may not be later than the 60th day from the date of submission of the request.
2. Mediation shall be conducted if a party, within 14 days of the date of the notification referred to in section 1, has agreed to participate in mediation.

. . .

Mediation shall last no longer than 60 days, unless the parties agree otherwise.

Art. 99^{15} 1. In case of failure to reach an agreement, any of the parties to the mediation may, within 30 days from the date of delivery of the minutes from the mediation, submit a request to the President of UKE to issue a ruling on the amount of remuneration for the use of the right referred to in Art. $99^{7}(2)$ or on the manner of determining the amount of such remuneration.
3. The ruling on the amount of remuneration shall cover the period from the date on which the service provider commences using the press publication within the scope of the right referred to in Art. 99^{7} paragraph 2, to the date of issuing the ruling.
4. In the event that the party does not participate in mediation or the parties do not conclude an agreement without conducting mediation, the President of the UKE may, at the request of the party, issue a ruling on the amount of remuneration for using the right referred to in Art. $99^{7}(2)$, or on the method of determining the amount of such remuneration without conducting mediation.

. . .

10. The ruling indicating the method of determining the amount of remuneration for the use of the right referred to in Art. $99^{7}(2)$ shall also specify the amount of remuneration for the period of 12 months, counted from the date on which the service provider commences using the press publication within the scope covered by the publishers rights. In the event that the use of the rights lasts for less than 12 months, the remuneration shall be determined in proportion to the period of use of the rights.

(*Continued*)

Table 3.4 (Continued)

*Art. L218-3–L218-4 of the French Intellectual Property Code**	*Art. 99^{11}–99^{17} of the Polish Copyright Act***
	Art. 99^{16}1. The provisions of the Act of 14 June 1960 – the Code of Administrative Procedure on the exclusion of an employee and an authority from the proceeding, handling matters, deliveries, summonses, fees and costs, deadlines and proceedings shall apply accordingly to the proceedings referred to in Art. 99,[15] with the exception of provisions on appeals and complaints. 2. The judgment is final and enforceable by way of court execution, provided that the remuneration is due. 3. The method of determining the amount of remuneration for exercising the right referred to in Art. 99^{7}(2) indicated in the judgment, shall be included in the agreement on exercising this right. Art. 99^{17}1. A party may file an objection to a ruling of the President of the UKE within 14 days of the date of delivery of the ruling. The objection shall be filed with a court of general jurisdiction via the President of the UKE. Filing an objection within the deadline is equivalent to requesting that the case be referred to the court with jurisdiction over the place of residence or registered office of the publisher of the press publication. … 7. The objection may concern the entire ruling or its part or the decision on costs. 8. If the objection is upheld, the court shall amend the contested ruling of the President of the UKE in whole or in part and shall rule on the merits of the case. 10. The court shall issue a ruling on the objection within 18 months of the date of transfer of the case files together with the objection. The court of second instance shall examine the appeal within 12 months of the date of presentation of the case files by the court of first instance together with the appeal.***

Note: *English version by the author. French version of Art. L218-3 and L218-4 of French Intellectual Property Code, https://www.legifrance.gouv.fr/codes/article_lc/LEGIARTI000038826732, accessed: 18.07.2023. **English version by the author. Polish version of Art. 99^{11}–99^{17}: https://isap.sejm.gov.pl/isap.nsf/download.xsp/WDU19940240083/U/D19940083Lj.pdf, accessed: 21.11.2024. *** For further analysis of the mediation mechanism introduced in Artis. 99^{12}–99^{17} of the Polish Copyright Act applicable in cases of difficulty reaching an agreement between press publishers and ISSPs, see Section 8 of this chapter.

important features of a contract."[84] As the subject matter to which the rights are transferred is expected to generate profit for the entities exploiting it, and given the investments and risks involved in its creation, compensation is justified. However, authorisation can also be granted without remuneration or in exchange for alternative benefits, such as a better display position of the press publication in a search service or on a news aggregator.

5.1. Remuneration for the exploitation of a press publication

The EU legislature did not provide specific guidelines on how remuneration for the use of press publications by ISSPs should be determined. Nor are MSobligated to establish such rules unless they deem it necessary to ensure the effectiveness of press publishers' protection. A MS's decision to regulate the method of calculating remuneration may be driven by the need to protect press publishers, who often have a weaker negotiating position compared to ISSPs, from being forced into unbalanced contractual terms for the use of their press publications.

According to Art. L218-4 of the French Intellectual Property Code, the remuneration obtained by press publishers **is based on the revenue from the exploitation of press publications, whether direct or indirect, or, if such revenue cannot be determined, it is assessed on a flat-rate basis.**[85] During the legislative process in France, it was emphasised that, given the rapid evolution of business models, it was important to target direct and indirect revenues linked to the economic value of a press publication within a broader ecosystem, without establishing overly precise thresholds.[86] Direct revenue comes mainly from advertising revenue generated through the sale of space to advertisers. For example, Google derives revenue from the display of press publications, particularly within its Google Search service, by leveraging users' data collected across its services.[87] Additionally, Google earns indirect revenue from its advertising intermediation services, which it offers to press publishers and are partly based on user data.[88] However, it has not been

84 S. Dussolier et al., *Contractual Arrangements Applicable to Creators: Law and Practice of Selected Member States*, Study, European Parliament (2014), 36, https://www.europarl.europa.eu/meetdocs/2009_2014/documents/juri/dv/contractualarangements_/contractualarangements_en.pdf, accessed: 24.101.2024.

85 English version by the author, French version, https://www.legifrance.gouv.fr/codes/article_lc/LEGIARTI000006278963, accessed: 19.07.2023.

86 Ministère de la Culture, *Droit voisin au profit des agences de presse et des éditeurs de presse. Recueil des travaux préparatoires de la loi n° 2019-775 du 24 juillet 2019 tendant à créer un droit voisin au profit des agences de presse et des éditeurs de presse,* Service de la coordination des politiques culturelles et de l'innovation Mission de la politique documentaire (2019), 105, https://www.culture.gouv.fr/fr/content/download/219602/pdf_file/Droit_voisin_agences_editeurs_presse.pdf?inLanguage=fre-FR&version=4, accessed: 07.01.2025.

87 FCA Decision of April 9, 2020 on interim measures.

88 FCA Decision of April 9, 2020 on interim measures, 17–18.

specified whether remuneration should be calculated proportionally or as a fixed percentage of the ISSPs' revenues.

Moreover, the French legislature, in Art. L.218-4 of the French Intellectual Property Code, established that the determination **of remuneration must consider elements such as:**

- **the human, material and financial investments made by press publishers and press agencies;**
- **the contribution of press publications to political and general information; and**
- **the extent to which press publications are used by online public communication services.**

The list of criteria is not exhaustive, and the elements do not have to be taken into consideration cumulatively. Among the factors to be taken into account, the contribution of press publications to **political and general information** should be considered. During the legislative process, it was explained that the explicit mention of political and general information was justified by its important role in developing, strengthening and defending democracy.[89] However, the legislature's intention was not to exclude press publications covering other topics.[90] Among the arguments in favour of this differentiation, it has been noted that press publications on political and general information are of particular interest to Google News.[91] In France, the special emphasis on political and general information has a long-standing tradition. The Conseil Constitutionnel, in its 1984 decision, explicitly recognised the constitutional value of pluralism in the daily newspapers that provide political and general information.[92]

This provision has faced criticism, particularly regarding the risk of differentiating remuneration for press publishers based on the topic of their publications. Concerns have also been raised about potential inconsistencies with the wording of Recital 54 of the CDSM Directive and the negative impact such differentiation could have on media pluralism.[93] In its defence, the French legislature emphasised that press publications should **contribute** to political and general information. However, it did not clarify how this contribution should be measured.[94]

Remuneration owed to press publishers can also be assessed **on a flat-rate basis** under French law, which applies when calculating remuneration based on revenues from press publication exploitation is not feasible. This system is similar

89 Ministère de la Culture, *Droit*, 160.

90 Ministère de la Culture, *Droit*, 196.

91 See: Ministère de la Culture, *Droit*, 223.

92 Conseil Constitutionnel, 11 Octobre 1984, Décision n° 84-181 DC, Loi visant à limiter la concentration et à assurer la transparence financière et le pluralisme des entreprises de presse, para. 38.

93 Ministère de la Culture, *Droit*, 243–244.

94 See Chapter 4 for the analysis of the provision from the perspective of protection of media pluralism.

to a global envelope allocated by a digital platform to a geographical area, which is then distributed among various beneficiaries. However, this method of determining remuneration may create a risk of conflating different types of agreements that ISSPs offer to press publishers and press agencies, particularly in the form of partnerships. As a result, press publishers often lack clarity on how much of their remuneration originates from the exercise of their related rights. Those publishers who do not join the partnership proposed by ISSPs may either receive no remuneration at all or significantly lower amounts. This situation also affects the obligation to share remuneration with authors of contributions to press publications. Because press publishers do not have a clear breakdown of the remuneration they receive for the use of their press publications, a question arises regarding how to calculate the share owed to authors.

For example, in France, Google made the negotiation on remuneration under publishers' rights conditional on joining a new global partnership called Publisher Curated News, which includes the Showcase service.[95] The launch of this new service would not have raised any problem in relation to the application of the press publishers' related rights if not for the fact that the contract proposed by Google for the use of all press publications did not distinguish between revenues generated from the use of works and other subject matter under the Showcase service and revenues derived from the use of press publications protected under publishers' rights.[96] For many publishers, joining the Showcase service was the only guarantee that they would receive remuneration, as Google refused to negotiate remuneration solely on the basis of press publishers' related rights. Moreover, "Google repeatedly suggested that remuneration for current uses of press content on its services is likely to be insignificant or even non-existent,"[97] which means that, despite repeated requests from press publishers, Google had no intention of negotiating and paying them and news agencies under the press publishers' related rights.[98]

In Poland, a non-exhaustive list of factors that could be taken into account by contracting parties has been provided. Among these factors are the revenues derived directly or indirectly by the service provider from the reproduction or making available of press publications. Special attention should be given to advertising

95 Showcase service was launched in October 2020 and was conceived as a new service based on the reuse of news articles which were previously not available on Google's portals. Showcase service implies news obligations for publishers which consist of creating, organising and completing a number of modules in order to provide press content on a daily basis. In the framework of this new service, press publishers agree to allow the users to access the content which is normally paid on the press publishers' website, for free on the Google's services. See: FCA Decision of July 12, 2021 on non-compliance with the interim measures of April 9, 2020.

96 FCA Decision of July 12, 2021 on non-compliance with the interim measures of April 9, 2020, 83.

97 FCA Decision of July 12, 2021 on non-compliance with the interim measures of April 9, 2020, 86.

98 French Competition Authority considered such practices as the failure to comply with the order to negotiate in good faith, to comply with obligations to communicate to publishers and news agencies the information necessary for a transparent evaluation of the remuneration due and to remain neutral in negotiations. See: FCA Decision of July 12, 2021 on non-compliance with the interim measures of April 9, 2020, 83, 114–115.

revenues and the duration of a press publication's use. The amount of remuneration can also be calculated based on the type of press publication. However, the legislature did not specify which types of press publications warrant higher remuneration, which could create uncertainty and potentially lead to abuses by the more powerful negotiating party.

5.2. Information claims

According to Art. L.218-4 of the French Intellectual Property Code, the ISSPs are required to provide press publishers and press agencies with all information related to the use of press publications by their users as well as any other details necessary for a transparent evaluation of remuneration and its distribution. In Poland, the law provides more details regarding the type of information that must be disclosed. According to Art. 99[11] of the Polish Copyright Act, publishers are entitled to receive up-to-date information from the service provider and to have access to the service provider's documentation but only to the extent necessary to determine the remuneration owed for the exercise of publishers' rights. It should be specified that the right to request information is subsidiary to the publisher's main claim, such as the payment of remuneration.[99] The request must clearly detail the specific information required, including the type of information, the time period the specific press publication concerned, ensuring that the ISSP understands exactly what information must be provided. This prevents ISSPs from circumventing the request by supplying overly general information. There is a risk that simply repeating the legal provision – stating that the information must be up-to-date or necessary for determining remuneration – will be too vague, potentially resulting in the publisher not receiving the expected information. The requirement in Polish law that the information and data obtained by the publisher shall be processed only for the purpose of determining the remuneration owed serves to functions: to protect the ISSPs' business and to enhance the share of data.

Access to information on the use of press publications by ISSPs is essential for calculating remuneration, and, in most cases, platforms are the sole holders of this data. The problem arises when an ISSP refuses to provide the necessary data or limits access, leading to incomplete calculations. Neither the French nor Polish implementations include a specific mechanism to address non-compliance with the obligation to provide data. This creates a risk that the effectiveness of press publishers' rights may be insufficiently safeguarded. A lack of information or rudimentary disclosure regarding the use of press publications could result in remuneration amounts that do not accurately reflect what publishers are actually owed.

99 See: Directive 2004/48 of the European Parliament and the Council of April 29, 2004 on the enforcement of intellectual property right.

To conclude:

- French and Polish legislatures introduced non-exhaustive lists of factors that may be considered when determining remuneration for press publishers. These factors include human, material and financial investments made by press publishers in French law, the length of press publication use in Polish law and direct and indirect revenues from the use of press publication or the type of press publications in both legislations. While the inclusion of such factors is important for strengthening the negotiating position of press publishers, the last factor, favouring a specific type of press publication, may lead to interpretative uncertainties and create opportunities for abuse by the more powerful negotiating party.
- to calculate remuneration, the provision of data by ISSPs is necessary. However, neither Polish nor French law includes a specific mechanism to address situations in which ISSPs fail to provide such data or do so only partially. This lack of enforcement measures may be seen as a threat to the effectiveness of press publishers' protection.

6. Collective management of publishers' rights

6.1. Definition and role of collective management organisations

According to Art. 3(2) of the Polish Act on collective management,[100] a collective management organisation is a society that associates the right holders or entities representing the right holders. Its primary statutory objective is the collective management of copyright or related rights for the benefit of the right holders within the scope of the authorisation granted to it by the Minister competent for Culture and National Heritage Protection.[101]

Such an organisation performs various function, including taking over the rights for collective management, negotiating contracts for the use of works or subject matter collecting remuneration, distributing and paying revenues, monitoring the use of protected content, enforcing copyright or related rights and exercising other rights and obligations under the Polish Copyright Act.[102] Similarly, according to Art. L321-1 of the French Intellectual Property Code, collective management organisations are legal entities, established in any legal form, whose main purpose is manag-

100 Ustawa z dnia 15 czerwca 2018 r. o zbiorowym zarządzaniu prawami autorskimi i prawami pokrewnymi, Dz.U. 2018 poz. 1293, https://isap.sejm.gov.pl/isap.nsf/download.xsp/WDU20180001293/T/D20181293L.pdf, accessed: 19.07.2023, hereinafter: Act on collective management.

101 English version by the author. Polish version of Art. 3(2) of the Act on collective management: https://isap.sejm.gov.pl/isap.nsf/download.xsp/WDU20180001293/T/D20181293L.pdf, accessed: 19.07.2023.

102 English version by the author. Polish version of Art. 3(2) of the Act on collective management of copyright and related rights: https://isap.sejm.gov.pl/isap.nsf/download.xsp/WDU20180001293/T/D20181293L.pdf, accessed: 19.07.2023.

ing copyright or related rights on behalf of multiple right holders for their collective benefit either by virtue of legal provisions or through contractual agreements.[103] The role of such an organisation is to authorise the use of works or other subject matter on behalf of the right holders, collect their remuneration and redistribute it to them after deducting management fees.[104] Additionally, these organisations are responsible for pursing claims in cases of copyright or related rights infringements.

Collective management organisations act as intermediaries in the collection of levies, which may be imposed as a tax on copying equipment or paid as a fixed amount by users, such as companies, libraries or universities, to the collecting organisations. These dues are then divided proportionally among right holders based on for example the frequency of use of their works.

6.2. Nature of the intermediation of collective management organisations

The intermediation of collective management organisations can either be mandatory or optional. In the case of mandatory intermediation, the ability to obtain permission to use the work or other subject matter directly from the right holder is totally or partially excluded. Likewise, right holders may be restricted from licensing their works individually. The introduction of mandatory intermediation is justified by the practical challenges of managing intangible rights. In many cases, individual right holders are unable to enforce their rights – for example, in collecting remuneration for the use of their works or subject matter – due to the sheer number of users.[105]

According to the European Commission,

> Member States are not allowed to implement art. 15 of the CDSM Directive through a mechanism of mandatory collective management. Imposing mandatory collective management would deprive publishers of this exclusive right by precluding publishers' choice to authorise or prohibit the use of their publication.[106]

According to Art. L.218-3 of the French Intellectual Property Code quoted in Table 3.5, press publishers may entrust the management of their rights to one or more collective

103 English translation by the author. French version of Art. L321-1 (I) of French Intellectual Property Code: https://www.legifrance.gouv.fr/codes/article_lc/LEGIARTI000033687876, accessed: 25.08.2023.

104 C. Bernault, J-P. Clavier, "Fiche 18. La gestion collective du droit d'auteur, Fiches de Droit de la propriété intellectuelle," (2016): 104–109, https://www.cairn.info/fiches-de-droit-de-la-propriete-intellectuelle--9782340014107-page-104.htm, accessed: 25.08.2023.

105 See: M. Ficsor, "Collective rights management from the viewpoint of international treaties, with special attention to the EU 'Acquis'," in *Collective Management of Copyright and Related Rights*, ed. D. Gervais (Wolters Kluwer, 2016), 47.

106 Answer given by Mr Breton on behalf of the European Commission: European Parliament, "Parliamentary question – E-004603//2020(ASW)," November 09, 2020, https://www.europarl.europa.eu/doceo/document/E-9-2020-004603-ASW_EN.html, accessed: 22.11.2022; see also: U. Furgał, "The EU press publishers' right: Where do member states stand?," *Journal of Intellectual Property Law & Practice* 16, no. 8 (2021): 890.

Table 3.5 Management of publishers' rights

*Art. L218-3 of the French Intellectual Property Code**	*The Polish Copyright Act*
The rights of press publishers and press agencies resulting from Art. L. 218-2 can be assigned or licensed. Such right holders can entrust the management of their rights to one or more collective management bodies governed by Title II of Book III of this Part.	–

Note: *English version by the author. French version of Art. L218-3 of the French Intellectual Property Code: https://www.legifrance.gouv.fr/codes/article_lc/LEGIARTI000038826732, accessed: 18.07.2023.

management organisations or negotiate directly with ISSPs. However, the intermediation of a collective management organisation is not mandatory. Similarly, in Poland, the legal grounds for implementing the CDSM Directive clarify that the exercise of the publishers' rights will not be subject to mandatory collective management. However, according to Art. 5 of the Act on Collective Management , a representative collective management organisation will have the ability to grant licenses with extended effect.[107]

Collective management organisations are often criticised for their complex functioning and lack of transparency in how funds are collected and distributed.[108] The intermediation of a collective management organisation entails costs, which can deduce the profits of press publishers. Moreover, negotiations conducted on behalf of multiple publishers tend to be more standardised and schematic,[109] which may not align with the specific needs of certain press publishers.[110] It should be

107 Kancelaria Prezesa Rady Ministrów, "Projekt ustawy o zmianie ustawy o prawie autorskim i prawach pokrewnych oraz niektórych innych ustaw," 2024, https://www.gov.pl/web/premier/projekt-ustawy-o-zmianie-ustawy-o-prawie-autorskim-i-prawach-pokrewnych-oraz-niektorych-innych-ustaw3, accessed: 05.02.2024. ECL is based on a licence initially concluded between a CMO and a user, which is extended by national law to also cover rightholders who are not members of the CMO. See: European Commission, *Commission Staff Working Document Report on the Use of Collective Licensing Mechanisms with an Extended Effect under Article 12(6) of Directive 2019/790/EU on Copyright and Related Rights in the Digital Single Market* (SWD (2021) 337 final 2021), 5, https://data.consilium.europa.eu/doc/document/ST-14480-2021-INIT/en/pdf, accessed: 07.01.2025.

108 See for example: S. Depreeuw, "Mandatory collective management of copyright: When the road to deadlock is paved with good intentions," Kluwer Copyright Blog, February 09, 2022, https://copyrightblog.kluweriplaw.com/2022/02/09/mandatory-collective-management-of-copyright-when-the-road-to-deadlock-is-paved-with-good-intentions/, accessed: 02.10.2023.

109 S. von Lewinski during a discussion at the Max Planck Institute for Innovation and Competition, 17.10.2023.

110 French collective management organisation (OGC) called "Société des droits voisins de la presse" (DVP) dedicated to defending the related rights of press publishers and press agencies has been created in 2021. It has been considered that the creation of such a body will have pro-competitive effects for press organs by strengthening their bargaining power vis-à-vis players in a dominant position, particularly digital platforms and limiting the distortion between press publishers by not favouring the big publishers and allowing the smaller ones to be defended. DVP signed an agreement with Google in 2023 and with Meta in 2024. See: DVP, "La Société des Droits Voisins

noted that mandatory intermediation could unify and strengthen the negotiating position of press publishers against powerful ISSPs. Conversely, negotiating independently weakens publishers' bargaining power and increases their dependence on ISSPs, given their market position.[111]

In my opinion, the introduction of mandatory intermediation could constitute a remedy against the imposition of unfavourable negotiating conditions by ISSPs, as it would strengthen the bargaining power of press publishers. However, given the significant differences in the interests of press publishers, as demonstrated in Chapter 1 of this monograph, and the various methods of achieving fair remuneration, I find that optional intermediation is a more suitable approach for the exercise of publishers' rights. It is worth noting that mandatory intermediation was introduced in Spain's regulation on press publishers[112] before the adoption of the CDSM Directive. The lack of mandatory intermediation in EU law may be seen as an attempt to regulate the issue differently, hoping that the result will be more effective.

Practice has shown that large and well-known press publishers, such as Le Monde, preferred to negotiate individually with ISSPs and had the bargaining power to negotiate and achieve tailored agreements.[113] At the same time, a different trend emerged among smaller press publishers, who sought to strengthen their position by turning collective management organisations to exercise their rights.[114] Additionally, some press publishers chose not to exercise their exclusive rights at all. Therefore, given this complex landscape, in which different types of press publishers pursue different interests, the introduction of mandatory intermediation would not be a suitable solution.

In Poland, a representative collective management organisation, according to the provisions of the Act on Collective Management, has the authority to grant a license with extended effect.[115] According to Art. 10(1) of the Act on Collective Management, a representative collective management organisation is one that holds exclusive authorisation to collectively manage the rights of a specific category of right holders for a particular type of works or subject matter within a

de la Presse signe un accord avec Meta," June 25, 2024, https://www.dvpresse.fr/signature-avec-meta/, accessed: 02.12.2024 ; DVP, "La Société des Droits Voisins de la Presse (DVP) annonce la signature d'un premier accord avec Google," October 17, 2023, https://www.dvpresse.fr/la-societe-des-droits-voisins-de-la-presse-dvp-annonce-la-signature-dun-premier-accord-avec-google/ ,accessed: 02.12.2024.

111 See: D. Gervais, *Collective Management of Copyright and Related Rights* (Wolters Kluwer, 2016).

112 See Chapter 2.

113 See: Media Specs, ""Apig": l'Alliance de la presse française contre les GAFA," September 20, 2018, https://www.mediaspecs.fr/apig-lalliance-de-la-presse-francaise-contre-les-gafa/, accessed: 18.07.2023.

114 A. de Rochegonde, "Le long chemin des droits voisins, Stratégies. Les medias des nouveaux modelès," Stratégies, May 23, 2022, https://www.strategies.fr/actualites/medias/LQ594241C/le-long-chemin-des-droits-voisins.html, accessed: 17.10.2023.

115 According to Art. 5a of the Polish Act on Collective Management.

specific field of exploitation. As explained by O. Bulayenko et al., the extended effect of a collective licence

> allows a representative collective management organisation, subject to statutory conditions and safeguards, to conclude licences covering the rights not only of rightholders who have given this collective management organisation an explicit authorisation to represent them, but also rightholders who have not given the organisation any authorisation to exercises their rights.[116]

This means that a representative collective management organisation can negotiate the licences on behalf of press publishers who have not given the collective management organisation an explicit authorisation to exercise their rights.

The Polish legislature did not provide explanation for its choice to introduce this licensing structure in relation to press publishers. M. Czajkowska-Dąbrowska points out that such a mechanism is adopted when it would not be possible for collective management organisations to obtain authorisation from all right holders or in order to ease the burden on users by ensuring access to protected cultural goods.[117] It could be presumed that Polish legislature's objective in applying this model to press publishers was to facilitate the exercise of publishers' exclusive rights.

On November 14, 2024, the Polish Minister of Culture decided that Repropol would be granted the right to collectively manage publishers' rights as the only collective management organisation for copyright or related rights in Poland.[118]

To conclude:

- the introduction of mandatory intermediation could constitute a remedy against the imposition of unfavourable negotiating conditions by ISSPs, as it would strengthen the bargaining power of press publishers. However, given the significant differences in the interests of press publishers, optional intermediation remains the more suitable path approach for exercising publishers' rights. Poland's introduction of the licence with extended effect presents a compromise between optional and mandatory intermediation.[119]

116 O. Bulayenko et al., *Study on Emerging Issues on Collective Licensing Practices in the Digital Environment*, Final Report, European Commission (2018), 130, https://www.ivir.nl/publicaties/download/Study_on_collective_practices_in_the_digital_environment.pdf, accessed: 05.02.2024.

117 See: L. Guibault, "Extended collective licensing for the use of out-of-commerce works in Europe: A matter of legitimacy vis-à-vis rights holders," *International Review of Intellectual Property and Competition Law* (IIC) 49 (2018).

118 See: Repropol, "Repropol uzyskał rozszerzenie zezwolenia i może reprezentować Wydawców w negocjacjach z Big Techami," November 23, 2024, https://repropol.pl/aktualnosci/repropol-na-podstawie-rozszerzonego-zezwolenia-na-prawa-pokrewne-wydanego-przez-ministerstwo-kultury-i-dziedzictwa-narodowego-moze-reprezentowac-wydawcow-w-negocjacjach-z-big-techami/, accessed: 08.01.2025.

119 According to L. Guibault: "to make mass digitisation economically viable in practice, a solution must be found in order to cover as many rights owners as possible, including non-members. In principle, this can be achieved in one of three ways: (1) mandatory statutory licensensing, (2) voluntary

7. Competition law – an alternative tool to ensure the effectiveness of publishers' rights in France

The question arises as to whether the rapid implementation of Art. 15 of the CDSM Directive in France, as the first country in the EU to do so, can guarantee its effectiveness. In this legal context, I understand effectiveness as a regulation's ability to be respected and achieve its intended or desired result.[120] This section presents a case study on the legal situation of press publishers in France following the adoption of publishers' rights, which strove to ensure effective protection through the use of competition law. Its objective is to identify the deficiencies, inaccuracies and grey areas in the French implementation that have been revealed in practice and couldundermine its effectiveness. Despite the protection that has been granted, press publishers in France have not been able to make use of it, which raises questions about the regulation's purposefulness. This analysis will be crucial for evaluating the implementation of publisher's rights in other Member States that followed France's lead, assessing whether the problems identified have been addressed and, if so, how. I focused on the study of the case of French press publishers against Google. The rationale for this choice lies in the scale of this dispute, the significance of the decisions made by the French Competition Authority (hereinafter: FCA) and their impact on the effectiveness of publishers' rights.[121]

7.1. Case presentation

In France, press publishers who sought remuneration for the use of their press publications by ISSPs under the new law faced unfair conditions due to Google's "quasi-monopolistic" position in the search engine market.[122] In response to the implementation of the publishers' rights, Google forced press publishers to choose between granting the platform free authorisation to reuse their press publication or seeing their publications delisted or downgraded, which could threaten the viability of their businesses.[123] While press publishers could authorise the use of their press publications at no charge, this decision should come from their own choice rather

opt-in agreements, and (3) Extended Collective Licensing (ECL) schemes. ECL is less intrusive than the first option while at the same time still providing large scale coverage that opt-ins cannot achieve," in L. Guibault, "Extended," 918.

120 See: Cambridge Dictionary, "Effectiveness," https://dictionary.cambridge.org/dictionary/english/effectiveness, accessed: 06.10.2023.

121 A dispute between Google and press publishers on the adequate remuneration for press publishers took place also in Germany but the German Competition Authority refrained from examining this in detail and has not intervened. See: Bundeskartellamnt, "Improvements for publishers using Google News Showcase," December 21, 2022, https://www.bundeskartellamt.de/SharedDocs/Meldung/EN/Pressemitteilungen/2022/21_12_2022_Google_News_Showcase.html?nn=3591568, accessed: 08.11.2023.

122 FCA, Decision of April 9, 2020 on interim measures, 43.

123 FCA, Decision of April 9, 2020 on interim measures, 43.

than being imposed by a dominant platform exploiting market dependence to avoid paying for compensation.

Google's practices could be described as an attempt to circumvent publishers' rights, effectively undermining their purpose. Despite the legal protection granted, press publishers were forced to authorise the free use of their press publications to safeguard their business interests, leaving them in the same position as before the law's implementation. In response, some French press publishers filed complaints to the FCA, challenging Google's conduct in the press sector. They argued that Google's application of publishers' rights constituted an abuse of dominant position, in violation of Art. L. 420-2 of the French Commercial Code (Code de commerce) and Art. 102 of the TFEU.[124] Additionally, they claimed that Googles actions amounted to an abuse of economic dependency. The complainants requested interim measures to be imposed, forcing Google to enter into good-faith negotiations with press publishers.

The question arises as to why several unions representing French press publishers, namely, Syndicat des Éditeurs de la Presse Magazine, Alliance de la Presse d'Information Générale and the Agence France-Presse, decided in November 2019 to pursue a competition law approach rather than claiming an infringement of related rights.

Infringement of intellectual property rights constitutes a tort,[125] which occurs when there is an encroachment into exclusive rights of the right holder, provided that the user cannot prove that their use is based on a legally effective title against the right holder.[126] In the context of the online use of press publication by ISSPs, an infringement occurs when such use takes place without the authorisation of press publishers and without legal justification. In such cases, a press publisher may claim infringement of their exclusive rights and seek legal remedies, including the cessation of unauthorised use; rectification measures, such as a public statement acknowledging the infringement; and notification to ISSP users. Additionally, they can claim compensation for damages and lost profits, particularly when the press publication has already been widely disseminated to the public.[127]

124 One of the conditions for the application of Art. 102 TFEU is that the anti-competitive practice has an effect on trade between Member States (cross-border aspect). Where there is such an effect, the EU competition law applies, where there is not, the national competition rules apply. Thus, it may be that a practice partly has a cross-border impact and partly a purely national impact, with the result that the authorities can apply both legal bases. The due attention should be paid to not to punish twice for the same breach according to the *ne bis in idem* principle.

125 M. van Eechoud, *Choice of Law in Copyright and Related Rights. Alternatives to the Lex Protectionis* (Kluwer Law International, 2003), 206.

126 A. Drzewicki, "Komentarz do art. 79 Ustawy o prawie autorskim i prawach pokrewnych," in *Ustawa o prawie autorskim i prawach pokrewnych. Komentarz*, ed. E. Ferenc-Szydełko (Wydawnictwo C.H. BECK, 2021, LEGALIS), point 1.

127 See: the provisions included in book III: General provisions relating to copyright, related rights and the rights of database producers (Art. L311-1 to L343-7) of the French Intellectual Property Code specifying the claims in case of the infringement of rightholder's rights.

In the case discussed, Google's practices often operated on the borderline between infringement and non-infringement.[128] This is due to Google's classification of all headlines as short excerpts exempt from protection, the calculation of higher remuneration for publishers covering political and general issues and displaying press publications from press publishers who did not decide to waive their rights in lower ranking positions. While these practices were undeniably detrimental to the interests of press publishers, they did not always constitute a *per se* infringement of publishers' rights. For this reason, press publishers sought an alternative mechanism to ensure the effectiveness of related rights in France, turning to competition law as a means of enforcement. However, it should be noted that some press publishers have still pursued legal action under copyright infringement claims against online platforms, meaning this path is not completely abandoned. For example, in November 2024, around 50 mostly regional French press publishers filed infringement actions against Microsoft, seeking several million euros in compensation for the use of their press publications under publishers' rights.[129] That same month, press groups, including Le Figaro, Le Monde, Le Parisien and Les Echos, also announced legal action against X (formerly Twitter), accusing the platform of using their content without payment.[130]

As to the relationship between the claims for infringement of copyright and related rights and claims concerning the abuse of a dominant position or unfair competition practices is distinct in nature, cause and purpose. The former aims

128 For example, in some case the negotiations under the related rights of press publishers were possible only if press publishers joined the Showcase services. In theory therefore, press publishers could enforce their rights but in practice, the additional conditions had to be met. See: P. Mouron, "L'Autorité de la concurrence au secours du droit voisin des éditeurs et agences de presse," *Revue européenne des médias et du numérique* no. 54 (2020): 10–14, https://amu.hal.science/hal-02885794/document, accessed: 05.08.2023 ; O. Wang, "Droit voisin des éditeurs de presse et concurrence: quelles perspectives après l'affaire," *Google* ?," Dalloz, September 27, 2022, https://www.dalloz-actualite.fr/node/droit-voisin-des-editeurs-de-presse-et-concurrence-quelles-perspectives-apres-l-affaire-google, accessed: 05.08.2023.

129 Le Monde, "Microsoft: une cinquantaine d'éditeurs de presse assignent le géant américain en justice concernant les droits voisins," November 08, 2024, https://www.lemonde.fr/economie/article/2024/11/08/droits-voisins-une-cinquantaine-d-editeurs-de-presse-assignent-en-justice-microsoft_6383770_3234.html, accessed: 08.12.2024; APIG, "Les éditeurs de presse d'information engagent des actions judiciaires contre Microsoft pour faire respecter la loi sur le droit voisin," November 08, 2024, 2024, https://www.alliancepresse.fr/actualite/les-editeurs-de-presse-dinformation-engagent-des-actions-judiciaires-contre-microsoft-pour-faire-respecter-la-loi-sur-le-droit-voisin/, accessed: 08.12.2024.

130 According to the press publishers, unlike Google and Meta, X/Twitter has never agreed to open negotiations with publishers in order to comply with the legal framework on copyright and related rights, despite several months of approaches and then amicable reminders. See: La Croix, "Droits voisins: le réseau X attaqué en justice par plusieurs groupes de presse," November 12, 2024, https://www.la-croix.com/droits-voisins-le-figaro-le-monde-et-d-autres-journaux-trainent-x-au-tribunal-20241112, accessed: 08.12.2024.

to remedy the infringement of an intellectual property rights, while the latter seeks to eliminate misconduct or behaviour that is contrary to honest commercial practice. According to French case law, infringement and unfair competition claims may be pursued jointly, provided that the infringing act and the unfair competition act are separable and that one is not merely accessory to the other.[131]

In response to the press publishers' complaint, the FCA issued a decision in April 2020, stating that "Google has not entered into any negotiations with publishers and news agencies with a view to defining the conditions for displaying and paying for their content that is protected under the press publishers' related rights."[132] Instead, Google imposed the choice: either allow the use of protected content for free or face a limitation in which only headlines and hyperlinks would be displayed. Given that publishers' revenues are highly dependent on the visibility of their content on Google services, press publishers had no choice but to comply with the display policy imposed by Google. Those, who decided to enforce their rights faced downgrading of their content or limited visibility, leading to significant losses in traffic and revenue.

> According to the La Dépêche Group, Google did not contextually display the Group's content on 24 October 2019. This is alleged to have resulted in a more than 50% reduction in visits from search engines on the day in question compared to the average for that month. According to tests carried out by the Figaro Group, a link listed without a photo or description on Google, experiences a downturn in its click performance of about 50%. Since traffic from Google Search accounts for around 50% of traffic of figaro.fr according to the publisher, the impact on Internet audiences could therefore potentially amount to a drop of 25%.[133]

Google's application of publishers' rights was deemed to have complicated press publishers' situation even more than before their legal protection was introduced.[134] The FCA found that Google's practices **were likely to constitute an abuse of dominant position** and imposed interim measures, which remained in force until

131 See: Cour de cassation, civile, Chambre commerciale, 19 janvier 2010, 08-15.338 08-16.459 08-16.469, Inédit, rectifié par un arrêt du 4 mai 2010, https://www.legifrance.gouv.fr/juri/id/JURITEXT000021734255/, accessed: 24.07.2023.

132 FCA, Decision of April 9, 2020 on interim measures, 46.

133 FCA, Decision of April 9, 2020 on interim measures, 32.

134 FCA, Decision of April 9, 2020 on interim measures, 56.

the FCA published its decision[135] on July 12, 2021.[136] In its ruling, the FCA found that Google failed to comply with:

- the order to negotiate in good faith;[137]
- the obligation to communicate to publishers and news agencies the information necessary for a transparent evaluation of the remuneration due;[138]
- the obligation of neutrality in negotiations with news publishers and news agencies;[139]
- the order to ensure that the existence and outcome of the negotiations provided for in the injunctions did not affect the indexing, classification or presentation of the protected content reused on Google's services.[140]

The FCA imposed a penalty of 500 million euros on Google and ordered the company to "make an offer of remuneration that meets the requirements of the press publishers' related right and the Decision for the current use of protected content on Google's services to those complainants who make a formal request

135 Google has been ordered: to negotiate in good faith within 3 months of the request to open negotiations with any news publishers and to achieve the result of the negotiations in the form of setting the remuneration due to the latter; to provide news publishers with the information required for the transparent assessment of the remuneration; to continue to display textual extracts and enriched extracts from news publishers during the negotiation period; to respect the principle of neutrality in the way in which news publishers' protected content is indexed, classified and presented on Google's services during negotiations on related rights and in negotiations on related rights in respect of any other economic relationship Google may have with news publishers and news agencies; and to provide the Authority with monthly reports on the manner in which it is complying with the decision.

136 See: M. Kowala, M. Malaga, "Press publishers' right and competition law. Case comment on the French Competition Authority's decisions against Google," *Yearbook of Antitrust and Regulatory Studies* 17, no. 30 (2024).

137 Despite the repeated request of the French press publishers, Google did not aim to negotiate and pay press publishers for the use of press publications. By linking the negotiations of the remuneration resulting from the publishers' right to the negotiation of the remuneration from the services like Showcase it made it not very transparent and conditional on participation in other services of Google.

138 FCA noted that this communication was partial, late, fragmented and not sufficient because not allowing "the complainants to make the link between Google's use of protected content, the revenue it derives from it and its financial proposal(s)." See: FCA, Decision of July 12, 2021 on non-compliance with the interim measures of April 9, 2020.

139 FCA found that the tech giant did not allowed press publishers to negotiate a separate remuneration for the use of press publications under the publishers' rights which constitutes a violation of the discussed Injunction see: FCA, Decision of July 12, 2021 on non-compliance with the interim measures of April 9, 2020, 93.

140 Google violated the obligation by linking the negotiations on the remuneration resulting from publishers' rights to the negotiations on the remuneration resulting from the services such as Showcase since the absence on latter meant a worse visibility for the press publisher. See: FCA, Decision of July 12, 2021 on non-compliance with the interim measures of 9 April, 2020, 115.

to re-open negotiations."[141] Google paid the fine and proposed commitments to address the FCA's concerns, including:

- negotiating in good faith with press publishers and news agencies that request it, ensuring that remuneration for the reproduction of protected content on its services is determined according to transparent, objective and non-discriminatory criteria;
- providing the necessary information for a transparent evaluation of the proposed remuneration and making a remuneration offer within three months of the start of negotiations;
- taking the necessary steps to ensure that negotiations do not affect the indexation, ranking or presentation of protected content and that they do not affect any other economic relationships that may exist between Google and news publishers or news agencies.[142]

These commitments were accepted by the FCA, which closed the proceedings June 21, 2022.[143] Unfortunately, this decision did not end the press publishers vs. Google dispute, as Google failed to comply with its commitments. In response, the FCA issued a new decision on March 15, 2024,[144] imposing a €250 million fine on Google for breaching its commitments to conduct negotiations in good faith; to provide publishers with the information necessary for a transparent assessment of their remuneration for the use of press publications under the publishers' rights; and to take the indispensable measures to ensure that negotiations do not affect other economic relations between Google and press publishers.[145] The FCA found that Google failed to comply with its obligation to negotiate a remuneration offer for the use of press publications on its services, in accordance with transparent, objective

141 This is the heaviest fine imposed by the Autorité de la concurrence for non-compliance with its injunctions, and the second highest imposed on an individual company in France. See: T. Gaudiaut, Les GAFA dans le viseur de l'Autorité de la concurrence, July 23, 2021, Statista, https://fr.statista.com/infographie/25325/plus-grosses-amendes-antitrust-infligees-a-une-entreprise-en-france/, accessed: 24.07.2023.

142 FCA, "Dans le cadre de l'instruction au fond du dossier sur les droits voisins, Google propose des engagements. L'Autorité les soumet à consultation publique," December 15, 2021, https://www.autoritedelaconcurrence.fr/fr/communiques-de-presse/dans-le-cadre-de-linstruction-au-fond-du-dossier-sur-les-droits-voisins, accessed: 24.07.2023.

143 FCA, "Related rights: The Autorité accepts Google's commitments," June 21, 2022, https://www.autoritedelaconcurrence.fr/en/press-release/related-rights-autorite-accepts-googles-commitments, accessed: 24.07.2023.

144 Decision of March 15, 2024 of FCA on non-compliance with the commitments set out in the Decision of June 21, 2022 concerning practices implemented by Google in the press sector, https://www.autoritedelaconcurrence.fr/sites/default/files/integral_texts/2024-03/24d03vf.pdf, accessed: 21.03.2024 (hereinafter: FCA, Decision of March 15, 2024 on non-compliance with the commitments of June 21, 2022).

145 FCA, Decision of March 15, 2024 on non-compliance with the commitments of June 21, 2022, 12–15.

and non-discriminatory criteria, within a period of three months.[146] Notably, in this decision, the FCA also considered publishers' accusations regarding the launch of Google's artificial intelligence service, Gemini. The FCA determined that Google had failed to inform publishers about the use of their content by Gemini, thereby violating its transparency commitment.[147] It is difficult to say whether this decision will end the ongoing dispute that began in 2019. Because Google did not contest the facts, it benefited from the settlement procedure and has proposed a series of corrective measures to address some of the breaches identified by the FCA,[148] which is promising.

7.2. Case study

Several problems arising from the wording of the French implementation of Art. 15 of the CDSM Directive, as revealed in practice, are likely to undermine the effectiveness of publishers' rights.

First, given the specific relationship between ISSPs and press publishers, the French legislature could have introduced a mechanism protecting press publishers from exploiting their dependence on ISSPs, such as assistance from an independent body in cases when platforms refuse to negotiate. The need of such a solution has been confirmed in practice, as publishers asked the FCA to mediate. However, it is important to acknowledge that the objective of the related rights regime, as chosen by the EU legislature, was not to prevent the abuse of a dominant position or address economic dependency but, rather, to recognise and protect the organisational and financial contribution of publishers in the production of press publications.

Second, under the French transposition of Art. 15 of the CDSM, press publishers are entitled to request from ISSPs the information necessary to calculate their remuneration.[149] However, the safeguard for transparency in this calculation, as adopted by the French legislature, may be insufficient. There is no clear specification on which information should be provided, nor is there a mechanism to address non-compliance. As a result, remuneration amounts calculated based on data provided in a discretionary manner by platforms may not reflect the actual remuneration due to publishers. For example, as shown in the case study, Google provided only fragmented and insufficient information, making it difficult to establish a clear link between the use of press publications and the revenues derived. This lack of transparency affected the accuracy of remuneration calculations and could potentially undermine the effectiveness of publishers' rights.

146 FCA, Decision of March 15, 2024 on non-compliance with the commitments of June 21, 2022, 12–15.

147 FCA, Decision of March 15, 2024 on non-compliance with the commitments of 2112-15.

148 FCA, "Related rights: the Autorité fines Google €250 million," March 20, 2024, https://www.autoritedelaconcurrence.fr/en/article/related-rights-autorite-fines-google-eu250-million, accessed: 08.12.2024.

149 See Section 5.1 of this chapter.

Third, the French legislature did not use its margin of discretion while transposing Art. 15 of the CDSM Directive to safeguard the position of press publishers negotiating remuneration under the new law. The legislature could have strengthened the position of negotiation press publishers by introducing, for example, an obligation preventing platforms from stopping the display of their publications. If such a safeguard were in place, press publishers would not have experienced a decline in the visibility of their publications that resulted in losses in revenue, and publishers would not have been deterred from asserting their rights.

Finally, in my opinion, the wording of the exclusion of very short extracts from publishers' protection in both the CDSM Directive and French law leaves considerable interpretative doubts regarding how its precise meaning. This lack of clarity has allowed ISSPs to classify all headlines as very short extracts, thereby excluding them from protection,[150] which calls into question the effectiveness of publishers' rights. Although the French legislature introduced some specifications to clarify the concept, they remain too vague to eliminate interpretative uncertainties. As a result, determining whether an infringement of related rights has occurred requires a case-by-case analysis. The legislature, both at the EU and French levels, could have clarified that short extracts are not necessarily synonymous with headlines. However, such an approach might have been criticised for excessive descriptiveness. Google's practice of classifying all headlines as very short extracts highlights the need for a clear and tangible standard, or yardstick, to determine, in each case, what qualifies as a very short extract, without requiring legal action and court interpretation. However, due to the lack of sufficient regulation, the yardstick imposed by platforms negatively impacts the interests of press publishers, as it fails to consider the actual content of very short extracts.

In conclusion, while press publishers were granted protection, its formulation, along with inaccuracies and deficiencies, allowed ISSPs to circumvent it and exploit its shortcomings to impose their own conditions for the use of press publications. This ease with which the law implementing Art. 15 of the CDSM Directive was circumvented largely stemmed from **the market position of ISSPs and the dependence of publishers' interests on them**.

Some remuneration agreements between press publishers and Google have been concluded following the FCA's decision. According to Google,

> it is the first and only platform to have signed a significant number of licensing agreements with 280 French news publishers … These cover more than 450 of their publications – and pay publishers tens of millions of euro a year.[151]

150 According to the FCA: Google "systematically and indiscriminately" considered the headlines of press publications as meeting the criteria from provision from Art. L. 211-3, para. 2 on Intellectual Property Code despite the fact that such practices could constitute an infringement of the said provision. See: FCA, Decision of April 9, 2020 on interim measures, 58.

151 S. Connal, "Un accord afin de régler un différend qui dure depuis trop longtemps," Google Blog France, March 20, 2024, https://blog.google/intl/fr-fr/nouvelles-de-lentreprise/chez-google/accord-regler-differend-qui-dure-depuis-trop-longtemps/, accessed: 08.12.2024.

Google successively signed agreements with AFP[152] at the end of 2021.[153] On April 14, 2022, Google announced that it had reached an agreement with the magazine publishers' union (SEPM), which represents 80 publishers and more than 400 titles, securing €20 million a year in remuneration under the publishers' law.[154] In 2023, an agreement was signed between Google and DVP.[155]

Details of these agreements, particularly regarding remuneration amounts, are mostly not publicly available. Several of these agreements were subject to confidentiality clauses between the contracting parties. This is the case of the agreement between Alliance of the General Information Press (in French: APIG) and Google, concluded in March 2022, the details of which remain confidential.[156]

The lack of transparency regarding negotiated remunerations and their conditions hinders research into the effectiveness of publishers' rights. It is difficult to compare the actual amounts obtained by press publishers to assess whether the remuneration received can genuinely contribute to improving the press sector. Additionally, much of the available data does not come from official sources and is often communicated inconsistently, selectively or not at all.

To conclude:

- the lack of mechanisms protecting press publishers from exploiting their dependence on ISSPs, the insufficient safeguards ensuring transparency in remuneration calculations and or the imprecise definition of press publication are key shortcomings of the French implementation that are likely to undermine the effectiveness of publishers' rights.
- the circumvention of publishers' protection in many cases did not constitute an infringement of publishers' rights but, rather, stemmed from the significant market position of ISSPs and the economic dependency of press publishers. This reality justifies the choice of French publishers to seek protection through competition law mechanisms.
- the lack of transparency regarding agreements and their conditions hinders research into the effectiveness of publishers' rights. While the FCA's intervention facilitated good-faith negotiations and let to some agreements, the absence of detailed data or the selective disclosure of information makes it difficult, if not impossible, to assess the effectiveness of the protection introduced.

152 French Press Agency, from French: Agence France Presse.

153 Google, "L'Agence France-Presse et Google signent un accord sur les droits voisins," November 17, 2021, https://blog.google/intl/fr-fr/nouvelles-de-lentreprise/chez-google/afp-google/, accessed: 08.01.2025.

154 UPP, "Accord entre Google et la presse magazine sur les droits voisins," April 21, 2022, https://www.upp.photo/fr/news/accord-entre-google-et-la-presse-magazine-sur-les-droits-voisins-3022, accessed: 08.12.2024.

155 See: Section 6 of this chapter.

156 C. Cohen, "Droits voisins: Google signe avec la presse d'information," Le Figaro, no. 24114, Europresse, 2022.

- the dispute before the FCA and its decisions should be seen as a catalyst that broke the negotiation impasse. Unfortunately, it has not yet resolved the broader conflict between press publishers and online platforms. While some agreements have been signed, the dispute between Google and press publishers before the FCA remains ongoing, and new lawsuits against X and Microsoft were filed by press publishers in November 2024.

8. Mechanisms to ensure the effectiveness of the publishers' rights in other Member States

The shortcomings of the France's implementation of publishers' rights likely undermined the regulation's effectiveness, serving as a lesson for MS that implemented publishers' protections afterward. In response, these MS introduced special control and replacement mechanisms to anticipate and prevent ISSPs from circumventing publishers' protections, in some cases drawing inspiration from common law solutions. This analysis examines the mechanisms introduced in Belgium, Spain, Italy, the Czech Republic and, finally, Poland, the last Member State to implement the CDSM Directive.[157] The objective is to assess how the margin of discretion in implementing Art. 15 of the CDSM Directive was used by MS after France and to identify the legal solutions which may ensure the regulation's effectiveness.

8.1. Lack of mechanisms protecting press publishers from exploiting their dependence on ISSPs in the French implementation

In Italy, the Communications Regulatory Authority[158] determines the criteria for the calculating the remuneration (fair compensation[159]) owed to press publishers and sets the amount in case the parties fail to reach an agreement, in accordance with Art. 43 bis (10) of copyright law (Legge sul diritto d'autore).[160]

Belgium also introduced an assisted negotiation mechanism similar to contractual arbitrage. According to Art. XI.216/2 §2 of the Code of Economic

157 For the wording of provisions from Arts. 99^{12}–99^{17} of the Polish Copyright Act applicable in case of the difficulty to reach the agreement between press publishers and ISSPs, see Section 5 of this chapter.

158 Autorità per le Garanzie nelle Comunicazioni (AGCOM) is the national regulatory agency for the communication industries in Italy.

159 In the framework of the Italian implementation the obligation to pay the fair compensation has been introduced which can be understood as a right to remuneration granted to press publishers. However, press publishers, in the CDSM Directive were granted the exclusive rights and not the right to remuneration which may lead to the conclusion that the Italian implementation goes beyond the margin of appreciation granted to Member States in the implementation of the publishers' right. See the further analysis of the issue in Chapter 4.

160 English version by the author. Italian version of Art. 43 bis (10) of Legge sul diritto d'autore, https://www.altalex.com/documents/codici-altalex/2014/06/26/legge-sul-diritto-d-autore#titolo1, accessed: 15.11.2022.

Law (Code de droit économique), press publishers and ISSPs must negotiate in good faith with regarding the use of press publication and the corresponding remuneration. If no agreement is reached, the more diligent party may initiate a dispute resolution procedure before the Belgian Institute for Postal Services and Telecommunications,[161] which issues a binding administrative decision on the remuneration for the use of press publication.[162]

In Poland, according to Art. $99^{12}(2)$ of the Copyright Act, if an agreement on the use of press publications by ISSPs is not reached within three months of one party submitting an offer, either party may request mediation from the President of the Office of Electronic Communications (hereinafter: President of UKE)[163] to determine remuneration. Mediation occurs only if both parties agree to participate. However, if mediation fails or party refuses to participate, the President of the UKE may, at the request of a party, issue a ruling on the remuneration for the use of press publications by ISSPs. The ruling is final, meaning that there is no appeal under the administrative procedure and is enforceable by way of court execution, provided that the remuneration is due. According to Art. 99^{17} of the Polish Copyright Act, a party may file an objection to the ruling within 14 days of the date of receiving the ruling. The objection can challenge the entire ruling, a specific part or the decision on costs. If upheld, the court will amend the contested ruling in whole or in part and decide on the merits of the case.

There are some similarities between the introduction of recourse to an intermediating institution in the discussed legislations and the solutions provided in the Australian News Media Bargaining Code.[164] Adopted in February 2021, the code is a mandatory framework designed "to address bargaining power imbalances between digital platform services and Australian news businesses."[165] Its objective

161 The BIPT is the federal regulatory body responsible for regulating the electronic communications market, the postal market, the electromagnetic spectrum of radio frequencies as well as the audiovisual media services and the video-sharing platform services in the bilingual Brussels-Capital Region. See: BIPT, https://www.bipt.be/operators/bipt, accessed: 09.01.2025.

162 English version by the author. French version of Art. XI.216/2 §2 of the Code of Economic Law, https://www.ejustice.just.fgov.be/eli/loi/2013/02/28/2013A11134/justel, accessed: 24.07.2023.

163 From Polish: Urząd Komunikacji Elektronicznej. The President of the Office of Electronic Communications (UKE) is a regulatory authority responsible for telecommunications and postal activities and frequency resources management. It's also a supervisory authority responsible for controlling compliance of products emitting or vulnerable to emission of electromagnetic field, including radio equipment placed on the market in Poland. See: UKE, https://uke.gov.pl/en/about-us/, accessed: 09.01.2025.

164 Hereinafter: the Code. In June 2023 Canadian Online News Acts has been adopted the solution of which mirrors those provided in Australian Code. See: K. Walker, "An update on Canada's Bill C-18 and our Search and News products," Google Canada Blog, November 29, 2023, https://blog.google/intl/en-ca/company-news/outreach-initiatives/an-update-on-canadas-bill-c-18-and-our-search-and-news-products/, accessed: 26.07.2023.

165 The Parliament of the Commonwealth of Australia, Revised Explanatory Memorandum to Treasury Law Amendment (News Media and digital platforms mandatory bargaining code) Bill 2021, 9, https://www.accc.gov.au/system/files/Revised%20explanatory%20memorandum.pdf, accessed: 25.07.2023, hereinafter: Revised Explanatory Memorandum.

is to incentivise news media businesses[166] and digital platforms to reach agreements for remuneration for news content displayed on digital platform services.[167] If the parties fail to reach an agreement, the code establishes a procedure for an abitral panel to determine the remuneration owed to press publishers for the use of their publications. The bargaining parties must participate in the arbitration in good faith,[168] and failure to comply may result in a maximum civil penalty under Australian law. Belgium has also introduced an explicit obligation to negotiate in good faith, but its legislation does not specify the consequence of non-compliance. In Spain's implementation, negotiations for authorising the use of press publication must adhere to the principles of good contractual faith, due diligence, transparency and respect for free competition rules, explicitly prohibiting the abuse of a dominant position.[169]

Under the Australian Code, each bargaining party must submit a final remuneration offer to the arbitral panel, which selects one unless it deems none to be in the public interest.[170] The parties must comply with the panel's decision,[171] and failure to do so may result in a civil penalty under Australian law.[172] A similar mechanism is implemented in Italy, though the Italian Communication Authority's determination of remuneration does not explicitly specify the consequences of non-compliance. Such specifications are provided in the Czech Republic's implementation of Art. 15 of the CDSM Directive. According to §105(1)(g) of Czech Copyright law (autorský zákon), which has been criticised, especially by online platforms,[173] an ISSP commits an infringement if it fails to obtain authorisation to use a press publication as required by §87b(9).[174] Competent authorities can impose fines based on the severity of the violation, up to a maximum 500,000 CZK or 1% of the total global turnover for the previous financial year. According to the Czech Ministry of Industry and Trade, this maximum fine is neither disproportionate nor unique

166 The terminology used in this point is the terminology from the News Media and digital platforms mandatory bargaining code.

167 Revised Explanatory Memorandum, 7.

168 Section 52ZS of Treasury Law Amendment (News Media and digital platforms mandatory bargaining code) Bill 2021 (the Australian Code), https://www.accc.gov.au/system/files/Final%20legislation%20as%20passed%20by%20both%20houses.pdf, accessed: 25.07.2023.

169 Art. 129 bis (3) of Ley de Propiedad Intelectual, https://www.boe.es/buscar/act.php?id=BOE-A-1996-8930#:~:text=La%20propiedad%20intelectual%20est%C3%A1%20integrada,las%20establecidas%20en%20la%20Ley, accessed: 15.08.2023

170 Section 52ZX(7) of the Australian Code.

171 Section 52ZZE of the Australian Code.

172 Sections 76(1)(a)(iaa), (1A)(b) and (4A)(h) of the Australian Code.

173 Google Search Central, "Updates to Google's services in Czechia in Light of the Czech transposition of the European Copyright Directive," December 12, 2022, https://developers.google.com/search/blog/2022/12/google-services-in-czechia, accessed: 09.12.2024.

174 Translation by the author. Czech version of Art. 87b, 105 of autorský zákon, https://www.zakonyprolidi.cz/cs/2000-121, accessed: 09.12.2024.

within the EU legal system, as similar penalties exist under the GDPR (up to 4% of global turnover) and the Digital Services Act (up to 6% of global turnover).[175]

Regarding the effectiveness of the solutions introduced in Australia, despite initial backlash against the Australian Code from digital platforms, including Google's threat to withdraw search services in Australia and of Meta's threat to shut down news feeds, [176] the Code has resulted in payments exceeding AU$200 million from these platforms to news publishers. It has been regarded as an effective tool for facilitating negotiations between news organisations and digital platforms.[177] In 2023, Canada adopted the Online News Act, which mirrors some of the mechanisms in the Australian Code to strengthen publishers' barging positions. However, it should be noted that copyright and competition law regimes differ significantly. Additionally, Australia's legal solutions are rooted in common law, which differs from the continental legal system. Therefore, legal solutions inspired by common law should be adapted to continental law with caution.

8.2. Failure to safeguard the situation of press publishers negotiating remuneration for the use of press publications

To prevent practices like those seen in France, in which Google offered the inferior display conditions to publishers that entered negotiations on remuneration for the use of press publications, the Italian legislature introduced a requirement that ISSPs must not limit the visibility of negotiating press publishers in search results during negotiations. Any unjustified restrictions as regards display conditions during this process may be evaluated to ensure compliance with the obligation to negotiate in good faith.[178]

Although the Italian solution does not impose financial sanctions for non-compliance, it represents an important step toward safeguarding the regulation's effectiveness. However, a practical issue arises: how can a press publisher prove that the visibility of their press publications has been reduced when ISSPs control the display data? A potential solution would be to extend the right to request information to include access to such data. According to media reports, several press publishers in Italy have already reached agreements without major changes

175 Ministry of Industry and Trade of Czech Republic, *Report on the Improvements of the IPR Protection and Enforcement in the Czech Republic in 2022: 2023 Special 301 Review*,https://downloads.regulations.gov/USTR-2022-0016-0073/attachment_1.pdf, accessed: 09.12.2024.

176 A. Schiffrin, "Platforms push back against laws like Australia's Media Bargaining Code," CEPR, July 20, 2022, https://cepr.org/platforms-push-back-against-laws-australias-media-bargaining-code, accessed: 26.07.2023.

177 R. Sims, "Instruments and objectives: Explaining the News Media Bargaining Code," Judith Neilson Institute for Journalism and Ideas, 3, 2022, https://jninstitute.org/wp-content/uploads/2022/05/Rod-Sims_News-Bargaining-Code_2022.pdf, accessed: 26.07.2023.

178 English version by the author. Italian version of Art. 43 bis (9) of Legge sul diritto d'autore, https://www.altalex.com/documents/codici-altalex/2014/06/26/legge-sul-diritto-d-autore#titolo1, accessed: 15.11.2022.

to Google's display policy or legal disputes.[179] In Spain, an additional obligation has been introduced to safeguard the editorial independence of publishers of press publications.[180]

The Czech legislature went a step further by introducing §87b(14)(b) of the copyright law, which prohibits ISSPs from circumventing publisher's rights. Specifically, ISSPs must not **arbitrarily restrict or regulate** an information society service in a discriminatory manner to avoid the need for authorisation to use a press publication from a particular publisher, unless there is a fair reason for such a restriction or regulation. This provision applies only when the ISSP is a dominant player in the market for the restricted or regulated service. If circumvention is established, the fine – similar to the penalty for violating Art. 87b(9) of the Czech copyright law, as discussed in Section 8.1. of this chapter – can be imposed under §105(1)(g) of the Czech copyright law.[181]

The Czech legislation aims to counteract practices like those seen in France, in which Google limited displayed content to only a headline and a link. However, this raises the question of whether such a measure interferes with the freedom to conduct business. The legislature clarifies that the provision applies only to major market players and only when restrictions are imposed without a fair reason. In line with the principle of proportionality, the measure seeks to balance conflicting interests without unduly harming platforms. Instead, it aims to protect publishers from the exploitation of market dominance. Given that press publishers are the weaker parties in these disputes and play a key role in fostering a democratic information society, providing them with legal support appears to be justified.

Poland, the last country to implement Art. 15, has not included any safeguards for negotiating press publishers. Given the documented practices of platforms and their negative impact on publishers, this omission should be understood as a shortcoming. While the Czech approach may be considered radical, the Polish legislature could have drawn inspiration from the Italian model. The absence of regulation in this area may stem from a desire to avoid provoking platforms, preventing them from taking even more drastic measures against dependent publishers. Time will tell if this was the right choice.

8.3. Insufficient safeguards for the transparency of the remuneration calculations for press publishers

The Italian implementation, like the French one, includes the obligation for ISSPs to provide the data necessary to determine publishers' remuneration for the use of

179 The Economic Times, "Google agrees to pay Italian publishers for news," March 25, 2021, https://economictimes.indiatimes.com/tech/technology/google-agrees-to-pay-italian-publishers-for-news/articleshow/81683034.cms?utm_source=contentofinterest&utm_medium=text&utm_campaign=cppst,accessed: 07.01.2025.

180 See: 129 bis (3) of Ley de Propiedad Intelectual.

181 English version by the author. Czech version of Art. 87b, 105 of autorský zákon, https://www.zakonyprolidi.cz/cs/2000-121, accessed: 09.12.2024.

press publications. However, the Italian legislature goes a step further by stipulating that if the required data is not provided within 30 days of the request, the Authority may impose an administrative sanction of up to 1% of the defaulting party's turnover from the last financial year closed prior to the dispute notification.[182] Similarly, the Czech legislature has introduced a fine of up to CZK 500,000 or up to 1% of the total annual worldwide turnover from the previous financial year, whichever is higher, for failing to provide the data necessary to calculate remuneration.[183]

Given the reluctance of some ISSPs in France to provide data and the manner in which they have done so, as discussed earlier in this chapter, the introduction of a sanction is a significant step toward improving compliance. It enhances the provision of necessary data for determining remuneration and helps safeguard the effectiveness of publishers' rights.

The Belgian legislature, Art. XI.216/2 §3 of the Code of Economic Law, mandates that ISSPs must provide press publishers, upon written request, with **up-to-date, relevant and complete** information regarding the exploitation of their press publications. This allows publishers to assess the value of their rights. Specifically, ISSPs must disclose **the number of consultations of press publications and the revenues generated from their exploitation.**[184] The requested information must be provided within one month from the day after the publisher's notification and may not be used for any purpose other than assessing the value of the rights. The information provided will be treated as strictly confidential. Although the legislature has specified the types of data that may be requested, the applicant should still clearly specify and elaborate on the exact information needed to ensure a precise and comprehensive request.

In Art. 99[11] of the Polish Copyright Act it is specified that the press publisher shall have the right to:

1) receive **up-to-date** information from the service provider,
2) have access to the service provider's documentation to the extent necessary to determine the amount of remuneration owed for the exercise of publishers' rights.

The information and data obtained by the publisher pursuant to Paragraph 1 shall be used exclusively for determining the remuneration owed to the publisher.

When requesting information from an ISSP under Art. 99,[11] the applicant must specify in detail the type of information being requested. Simply stating that the

182 English version by the author. Italian version of Art. 43 bis (12) of Legge sul diritto d'autore, https://www.altalex.com/documents/codici-altalex/2014/06/26/legge-sul-diritto-d-autore#titolo1, accessed: 15.11.2022.

183 According to Art. 105b of autorský zákon, https://www.zakonyprolidi.cz/cs/2000-121, accessed: 09.12.2024.

184 English version by the author. French version of Art. XI.216/2 §3 of the Code of Economic Law, https://www.ejustice.just.fgov.be/eli/loi/2013/02/28/2013A11134/justel, accessed: 24.07.2023.

information should be up-to date will likely be insufficient to obtain detailed data on the use of press publications. Unlike the Belgian legislature, the Polish legislature did not explicitly require that the information be complete. However, this should not be an issue if the data request is formulated comprehensively. The provision stating that information obtained from ISSPs will be used solely to determine the amount of remuneration is intended to address concerns raise by ISSPs, who may be reluctant to share data due to fears of misuse that could compromise business confidentiality.

To conclude:

- in some MS, independent bodies play a crucial role in determining remuneration when the parties fail to reach an agreement. Given the relatively weak bargaining position of press publishers – due to the significant market power of certain ISSPs and publishers' economic dependence on them – the involvement of public bodies can enhance the effectiveness of publishers' protection. However, there is a risk that such measures could exceed the margin of discretion granted to MS in implementing the CDSM Directive, which should be carefully considered.
- the Italian legislature introduced an obligation preventing ISSPs from limiting the visibility of publishers' content in search results during negotiations. Similarly, the Czech legislature implemented sanctions for arbitrarily restricting or regulating an information society service. These legal measures are designed to strengthen publishers' negotiating position.
- because ISSPs hold the information necessary to calculate the remuneration owed to press publishers, measures requiring that the data provided be up-to-date, relevant and complete, as in Belgium, or at least up-to-date, as in Poland, are important for facilitating data provision. In any case, applicants should specify their data requests as precisely as possible. In Italy, failure to provide such data results in an administrative pecuniary sanction imposed by an independent body. Similarly, the Czech Republic has introduced sanctions, which may effectively compel ISSPs to comply with data requests.

9. Conclusion

Press publishers are granted exclusive rights of *erga omnes* nature, though their practical scope is limited, allowing claims to be directed only against a specific group, namely ISSPs using press publications in the online environment. This restriction benefits the free flow of information, as publishers' rights do not extend to users who are not ISSPs. ISSPs include any natural or legal persons providing an information society service for remuneration, broadly defined to encompass income generated from advertisements or personal data, provided remotely, electronically and at the individual request of a service recipient. Press publishers have been granted reproduction and making available rights, interpreted broadly based on several criteria established by the CJEU.

The freedom to use a press publication applies to individual users who access press content for private or non-commercial purposes and are not ISSPs. The exclusion of private or non-commercial uses should be understood as an alternative criterion. A systemic and purposive analysis of this exclusion suggests "individual users" should be interpreted broadly, potentially including legal persons, such as non-profit organisations.

Mandatory intermediation by collective management organisations has not been required, reflecting the significant differences in press publishers' interests. From a research perspective, evaluating the effectiveness of the publishers' rights would require studying and comparing agreements between press publishers and ISSPs to assess the impact on the regulation's intended objectives. However, such an analysis depends on access to information about the agreements reached between the parties.

The analysis of French publishers' case revealed that press publishers' rights, both at the EU and French levels, lacked mechanisms to protect press publishers from exploitation of their dependence on ISSPs and the negative effects of market power imbalances between the two actors. The absence of such measures allowed the regulation to be circumvented, ultimately undermining its effectiveness and intended purpose.

A clear trend has emerged in the implementation of Art. 15 of the CDSM Directive following the French example. To ensure the effectiveness of publishers' protections, some MS have introduced mechanisms to strengthen press publishers' negotiating positions. This approach is justified by the specific relationship between ISSPs and press publishers, the imbalance in bargaining power and the dominant market position of platforms, which enables them to dictate terms for the use of press publications. The analysis of the French case in this chapter demonstrated that granting exclusive rights alone, without additional safeguards, may be insufficient to achieve the objectives behind publishers' rights, namely, safeguarding media pluralism and ensuring the free flow of information.

4 Press publishers' rights in the context of access to information and media pluralism – conclusions and recommendations

1. Introduction

The final chapter assesses the related rights of press publishers in the context of market realities. It then examines whether these rights interfere with fundamental rights and, if so, whether such interference is justified. A key part of the analysis involves determining the extent of MS' discretion in implementing Art. 15 of the CDSM Directive and how freely they can choose the means to achieve the law's objectives. This evaluation is crucial for the final stage of the analysis, which focuses on identifying potential threats posed by press publishers' rights to media pluralism and the free flow of information at both the EU level and within the national laws discussed. Additionally, the objective is to propose remedies that are crucial at the stage of applying the law and to identify key elements that contribute to balancing the protection of the publishers' interests with the free flow of information and media pluralism. The proposed mechanisms will serve as a source of inspiration for future regulations concerning the relationship between various media and their impact on freedom of expression and information flow.

2. Press market realities

This section aims to assess publishers' rights within the context of press market realities, focusing on the economic consequences of their adoption. It explores the relationship between press publishers and ISSPs as well as the dynamics among different press publishers following the adoption of these rights. In this monograph, press market realities are defined as the interdependencies among various actors shaping press sector, influencing business models and determining the methods of information production and dissemination.[1]

1 Definition formulated on the basis of criteria established in: European Commission, *Market Definition in the Media Sector – Economic Issues*, Report by Europe Economics for the European Commission, Report by Bird & Bird for the European Commission, Directorate-General for Competition, Information, communication and multimedia 2002, https://op.europa.eu/en/publication-detail/-/publication/e438a087-8dd9-450d-85f4-bf3a02b98ca9/language-en, accessed: 08.01.2025.

DOI: 10.4324/9781003599494-4

2.1. Publishers' rights – an answer to market failure?

It is widely recognised that the press industry is facing a stage of market failure.[2] This term, understood as a market's inability to deliver an optimal outcome, refers to situations in which "less welfare is created than could be created given the available resources. The social task then becomes to correct the failure."[3] R. M. Hilty and V. Moscon describe market failure as occurring when third parties benefit from goods or services in a way that prevents the original investors from generating profit.[4] The EU legislature identified press publishers as victims of such practices by ISSPs and introduced publishers' rights as a means to address this market failure. These rights were designed to provide press publishers with "an efficient tool against aggregators" and a mechanism to fight the "mass exploitation of press publications in the digital economy."[5]

Because the remuneration amounts paid by ISSPs to press publishers under the new law are often confidential, evaluating and comparing the conditions received by different press publishers is challenging. This lack of transparency also makes it difficult to assess whether the objectives of publishers' rights are being met. As a result, it is impossible to conclude whether the adoption of related rights effectively addressed the market failure.

While proposing a solution to address market failure, the EU legislature focused on legally regulating the use of press publications by ISSPs and strengthening the legal position of press publishers in response to competition from online platforms in the dissemination of information. However, other factors contributing to the challenges faced by the press sector – as identified in the first chapter of the monograph, such as technological issues in implementing subscription models, struggles in adapting business models to the digital environment and the lack of effective measures to counter readers' reluctance to pay for subscriptions – were not addressed by the introduction of publishers' rights. Publishers' rights are supposed to generate additional revenue, which, in turn, should improve the overall welfare of the press sector. However, given the broader challenges faced by the industry, this approach may be seen as a piecemeal solution rather than a comprehensive remedy.

Publishers' rights target ISSPs and may be seen as burdens that make the use of press publications more costly and complex. This could discourage platforms from investing in the reuse of press content[6] and push them toward developing business models based on their own information production, a trend likely to accelerate

2 See: P. Napoli, *Social Media and the Public Interest: Media Regulation in the Disinformation Age, New York Chichester* (West Sussex: Columbia University Press, 2019); P. Walters, "A public good: Can government *really* save the press?," *Sage Journals* 23, no. 8 (2020), https://journals.sagepub.com/doi/full/10.1177/1464884920982404, accessed: 09.10.2023.

3 E. Baekkeskov, "Market failure," Britannica, https://www.britannica.com/money/topic/market-failure, accessed: 09.10.2023.

4 R. M.Hilty, V. Moscon, *Modernisation*, 4.

5 T. Höppner, *The Proposed*, 4.

6 J. Moeller, N. Helberger, "Beyond," 24–25.

with the increased use of artificial intelligence (AI). A legislative approach that fails to consider the interdependencies between press publishers and ISSPs, as demonstrated in the first chapter, as well as the important role of online platforms in dissemination of information, risks being counterproductive. [7]

2.2. *Publishers' rights and the vertical complementarity between ISSPs and press publishers*

In response to the adoption of publishers' rights in France, Google gave press publishers a choice: either allow their content to be displayed for free or restrict it to hyperlinks and headlines if they chose to enforce their rights. Under Google's new display policy, press publishers decide the length of the excerpts shown. However, the majority opted not to impose restrictions.[8] From a practical standpoint, this indicates that most press publishers chose not to enforce their rights, allowing Google to use full articles excerpts out of concern that limiting display could reduce their visibility and, consequently, harm their revenue. Such decisions can be explained by the relationship of vertical complementarity between ISSPs and press publishers.[9] Displaying text with an accompanying image improves publishers' visibility in the digital environment, resulting in higher click-through rate and, consequently, greater profits. *A contrario*, displaying only hyperlinks or, even worse, removing publishers from ISSPs services altogether significantly reduces website traffic and revenue, as demonstrated in Section 7.1. of Chapter 3 in the case of French press publishers.[10] This confirms the interdependencies established in Chapter 1 between the interests of press publishers and ISSPs, highlighting the strong dependence of publishers on online platforms.[11]

Although some French press publishers managed to reach agreements with Google following intervention of the authorities and the penalty imposed on the company,[12] the interdependencies between ISSPs and publishers continue to shape their relationship. I have identified several threats in this regard. First, ISSPs may offer press publishers lower remuneration in exchange for better display positioning. Second, online platforms may use the publishers' dependence to influence the type and subject matter of content published by press publishers.

7 See: H. Coster, "As Google pushes deeper into AI, publishers see fresh challenges," Reuters, October 19, 2023, https://www.reuters.com/technology/google-pushes-deeper-into-ai-publishers-see-fresh-challenges-2023-10-19/, accessed: 23.10.2023.
8 FCA, Decision of April 9, 2020 on interim measures, 55.
9 See Chapter 1.
10 Decision of FCA of April 9, 2020 on interim measures, 30–32.
11 See Chapter 1.
12 S. Missoffe, "Google a signé plus de 150 contrats portant sur les droits voisins, tandis que l'Autorité de la Concurrence accepte ses engagements," Google Blog France, July 22, 2022, https://blog.google/intl/fr-fr/nouvelles-de-lentreprise/chez-google/google-a-signe-plus-de-150-contrats-portant-sur-les-droits-voisins-tandis-que-lautorite-de-la-concurrence-accepte-ses-engagements/, accessed: 08.08.2023.

To calculate the remuneration for the use of press publications, information from both press publishers and ISSPs is required. The data provided by ISSPs includes details on their profits from displaying press publications or excerpts, the number of impressions and the number of clicks, among other metrics. Because ISSPs control this data, press publishers are dependent on them to determine their remuneration. The final amount depends on the figures reported for clicks, visits and impressions, making publishers heavily dependent on the accuracy and transparency of ISSP-provided data.

The risk of discretion and fragmented reporting of data, which impacts the interests of press publishers, must be pointed out. With the rapid advancement of new technologies and the emergence of new methods for using press publications, press publishers increasingly argue that the data shared by ISSPs does not accurately reflect the actual state of affairs.[13]

2.3. Publishers' rights and two speed press industry

The adoption and exercise of publishers' rights in France highlighted and sharpened the differences in the interests of press publishers. For some, enforcing these rights was less beneficial than maintaining the existing relationship with ISSPs.[14] This was particularly true for smaller publishers with weaker negotiating power and those covering topics unrelated to politics or general information, as these factors influenced remuneration. Moreover, large press publishers enjoyed a more privileged negotiating position with Google,[15] which further contributed to the fragmentation of the press market. A report on the implementation of publishers' rights in France noted that the lack of cooperation among press publishers resulted in the signing of individual and bilateral agreements rather than a collective bargaining approach. These agreements primarily benefited the largest players in the sector, who are, however, a minority.[16] This outcome reinforces a "winner-takes-all" dynamic.[17] Additionally, the criteria used to calculate press publishers' remuneration can further contribute to market fragmentation.

If remuneration criteria favour large publishers with extensive journalistic staff and significant investments, this negatively impacts small and niche publishers,

13 Statement of Irene Lanzaco for Press Gazette. Future of Media see in: A. Majid, "Publishers square up for new battle with Google in Spain," Presse Gazette. Future of Media (2023), https://pressgazette.co.uk/platforms/google-news-spain-facebook-challenge/, accessed: 12.03.2025.

14 See: A. Mendoza-Caminade, "Le droit voisin des éditeurs de presse et des agences de presse à l'épreuve de la puissance des plateformes en ligne: la longue marche vers l'effectivité du droit," *Revue Lamy de la concurrence* no. 106 (2021).

15 See the detailed analysis of the agreements reached by Google and press publishers in France in: Ch. Papaevangelou, N. Smyrnaios, "Regulating dependency: The political stakes of online platforms' deals with French publishers," *Anàlisi: Quaderns de Comunicació i Cultura* no. 68 (2023): 117–134, https://shs.hal.science/halshs-03747847/document, accessed: 08.08.2023.

16 V. Duby-Muller, L. Garcia, *Rapport*, 28–29.

17 See Chapter 1.

further deepening the divide between successful large publishers and smaller ones struggling to stay in the market.[18]

2.4. Publishers' rights and AI

In December 2023, *The New York Times* sued OpenAI and Microsoft for the unauthorised reproduction of its publications during the training of a GPT model. The newspaper alleged that Microsoft, through Bing Chat (recently rebranded as "Copilot"), and OpenAI, through ChatGPT, were attempting to free ride on "The *Times's* massive investment in its journalism by using it to build substitutive products without permission or payment."[19] Similarly, in November 2024, Canadian press publishers filed a lawsuit against OpenAI for using news content to train its ChatGPT generative AI system. According to the publishers, "OpenAI is capitalizing and profiting from the use of this content, without getting permission or compensating content owners."[20] In the EU, despite the adoption of the publishers' rights, concerns about their ineffectiveness in addressing challenges posed by AI's use of press publications are growing. For example, during a dispute before the FCA, press publishers alleged that they were neither informed no able to verify whether their press publications had been used to train Google's AI, Gemini. Additionally, they expressed frustration over the lack of effective technical tools to prevent the use of their materials by AI[21] and the absence of remuneration for such usage.

Some commentators argue that the press industry plays a crucial role in AI development, as it possesses highly valuable assets: "text data for training models and ethical principles for creating reliable and trustworthy systems."[22] In EU copyright law, the legal basis for using press publications for AI training can be found in Articles 3 and 4 of the CDSM Directive, which introduce the text and data mining (TDM) exceptions and apply to press publishers' rights. According to Art. 4 of the CDSM Directive, Member States must establish an exception or limitation to the reproduction right, allowing for reproductions and extractions of lawfully accessible works for TDM purposes. These reproductions and extractions may be retained for as long as necessary to fulfil the purposes of text and data mining.

18 See for example the factors established by the Italian legislator, section 4.5, Chapter 4.

19 United States District Court, Southern District of New York, The New York Times Company v. Microsoft Corporation et al., filed 27.12.2023, 2, https://nytco-assets.nytimes.com/2023/12/NYT_Complaint_Dec2023.pdf, accessed: 22.04. 2024.

20 AP, "Canadian news publishers sue OpenAI over alleged copyright infringement," November 29, 2024, https://apnews.com/article/canada-news-publishers-lawsuit-chatgpt-3e1790fcf4c9f001f1d32609c4d547af, accessed: 23.12.2024.

21 FCA, Decision of March 15, 2024 on non-compliance with the commitments of June 21, 2022, 36-40.

22 M. Adami, "Is ChatGPT a threat or an opportunity for journalism? Five AI experts weigh in," March 23, 2023,https://reutersinstitute.politics.ox.ac.uk/news/chatgpt-threat-or-opportunity-journalism-five-ai-experts-weigh, accessed: 23.11.2023.

The application of this exception to the development and training phase of large generative models is confirmed in Recital 105 of the AI Act.[23] As a result, any publicly available press publication that does not include an appropriate reservation of rights – such as through machine-readable means (e.g., metadata) or in the terms and conditions of a website or service – can be used for AI training without the press publishers' authorisation. Furthermore, Art. 4 of the CDSM Directive does not provide for any remuneration for the use of content for this purpose.

It is hoped that several concerns raised by press publishers, especially those regarding transparency of AI's use of their press publications and the effectiveness of the opt-out mechanism, will be addressed with the adoption of the General-Purpose Artificial Intelligence Code of Practice. This initiative aims to facilitate the implementation of rules governing general-purpose AI models under the AI Act, which will come into effect in August 2025.[24] Regarding remuneration, some press publishers have already signed agreements with ISSPs for the use of their press publications.[25] However, a more systemic discussion on this matter is necessary.

To conclude:

- publishers' rights were introduced to address market failure in the press sector. However, due to the confidentiality of agreements between press publishers and ISSPs, it is impossible to conclude whether these rights have effectively achieved this goal. The EU legislature's approach focused on strengthening press publishers' legal position regarding the use of their press publications by ISSPs. From a broader perspective, however, this legislative step is a piecemeal solution, as it does not address other issues challenging the welfare of the press industry, such as technological difficulties in implementing subscriptions, adapting business models and overcoming readers' reluctance to pay for content. As a result, it may be insufficient to fully remedy the market failure. Moreover, there is a risk that publishers' rights will contribute to the fragmentation of the press market and reinforce a "winner-takes-all" dynamic. At the same time, AI presents both opportunities and challenges to the press sector, highlighting the need for a systemic discussion on the use of press publications in AI.

23 For the further analysis see: M. Kowala, "Protection."

24 European Commission, "General-Purpose AI Code of Practice," https://digital-strategy.ec.europa.eu/en/policies/ai-code-practice, accessed: 23.12.2024.

25 Y. Bourgin, "Droits voisins: un accord conclu au Monde, 25% seront reversés aux journalistes," L'UsineDigitale, June 10, 2024, https://www.usine-digitale.fr/article/droits-voisins-un-accord-conclu-au-monde-25-seront-reverses-aux-journalistes.N2214416, accessed: 23.12.2024 ; M. Alcaraz, "OpenAI signe un accord avec le groupe de presse Condé Nast," LesEchos, August 21, 2024, https://www.lesechos.fr/tech-medias/intelligence-artificielle/openai-signe-un-accord-avec-le-groupe-de-presse-conde-nast-2114539, accessed: 23.12.2024.

3. Obligation to respect freedom of expression and information in light of the adoption of the press publishers' rights

3.1. The press publishers' rights as a limitation of the exercise of the right to freedom of expression and information

As demonstrated in the analysis conducted in the first chapter, fundamental rights interact with each other – they can be complementary and conflicting, sometimes creating paradoxical situations.[26]

Publishers' rights were adopted with the objective of preserving access to information, ensuring its free flow and safeguarding media pluralism. However, extending exclusive rights to a new category of right holders, press publishers, may also limit access to information. By granting publishers the power to authorise or prohibit access to content within press publications, these rights could be seen as **an interference with freedom of expression**.

3.2. Justifications for the limitation of the exercise of the right to freedom of expression and information

For an interference with fundamental rights to be considered justified,[27] it must meet specific criteria: it must be prescribed by law, pursue a legitimate aim and comply with the principle of proportionality. The purpose of this section is to assess whether the publishers' rights constitute a justified interference with freedom of expression and information.

3.2.1. Prescription by law

Publishers' protection is prescribed by law, as established in the CDSM Directive. As noted in the first chapter, the law should be formulated with sufficient precision. While the analysis of press publishers' rights in previous chapters has highlighted several interpretative doubts, these can be clarified through case law and practice. Moreover, these uncertainties do not call into question the essence of the law.

The EU legislature justified its competence to adopt the publishers' rights under Art. 114 of the TFEU, aiming to harmonise the legal framework and ensure the proper functioning of the internal market. While the regulation indirectly addresses media pluralism – one of its intended effects – it remains within the EU's legislative competence and does not extend beyond its designated scope in this field.[28]

3.2.2. Legitimate aim

Interference with fundamental rights must align with objectives of general interest. The adoption of publishers' rights aimed to:

26 See Chapter 1, Section 2.3.
27 See: Chapter 1, Section 2.5.
28 See: Chapter 1, Section 3.

- strengthen the bargain position of press publishers;
- increase press publishers' revenues to help recoup their investments and ensure the sustainability of press publishing industry;
- foster the availability of reliable information and strengthen freedom of expression and media pluralism.

The EU legislature highlighted that press publishers suffered from the decline in print newspaper revenues, competition with online platforms and challenges in transitioning to the digital landscape. However, this raises the question of whether experiencing difficulties due to competition or technological transformation should automatically warrant legal protection. The answer is no, unless there is a compelling justification for introduction of such protection. For press publishers, this justification lies in their role in disseminating information and providing access to reliable content, which is essential for the functioning of democratic society.

The prosperity of the press sector serves as a safeguard for media pluralism and the free flow of information. Therefore, the protection of press publishers constitutes a legitimate aim, justifying the interference with freedom of expression. However, because the adoption of publishers' rights both interferes with and seeks to promote freedom of expression, this reflects the paradox of rights being simultaneously complementary and conflicting.

3.2.3. Proportionality

3.2.3.1. EFFECTIVENESS

In regard to the criterion of effectiveness, it is essential to assess whether the adoption of publishers' rights is suitable for achieving the intended objectives. Before the adoption of the CDSM Directive, press publishers claimed that their bargaining position was weak because they were not recognised as right holders under EU law.[29] In response, the EU legislature extended exclusive rights to press publishers, aiming to strengthen their ability to negotiate agreements with ISSPs. This measure was expected to lead to higher revenues for press publishers, which, in turn, would contribute to a more sustainable press sector, benefiting the free flow of information and media pluralism. However, it should be noted that in its Impact Assessment, the European Commission did not provide detailed data or specific calculations regarding the impact of publishers' rights on increasing press publishers' revenues.[30] While it can be assumed that granting related rights may generate revenue for publishers, making the measure potentially suitable for achieving its objective, the lack of concrete data makes it difficult to determine the scale of these revenues and the effectiveness of the adopted measures.

29 See: European Commission, *Impact Assessment*, 157–158.

30 See: Chapter 2, Section 3.

3.2.3.2. NECESSITY

When adopting new legislation, the EU legislature must ensure that no less intrusive measure could achieve the legitimate goal while causing less harm to the affected fundamental rights. In this case, the EU legislature determined that the adoption of publishers' rights was necessary to address a pressing social need, thereby justifying the interference with fundamental rights.

In the Impact Assessment, three alternative solutions were proposed to address the challenges faced by press publishers.[31] Option 1 focused on encouraging stakeholder dialogue and cooperation to find solutions concerning the dissemination of press publications. Option 2 proposed introducing a related right in EU law to cover digital uses of press publications. Option 3 expanded on Option 2 by allowing MS to grant press publishers the right to claim compensation for such uses under an exception.

It was noted that the third option "is the most proportionate as it allows addressing in a targeted way and in their own merits the specific problems faced by different categories of publishers, without going beyond what is needed to achieve this objective."[32] This option was expected to increase the protection of press publications and promote the quality of journalistic content.[33]

However, the legislature did not provide details on how these conclusions were reached, nor did it specify the methods or tools used in the assessment. S. Karapapa pointed out that even though

> the Commission offers statistical evidence on the extent of the so-called newspaper crisis, the claims on the casual relationship between the introduction of a press publishers intellectual property right and the increase in the revenues of the press leading to media diversity are neither supported nor substantiated with data.[34]

It should be noted that no alternative regulatory approaches beyond the related rights' regime were considered.[35] The EU legislature's decision can be explained by the rationale behind the adoption of these rights, which was to reward press publishers for their investment, ensure the wider dissemination of works included in press publications and protect press publishers from the threat of piracy by ISSPs.

31 See: European Commission, *Impact Assessment*, 161–164.

32 European Commission, *Impact Assessment*, 173.

33 European Commission, *Impact Assessment*, 170. See also: European Commission, Proposal, Explanatory Memorandum, 9.

34 S. Karapapa, "The press publication right in the European union: An overreaching proposal and the future of news online," in *Non-Conventional Copyright: Do New and Non-Traditional Works Deserve Protection?*, ed. E. Bonadio and N. Lucchi (Edward Elgar, 2018), 7.

35 For example, the EU legislator did not envisage the introduction of taxation model, see: P. Keller, "The press publishers right will fail – to support the media we should tax information aggregators instead," Shared Digital Europe, April 30, 2020, https://shared-digital.eu/as-predicted-the-new-press-publishers-right-is-a-failure-lets-make-information-aggregators-pay-news-media-producers-for-real/, accessed: 04.11.2023.

While this choice of legal framework appears justified, it does not fully address the consequences of the complex relationship between press publishers and ISSPs. In particular, it overlooks the unresolved challenges stemming from the ISSPs' dominant market position and the impact this imbalance has on press publishers.

3.2.3.3. PROPORTIONALITY (IN A NARROW SENSE)

According to Recital 84 of the CDSM Directive, "this Directive respects the fundamental rights and follows the principles recognised in particular by the Charter." In regard to related rights of press publishers, the Explanatory Memorandum asserts that "the proposal is proportionate as it only covers press publications and digital uses."[36] However, I have identified an important missing point in the assessment of these rights. While balancing the various interests at stake, the EU legislature did not account for the positive effect news aggregators on press publishers, particularly for small and local publishers, for whom visibility on such platforms is of vital importance.[37] The legislature did not analyse how this relationship would be affected by the introduction of the new rights. While this identified deficiency does not necessarily mean that the regulation fails the proportionality test, it is, in my opinion, legitimate to conclude that it may affect, in the later stages, the effectiveness of the granted protection.

It should be noted that the extension of exclusive rights has been balanced with the exceptions and limitations. Additionally, publishers' rights apply against a specific category of entities, ISSPs, meaning that individual users are not directly affected by this regulation. The scope of publishers' rights is also limited. The definition of the subject matter of protection extends only to protected content. These elements serve as safeguards for the free flow of information, aiming to balance the expanded protection granted by extending exclusive rights to new actors.

The core of the right to receive information, as established in Chapter 1, is the public's right to be adequately informed, particularly on matters of public interest. This means that access to available information cannot be unjustifiably restricted. Despite the introduction of publishers' rights, the public can still access publicly available information, ensuring that the fundamental right to be informed is preserved. Media, as a key player in information dissemination, should remain pluralistic to ensure the free expression of diverse ideas and viewpoints. However, the new layer of protection may limit access to information if, for example, ISSPs choose not to display press publications, if press publishers refuse to authorise their use or if the amount of information displayed on ISSPs is significantly reduced. This does not, however, mean that the public will lose access to information entirely or to significant extent. Rather, it suggests that they may need to seek

36 It is not further specified what should be covered in addition to press publications and digital uses to make the proposal disproportionate. See: European Commission, Proposal, Explanatory Memorandum.

37 See: S. Athey, M. Mobius, J. Pal, "The impact."

alternative sources. Because the core of the right to receive information – an essential component of freedom of expression – remains intact, it can be, in my opinion, concluded that the principle of proportionality is upheld, and the interference with freedom of expression is justified.

To conclude:

- the adoption of publishers' rights constitutes a justified interference with freedom of expression. This conclusion is supported in practice, as no action for annulment of the act has been brought under Art. 263 of the TFEU. Furthermore, the time limit for initiating such an action has already expired, according to Art. 263(6) of the TFEU.
- although the adoption of publishers' rights does not infringe upon the core of freedom of expression, the EU legislature's assessment prior to their adoption exhibited certain deficiencies. I identified a lack of examination in the following areas:
  - the market position of ISSP and the extent of press publishers' dependence on online platforms
  - the impact of the publishers' rights on ISSPs' activities that facilitate the dissemination of information and increase content diversity in the online environment.
  - the need for safeguards against ISSPs imposing unfavourable negotiating conditions and exploiting market asymmetries. despite indications that such practices could arise, given Google's reaction to the introduction of press publishers' rights in Spain in 2014.
- the insufficient assessment of the related rights before their adoption, while not affecting the validity of publishers' rights, may render the regulation incomplete, lacking important mechanisms, and ineffective. Addressing some of these shortcomings will largely depend on how MS exercise their margin of discretion in implementing the CDSM Directive.

3.3. Scope of Member States' margin of discretion in the implementation of press publishers' rights

The objective of this section is to determine the scope of MS' margin of discretion in implementing Art. 15 of the CDSM Directive. This analysis aims to identify the types of legal interventions that can be adopted to address the insufficiencies in Art. 15, as identified in the analysis conducted in previous chapters.

Directives, as legal instruments of the EU, provide a degree of flexibility within EU law. They are binding regarding the objectives to be achieved but allow MS some extent of discretion in selecting the methods and forms of implementation.[38] The scope of this discretion includes choosing among the options provided in the Directive, further specifying EU legal norms or adopting more stringent

38 P. Craig, G.de Burca, *EU Law, Text, Cases and Materials* (Oxford University Press, 2008), 106–107.

standards.[39] The CJEU provides guidance on how MS should implement directives. In its judgement on Poland's action for the annulment of Art. 17 of the CDSM Directive, the Court stated,

> Member States must, when transposing Article 17 of Directive 2019/790 into their national law, take care to act on the basis of an interpretation of that provision which allows a fair balance to be struck between the various fundamental rights protected by the Charter. Further, when implementing the measures transposing that same provision, the authorities and courts of the Member States must not only interpret their national law in a manner consistent with that provision but also make sure that they do not act on the basis of an interpretation of the provision which would be in conflict with those fundamental rights or with the other general principles of EU law, such as the principle of proportionality.[40]

When adapting this reasoning to the implementation of Art. 15 of the CDSM Directive, it should be noted that MS must adopt an interpretation of the implemented provisions that ensures a fair balance between various fundamental rights. Moreover, transposition entails additional obligations: once the provision is implemented, national law must be interpreted consistently with it, ensuring that its application does not conflict with fundamental rights or the general principles of EU law.

Publishers' rights are an example of maximum harmonisation, meaning that the level of protection granted to press publishers at the national level cannot be more or less extensive than what is established by the Directive. As a result, in every MS, press publishers must be granted exclusive rights to authorise and prohibit reproduction and making available of press publications as stipulated in Art. 15(1) of the CDSM Directive. Furthermore, according to Art. 15(2), these rights must not affect any rights already granted under EU law to authors and other right holders concerning the works and other subject matter included in a press publication.

Nevertheless, MS are free to specify the circumstances under which authorisation for the use of press publication is granted. In implementing the Art. 15, they should adopt solutions that increase of press publishers' revenue and allow them to recoup their investments, as these are the objectives of the new law. Given the identified risk of ISSPs imposing unfavourable negotiating conditions – particularly in light of the 2014 Spanish case – national legislatures should introduce necessary safeguards to prevent such practices. The objective of MS should be to ensure the effectiveness of the publishers' rights.

39 See: S. Princen, H. Smekal, R. Zbíral, "Mapping the legal scope for flexible implementation in EU directives," RSC 2022/46 Robert Schuman Centre for Advanced Studies Integrating Diversity in the European Union (InDivEU) (2022), 8.

40 CJEU, Republic of Poland v European Parliament, Council of the European Union, Case C-401/19, April 26, 2022, para.99. See also: CJEU, Promusicae v. Telefónica de España SAU, Case C-275/06, January 29, 2008, para. 68.

As established in the previous section, at the EU level, the impact of publishers' rights on increasing press publishers' revenues and enabling them to recoup their investments has not been sufficiently examined. While national legislatures cannot adopt a different legal regime or expand the scope of protection beyond what is provided in the Directive, they can adopt more stringent standards and more specific solutions to facilitate the process of obtaining remuneration for the authorisation of press publication use.

Because one of the objectives of adopting publishers' rights was to foster the availability of reliable information and strengthen freedom of expression and media pluralism, MS could consider introducing reporting obligations for agreements reached with press publishers. Additionally, they could require ISSPs to conduct audits to ensure compliance with the adopted provisions. Such measures could be justified by the public interest in protecting the free flow of information and safeguarding media pluralism. Furthermore, MS should carefully define the subject matter of protection and clarify exclusions from its scope to prevent any unintended restrictions on access to information. By doing so, they can eliminate potential risks while ensuring that the regulation effectively fulfils its intended objectives while maintaining to access to information and media pluralism.

To conclude:

- the margin of discretion for MS in implementing publishers' rights is limited due to the principle of maximum harmonisation. The transposition of Art. 15 of the CDSM Directive should include legal safeguards and, where necessary, introduce more specific and stringent standards to effectively achieve the Directive's objectives. However, this must be done without exceeding the discretion granted to MS in implementing the provision.

4. Legal framework in the EU and national laws for access to information and press publishing activity after the adoption of press publishers' rights – toward a balanced model of interpretation

The adoption of press publishers' rights has introduced changes to the legal framework governing access to information. This section aims to examine how the scope of protection under the copyright and related rights regime has evolved in the context of press publishing, specifically focusing on the new subject matter since the adoption of the publishers' rights, the holder of protection and its scope.

One of the objectives of press publishers' rights was to foster the availability of reliable information and strengthen freedom of expression and media pluralism. However, the analysis conducted in this monograph has revealed that certain risks to the free flow of information and media pluralism may arise from the scope and wording of Art. 15 of the CDSM Directive and its national implementations. This section aims to analyse the risks and dangers associated with publishers' rights, explaining how may threaten freedom of expression and proposing legal remedies to limit their counterproductive effects. The analysis will be based on the assessment of the criteria of media pluralism established in Chapter 1.

4.1. Subject matter of protection

4.1.1. Definition of press publication and scope of public domain

Public domain exists *de facto* and is primarily understood through a negative[41] approach, meaning it encompasses anything not covered by copyright protection. Public domain guarantees absolute and unrestricted enjoyment of the materials it contains. As the name suggests, the public domain consists of elements that belong to everyone. Public domain serves as a foundation for intellectual process, fostering innovation and creation. It guarantees unrestricted access to ideas, facts, principles and methods – key drivers of societal development. Additionally, it includes materials that do not meet the copyright protection requirements. A subject matter qualifies as a work only if it meets certain criteria, such as a degree of originality and, under certain legislation, individuality or fixations of the expression. If an expression does not have these features, it falls into the scope of public domain. Another component of public domain consists of works for which copyright protection has expired.[42] It also includes elements excluded from copyright protection on public policy grounds,[43] such as news of the day, miscellaneous facts or official acts. Finally, works can enter the public domain through the voluntary act of the author of the work relinquishing their rights.

The public domain aims to foster creative development, enhance economic benefits related to the reuse of unprotected works or elements that were never protected. The informative and cultural heritage rationales underlying the public domain are particularly relevant to this monograph, as public domain facilitates access to information.[44]

According to C. Geiger, O. Bulayenko and G. Frosio, "lifting materials out of the public domain has unwanted consequences, impinging greatly on freedom of expression and democratisation, while favouring centralisation of information."[45] The adoption of protection for a new subject matter can limit the scope of public domain, as elements that were previously unprotected become subject to exclusive rights.

41 See: M. Birnhack, "More or Better? Shaping the public domain," in *The Public Domain of Information,* ed.
P.B. Hugenholtz, L. Guibault (Kluwer Law International 2005), 59–86.

42 The term of protection for copyright has be harmonised at 70 years after the death of the author or 70 years after the work is lawfully made available to the public within the EU law in the Term Directive.

43 See: S. Dusollier, *Scoping Study on Copyright and Related Rights and the Public Domain* (WIPO, 2010), 20

44 A. Niewęgłowski, Komentarz do art.4 in Prawo autorskie, Komentarz, ed. A. Niewęgłowski (Wolters Kluwer, 2021, LEX), point. 2.

45 O. Bulayenko, O., G. Frosio, Ch.Geiger, "Opinion," 17.

The adoption of related rights for press publishers adds an additional layer of protection. Elements already protected by copyright, such as photographs, videos, literary expressions, when assembled into a press publication under Art. 2(4) of the CDSM Directive, also become subject to press publishers' related rights.[46] Consequently, the same subject matter may be protected under two different legal frameworks, with two distinct right holders independently controlling its use. To illustrate, a photograph included in a press publication will remain protected by copyright while also falling under the related rights regime.

However, based on the interpretation of the definition of "press publication" provided in Chapter 2, the press publishers' protection does not extend to unprotected elements. These elements remain freely available for reuse by anyone, for example by journalists writing new press items or by internet users creating new content. The possibility of reusing public domain materials is, therefore, not restricted by the definition of press publication under Art. 2(4) of the CDSM Directive. In conclusion, the scope of public domain is not limited due to the introduction of the protection of a new subject matter thanks to its specific structure.

The EU legislature based the new subject matter on the subject matters already protected under the copyright and related rights regime. For example, press publishers' protection does not apply to news of the day or AI-generated images, which, despite their potential inclusion in a press publication, can be used freely. While access to protected elements is restricted from the perspective of the free flow of information, the adoption of this new subject matter within the related rights regime does not extend the scope of these restrictions. This is an important safeguard for access to information.

The purpose of adopting press publishers' rights was to reward the publishers for their efforts and investments in publishing press publications. A purposive interpretation of this protection would, therefore, support the view that exclusive rights should also extend to the use of unprotected elements of press publications to effectively safeguard the interests of press publishers. However, it should be noted that the effectiveness of publishers' protection in this regard would significantly limit the scope of public domain by extending exclusive rights to elements that would otherwise remain freely accessible.

Accordingly, based on the results of the linguistic interpretation, I conclude that press publishers' protection applies only to the protected elements of a press publication.

The scope of the definition of press publication has been criticised as being too broad. One reason for this criticism is that it encompasses press publications that provide information to the general public not only on news but also on other

46 The protection does not extend to the mere facts according to recital 57 of the CDSM Directive. It should be seen as a reference to the idea/expression dichotomy according to which ideas, procedures, methods of operation or mathematical concepts as such are not be protected. What is protected by copyright is the expression of the idea or a fact but not the idea or fact as such.

topics.[47] According to M. M. Eechoud "the addition of 'other topics' extends it to virtually every domain of commercial, government and citizen publishing."[48] However, if press publishers' rights applied only to press publications exclusively covering news, there would be a differentiation in the scope of protection of press publishers, favouring a particular group of publishers that cover particular topic. Such a distinction would result in further widening of disparities in the press sector and would not be conducive to achieving the objectives of the new law. Moreover, it should be remembered that publishers' rights do not protect the information itself but, rather, the collection of protected elements that provide information. The purposive analysis of the provision leads to the conclusion that the broadly defined subject matter of press publishers' protection, in terms of the topics covered by press publication, supports the objectives of the regulation and does not negatively impact the free flow of information.

I see that another safeguard for the free flow of information lies in the explicit exclusion of very short extracts of press publication and individual words from protection, according to Art. 15(1) of the CDSM Directive. Although the legislature has introduced a new subject matter of protection, a certain minimum threshold has been established for protection to apply. This means that anything that does not meet this minimum criterion is not subject to protection and, therefore, remains freely accessible, without being controlled by the right holder. It is beneficial to the free flow of information. A separate issue, which will be discussed later in this chapter, concerns the scope of the area excluded from protection and the criteria for determining its boundaries.

4.1.2. Press publication as a (collective) work

A press publication is a collection primarily composed of literary works of a journalistic nature, but it may also include other works or other subject matter. Given that it consists of a compilation of different elements, it is necessary to examine whether a press publication could qualify as a collective work[49] and, if so, what the implications are for the dual protection granted to press publishers in such cases.

A press publication consists of at least two works and other subject matters. It may also contain non-protected elements, but the publishers' protection will not extend to those elements. Collective work, as discussed in Chapter 2 based on the Polish and French legal frameworks, similarly must include at least two works and may also include also non-protected elements. A press publication consists of works of a specific journalistic nature and is intended to provide the general public with information on news or other topics. Neither the French nor Polish legislature has specified such requirements for a collective work, but there is nothing to prevent a specific collective work from meeting these criteria.

47 See: S. Karapapa, "The press," 316–339.
48 M.M. van Eechoud, "A publisher's," 34.
49 See Chapter 2, Section 3.2.

A press publication is a collection constituting an individual item within a periodical or regularly updated publication released under a single title. A collective work, as a result of the publisher's effort in compiling and organising it elements, will also be considered a distinct item – a work within the meaning of copyright law. The specificity of a press publication lies in the requirement that it must be published within a periodical or regularly updated publication.

For a collective work to qualify for protection, it must possess a creative nature. The selection, combination and arrangement of its elements must result in a creative outcome. This contrasts with the related rights regime in which protection is not dependent on the creative features of literary or artistic expression. This is an important difference between the compared subject matters. Although a press publication may have a creative nature, this is neither required nor assessed for it to receive protection under the new law.

According to French law, the adoption of publishers' protection aims to reward the engagement of press publishers, which includes initiative, editorial responsibility and control. According to the Polish implementation of the CDSM Directive, the publisher's role consists of exercising actual and legal control over the selection of the content that is disseminated.[50] Emphasis in both national legislations and the Directive is placed on exercising control over the publication process. This suggests that while it is less likely – though, of course, not impossible – for the publisher to be involved in a creative capacity, the selection of content elements will often be up to the editor-in-chief or journalist.[51] A press publisher is responsible for controlling the selection and arrangement of the elements of a press publication. I understand this responsibility as including the acceptance of materials submitted for publication and financing the creation, production and distribution of the press publication.

The publishers' involvement in creating a collective work includes initiating, organising and providing technical and financial support; bearing the risks and responsibilities of the final form of the work; defining the conceptual framework; and selecting and arranging its elements. The latter, in particular, demonstrates involvement of a creative nature. For protection under the related rights regime it is irrelevant whether press publisher's involvement is creative. For copyright protection to apply, the press publisher must be involved in a creative way. Therefore, it cannot be ruled out that a press publisher's involvement in the creation of a press publication may be creative, allowing them to receive copyright protection on this basis. This means that, depending on whether the criteria for protecting a collective work are met, a press publication may be considered a collective work. In such cases, there will be a double layer of protection, granting the press publisher exclusive rights to both the press publication and collective work. However, if the creative criterion is not met, this additional layer of protection will not apply.

50 See: Chapter 2, Section 5.
51 See Chapter 1.

From a practical perspective, a major challenge in enforcing rights to a collective work has been the need to prove legal ownership of all its elements before the court in order to seek protection.[52] Under the related rights regime, it is not necessary to prove legal ownership of the elements within a press publication. Instead, it is sufficient to demonstrate that the work in question is included in a press publication, making it easier for publishers to pursue their claims. In conclusion, the adoption of the publishers' rights simplifies the process of obtaining injunctive relief or initiating infringement proceeding in court by eliminating the need to demonstrate the transfer of rights from the authors of the respective works included in a press publication or to prove the grant of an exclusive license. The adoption of publishers' rights **complements** the protection of press publishers in cases in which a press publication does not meet the criteria for a collective work. It also serves a complementary function in legal systems in which the concept of a collective work is not recognised.

The specificity of publishers' rights lies in the fact that the same subject matter can fall under both copyright protection and the related rights regime. A press publication can qualify as a copyright-protected work while also being protected under the related rights regime. This is not the case for phonograms or broadcasts. A phonogram, as defined as Art. 3(b) of the Rome Convention, refers to any exclusively aural fixation of sounds from a performance or other sounds. It is a distinct subject matter of related rights protection, separate from the subject matter of copyright protection, which covers the sound of the performance or other sound itself. A broadcast, as defined in Art. 3(f) of the Rome Convention, refers to the transmission by wireless means for public reception of sounds or of images and sounds. It constitutes a distinct from the sounds or images and sounds it transmits, which are protected by copyright. A press publication protected under the related rights regime can also be a subject matter protected by copyright. Therefore, **a clear distinction** must be made between a press publication protected under copyright for its originality and a press publication protected under related rights to reward the press publisher's involvement in its dissemination.

To conclude:

- the construction of publishers' rights, which apply only to the use of press publications based on the protected elements, serves as a safeguard against restricting the free flow of information by preventing the extension of protection to public domain elements. Another safeguard is the minimum threshold for protection, which excludes individual words and very short extracts of press publications from being protected.
- unlike some subject matters of related rights, such as phonograms or broadcasts, the specificity of press publishers' related rights lies in the fact that the subject matter of protection can overlap with the subject matter of copyright protection.

52 M. van Eechoud, "A publisher's," 27.

- a press publication protected under the related rights regime can also be considered a collective work, as regulated in French or Polish law, if it meets the criteria for collective work protection. In such a situation, there will be a multiplication of layers of protection. The press publisher will hold exclusive rights both to the press publication and to the collective work. Following the adoption of the related rights of press publishers, they are recognised as original right holders, meaning they can more easily get injunctive relief or initiate infringement in court. This is because they do not need to demonstrate the transfer of rights from the authors of the respective works included in a press publication or provide proof of an exclusive license grant. The adoption of the publishers' rights serves a complementary function in legal systems in which collective work is not recognised.

4.2. Holder of protection

Since the adoption of the CDSM Directive, protection resulting from the reproduction and making available rights has been extended to publishers of press publications. They have become another category of right holders, alongside authors, performers, phonogram producers, producers of the first fixation of films, and broadcasting organisations, with the authority to control access to information included in works and other subject matter.

As observed above, the subject matter of protection under publishers' rights is based on subject matters already protected. However, granting exclusive rights to a new category has led to the emergence of a new group of actors who control access to the information contained in these subject matters. Therefore, despite secondary nature of a press publication, as it is based on already existing subject matters, the addition of a new group of actors controlling access to these subject matters further contributes to restricting access to the information they contain. Protection applies to all publishers of press publication established in a Member State. Any entity that meets the criteria of a press publisher and publishes a press publication is entitled to the protection granted under related rights.

However, it should be noted that a press publisher's control over the use of press publications applies only when they are used by ISSPs. The *erga omnes* character[53] of related rights, in practice, limited to the online environment and applies specifically to ISSPs, against whom these rights are enforced. This **limits** the scope of entities against whom the right is directed.

Individual internet users who access press publications, for their own non-commercial needs, without engaging in activities that classify them as ISSPs, can use press publications without restriction. Because the right applies only against ISSPs, users **are not directly affected by the regulation**. However, users remain the main audience of ISSPs, whose objective is to provide information to the public. Indirectly, **the introduction of a new category of entities controlling access to**

53 See Chapter 3, section 2.

information in press publications may negatively impact individual users and the framework of their access to information. There are numerous examples of situations in which users may be indirectly affected by the adoption of the rights. This occurs when a press publisher refuses to authorise the use of a press publication under their rights when an ISSP decides not to make a press publication available due to the high remuneration required by the press publisher. The *erga omnes* nature, though limited in practice to ISSPs, helps reduce the negative impact of this extension on the flow of information. However, it does not eliminate it entirely, as the targeted entities play a significant role in disseminating information.[54]

To conclude:

- the extension of protection through reproduction and making available rights to publishers of press publications introduces a new category of right holders who are empowered to control public access to the information included in works, other subject matters and elements of press publication.
- a press publisher's control over the use of press publications applies only when used by ISSPs. The practical *non-erga omnes* nature of these related rights limits the range of entities against whom they are directed, meaning that users are not directly affected by the regulation. However, due to the significant role of ISSPs in information dissemination, an indirect negative impact on public access to information must be acknowledged.

4.3. Exclusive rights

The objective of exclusive rights is to incentivise the production and dissemination of intellectual works. Some scholars view exclusive rights as complementary to competition law, which is "by nature devoted to regulating competitor relations."[55]

The threat to the effectiveness of publishers' rights arises on the competition law's ground and relates to anti-competitive practices by ISSPs. Related rights are insufficient for addressing anti-competitive practices. The related rights regime protects investment, aiming to reward the right holder for their specific contribution. The objective of competition law also relates to investment, but it does not explicitly protect it. Instead, it regulates competitor behaviour, particularly in cases in which one entity seeks to take over or exploit another's investment.[56] Granting exclusive rights to press publishers serves to protect the investments they have made. However, this does not mean protection against unfair market practices.

54 See Chapter 1, section 5.4.

55 V. Moscon, "Use and abuse of neighbouring rights and the growing need for a sound understanding: The case of online news protection in Europe," in *The* Object *and* Purpose *of* Intellectual Property, ed. S. Frankel (Edward Elgar Publishing, 2019), 309.

56 See: V. Moscon, "Use," 324.

leading to the conclusion that the choice of legal regime may hinder the achievement of the intended objectives of publishers' rights.

In the context of access to information, granting exclusive rights to a new group of actors gives them the power to control access to the information included in press publications. The risk is not only in granting these rights to a new group but also in the broad interpretation of the scope of protection, which may present additional challenges. It is important to note that a broader interpretation of exclusive rights reduces the scope of permissible use of a work/subject matter without infringement. In other words, the broader the interpretation of exclusive rights in relation to the use of a press publication, the fewer instances in which the use of press publications will fall outside the scope of these rights. Moreover, the broader the interpretation, the greater the likelihood of interfering with the normal use and simple enjoyment of the work/subject matter, which, in principle, should not fall within the scope of the exclusive rights.

Due to the broad interpretation of the reproduction right and the uncertain legal classification[57] of several activities, important for media organisations, such as scanning, storing and indexing press publications, ISSPs may choose to refrain from engaging in these activities to avoid potential legal consequences. As a result, the final outcomes of such activities may never reach the readers or may do so only to a limited extent, potentially hindering the free flow of information. I agree with C. Sganga, who points out that the purpose of ensuring an adequate reward for right holders, anchored in property logic, take precedence over other arguments that "could support a more careful balance between exclusivity, access and new creations."[58] This observation leads to the conclusion that a broad interpretation of the reproduction right, while serving the interests of its beneficiaries, may pose a risk to the interests of those who access and use the works.[59]

As regards the making available right,one example is the evolving interpretation of deliberate intervention to enable access to a work, which is one of the factors assessed in determining whether an act of communication to the public of which making available right is part, has occurred. In subsequent CJEU judgements, the concept of deliberate intervention by a user has evolved into a mere facilitation of access, which is now considered sufficient for an act of communication to the public to occur. In other words, a user's engagement in providing public access to a work does not need to be substantial to meet the criteria of the act of communication to the public under Art. 3 of the InfoSoc Directive. The mere provision of a product giving access to a work can already be considered an act of communication to the public. Press publishers' rights apply only toagainst ISSPs, meaning that the outlined doubts and interpretive concerns will impact only their situation.

57 For example, the doubts as to whether the requirements from Art. 5(1) of the InfoSoc Directive are met or not.

58 C. Sganga, *Propertizing European Copyright. History, Challenges and Opportunities* (Edward Elgar Publishing, 2018),126.

59 P. Jougleux, "Access to works protected by copyright law," in *Pluralism or Universalism in International Copyright Law*, ed. T.E. Synodinou (Wolters Kluwer, 2019), 643–650.

Granting exclusive rights to additional actors expands the list of entities controlling access to information.[60] The adoption of publishers' rights, from the perspective of access to information, should be viewed negatively as it risks disrupting the flow of information unless it is sufficiently balanced with exceptions and limitations. However, it must be acknowledged that limiting the scope of publishers' rights to apply only against a specific group of actors mitigates to some extent this negative impact.

To conclude:

- granting exclusive rights to press publishers serves to protect their investments but does not shield them from unfair market practices by online platforms on which they depend. There is a risk that the granting exclusive rights without complementary mechanisms to prevent the abuse of a dominant position, the imposition of unfair negotiating conditions or the exploitation of market dependencies may be insufficient to ensure the effectiveness of the publishers' protection.
- the grant of exclusive rights to press publishers should be understood as a grant of power to control access to the information included in press publications. As the exclusive rights of reproduction and making available to the public are broadly interpreted, the scope of permissible uses of a press publication without infringement become narrower. However, the negative impact on the free flow of information is limited in this case because publishers' rights apply only to ISSPs and not individual users.

4.4. *Exclusions from the scope of protection*

The protection granted to press publishers does not extend to hyperlinking or to the use of individual words and very short extracts of press publications. These exclusions serve as safeguards for the free flow of information, helping to **balance the restrictive effects of exclusive rights**. However, the extent to which this balancing effect occurs depends on how these exclusions are interpreted.

4.4.1. *Hyperlinks*

A narrow interpretation of hyperlinks and very short extracts of press publication would result in less information being accessible to the public. In the case of hyperlinks, if their interpretation is limited to the URL address, the audience will not see the short excerpts from press publications that are often displayed alongside the link. Given that many people rely on online platforms as a source of information, and that for some, reading the short excerpt is sufficient, the restriction of available

60 According to A. Strowel and F. Tulkens, the nature of the exclusive right known as copyright has evolved towards a right to control access as we move into the digital age. See: A. Strowel, F. Tulkens, "Freedom," 303.

information compared to what was accessible before the adoption of related rights may reduce plurality of media and hinder the free flow of information. The CJEU highlighted the particular importance of linking in the context of freedom of expression and information under Art. 11 of the Charter.[61] It highlighted the role of hyperlinks in facilitating the exchange of opinions and information on the internet, recognising their significance in a digital environment marked by the availability and exchange of immense amounts of information.[62] Therefore, the conclusion is that a narrow interpretation of hyperlinks will contribute to the effectiveness of publishers' protection but may negatively impact the free flow of information. A compromise would be to specify within the implementing provisions that a hyperlink may include individual words and very short extracts of a press publication, as long as they do not substitute reading the full publication. The assessment criteria for this should be the same those for used for the exclusion of individual words and very short extracts.

4.4.2. *Individual words and very short extracts of press publication*

A restrictive interpretation of very short extracts of press publication excluded from protection resulting under publishers' rights has been advocated by many academics and national legislators implementing the CDSM Directive to ensure more effective protection of press publishers.[63] Their objective is to interpret very short extracts in a narrow sense to minimise the use of press publications that do not fall within the scope of exclusive rights. In practice, this means that less information will reach the public. Moreover, because the criteria for determining what qualifies as a very short extract and how short it must be to fall within the exclusion remain subjective and difficult to measure, despite some national efforts to define the term more precisely,[64] ISSPs may choose to shorten the information displayed to the public. This could be done to avoid infringing publishers' rights or to circumvent the need for authorisation, which could lead to additional costs. As a result, the information reaching the audience will be significantly shorter than what would have been available if short extracts had not been interpreted in a restrictive manner.

61 See: CJEU, Svensson, para. 18.

62 CJEU, GS Media, para. 45.

63 See: Ch. Angelopoulos, *Articles 15 & 17 of the Directive on Copyright in the Digital Single Market, Comparative National Implementation Report*, https://informationlabs.org/wp-content/uploads/2022/09/Angelopoulos-Report-Full-Report.pdf, accessed: 20.12.2024.

64 In Bulgaria it has been specified that the very short extract is: "the title of the publication, together with the first up to 100 consecutive characters of the text, which may be accompanied by a preview image in small format with a resolution of up to 128 by 128 pixels and part of a sound file or a video clip of up to three seconds." See: A. Lazarova, "The last in line: Bulgaria implements the CDSM Directive", Kluwer Copyright Blog, December 27, 2023, https://copyrightblog.kluweriplaw.com/2023/12/27/the-last-in-line-bulgaria-implements-the-cdsm-directive/, accessed: 20.12.2024.

The qualitative criteria introduced in some MS to assess the impact of press publication use on the interests of press publishers will be useful in the judicial evaluation of whether a specific act constitutes an infringement of publishers' rights or meets the requirements for exclusion from protection. However, the assessment of these criteria will be conducted on a case-by-case basis, meaning that predictability and certainty are not guaranteed. Moreover, the significant litigation costs involved may serve as a disincentive for some press publishers, especially small and local publishers, who are in a weaker financial position compared to technology giants, making it more difficult for them to assert their rights. The lack of a specific threshold also negatively affects ISSPs, which operate in a highly automated way. The complex and evaluative criteria for determining what qualifies as very short extracts of a press publication are difficult to translate into algorithms, creating challenges for automated content processing.

A possible remedy would be the adoption of a quantitative threshold. While this would limit flexibility, it would provide more certainty and commonality in interpreting this exclusion. A possible solution could be to set a character limit. I believe that a limit of around 100 characters could strike a compromise between the interests of publishers, who want ISSPs to use only the shortest possible extracts outside the scope of the publishers' rights, and the interests of platforms, which seek to make these extracts as long as possible. It should not be forgotten that the user is also part of this equation and, therefore, proper attention must be given to safeguarding the free flow of information.

To illustrate, the Guardian headline (December 12, 2024), "Macron swears amid furious exchange with cyclone-hit Mayotte islanders,"[65] has 70 characters. This headline conveys key information about the content of the article but does not, in my opinion, deter the reader from reading the entire article on the press publication's website. Consequently, the assessment of whether a headline should be considered a very short extract of a press publication that is excluded from protection is complex. The use of quantitative criterion would facilitate the assessment. The headline in the example above can be considered a short extract that is excluded from publishers' protection under the proposed threshold. In the judgement of the Amsterdam District Court of October 30, 2024,[66] concerning the provision of a service mainly aggregating RSS feeds of newspaper publishers,[67] a quantitative threshold of 150 characters was proposed to qualify an excerpt as a short extract of a press publication. At present, there are few rulings on this issue,

65 R. Savage, "Macron swears amid furious exchange with cyclone-hit Mayotte islanders," The Guardian, December 20, 2024, https://www.theguardian.com/world/2024/dec/20/emmanuel-macron-swears-amid-furious-exchange-with-cyclone-hit-mayotte-islanders, accessed: 20.12.2024.

66 Amsterdam District Court of 30 October 2024, ref. C/13/737 170 / HA ZA 23-690, https://www.technollama.co.uk/can-a-dutch-case-about-rss-teach-us-anything-about-ai-copyright, accessed: 20.12.2024.

67 The defendant (HowardsHome) took article notifications from publicly available RSS feeds and allowed its customers to view, search and further process individual notifications (hyperlink and article digest, sometimes also an image posted by the publisher) on its own portal and via an API.

but this will certainly change over time. I acknowledge that the adoption of a quantitative threshold is regarded with reluctance, as it may be seen as a constraint on flexibility.[68] This is not a miracle solution, but its advantage is certainty. It can be expected that a trend will emerge in which courts introduce numerical thresholds in case law to determine whether an excerpt is excluded from protection, especially in jurisdictions in which no definition or only a descriptive definition of very short extracts of press publication has been provided.

4.4.3. Private or non-commercial uses of press publications by individual users

Art. 15 of the CDSM Directive specifies that press publishers' protection does not apply to private or non-commercial uses of press publications by individual users. It applies to the online use of press publications by ISSPs. Therefore, the question may be asked as to which category the use of a press publication by non-profit organisations falls into. In this regard, two scenarios are worth considering.

The first is based on a narrow interpretation of individual users, as reflected, for example, in the Polish implementation of the CDSM Directive. According to this implementation, protection does not apply to personal use that is not related to any business activity. As observed earlier, it is difficult to attribute personal use to any organisation, which, consequently, means that the activities of non-profit organisations are explicitly excluded from the scope of the exclusion. Because such activity is excluded from the exclusion, and, at the same time, the publishers' rights do not clearly apply to it, it is difficult to determine unequivocally the legal qualification of the activities of such organisations within the framework of publishers' rights. This can have a negative impact on the free flow of information, as non-profit organisations often play an important role in the dissemination of information.[69]

Lack of certainty regarding the legal qualification of the use of press publications means that such organisations will be less likely to use press publications republication or further elaboration.[70] The scale of the threat depends on how important non-profit organisations are as actors in disseminating information and the size of the audience they reach. The same applies to the use of press publications by libraries.

The second scenario is based on the broad interpretation of individual users, which also encompasses, for example, non-profit organisations using press publications within the scope of the exclusion from publishers' protection. I advise adopting this interpretation, as the new rights will either not change or will positively influence access to information.

68 See: U. Furgał, "The emperor has no clothes: How the press publishers' right implementation exposes its shortcomings," *GRUR International* 72, no. 7 (2023): 650–664.

69 See for example the scope of the activity of the Polish foundation Panoptykon.

70 In this analysis I left aside the examination of what kind of exceptions and limitations could apply in case of the use of press publications by non-profit organisations.

To conclude:

- the exclusions for the use of the very short extracts of press publication and acts of hyperlinking from the scope of publishers' protection serve as safeguards for the free flow of information, balancing the restrictive effect caused by the mere adoption of exclusive rights. However, a restrictive interpretation of these exclusions undermines this balancing objective and may become an obstacle to the free flow of information by limiting the amount of information that reaches the audience.
- the difficulty in legally qualifying the use of press publications by, for example, non-profit organisations, due to the vague wording of the exclusion in the CDSM Directive and its national implementations, can impact the activity of such organisations that contribute to the dissemination of information. This may lead to their reluctance to use press publications and, consequently, may disrupt the free flow of information.

4.5. Conditions for calculation of remuneration

The conditions for calculating remuneration for press publishers, due to the use of press publications by ISSPs, were regulated by some Member States as part of the implementation of the CDSM Directive.

According to the second paragraph of Art. L218-4 of the French Intellectual Property Code, the determination of the amount of remuneration must take into account, among others, **the contribution of press publications to political and general information** and the extent to which press publications are used by online public communication services.[71] Accordingly, press publishers that publish on political and general information are likely to receive higher remuneration, while those covering topics unrelated to these areas, often small and niche publishers, are likely to receive less. For these publishers, lower remuneration can significantly affect their business.

The adoption of such a factor influencing the amount of remuneration can be seen as a tool in hand for ISSPs to differentiate between press publishers based on the subject matter of their publications, potentially disadvantaging publishers that focus on niche subjects. To illustrate, the distinction introduced by the French legislature became a basis for discriminatory treatment by Google, which excluded from remuneration press publishers and news agencies that did not have a "political and general information" qualification. Google explained that it

> does not deny that the related right covers non-IPG[72] press publications, (but) it does not require Google (or any other party) to purchase any content.

71 English version by the author. French version of art. L218-4 of French Intellectual Property Code, https://www.legifrance.gouv.fr/codes/article_lc/LEGIARTI000038826736, accessed: 11.08.2023.

72 Political and general information, from French: Information Politique et Générale.

> (However,) as regards non-IPG content, Google considers that it has no commercial interest in taking out paying licences for this type of content in view of the many equivalent alternatives widely available on the Internet.[73]

The FCA, which settled the dispute between French press publishers and Google, noted that under Art. L.218-4 of the French Intellectual Property Code, the contribution of press publications to political and general information is one of factors to be considered for benefiting from related rights, but its fulfilment is not mandatory. The list of factors provided in the provision is not exhaustive; therefore, "the contribution to the IPG cannot be the sole criterion for remuneration. The provision from art. L.218-4 opens the possibility to individual handling of remuneration, and not general and undifferentiated as Google does."[74]

Taking into account the objectives of the regulation and the wording of Art. 15 of the CDSM Directive, which does not provide for differentiated treatment of press publishers, specifications such as the one introduced in France give platforms the means to engage in practices that undermine the objectives of the publishers' rights.

In the Polish implementation, some inspiration from the French provision can be seen. According to Art. 99[12] when determining remuneration for the use of a press publication, the parties must take into account all relevant circumstances, in particular for example **the type** of press publications reproduced or made available to the public. The Polish legislation distinguishes itself in that it does not specify which types of press publications are meant or how they should impact the amount of remuneration, making the provision ambiguous and potentially opening the way for platforms to abuse the law.

In Italy, when determining the criteria for calculating remuneration, Art. 43 bis (8) of the Legge sul diritto d'autore states that factors such as the length of **press publisher's activity, market relevance**, number of journalists employed, number of online consultations of press publications, costs of technological and infrastructure investments and the economic benefits derived by both parties in terms of visibility and advertising revenues should be considered.[75] Calculating remuneration based on the length of the press publisher's activity or market relevance favours experienced and large publishers and disadvantages beginners as well as small and niche press publishers who, despite producing valuable content, will receive lower remuneration. Such wording of the conditions for remuneration **exacerbates disparities** within the press sector. As a result, due to the differential treatment and lower remuneration for the use of their press publications, affected publishers may be forced to reduce their activities or even cease operations due to financial difficulties and a weaker market position compared to large, more

73 FCA, Decision of July 12, 2021 on non-compliance with the interim measures of April 9, 2020, 50.

74 FCA, Decision of July 12, 2021 on non-compliance with the interim measures of April 9, 2020, 94.

75 English version by the author. Italian version of art. 43 bis (8) of the Legge sul diritto d'autore: https://www.altalex.com/documents/codici-altalex/2014/06/26/legge-sul-diritto-d-autore#titolo1 ,accessed: 15.11.2022.

established press publishers. To safeguard media pluralism, the visibility and the real accessibility of information coming from **different** media organisations is necessary.[76]

The differences in remunerations resulting from the legal solutions introduced in France and Italy can contribute to the imbalances in the press sector and further accentuate existing inequalities. Media pluralism requires a guarantee **of access to and consumption of** a wide range of viewpoints across a variety of platforms and media owners.[77] Favouring of content from certain press publishers, leading to over-representation of some media outlets and under-representation of others, reinforces a winner-takes-all dynamic. As a result, the range of information that readers can actually access and consume will be reduced. It does not strive to optimise the number of press publishers, which would be beneficial to safeguarding media pluralism,[78] and, in my opinion, it represents a significant threat to media pluralism.

While determining the factors on which remuneration should be calculated, the focus should be on the use of the press publication. As this use generates profits for ISSPs, it is justified to share those profits with press publishers within the framework of their exercise of exclusive rights. The calculation of this remuneration should be based on criteria such as the number of ISSP services on which the press publications are displayed, as well as the number of times these publications have been displayed and searched for on those services. The indirect revenues of ISSPs from the use of press publications should also be taken into account, as has been done in the French transposition. For the sake of balance, the extent to which the use of press publications by ISSPs contributes to the profits of press publishers, in the form of clicks and visits to their websites, should also be considered. Every activity aiming at disseminating information is important from the perspective of public debate and access to information, as noted in Chapter 1. Therefore, the criteria discussed should not discourage platforms from continuing their role in the dissemination of information.

To conclude:

- the effectiveness of the protection granted by publishers' rights, particularly in relation to the free flow of information and media pluralism, may be threatened by criteria focused on the press publisher. These include factors such as the topic of the press publications and the publisher's popularity, size or length of service. Such criteria could result in a differentiation among press publishers that the EU legislature did not intend, reinforcing a winner-takes-all dynamic that leads to the over-representation of some press publishers and under-representation of others – an outcome unfavourable to protection of media pluralism. As a result, the objectives of the law could not be achieved.

76 See the introduction to Chapter 1.
77 See: Ofcom, *Measuring*, 8.
78 See Chapter 1.

4.6. Information claim

To determine the remuneration owed to press publishers, access to data, which, in most cases, is held by ISSPs, is necessary. According to Irene Lanzaco, director general of the Spanish news industry trade body, Asociación de Medios de Información (AMI), representing, for example, *El Pais* and *El Mundo*,

> There is a lot of information on Google's side and very little, if any, information on the side of the publishers. This means that Google is able to capture and monetise valuable audience data coming out from news and only the tech giant really knows how much news is worth to them.[79]

This example shows that aspects of data value capture should be taken into account when legislating on the functioning of online platforms. Solutions that specify the types of data ISSPs must provide, such as those introduced in Poland and Belgium, or go even further, as in Italy or the Czech Republic, by imposing penalties for failure to provide data are necessary to redress market imbalances and strengthen the bargaining position of press publishers.

However, the press publishers' struggle to access the necessary information for calculating their remuneration can be long and challenging. For example, in May 2024, the Paris Court of First Instance ordered X to provide publishers of *Le Figaro*, *Le Parisien*, *Les Echos*, *Le Nouvel Obs* and the *Le Monde* group, within two months, with a series of commercial data enabling them to assess the revenue derived from their content. This included data on the number of views, click rates, the average number of engagements (retweets, quotes, replies, likes, shares, etc.), and the advertising revenue generated in France on X in relation to these publications, to calculate the remuneration owed under publishers' rights. The platform was also required to provide a description of its publication display algorithms.[80] The provision of this said data was seen as an important step toward facilitating negotiations on remuneration for the use of press publications by the ISSP. However, five months later, with no data from X, the press publishers decided to sue the platform for violating their rights. According to the publishers, X "has not yet complied" with the court's decision, "demonstrating its continued intent to avoid its legal obligations."[81]

Another complaint, this time against Microsoft, was filed with the Paris Court of First Instance by 50 French press publishers in November 2024. These media

79 Statement of Irene Lanzaco for Press Gazette. Future of Media see in: A. Majid, "Publishers square up for new battle with Google in Spain," Presse Gazette. Future of Media, (2023), https://pressgazette.co.uk/platforms/google-news-spain-facebook-challenge/, accessed: 12.08.2023.

80 Tribunal Judiciaire de Paris, Ordonnance de Référé, May 23, 2024, N° RG 23/55581 – N° Portalis 352J-W-B7H-C2JUY, Dalloz-Actualité, https://www.dalloz-actualite.fr/sites/dalloz-actualite.fr/files/resources/2024/06/23_mai_2024_-_2355581.pdf, accessed: 21.12.2024.

81 A. Chrisafis, "French news titles sue X over allegedly running their content without payment," The Guardian, November 12, 2024, https://www.theguardian.com/world/2024/nov/12/french-news-titles-sue-x-over-allegedly-running-their-content-without-payment, accessed: 21.12.2024.

outlets are calling on Microsoft to negotiate in good faith under the publishers' law. The platform is refusing to provide factual information essential for an objective assessment of the remuneration owed to press publishers, despite being legally obligated to do so. Despite repeated requests over the years, Microsoft continues to shirk this obligation, according to a press release from Apig, which emphasised that respect for press publishers' rights is a vital issue for the survival and independence of news media and the funding of professional journalism, especially in a context marked by the massive dissemination of disinformation.[82]

Based on these examples, reflecting on how to make the information claim more effective becomes crucial to ensuring publishers' protection, as without access to data on the use of press publications, the calculation of remuneration becomes impossible. I am not sure that specifying in the legislation what data must be provided (such as up-to-date, complete or relevant information) will make any difference because the applicant is already required to specify in the information claim what data are being requested, and this must be done as precisely as possible. Legislation that introduces penalties for failure to provide data is more likely to motivate platforms to comply. Although, in the Paris Court of First Instance ruling discussed above, X's failure to share information on the use of press publications was also subject to a penalty, yet the platform has still not provided the data, at least so far.

Poland, in an effort to ensure the effectiveness of publishers' protection and to anticipate the behaviour demonstrated by platforms toward French press publishers regarding the provision of data, introduced some supplementary measures. In Art. 99^{15}(4) of the Polish Copyright Law a provision has been introduced according to which, when a party fails to enter into mediation or if the parties fail to reach an agreement without mediation, the President of UKE may, at the request of a party, rule on the amount of remuneration for the use of the right referred to in Art. 99^{7}(2) or on the method for determining that remuneration without mediation. In order to determine the amount of remuneration or the method for calculating it, the President of UKE may appoint **an expert**. The expert's determination of the information necessary to calculate the remuneration, along with the independent body's ruling, helps to circumvent the issue of obtaining data directly from the platforms. Separate issues remain as to whether such a solution will be effective, whether its introduction stays within the margin of discretion allowed when implementing Art. 15 of the CDSM Directive and, finally, whether platforms will comply and pay the remuneration.

82 APIG, "Les éditeurs de presse d'information engagent des actions judiciaires contre Microsoft pour faire respecter la loi sur le droit voisin," November 8, 2024, https://www.alliancepresse.fr/actualite/les-editeurs-de-presse-dinformation-engagent-des-actions-judiciaires-contre-microsoft-pour-faire-respecter-la-loi-sur-le-droit-voisin/, accessed: 21.12.2024.

To conclude:

- the lawsuits filed by French press publishers against Microsoft and X illustrate the difficulty publishers face in obtaining information on the use of their press publications by ISSPs, highlight the reluctance of platforms to negotiate in good faith and call into question the effectiveness of the protection introduced in Art. 15 of the CDSM Directive. To strengthen the bargaining position of press publishers, some MS implementing the CDSM Directive after France have introduced additional mechanisms to make the information claim more effective. Measures such as the possibility of expert assessment of the requested data, the imposition of penalties for failure to provide data or top-down fixing of remuneration may motivate ISSPs to share information on the use of their press publications. However, the effectiveness of these solutions must be confirmed in practice, as well as their compliance with the EU law by the CJEU.

4.7. Mediation mechanism

In view of the threat of the abuse of dominant position and the exploitation of publishers' economic dependence, some MS have introduced mechanisms aimed at redressing the power imbalance between the negotiating parties in the exercise of publishers' rights. The involvement of an independent body to assist in cases in which the parties face difficulties in reaching an agreement has been discussed, but some MS have gone a step further by entrusting an independent body with the authority to determine the remuneration. In Italy, it has been explicitly stated that for the use of press publications, ISSPs shall pay a fair compensation.[83] In the Czech Republic, ISSPs are required to pay the publisher a reasonable remuneration for granting the authorisation to exercise the right to use the press publication.[84] It should be acknowledged, however, that press publishers were not granted a remuneration right aimed at securing the economic interest of right holder but, rather, exclusive rights conferring the power to authorise or prohibit the reproduction and making available of press publications. Exclusivity means that, for ISSPs to use a press publication, the consent of the right holder is required. This consent is typically granted in exchange for remuneration, but the parties may agree otherwise; for example, the use may be authorised in exchange for better visibility or even free of charge.

A remuneration right does not confer a monopoly over the use of a subject matter, but for some scholars, it serves as a response to problems resulting from the exercise of exclusive rights, such as "lack of bargaining power, complex exploitation markets, fear of being black-listed"[85] and a solution to "the blocking

83 English version by the author. Italian version of Art. 43 bis (8) of the Legge sul diritto d'autore, https://www.altalex.com/documents/codici-altalex/2014/06/26/legge-sul-diritto-d-autore#titolo1, accessed: 15.11.2022.

84 Translation by the author. Czech version of Art. 87b (9), https://www.zakonyprolidi.cz/cs/2000-121, accessed: 09.12.2024.

85 R. Xalabarder, "The principle," 24.

effects of exclusivity since they guarantee access and thus enhance acceptance of copyright norms amongst the general public."[86] However, in the case of press publishers, the EU legislature decided to grant them exclusive rights, and due to the principle of maximum harmonisation, the same scope of protection must be provided at the national level when implementing Art. 15 of the CDSM Directive. Therefore, it is legitimate and justified to ask whether the explicit obligation to pay remuneration introduced in some Member States exceeds the margin of discretion allowed in implementing Art. 15 of the CDSM Directive and whether it conflicts with the EU law. In December 2023, the Tribunale Amministrativo Regionale per il Lazio (Sezione Quarta) submitted a request for a preliminary ruling, asking the CJEU whether Art. 15 of the CDSM Directive should be interpreted as precluding the introduction of the following provisions within the framework of its national implementation:

a) introduction of the obligation of remuneration (fair compensation);
b) provision of the obligation to enter into negotiations with publishers and not to restrict the visibility of the publisher's content in search results pending the finalisation of the negotiation; provision of the information necessary for the purposes of determination of a fair compensation;
c) grant to an independent body a supervisory and sanctioning power, the power to identify the reference criteria for determining fair compensation, the power to determine, in the event of failure to reach agreement between the parties, the exact amount of fair compensation.[87]

The CJEU response to these questions will be invaluable in determining whether the introduction of such mechanisms, which undoubtedly help safeguard the effectiveness of publishers' protection, remains within or exceeds the margin of discretion granted to Member States in implementing the CDSM Directive.

Press publishers have been granted exclusive rights to authorise or prohibit the online use of their press publications by ISSPs, but this does not imply that ISSPs are obligated to enter into negotiations. U. Furgał explains that "digital intermediaries are obliged not to behave in a way covered by the publishers' monopoly unless they acquire publishers' consent. That does not mean, however, that they must seek publishers' consent whenever a publisher requests them to do so."[88] The choice of the related rights regime may indicate that the EU legislature either did not intend to impose an obligation on ISSPs to negotiate or did not anticipate the level of difficulty press publishers would face in enforcing the new law and, therefore,

86 O. Bulayenko, Ch. Geiger, "Creating statutory remuneration rights in copyright law: What policy options under the international legal framework?," *Centre for International Intellectual Property Studies Research Paper*, no. 2020-05 (2020), 58.

87 Il Tribunale Amministrativo Regionale per il Lazio, Sezione Quarta, N. 18790/2023 REG.PROV. COLL. N. 07093/2023 REG.RIC., 12.12.2023, point 21, https://drive.google.com/file/d/1VbN_nAwpL2q7zZTFGLRyJ2f28JEBVltv/view, accessed: 31.01.2024.

88 U. Furgał, "The emperor," 659.

chose to limit the intervention to the related rights framework. In Poland, a party must agree to mediation, but if it chooses not to participate in mediation or does not enter into negotiations, it harms its own position because the remuneration will be set by the UKE.

In the Belgian case, similarly to the Italian implementation, the parties are obligated to negotiate, which raises questions about potential restrictions on contractual freedom and negotiating autonomy. This could lead to arguments that such an obligation constitutes a limitation on the freedom to contract. Although this freedom is not absolute and its limitation may be justified on the grounds of protecting freedom of expression, concerns can still be raised as to whether the interference with contractual freedom goes too far. This issue was raised by Google and Meta, which, at the end of January 2023, filed actions before the Belgian Constitutional Court seeking the annulment of the Belgian law of June 19, 2022, which transposed the CDSM Directive. The platforms claimed that the contested law creates an excessive burden on ISSPs, violating the general principle of freedom of trade and industry and, in particular, the freedom of contract by imposing conditions under which the agreements with press publishers must be concluded.[89] In September 2024, the Constitutional Court issued a ruling and referred 13 questions to the CJEU, focusing on the obligation to negotiate and the requirement to pay remuneration to press publishers.[90]

Factors such as the relatively weak bargaining position of press publishers; the significant market power of some ISSPs, such as Google, X or Meta; and the economic dependence of publishers on these platforms justify the adoption of mechanisms that facilitate and assist in negotiations concerning the exercise of publishers' rights. The freedom of contract is not absolute, and the risk of abuse of dominant position by ISSPs can serve as an important justification for adopting such mechanisms. On the other hand, it raises the question of whether these measures exceed the margin of discretion of MS in implementing Art. 15 of the CDSM Directive and whether they interfere too extensively with contractual freedom. The objective of the legislature was, therefore, valid, and its achievement legitimate, but the choice of means by which this objective is intended to be achieved may be inappropriate in relation to the scope of protection granted to publishers under EU law.

In the public debate in Poland proceeding the implementation of Art. 15 of the CDSM Directive, the time-consuming nature and, consequently, low effectiveness

89 La Correspondance de la Presse, "Droits voisins / Belgique: Meta et Google conteste la loi belge qui selon eux porte atteinte à leur liberté de commerce et d'industrie; le législateur belge a 'placé toute une industrie dans une insécurité juridique majeure'," Europresse, March 13, 2023, https://www.lacorrespondancedelapresse.fr/2023-03-13, accessed: 08.01.2025.

90 Cour Consitutionelle, Arrêt n° 98/2024 du 26 septembre 2024, Numéros du rôle: 7922, 7924, 7925, 7926 et 7927, ECLI:BE:GHCC:2024:ARR.098, https://www.const-court.be/public/f/2024/2024-098f.pdf, accessed: 22.12.2024.

of the mediation procedure was raised as an argument against its introduction.[91] In response, the Polish implementation specifies that mediation shall not exceed 60 days, unless the parties mutually agree to extend the period. Afterward, the party has the right to appeal to the court, as the administrative procedure is designed as a single-instance procedure only. According to art. 99^{12}(12) of the Polish Copyright Law, the court's decision must be issued within 60 days from the date of filing the application for a decision, or within 30 days from the receipt of the expert's opinion, if one was appointed, but no later than 6 months from the date of filing the application. The aim of these specifications was to ensure a relatively short time for processing disputes and, thereby, to encourage parties to pursue the pursuit of dispute resolution accordingly.

The introduction of mediation mechanisms and involvement of an independent body to determine remuneration in cases in which the parties fail to reach an agreement were intended to strengthen the negotiating position of press publishers and to ensure the effectiveness of the protection granted to them. However, the consequences observed in some Member States seem to have had the opposite effect. In Poland, following the adoption of the publishers' rights, Meta changed the way publishers' content was displayed in September 2024. Previously, the title, main graphic and the beginning of the text appeared together with the link, which helped to attract users' attention. Currently, only the title is displayed. According to the platform, Poland has implemented its own interpretation of Art. 15, which it claims is not aligned with the scope or terms of the Directive, leading to a lack of clarity regarding how the new rules should be applied. As a result, Meta has changed the way it displays links to news articles on Facebook so that only the headline and hyperlink are shown, without images or text from the article.[92] This change is described as temporary pending the CJEU ruling on the Italian preliminary question.

For press publishers, Meta's action, which is one of the major distributors of press content, especially in the social media market, will have a negative impact on the entire sector. Meta is increasingly seen as a content censor, leveraging its dominant position.[93] The change in how content is displayed may have led to reduced interest in press publications and a decline in the number of views, thereby negatively affecting the interests of press publishers. In October 2024, the President of the Office of Competition and Consumer Protection (UOKiK) opened an investigation into the changes made by Meta, aiming to determine whether the platform

91 M. Kowala, *Media kontra platformy internetowe. Zasady wynagradzania i ich egzekwowanie*, Raport dla Fundacji im. Stefana Batorego (2024), media-kontra-platformy-internetowe-zasady-wynagradzania-i-ich-egzekwowanie, accessed: 08.01.2025.

92 Press, "Polskie media reagują na złośliwe działania Facebooka. 'Meta gra ostro'," September 23, 2024, https://www.press.pl/tresc/83710,polskie-media-reaguja-na-zlosliwe-dzialania-facebooka_-_meta-gra-ostro_, accessed: 22.12.2024.

93 Press, "Polskie."

may have abused its market position through these actions.[94] In Google Search, Discover, and News, Google decided to remove the display of previews of EU press publication content, such as snippets, thumbnails, and video previews, that might be protected under the new law in the Czech Republic.[95] This change can significantly reduce the attractiveness of the displayed content and, as a result, decrease the number of clicks and views, ultimately affecting revenues for press publishers.

To conclude:

- the introduction of such mechanisms, as seen in the examples of Poland and the Czech Republic, may lead to questions about their impact on media pluralism and the free flow of information. Because the content of press publishers is displayed in a limited way, it may negatively affect not only the press sector but also the recipients of information. There appears to be a form of media retaliation by platforms in response to the introduction of mediation mechanisms, which, in turn, adversely affect publishers' interests and limit access to information.

4.8. Safeguards for visibility and transparency

Considering the examples discussed above, the introduction of safeguards to ensure the visibility of content from press publishers engaged in negotiations with ISSPs is necessary. Any unjustified restriction on the display of such content during negotiations should be regarded as a breach of the duty to negotiate in good faith. The adoption of such a measure serves as a safeguard for the free flow of information. It helps reduce the risk that public will receive less information during ongoing negotiations. It addresses the potential misuse of press publishers' economic dependence by ISSPs pressuring them into accepting unfavourable or less favourable terms. Moreover, it protects press publishers against the imposition of negotiating conditions, and such a protection is desirable to help ensure the effectiveness of publishers' rights.

The adoption of publishers' rights in France was accompanied by a debate on the sources of funding for the press sector. It was noted that state aid, as a proportion of press sales, increased from 12.9% to 23.3% between 2008 and 2021, representing a significant burden on the public finance sector.[96] The adoption of publishers' rights was seen as a form of financial relief, shifting part of the burden of supporting the press sector from the state to private entities. However, this shift brings a potential threat to media pluralism, namely the risk of strengthening publishers' dependence on private actors.

94 UOKiK, "Meta – postępowanie wyjaśniające," October 22, 2024, https://uokik.gov.pl/meta-postepowanie-wyjasniajace, accessed: 22.12.2024.
95 Google Search Central Blog, "Updates."
96 V. Duby-Muller, L. Garcia, *Rapport*, 27.

One of the consequences of introducing related rights may be the intensification of control by ISSPs over the process of dissemination and creation of press publications. In this context, control is understood broadly as real influence over the informational content that reaches the audience, and it is exercised through the existing dependencies between press publishers and ISSPs. The remuneration resulting from the related rights of press publishers, as agreed between the parties, which is sometimes referred to as "private subvention,"[97] is considered by some academics to have the potential to create distortions of competition and inequalities[98] between press publishers. Other scholars view it as a means for online platforms to exert control over the production and dissemination of press publications, using it as a bargaining chip to offer lower remuneration in exchange for a better display position for press publishers.[99] To illustrate, in France, Google limited the visibility of press publications from publishers who sought to enforce their rights.[100] This had a proven negative effect on the traffic redirected to their websites and resulted in financial loses for those publishers.[101] Those who sought better display, which is important for their survival in the market, chose to forego remuneration. In contrast, those who insisted on enforcing their rights experienced a loss in visibility.

It should be recalled that online visibility and the real accessibility of information from media organisations[102] are increasingly important factors in safeguarding media pluralism. The control exercised by ISSPs over press publishers may take the form of making visibility conditional on non-payment of remuneration, on reducing the amount of remuneration or on the content and subject matter of press publications. Such practices can undermine the independence of press publishers and weaken safeguards for media pluralism.

To conclude:

- the confidentiality of the agreements reached between press publishers and ISSPs makes it very difficult or even impossible to assess the effectiveness of the press publishers' rights. Moreover, the lack of transparency regarding the amount of remuneration received by press publishers allows for discretionary calculation of the authors' share. For these reasons, I consider that disclosure of the details of agreements reached under the publishers' rights should be allowed, either at the request of a collective management organisation or at the request of the researcher, through a designated body, such as one appointed by the Ministry of Culture.

97 V. Duby-Muller, L. Garcia, *Rapport*, 50–51,

98 V. Duby-Muller, *Rapport*, 27.

99 T. Höppner, Post on Linkedin, 2022, https://www.linkedin.com/posts/thomas-höppner-7ba59a70_related-rights-the-autorité-accepts-googles-activity-6944995588136435712-zfaV, accessed: 10.08.2023.

100 See Chapter 5, Sections 3.2.3 (c), 3.3.

101 V. Duby-Muller, L. Garcia, *Rapport*, 31.

102 See the introduction to the first chapter.

- however, the obligation to disclose information contained in such agreements should be limited in scope. Otherwise, the interference with freedom of contract would be too significant. Therefore, I propose limiting the scope of entitled entities to collective management organisations, for the purpose of determining the authors' share, and to researchers. In the latter case, researchers should be vetted by an independent body and required to use the data exclusively for research purposes, treating it as strictly confidential.

5. Conclusion

The analysis conducted shows that the extension of protection under the related rights regime to a new subject matter – press publication – does not constitute a threat to access to information due to the safeguards for the free flow of information provided in Articles 2(4) and 15(2) of the CDSM Directive.

However, the explicit recognition of press publishers as holders of exclusive rights through the adoption of the publishers' rights introduces a new group of actors controlling access to the protected subject matter, which contributes to a limitation of access to the information contained therein. While the rights apply only against ISSPs, not directly against users, the indirect negative impact of this legislative approach on the framework of access to information should be acknowledged, particularly given the central role of ISSPs in disseminating information.

The assessment of the publishers' rights in the context of media pluralism and access to information revealed that the exclusions from the scope of protection – intended to balance the restrictive effect of the publishers' protection on the free flow of information – if understood in a **restrictive** manner, will fail to fulfil this balancing objective and may, instead, become an obstacle to the free flow of information by limiting the information that reaches the audience. Discriminatory conditions of remuneration introduced in some Member States can lead to over-representation of some media outlets and under-representation of others, reinforcing a winner-take-all dynamic that is unfavourable to the protection of media pluralism.

A press publication can be considered a collective work, as regulated in, for example, French or Polish law. In such cases, a multiplication of protection layers may occur. However, under publishers' related rights, it is not necessary to prove legal titles to the individual elements of a press publication, which makes it easier for press publishers, as original right holders, to institute infringement proceeding before the court. The adoption of publishers' rights is complementary to legislations in which the collective work is not recognised. As a result, the related rights enhance legal certainty and simplify the process of asserting the publishers' rights and defending their interests.

The adoption of mediation mechanisms, although justified by the need to strengthen the negotiating position of press publishers in the face of the strong market position of ISSPs, raises legitimate doubts regarding the compliance of such legal solutions with EU law. It is also uncertain whether such solutions will ensure the effectiveness of publishers' protection. In some MS, we are currently witnessing a form of media revenge by ISSPs, who, in retaliation for the introduction of such mechanisms, limit the visibility of press publications online. This is an undesirable phenomenon from the perspective of the free flow of information, the protection of media pluralism and the welfare of the press sector.

The analysis of the market realities leads to the conclusion that it cannot be clearly stated whether the introduction of publishers' rights effectively addresses the market failure. This difficulty arises, *inter alia*, from the fact that the agreements reached between press publishers and ISSPs are mostly confidential, which makes it impossible to determine how much the remuneration contributes to the improvement of press publishers' situation. The conducted research showed that the adoption of publishers' rights can lead to a strengthening press publishers' dependence on ISSPs and a greater emphasis on the differences between press publishers.

The related rights of press publishers constitute a justified interference with freedom of expression. The conducted analysis showed that the core of the right to receive information, understood as the public's right to be adequately informed, particularly on matters of public interest, is not affected.

Final conclusion

The EU legislature chose to support freedom of expression by applying tools from the domain of literary and artistic creation and dissemination, introducing protection for press publishers under the related rights regime. The grant of exclusive rights to press publishers was expected to improve their financial situation and, consequently, strengthen the press sector, leading to better access to information and enhanced protection of media pluralism. Intuitively, therefore, an objective outside the scope of the related rights regime could be achieved through its means. However, the mere extension of exclusive rights to a new category of actors represents a step toward restricting the access to information, as it creates a monopoly over the use of press publications. A paradox arises in that the new protection for press publishers, rather than enhancing access to information, may, in fact, limit it. To balance this effect, numerous safeguards have been introduced.

My research showed that the related rights of press publishers, in contrast to other related rights, are distinguished by a higher level of specificity. They are directed against a specific group of actors, namely ISSPs, and not against every user of press publication. They apply to the use of press publications in the online environment. The subject matter of protection must meet the criterion of being a collection consisting of protected elements, so unprotected elements from the public domain are not covered by the protection. The term of protection is significantly shorter compared to that of other related rights. All these specificities can be seen as safeguards for the flow of information in the context of extending exclusive rights to press publishers.

Moreover, acts of hyperlinking or the use of individual words or very short extracts of a press publication are excluded from the scope of protection arising from the publishers' rights, which contributes to limiting their scope. In this context, however, another paradox can be identified: a broad understanding of these exclusions will enhance the free flow of information, while a narrow understanding will contribute to more effective protection of press publishers. Ultimately, this is about weighing the interests at stake and deciding whether to tip the scales toward enhanced protection for press publishers or toward the free flow of information.

By discussing the functioning of press publishers and ISSPs supplying the services such as news aggregation, the analysis identified a high level of interdependence between these actors, along with significant market imbalances.

DOI: 10.4324/9781003599494-5

The mere granting of exclusive rights, without implementing mechanisms to secure the negotiating position of press publishers, as evidenced by the analysis of the French publishers' case, may not lead to an increase in the effectiveness of their protection. The research conducted showed that any legal changes, including those in the copyright and related rights regime concerning the online information communication environment, should take into account the dependencies and market power imbalances between the actors affected by the legislation. These factors are crucial to its effectiveness, and failure to properly consider them can lead to counterproductive outcomes.

Press publishers' rights were adopted to address market failure. However, as most agreements reached between press publishers and ISSPs remain confidential, it is impossible to determine whether revenues generated from the use of press publications have effectively improved the situation for press publishers and, consequently, strengthened the press sector, ensured access to reliable information and protected media pluralism. Consequently, the conclusion to be drawn from the analysis conducted in this monograph is that achieving the objectives of freedom of expression through regulation based on the related rights regime can be difficult. This is due to the very characteristics and purpose of the protection arising from the chosen legal regime as well as the market realities and the dependencies between actors involved. To say that it can be difficult does not mean that it is impossible, and the important task of weighing conflicting interests rests with the MS. The scope of their margin of discretion, however, is limited, as the publishers' rights represent a case of maximum harmonisation. Therefore, the protection granted to press publishers at the national level, as a result of the Directive's implementation, cannot be either more or less intense. Nevertheless, MS are free to specify the circumstances under which the authorisation for the use of press publications takes place. They should implement solutions that address the identified dependencies and market power imbalances in order to minimise the factors that could potentially undermine the effectiveness of the publishers' rights.

Based on the lessons learned from the French case, some MS introduced additional safeguards against the limitation of press publishers' visibility on ISSPs' services as well as mechanisms for arbitration and assistance in the negotiation process between press publishers and ISSPs. The Polish legislator was the last to implement the CDSM Directive. Although the delay in fulfilling the obligations under EU law warrants criticism, the Polish legislature was, in a sense, in a privileged position. It could draw lessons from both the legislative successes and failures of other MS in this area, using those insights to shape its implementation and avoid numerous threats to the free flow of information and media pluralism. This implementation includes a significant number of safeguards for the bargaining position of press publishers compared to the first, French implementation. At the same time, it could be described as moderate, as it does not introduce sanctions for non-payment of remuneration or for failure to provide information on the use of press publications, as has been done in other MS.

The effectiveness of publishers' protection cannot be ensured through measures that are not in conformity with EU law, as such measures will be easily contestable. Nevertheless, due to the significant market position of ISSPs, additional safeguards remain necessary. Described by some as a phenomenon of technofeudalism,[1] the market power of platforms and the weakness of other actors dependent on them make it difficult to introduce regulation that safeguards publishers' interests without simultaneously restricting the free flow of information in a network largely controlled by platforms. The lack of safeguards is problematic, as it contributes to the development of free riding practices of ISSPs. On the other hand, introducing safeguards is not an ideal solution either, as numerous examples show that platforms may use them as a pretext to limit the visibility of press content in order to avoid paying under publishers' rights. Perhaps if the mediation mechanisms had been explicitly provided for in the CDSM Directive itself, there would be no possibility of contesting them on the grounds of non-compliance with the EU law, removing one argument from the platforms.

One path to strengthen the position of press publishers negotiating with platforms under the new law is to seek support from competition authorities and invoke competition law in cases of abuse of dominance, bad faith negotiations or the imposition of unfair negotiating conditions. In some MS, the Competition Authority has already intervened to ensure the exercise of publishers' rights. This, however, presents another paradox: to effectively exercise exclusive rights under the related rights regime, it becomes necessary to rely on tools from competition law.

Another path is to seek systemic changes aimed at balancing the relationship between dominant online platforms and press publishers, who are dependent on these platforms and hold a weak negotiating position. For instance, in the United States, enforcing "structural remedies" that would prevent Google from using some of its products, such as Chrome, Android and Play, is being considered in order to weaken its position on the market.[2] It is worth seeking structural remedies in areas in which platforms depend on press publishers, using this dependency as a bargaining chip. It could be the use of press materials for AI training purposes, as ensuring high-quality and trustworthy AI output requires the high-quality training data, which press publications can provide. Moreover, publishers should be encouraged to seek agreements with platforms, as cooperation with ISSPs and visibility on their services bring benefits to press publishers.

I believe that the set of guidelines and warnings formulated in this monograph will be useful not only for legislators but also for users, NGOs, academics and

1 Y. Varoufakis, *Technofeudalism. What Killed Capitalism* (Vintage, 2024).
2 J. Simpson, "Google faces US government attempt to break it up," The Guardian, October 9, 2024, https://www.theguardian.com/technology/2024/oct/09/google-us-government-attempt-break-up-business-court-filing, accessed: 06.01.2025.

practitioners and will contribute to raising awareness about the complex relationship between the press sector and online platforms. I hope that legislators, wishing to regulate this complex relationship in the future, will choose the right words – words that will actually translate into effective action that is beneficial for media pluralism and the free flow of information.

Bibliography

Table of legislation

(The table includes also non-binding legal instruments.)

International treaties and conventions

Berne Convention: Berne Convention for the Protection of Literary and Artistic Works, of 9 September 1886 (completed at Paris on 4 May 1896, revised at Berlin on 13 November 1908, completed at Berne on 20 March 1914, revised at Rome on 2 June 1928, at Brussels on 26 June 1948, at Stockholm on 14 July 1967, at Paris on 24 July 1971, and amended on 28 September 1979).

Rome Convention: International Convention for the Protection of Performers, Producers of Phonograms and Broadcasting Organisations, done at Rome on October 26, 1961.

TRIPS: Agreement on Trade-Related Aspects of Intellectual Property Rights, 15 April 1994.

WCT: WIPO Copyright Treaty, adopted in Geneva on 20 December 1996.

WPPT: WIPO Performances and Phonograms Treaty, adopted in Geneva on 20 December 1996.

Council of Europe

ECHR: European Convention on Human Rights, signed in Rome on 4 November 1950.

Council of Europe, *Pluralisme des médias et enjeux de la concurrence* (IRIS spécial, Une publication de l'Observatoire européen de l'audiovisuel, 2020).

Committee of Ministers, Recommendation CM/Rec(2018) of the Committee of Ministers to member States on media pluralism and transparency of media ownership, https://search.coe.int/cm/Pages/result_details.aspx?ObjectId=0900001680790e13, accessed: 06.01.2023.

Committee of Ministers, Recommendation CM/Rec(2011)7 of the Committee of Ministers to member states on a new notion of media, https://search.coe.int/cm/Pages/result_details.aspx?ObjectID=09000016805cc2c0, accessed: 09.01.2025.

European Union

Treaties and charters

Charter: Charter of Fundamental Rights of the European Union, OJ C 364/1, 18.12.2000.

TEU: Treaty on European Union (Consolidated Version), Treaty of Maastricht, 7 February 1992, OJ EC C 325/5, 24.12.2020.

TFEU: Consolidated Version of the Treaty on the Functioning of the European Union, 5 September 2008, OJ C 326, 26.10.2020.

Regulations

Digital Services Act: Regulation (EU) 2022/2065 of the European Parliament and of the Council of 19 October 2022 on a Single Market For Digital Services and amending Directive 2000/31/EC, OJ L 277, 27.10.2022.

EMFA: Regulation (EU) 2024/1083 of 11 April 2024 establishing a common framework for media services in the internal market, OJ L, 2024/1083, 17.4.2024.

Directives

Audiovisual Media Services Directive: Directive 2010/13/EU of the European Parliament and of the Council of 10 March 2010 on the coordination of certain provisions laid down by law, regulation or administrative action in Member States concerning the provision of audiovisual media services, OJ L 95, 15.4.2010.

Directive on Technological Regulations: Directive (EU) 2015/1535 of the European Parliament and of the Council of 9 September 2015 laying down a procedure for the provision of information in the field of technical regulations and of rules on Information Society services, OJ L 241, 17.9.2015.

Database Directive: Directive 96/9/EC of the European Parliament and of the Council of 11 March 1996 on the legal protection of databases, OJ L 77/20, 27.03.1996.

CDSM Directive: Directive (EU) 2019/790 of the European Parliament and of the Council of 17 April 2019 on copyright and related rights in the Digital Single Market and amending Directives 96/9/EC and 2001/29/EC, OJ L 130, 17.5.2019.

Electronic Commerce Directive: Directive 2000/31/EC of the European Parliament and of the Council of 8 June 2000 on certain legal aspects of information society services, in particular electronic commerce, in the Internal Market, OJ L 178, 17.7.2000.

Enforcement Directive: Directive 2004/48/EC of the European Parliament and of the Council of 29 April 2004 on the enforcement of intellectual property rights, OJ L 157, 30.04.2004.

InfoSoc Directive: Directive 2001/29/EC of 22 May 2001 on the harmonisation of certain aspects of copyright and related rights in the information society, OJ L 167/10, 22.06.2001.

Rental and Lending Rights Directive: Council Directive 92/100/EEC, of 19 November 1992 on rental right and lending right and on certain rights related to copyright in the field of intellectual property, 1992 O.J. (L 346/61) as republished and amended by Directive 2006/115/EC of the European Parliament and of the Council of 12 December 2006 (codified version), 2006 O.J. (L 376/28).

Term Directive: Directive 2006/116/EC of the European Parliament and of the Council of 12 December 2006 on the term of protection of copyright and certain related rights, 2006 O.J. (L 372/12), as amended by Directive 2011/77/EU of the European Parliament and of the Council of 27 September 2011, 2011 O.J. (L 265/1).

Preparatory documents, proposals and Explanatory Memoranda

European Commission, *Impact Assessment on the modernisation of EU copyright rules Accompanying the document Proposal for a Directive of the European Parliament and of the Council on copyright in the Digital Single Market Print*, (SWD (2016) 301 final, 2016) 156, https://eur-lex.europa.eu/legal-content/EN/TXT/?uri=celex:52016SC0301, accessed: 27.10.2022.

European Commission, *Online News Aggregation and Neighbouring Rights for News Publishers*, Ref.Ares(2017)6256585-20/12/2017, (2017), (unreleased), https://www.asktheeu.org/en/request/4776/response/15356/attach/6/Doc1.pdf, accessed: 06.11.2023.

European Commission, Proposal for a Directive of the European Parliament and of the Council on copyright in the Digital Single Market – COM (2016)593, 14.9.2016 final 2016/0280 (COD), https://digital-strategy.ec.europa.eu/en/library/proposal-directive-european-parliament-and-council-copyright-digital-single-market, accessed:27.10.2022.

European Commission, *Staff Working Document Impact Assessment on modernization of EU copyright rules Accompanying the document Proposal for a Directive of the European Parliament and of the Council on the copyright in the Digital Single Market*, (SWD 2016 301 final, 2016).

European Commission, *Commission Staff Working Document Report on the use of collective licensing mechanisms with an extended effect under Article 12(6) of Directive 2019/790/EU on copyright and related rights in the Digital Single Market*, (SWD(2021) 337 final 2021), https://data.consilium.europa.eu/doc/document/ST-14480-2021-INIT/en/pdf, accessed: 07.01.2025.

European Commission Staff Working Document, Media pluralism in the Member States of the European Union, SEC(2007) 32.

CREATe, EU Copyright Reform, Evidence on the Copyright in the Digital Single Market Directive, 26 March 2019, 59, https://www.create.ac.uk/policy-responses/eu-copyright-reform/#table, accessed: 08.11.2022.

Communications

European Commission, *Communication from the Commission to the European Parliament, The Council, the European Economic and Social Committee and the Committee of the Regions Promoting a Fair, Efficient and Competitive European Copyright-Based Economy in the Digital Single Market, COM/2016/0592 Final*, (2016), https://eur-lex.europa.eu/legal-content/EN/TXT/?uri=CELEX%3A52016DC0592, accessed: 27.10.2022.

European Commission, *Market Definition in the Media Sector – Economic Issues*, Report by Europe Economics for the European Commission, Report by Bird & Bird for the European Commission, Directorate-General for Competition, Information, Communication and Multimedia, 2002, https://op.europa.eu/en/publication-detail/-/publication/e438a087-8dd9-450d-85f4-bf3a02b98ca9/language-en, accessed: 08.01.2025.

European Parliament, *Strengthening the Position of Press Publishers and Authors and Performers in the Copyright Directive*, Policy Department for Citizens' Rights and Constitutional Affairs Directorate General for Internal Policies of the Union, Study for the JURI Committee (2017).

Reports and studies

European Commission, *Study on media plurality* (Publication Office of the European Union, 2022), 12–13, https://op.europa.eu/en/publication-detail/-/publication/475bacb6-34a2-11ed-8b77-01aa75ed71a1/language-en/format-PDF/source-266738523, accessed: 02.03.2023.

European Commission, 2022 Rule of Law Report, https://commission.europa.eu/strategy-and-policy/policies/justice-and-fundamental-rights/upholding-rule-law/rule-law/rule-law-mechanism/2022-rule-law-report_en, accessed: 01.09.2023.

European Parliament, *The European Media Freedom Act: Media Freedom, Freedom of Expression and Pluralism*, 17–19, https://www.europarl.europa.eu/RegData/etudes/STUD/2023/747930/IPOL_STU(2023)747930_EN.pdf, accessed: 23.10.2023.

European Parliament, *Strengthening the Position of Press Publishers and Authors and Performers in the Copyright Directive*, (Policy Department for Citizens' Rights and Constitutional Affairs Directorate General for Internal Policies of the Union, Study for the JURI Committee, 2017).

Council resolutions and conclusions

Council, Resolution of 14 May 1992 on Increased Protection for Copyright and Neighbouring Rights (92/C 138/01), 1992.

Council of European Union, *Council Conclusions on Safeguarding a Free and Pluralistic Media System* (2020/C 422/08, 2020).

National laws

Poland

Ministerstwo Kultury i Dziedzictwa Narodowego, *Uzasadnienie do projektu ustawy o zmianie ustawy o prawie autorskim i prawach pokrewnych oraz niektórych innych ustaw*, (2020), https://bip.mkidn.gov.pl/media/pu_prawo_autorskie_20220620/Uzasadnienie_do_ustawy.pdf, accessed:19.11.2022.

The Constitution of the Republic of Poland of 2nd April, 1997, https://www.sejm.gov.pl/prawo/konst/angielski/kon1.htm, accessed: 02.03.2023.

Ustawa z dnia 4 lutego 1994 r. o prawie autorskim i prawach pokrewnych, t.j. Dz. U. z 2022 r. poz. 2509, z 2024 r. poz. 1222, 1254.

Ustawa z dnia 26 stycznia 1984 r. Prawo prasowe, Dz. U. 1984 Nr 5 poz. 24, t.j. Dz. U. z 2018 r. poz. 1914; Act of 26 January 1984 – Press Law, Dz. U. 1984 Nr 5 poz. 24, t.j. Dz. U. z 2018 r. poz. 1914.

Ustawa z dnia 6 marca 2018r. Prawo przedsiębiorców, Dz. U. 2018 poz. 646 t.j. Dz. U. z 2021 r. poz. 162, 2105, z 2022 r. poz. 24, 974, 1570.

Ustawa z dnia 11 marca 2004 o podatku od towarów i usług Dz. U. 2004 Nr 54 poz. 535, t.j. Dz. U. z 2022 r. poz. 931, 974, 1137, 1301, 1488, 1561, 2180.

Ustawa z dnia 18 lipca 2002 r. o świadczeniu usług drogą elektroniczną, Dz. U. z 2020 r. poz. 344.

Ustawa z dnia 15 czerwca 2018 r. o zbiorowym zarządzaniu prawami autorskimi i prawami pokrewnymi, Dz.U. 2018 poz. 1293.

France

Code de la propriété intellectuelle (dernière mise à jour le 20.10.2023/ Last update 20.10.2023), https://www.legifrance.gouv.fr/codes/texte_lc/LEGITEXT000006069414/, accessed: 21.05.2023.

Code des postes et des communications électroniques, https://www.legifrance.gouv.fr/codes/section_lc/LEGITEXT000006070987/LEGISCTA000006150573/#LEGISCTA000006150573, accessed: 12.01.2023.

LOI n° 2019-775 du 24 juillet 2019 tendant à créer un droit voisin au profit des agences de presse et des éditeurs de presse, https://www.legifrance.gouv.fr/jorf/id/JORFTEXT000038821358, accessed: 23.11.2022.

Loi n° 86-897 du 1 août 1986 portant réforme du régime juridique de la presse, https://www.legifrance.gouv.fr/loda/id/JORFTEXT000000687451, accessed: 09.01.2023.

Loi n° 47-585 du 2 avril 1947 relative au statut des entreprises de groupage et de distribution des journaux et publications périodiques, https://www.legifrance.gouv.fr/loda/id/JORFTEXT000000684244/, accessed: 11.11.2023.
LOI n° 2004-575 du 21 juin 2004 pour la confiance dans l'économie numérique, LOI n° 2004-575 du 21 juin 2004 https://www.legifrance.gouv.fr/jorf/id/JORFTEXT000000801164, accessed: 12.07.2023.

Germany

Urheberrechtsgesetz, https://dejure.org/gesetze/UrhG/87f.html, accessed: 15.08.2023.

Belgium

28 Février 2018, Code de droit économique, https://www.ejustice.just.fgov.be/eli/loi/2013/02/28/2013A11134/justel, accessed: 11.11.2023.

Spain

Ley de Propiedad Intelectual, 5 November 2014; version of the article from 2014, Spanish version: https://www.boe.es/buscar/act.php?id=BOE-A-1996-8930&b=52&tn=1&p=20190302#a32, accessed: 23.11.2022.

Italy

Legge sul diritto d'autore, https://www.altalex.com/documents/codici-altalex/2014/06/26/legge-sul-diritto-d-autore#titolo1, aceessed: 15.08.2023.

Czech Republic

Autorsky Zákon, https://www.zakonyprolidi.cz/cs/2000-121, accessed: 09.12.2024.

Australia

Australian News Media Bargaining Code, https://www.accc.gov.au/system/files/Final%20legislation%20as%20passed%20by%20both%20houses.pdf, accessed: 25.10.2023.
The Parliament of the Commonwealth of Australia, Treasury Law Amendment (News Media and Digital Platforms Mandatory Bargaining Code) Bill 2021, Revised Explanatory Memorandum, https://www.accc.gov.au/system/files/Revised%20explanatory%20memorandum.pdf, accessed: 25.07.2023.

Table of cases

(Alphabetically ordered. When available, citations refer to the European Case Law Identifier (ECLI).)

European Court of Human Rights (ECtHR)

Anheuser-Busch vs. Portugal: Anheuser-Busch Inc. v. Portugal (App. no. 73049/01), 11.01.2007, ECLI:CE:ECHR:2007:0111JUD007304901.

Appleby & Others v. the United Kingdom: Appleby & Others v. the United Kingdom (App. No.44306/98), 06.05.2002, CE:ECHR:2003:0506JUD004430698.
Ashby Donald: Ashby Donald and others v. France (App. no. 36769/08), 10.01.2013, ECLI :CE:ECHR:2013:0110JUD003676908.
Autronic AG: Autronic AG v. Switzerland (App No. 12726/87), 22.05.1990.
Cengiz and others v. Turkey: Cengiz and others v. Turkey, (App. Nos. 48226/10 and 14027/11), 01.12.2015, CE:ECHR:2015:1201JUD004822610.
Chassagnou and Others v. France: Chassagnou and Others v. France, (App.Nos.25088/94, 28331/95 and 28443/95), 29.04.1999.
Delfi AS v. Estonia: Delfi AS v. Estonia [GC], (App. No. 64569/09), 16.06.2015, ECLI:CE: ECHR:2013:1010JUD006456909.
Dima v. Romania: Dima v. Romania, (App. No. 58472/00), 26.05.2005, ECLI:CE:ECHR:2 006:1116JUD005847200.
Editions Plon v. France : Editions Plon v. France, (App. Nos. 58148/00), 18.05.2004.
Guerra and others v. Italy: Guerra and others v. Italy, (App.no. 116/1996/735/932), 19.02.1998, ECLI:CE:ECHR:1998:0219JUD001496789.
Haider v. Austria: Haider v. Austria, (App. No. 25060/94), 18.10.1995.
Handyside v. United Kingdom: Handyside v. United Kingdom, (App. No. 5493/72), 07.12.1976, ECLI:CE:ECHR:1976:1207JUD000549372.
Hatton and Others v. the United Kingdom, Hatton and Others v. the United Kingdom, (App. No. 36022/97), 08.07.2003, ECLI:CE:ECHR:2003:0708JUD003602297.
Kenedi v. Hungary: Kenedi v. Hungary, (App. No. 31475/05), 26 May 2009.
Kopecký v. Slovakia: Kopecký v. Slovakia, (App. No. 44912/98), 28.09.2004.
Lingens v. Austria: Lingens v. Austria, (App. No. 9815/82), 08.07.1986, ECLI:CE:ECHR: 1986:0708JUD000981582.
Magyar Jeti Zrt v. Hungary: Magyar Jeti Zrt v. Hungary, (App. No. 11257/16), 04.12.2018, ECLI:CE:ECHR:2018:1204JUD001125716.
Melnychuk v. Ukraine: Melnychuk v. Ukraine (App. No. 28743/03), 05.07.2005, ECLI:CE: ECHR:2005:0705DEC002874303.
Observer and Guardian v. The United Kingdom, Observer and Guardian v. The United Kingdom, (App. No. 13585/88), 26.11.1991, CE:ECHR:1991:1126JUD001358588.
OOO Regnum v. Russia, OOO Regnum v. Russia, (App. No. 22649/08), 08.09.2020, ECLI: CE:ECHR:2020:0908JUD002264908.
Özgür Gündem v. Turkey: Özgür Gündem v. Turkey, (App. No. 23144/93), 16.03.2000.
Tammer v. Estonia: Tammer v. Estonia, (App. No. 41205/98), 06.02.2001.
The Pirate Bay: Fredrik Neij and Peter Sunde Kolmisoppi (The Pirate Bay) v. Sweden (App. No.40397/12), 19.02.2013, ECLI:CE:ECHR:2013:0219DEC004039712.
Thoma v. Luxembourg: Thoma v. Luxembourg, (App. No.38432/9), 29.03.2001.
Remuszko v. Poland: Remuszko v. Poland, (App. No. 1562/10), 16.10.2013.
Sunday Times v. the United Kingdom: Sunday Times v. the United Kingdom, (App. No.6538/74), 26.04.1979, ECLI:CE:ECHR:1979:0426JUD000653874.
Társaság a Szabadságjogokért v. Hungary: Társaság a Szabadságjogokért v. Hungary, (App.No. 37374/05), 14.04.2009, CE:ECHR:2009:0414JUD003737405.
Verein gegen Tierfabriken Schweiz v. Switzerland: Verein gegen Tierfabriken Schweiz v. Switzerland, (App. No.24699/94), 28.06.2001, ECLI:CE:ECHR:2007:1004 JUD003277202.
Worm v Austria: Worm v. Austria, (App. No.83/1996/702/894), 29.08.1997.
Yıldırım v. Turkey: Ahmet Yıldırım v. Turkey (App. No. 3111/10), 10.12.2012, ECLI:CE:E CHR:2012:1218JUD000311110.
Youth Initiative for Human Rights v. Serbia: Youth Initiative for Human Rights v. Serbia, (App. No.48135/06), 25.06.2012.

Court of Justice of the European Union (CJEU): Judgements

ACI Adam: Case C-435/12, ACI Adam BV and Others v. Stichting de Thuiskopie and Stichting Onderhandelingen Thuiskopie vergoeding, 10.04.2014, ECLI:EU:C:2014:254.
Air Transport Association: Case C-366/10, Air Transport Association of America and Others, 21.12.2011, ECLI:EU:C:2011:864.
Alassini: Joined Cases C-317/08, C-318/08, C-319/08 and C-320/08, Alassini and Others, 18.03.2010, ECLI:EU:C:2010:146.
BestWater: Case C 348/13, BestWater International GmbH v. Michael Mebes, Stefan Potsch, 21.10.2014, ECLI:EU:C:2014:2315.
British American Tobacco: Case C-491/01, British American Tobacco (Investments) and Imperial Tobacco, 10.12.2002, ECLI:EU:C:2002:741.
C More Entertainment: Case C-279/13, C More Entertainment AB v. Linus Sandberg, 26.03.2015, ECLI:EU:C:2015:199.
Centro di Musicologia: Case C-386/04, Centro di Musicologia Walter Stauffer v. Finanzamt München für Körperschaften, 14.09.2006, ECLI:EU:C:2006:568.
Coty: Case C-580/13, Coty Germany GmbH v. Stadtsparkasse Magdeburg, 16.07.2015, ECLI:EU:C:2015:485.
Deckmyn: Case C-201/13, Johan Deckmyn and Vrijheidsfonds VZW v. Helena Vandersteen and Others, 03.09.2012, ECLI:EU:C:2014:2132.
Donner: Case C-5/11, Criminal Proceedings Against Titus Alexander Jochen Donner, 21.06.2012, ECLI:EU:C:2012:370.
Familiapress: Case C-368/95, Familiapress v. Bauer Verlag,26.06.1997, ECLI:EU:C:1997:325.
Filmspeler: Stichting Brein V Jack Frederik Wullems, Case C-527/15, 26.04.2017, ECLI:EU:C:2017:300.
Football Dataco: Case C-604/10, Football Dataco Ltd and Others v. Yahoo! UK Ltd and Others, 01.03.2012, ECLI:EU:C:2012:115.
Funke Medien: C-469/17, Funke Medien NRW GmbH v. Bundesrepublik Deutschland, 29.07.2019, ECLI:EU:C:2019:623
GS Media: Case C-160/15, GS Media B V Sanoma Media Netherlands BV, Playboy Enterprises International Inc., Britt Geertruida Dekker, 08.09.2016, ECLI:EU:C:2016:644.
Infopaq I: Case C-5/08, Infopaq International A/S v. Danske Dagblades Forening, 16.07.2009, ECLI:EU:C:2009:465.
Infopaq II: Case C-302/10, Infopaq International A/S v. Danske Dagblades Forening, 17.01.2012 (Order), ECLI:EU:C:2012:16.
Kadi: Joined Cases C-402/05 P and C-415/05 P, Yassin Abdullah Kadi and Al Barakaat International Foundation v. Council of the European Union and Commission of the European Communities, 3.09.2008, ECLI:EU:C:2008:461.
Levola Hengelo: Case C-310/17, Levola Hengelo BV v. Smilde Foods BV, 13.11.2018, ECLI:EU:C:2018:899.
L'Oréal v eBay: Case 324/09, L'Oréal SA and Others v. eBay International AG and Others, 12.07.2011, ECLI:EU:C:2011:474.
Luksan: Case C 277/10, Martin Luksan v. Petrus van der Let, 9.02.2012, ECLI:EU:C:2012:65.
Marco Del Corso: Case C- 135/10, Società Consortile Fonografici (SCF) v. Marco Del Corso, 15.03.2012, ECLI:EU:C:2012:140.
Meltwater: Case C-360/13, Public Relations Consultants Association Ltd v. Newspaper Licensing Agency Ltd and Others, 5.06.2014, ECLI:EU:C:2014:1195.
Metronome Musik: Case C- 200/96, Metronome Musik and Music Point Hokamp GmbH, 28 April 1998, ECLI:EU:C:1998:172.
Murphy: Joined Cases C-403/08 and C-429/08, Football Association Premier League Ltd and Others v. QC Leisure and Others (C-403/08) and Karen Murphy v. Media Protection Services Ltd (C-429/08), 4.10.2011, ECLI:EU:C:2011:631.

Nintendo: Case C-355/12, Nintendo Co. Ltd and Others v. PC Box Srl and 9Net Srl, Case 23.01.2014, ECLI:EU:C:2014:25.

Padawan: Case C-467/08, Padawan SL v. Sociedad General de Autores y Editores de España (SGAE), 21.10.2010, ECLI:EU:C:2010:620.

Painer: Case C-145/10, Eva-Maria Painer tegen Standard VerlagsGmbH en anderen, 1.12.2011, ECLI:EU:C:2011:798.

Papasavvas : Case C-291/1Sotiris Papasavvas v. O Fileleftheros Dimosia Etairia Ltd, Takis Kounnafi, Giorgos Sertis, 11.09.2014, ECLI:EU:C:2014:2209.

Pelham: Case C-476/17, Pelham GmbH and Others v Ralf Hütter, Florian SchneiderEsleben, 29 July 2019, ECLI:EU:C:2019:624.

Promusicae: Case C-275/06, Productores de Música de España (Promusicae) v. Telefónica de España SAU, 29.01.2008, ECLI:EU:C:2008:54.

Rafael Hoteles: Case 306/05, SGAE v Rafael Hoteles SA, 07.12.2006, ECLI:EU:C:2006:764.

Renckhoff: Case C-161/17, Land Nordrhein-Westfalen v. Dirk Renckhoff, 07.08.2018, ECLI:EU:C:2018:634.

Republic of Poland: Case C-401/19, Republic of Poland v. European Parliament, Council of the European Union, 26.04.2022, ECLI:EU:C:2022:297.

Satamedia: Case C-73/07, Tietosuojavaltuutettu v. Satakunnan Markkinapörssi Oy and Satamedia Oy, 16.12.2008. ECLI:EU:C:2008:727.

Scarlet Extended: Case C-70/10, Scarlet Extended SA v. Société belge des auteurs, compositeurs et éditeurs SCRL (SABAM), 24.11.2011, ECLI:EU:C:2011:771.

Sergejs Buivids: Case C–345/17, Sergejs Buivids v. Datu valsts inspekcija, 14.02.2019, ECLI:EU:C:2019:122.

Schmidberger: Case C-112/00, Eugen Schmidberger, Internationale Transporte und Planzüge v. Republik Österreich,, 12.06.2003, ECLI:EU:C:2003:333.

Soulier and Doke: Case C-301/15, Soulier and Doke, 16.11.2016, ECLI:EU:C:2016:878.

Spiegel Online: Case C516/17, Spiegel Online GmbH v. Volker Beck, 29.07.2019, ECLI:EU:C:2019:625.

Schrems: Case C311/18, Facebook Ireland and Schrems, 16.07.2020, ECLI:EU:C:2020:559.

Stichting de Thuiskopie: Case C-462/09, Stichting de Thuiskopie v. Opus Supplies Deutschland GmbH and Others, 16.06.2011, ECLI:EU:C:2011:397.

Svensson: Case C-466/12, Nils Svensson and others v. Retriever Sverige AB, 13.02.2014, ECLI:EU:C:2014:76.

Tom Kabinet: Case C-263/18, Nederlands Uitgeversverbond, Groep Algemene Uitgevers v. Tom Kabinet Internet BV et al., 19.12.2019, ECLI:EU:C:2019:1111.

TVCatchup: Case C-607/11, ITV Broadcasting Ltd and others v. TVCatchup Ltd, 07.03.2013, ECLI:EU:C:2013:147.

You Tube and Cyando: Case C-682/18, C-683/18, Frank Peterson v. Google LLC, YouTube Inc., YouTube LLC, Google Germany GmbH and Elsevier Inc. v. Cyando, 22.06.2021, ECLI:EU:C:2021:503.

Ulmer: Case C-117/13, Technische Universität Darmstadt v. Eugen Ulmer KG, 11.09.2014, ECLI:EU:C:2014:2196.

UPC Telekabel: Case C-314/12, UPC Telekabel Wien GmbH v. Constantin Film Verleih GmbH, Wega Filmproduktionsgesellschaft mbH, 27.03.2014.

Vereniging Openbare Bibliotheken: Case C-174/15, Vereniging Openbare Bibliotheken v. Stichting Leenrecht, 10.11.2016, ECLI:EU:C:2016:856.

Ziggo: Case C-610/15, Stichting Brein v. Ziggo BV, XS4ALL Internet BV, 14.06.2017, ECLI:EU:C:2017:456.

Court of Justice of the European Union (CJEU): Advocate General (AG) Opinions

Opinion AG in Funken Medien: Opinion of Advocate General Szpunar delivered on 25.10.2018, Case C-469/17, Funke Medien NRW GmbH v. Bundesrepublik Deutschland, ECLI:EU:C:2018:870.

Opinion AG in GS Media: Opinion of Advocate General Wathelet delivered on 7.04.2016 Case C-160/15, GS Media BV v. Sanoma Media Netherlands BV, Playboy Enterprises International Inc., Britt Geertruida Dekker ECLI:EU:C:2016:221.

Opinion AG in Painer: Opinion of Advocate General Trstenjak delivered on 12.04.2011, Case 145/10, Eva-Maria Painer tegen Standard VerlagsGmbH en anderen, ECLI:EU:C:2011:239.

Opinion AG in Pelham: Opinion of Advocate General Szpunar delivered on 12.12.2018, Case C476/17, Pelham GmbH and Others v. Ralf Hütter, Florian SchneiderEsleben, ECLI:EU:C:2018:1002.

Opinion AG in Republic of Poland: Opinion of Advocate General Saugmandsgaard Øe delivered on 15.07.2021 Case C-401/19 Republic of Poland v. European Parliament and Council of the European Union, ECLI:EU:C:2021:613.

Opinion AG in Stichting de Thuiskopie: Opinion of Advocate General Jääskinen delivered on 10.03.2011, Case C-462/09, Stichting de Thuiskopie v. Opus Supplies Deutschland GmbH and Others, ECLI:EU:C:2011:133.

Opinion AG in VG Bild-Kunst: Opinion of Advocate General Szpunar delivered on 10.09.2020, Case C-392/19 VG Bild-Kunst v. Stiftung Preußischer Kulturbesitz, ECLI:EU:C:2020:696.

Opinion AG in **YouTube/Cyando***:* Opinion of Advocate General Saugmandsgaard Øe delivered on 16.07.2020, Cases C682/18 and C683/18, Frank Peterson v. Google LLC, YouTube Inc., YouTube LLC, Google Germany GmbH and Elsevier Inc. v. Cyando, ECLI:EU:C:2020:586.

National case law

Poland

Polish Appellate Court in Warsaw: Judgement of 26 January 1995, I ACr 1037/94, LEX no. 535044.

Polish Appellate Court in Warsaw: Judgement of 18 November 1999, I ACa 792/99, LEX no. 535049.

Polish Supreme Court: Judgement of 15 November 2002, II CKN 1289/00, LEX no .78613.

Polish Appellate Court in Warsaw: Judgement of 11 May 2007, I Aca 1145/06, LEX no. 558375.

Polish Supreme Court, Decision of 26 July 2007, IV KK 174/07, LEX no. 287505.

Polish Constitutional Court, 12 May 2008, SK 43/05, LEX no. 376365.

Polish Supreme Court, Decision of 15 December 2010, III KK, LEX no. 784329.

Polish Constitutional Court, 23 June 2015 r., SK 32/14, LEX no. 1747331.

Court of Appeal in Gdańsk, 3 January 2019 r., V AGa 129/18, LEX no. 2763417.

Polish Supreme Court, 9 August 2019, II CSK 7/18, LEX no. 2652247.

France

Constitutional Council, 27 July 1982, decision n°82-141 DC, Law on audiovisual communication.

Constitutional Council, 11 October 1984, Decision no. 84-181 DC, Law to limit concentration and ensure the financial transparency and pluralism of press companies.

Constitutional Council, 27 July 2006, Decision no. 2006-540 DC of Copyright and related rights in the information society.
The Court of Cassation, Microfor vs. Le Monde, 30 October 1987, 86-11918.
The Court of Cassation, Req. 8 août 1861, Havas, Bullier et comp. v. Gounouilhou: DP 1862. 1. 13.
The Court of Cassation, 19 January 2010, 08-15.338 08-16.459 08-16.469.
The Court of Cassation, 16 December 1986, 85-10.838.
The Court of Cassation, 15 April 1986, 84-12.008.
The Court of Cassation, Mulholland Drive, 28 February 2006, 05-15.824.
The Court of Cassation, 30 January 1978, 75-92.001.
The Court of Cassation, 9 November 1983, 82-10.005.
Court of Appeal, 25 October 1990, 88/6738, 88/20948.
FCA Decision 20-MC-01 of 9 April 2020 on requests for interim measures by the Syndicat des éditeurs de la presse magazine, the Alliance de la presse d'information générale and others and Agence France-Presse, https://www.autoritedelaconcurrence.fr/sites/default/files/integral_texts/2020-06/20-mc-01_en.pdf, accessed: 12.01.2024.
FCA Decision 21-D-17 of 12 July 2021 on non-compliance with the injunctions issued against Google in Decision 20-MC-01 of 9 April 2020, https://www.autoritedelaconcurrence.fr/sites/default/files/attachments/2022-02/21-d-17_en.pdf, accessed: 08.12.2024.
Decision of 15 March 2024 of FCA on non-compliance with the commitments set out in the Decision of 21 June 2022 concerning practices implemented by Google in the press sector, https://www.autoritedelaconcurrence.fr/sites/default/files/integral_texts/2024-03/24d03vf.pdf, accessed: 21.03.2024.
Tribunal Judiciaire de Paris, Ordonnance de Référé, 23 May 2024, N° RG 23/55581 – N° Portalis 352J-W-B7H-C2JUY, Dalloz-Actualité, https://www.dalloz-actualite.fr/sites/dalloz-actualite.fr/files/resources/2024/06/23_mai_2024_-_2355581.pdf, accessed: 21.12.2024.

Belgium

The Court Appel of Brussels, Google Inc vs. Copiepresse, 2011.
Cour Consitutionelle, Arrêt n° 98/2024 du 26 septembre 2024, Numéros du rôle: 7922, 7924, 7925, 7926 et 7927, ECLI:BE:GHCC:2024:ARR.098.

Italy

Il Tribunale Amministrativo Regionale per il Lazio, Sezione Quarta, N. 18790/2023 REG. PROV.COLL.
N. 07093/2023 REG.RIC., 12.12.2023.

Netherlands

Amsterdam District Court of 30 October 2024, ref. C/13/737 170 / HA ZA 23-690, https://www.technollama.co.uk/can-a-dutch-case-about-rss-teach-us-anything-about-ai-copyright, accessed: 20.12.2024.

United States

United States District Court, Southern District of New York, The New York Times Company v. Microsoft Corporation et al., filed 27.12.2023, https://nytco-assets.nytimes.com/2023/12/NYT_Complaint_Dec2023.pdf, accessed: 22.04.2024.

Monographs and articles

Aguinis, H., S. J. Vaschetto, "Editorial Responsibility: Managing the Publishing Process to Do Good and Do Well," *Management and Organization Review* 7, no. 3 (2011).

Angelopoulos, Ch., *Articles 15 & 17 of the Directive on Copyright in the Digital Single Market, Comparative National Implementation Report*, https://informationlabs.org/wp-content/uploads/2022/09/Angelopoulos-Report-Full-Report.pdf, accessed: 20.12.2024.

Angelopoulos, Ch., "European Copyright and human rights in the digital sphere," in *Human Rights, Digital Society in the Digital Sphere*, ed. M. Susi, (Routledge, 2019).

Angelopoulos, Ch., "On Online Platforms and the Commission's New Proposal for a Directive on Copyright in the Digital Single Market," *SSRN*, (Centre for Intellectual Property and Information Law (CIPIL), University of Cambridge, 2017), https://papers.ssrn.com/sol3/papers.cfm?abstract_id=2947800, accessed: 16.08.2022.

Athey, S., M. Mobius, J. Pal, "The Impact of News Aggregators on Internet News Consumption: The Case of Localization," *National Bureau of Economic Research, NBER Working Paper No. 28746,* (2021), https://www.nber.org/system/files/working_papers/w28746/w28746.pdf, accessed: 03.02.2023.

Azzi, T., "Commentaire de la loi du 24 juillet 2019 tendant à créer un droit voisin au profit des agences de presse et des éditeurs de presse," *Dalloz IP/IT* 1 (2020).

Azzi, T., *Recherche sur la loi applicable aux droits voisins du droit d'auteur en droit international privé,* (L.G.D.J, 2005).

Badouard, R., "Pluralisme, indépendance, diversité : peut-on encore "sauver les médias" ?," *Participations* 2, no. 15 (2016).

Banterle, F., G. Ghidini, "Copyright, News, and "Information Products" Under the New CDSM Directive," ResearchGate, (2020), 6, https://www.researchgate.net/publication/342707640_Copyright_news_and_information_products_under_the_new_DSM_Copyright_Directive, accessed: 09.11.2022.

Barak, A., *Proportionality. Constitutional Rights and their Limitations*, (Cambridge University Press, 2012).

Bárd, P., J. Bayer, *A Comparative Analysis of Media Freedom and Pluralism in the EU Member States*, (European Parliament's Committee on Civil Liberties, Justice and Home Affairs, 2016), 34–36, https://www.statewatch.org/media/documents/news/2016/oct/ep-study-media-freedom-in-EU.pdf, accessed: 09.01.2025.

Barendt, E., *Freedom of Speech*, (Oxford University Press, 2005).

Barta, J., "Prawa pokrewne," in *Prawo autorskie, System Prawa Prywatnego*, ed. J. Barta, vol. 13, (C.H.Beck, 2017).

Barta, J., R. Markiewicz, "Postęp techniczny w mediach," in *Prawo mediów*, ed. J. Barta, R. Markiewicz, A. Matlak, (LexisNexis, 2005).

Barta J., R. Markiewicz, *Prawo autorskie* (Wolters Kluwer, 2016).

Bechtold, S., "Information Society Directive," in *Concise European Copyright Law*, ed. T. Dreier, B. Hugenholtz, (Kluwer Law International, 2006).

Bell E., et al., *The Platform Press. How Silicon Valley Reengineered Journalism*, (Tow Center for Digital Journalism, Columbia Journalism School, 2017).

Bently L., in *Copyright, Related Rights and the News in the EU: Assessing Potential New Laws*, Transcript of Conference, University of Amsterdam, (2016), 52, https://resources.law.cam.ac.uk/cipil/documents/potential_legal_responses_complete_transcript.pdf, accessed:27.10.2022.

Bernault, C., J.-P. Clavier, "Fiche 18. La gestion collective du droit d'auteur, Fiches de Droit de la propriété intellectuelle," (2016): 104–109, https://www.cairn.info/fiches-de-droit-de-la-propriete-intellectuelle--9782340014107-page-104.htm, accessed: 25.08.2023.

Bertrand, A. R., *Droit d'auteur*, (Paris Dalloz Action, 2010).

Birnhack, M., "More or Better? Shaping the public domain," in *The Public Domain of Information,* ed. P. B. Hugenholtz, L. Guibault, (Kluwer Law International, 2005).

Błońska, B., "Komentarz do art.11 Ustawy o prawie autorskim i prawach pokrewnych," in *Prawo autorskie i prawa pokrewne. Komentarz,* ed. W. Machała, R. Sarbiński, (Wolters Kluwer Polska, LEX, 2019).
Błońska,B., "Komentarz do art. 25 Ustawy o prawie autorskim i prawach pokrewnych," in *Prawo autorskie i prawa pokrewne. Komentarz,* ed. W. Machała, R. Sarbiński, (Wolters Kluwer Polska, LEX, 2019).
Boczkowski, P. J., E. Mitchelstein, *The News Gap: When the Information Preferences of the Media and the Public Diverge*, (The MIT Press, 2013).
Bodó, B., "Selling News to Audiences – A Qualitative Inquiry into the Emerging Logics of Algorithmic News Personalization in European Quality News Media," *Digital Journalism* 7, no. 8 (2019).
Bonadio, E., L. McDonagh, "Artificial Intelligence as Producer and Consumer of Copyright Works: Evaluating the Consequences of Algorithmic Creativity," *Intellectual Property Quarterly* 2 (2020).
Bossio, D., *Journalism and Social Media. Practitioners, Organisations and Institutions*, (Palgrave Macmillan, 2017).
Bowrey, K., *Copyright, Creativity, Big Media and Cultural Value. Incorporating the Author*, (Routledge, 2021).
Brogi, E. "Cascading Risks to Media Pluralism and a European Approach to Tackle Them, Henrich Böll Stiftung," The Green Political Foundation, October 10, 2022, https://www.boell.de/en/2022/10/10/cascading-risks-media-pluralism-and-european-approach-tackle-them.
Brogi, E., et al., "EU and Media Policy: Conceptualising Media Pluralism in the Era of Online Platforms. The Experience of the Media Pluralism Monitor," in *Research Handbook on Media Law and Policy*, ed. P. L. Parcu, E. Brogi (Edward Elgar, 2021).
Brosius, H. B., A. Graefe, M. Haim, "Burst of the Filter Bubble? Effects of Personalization on the Diversity of Google News," *Digital Journalism* 6, no. 3 (2018).
Bruguière, J. M., J. M. Deltorn, "Intelligences artificielles génératives. Y a-t-il exploitation des oeuvres,au sens du droit d'auteur ? N'y aurait-il pas d'autres modèles à considérer?," *Recueil Dalloz*, (2023).
Buiten,M., K. Heine M. Kerk, M. Senftleben, "New Rights or New Business Models? An Inquiry into the Future of Publishing in the Digital Era," *International Review of Intellectual Property and Competition Law* 48, no. 10 (2017).
Bulayenko, O., Ch.Geiger, "Creating Statutory Remuneration Rights in Copyright Law: What Policy Options Under the International Legal Framework?," Centre for International Intellectual Property Studies Research Paper, no. 2020-05, (2020).
Bulayenko, O., G. Frosio, Ch.Geiger, "Opinion of the CEIPI on the European Commission's Copyright Reform Proposal with a Focus on the Introduction of Neighbouring Rights for Press Publishers in EU Law," CEIPI Research Paper, (2016), https://papers.ssrn.com/sol3/papers.cfm?abstract_id=2921334, accessed: 27.10.2022.
Bulayenko, O., G. Frosio, Ch. Geiger, "The Introduction of a Neighbouring Right for Press Publisher at EU Level: The Unneeded (and Unwanted) Reform," *European Intellectual Property Review* 39, no. 4 (2017).
Bulayenko, O., et al., *Study on Emerging Issues on Collective Licensing Practices in the Digital Environment, Final Report,* (European Commission, 2018), 130, https://www.ivir.nl/publicaties/download/Study_on_collective_practices_in_the_digital_environment.pdf, accessed: 05.02.2024.
Bustos, R. Gisbert, "The Right to Freedom of Expression in a Democratic Society (Art. 10 ECHR)," in *Europe of Rights: A Compendium on the European Convention of Human Rights*, ed. J. G. Roca, P. Santolaya, Martinus, (Nijhoff Publishers, 2012).
Calboli, I., "Comparative Legal Analysis and Intellectual Property Law: A Guide for Research," in *Handbook of Intellectual Property Research. Lenses, Methods and Perspectives*, ed. I. Calboli, M. L. Montagnani, (Oxford University Press, 2021).

Calin M., et al., "Attention Allocation in Information. Rich Environments: The Case of News Aggregators," *Boston University School of Management Research Paper Series*, no. 4, (2013).

Calzada, J., R. Gil, "What Do News Aggregators Do? Evidence from Google News in Spain and Germany," *Marketing Science* 39, no. 1 (2020).

Caron, Ch., *Droit d'auteur et droits voisins,* (Lexis Nexis, 2017).

Castendyk, O., E. Dommering, A. Scheuer, *European Media Law*, (Kluwer Law International, 2008).

Castets – Renard,C., "Éditeur de contenus ou éditeur de services," *Victoires éditions, LEGICOM* 46, no. 1 (2011).

Ceron, W., M. F. de Lima Santos, "Artificial Intelligence in News Media: Current Perceptions and Future Outlook," *Journalism and Media*, (2022), https://www.mdpi.com/2673-5172/3/1/2, accessed: 23.06.2023.

Chiou, L., C. Tucker, "Content Aggregation by Platforms: The Case of the News Media," MIT Sloan Research Paper no. 6925-23, (2015).

Chönherr, F., Ch. Geiger, "The Information Society Directive," in *EU Copyright Law. A Commentary,* ed. I. Stamatoudi, P. Torremans, (Edward Elgar Publishing, 2014).

Christoffersen, J., *Fair Balance: Proportionality, Subsidiarity and Primarity in the European Convention on Human Rights*, Vol. 99, (Brill, 2009).

Christoffersen, J., "Human Rights and Balancing: The Principle of Proportionality," in *Research Handbook in Human Rights and Intellectual Property,* ed. Ch. Geiger, (Edward Elgar Publishing, 2016).

Cobos, T. L., "New Scenarios in News Distribution: The Impact of News Aggregators Like Google News in the Media Outlets on the Web," in *Present Scenarios of Media Production and Engagement,* ed. S. Tosoni et al., (Lumière Bremen, 2017).

Cornia, A., et al., *Pay Models in European News*, (Reuters Institute for Study of Journalism, 2017), https://reutersinstitute.politics.ox.ac.uk/sites/default/files/2017-07/Pay%20Models%20in%20European%20News%20Factsheet.pdf, accessed: 20.01.2023.

Cornia, A., R. K. Nielsen, A. Sehl, *Digital News Project. Private Sector Media and Digital News*, (Reuter Institute for Study of Journalism, 2016).

Craig, P., G. de Burca, *EU Law, Text, Cases and Materials*, (Oxford University Press, 2008).

Czarny – Drożdżejko, E., "The Subject-Matter of Press Publishers' Related Rights Under Directive 2019/790 on Copyright and Related Rights in the Digital Single Market," *International Review of Intellectual Property and Competition Law* (IIC) 51, no. 51 (2020).

Del Águila, A., A. Padilla, C. Serarols, "Value Creation and News Intermediaries on Internet: An Exploratory Analysis of the Online News Industry and the Web Content Aggregators," *International Journal of Information Management* 27, no. 3, (2007).

Derclaye, E., "Intellectual Property Rights and Human Rights: Coinciding and Cooperating," in *Intellectual Property and Human Rights*, Enhanced Edition of *Copyright and Human Rights,* ed. P. L. C. Torremans, (Kluwer Law International, 2008).

Derieux, E., *Droit des médias. Droit français, européen et international*, 8 edition, (LGDJ, 2018).

Derieux, E., "Droits voisins des éditeurs de presse : mesures conservatoires à l'encontre de Google," *Revue Lamy Droit de l'Immatériel*, no. 170, (2020).

de Rochegonde, A., "Le long chemin des droits voisins, Stratégies. Les medias des nouveaux modelès," Stratégies, May 23, 2022, https://www.strategies.fr/actualites/medias/LQ594241C/le-long-chemin-des-droits-voisins.html, accessed: 17.10.2023.

Diakopoulos, N., *Automating the News: How Algorithms Are Rewriting the Media*, (Harvard University Press, 2019).

Diaz- Noci, J., "Artificial Intelligence Systems-Aided News and Copyright: Assessing Legal Implications for Journalism Practices," *Future Internet*, (2020), https://www.mdpi.com/1999-5903/12/5/85, accessed: 23.06.2023.

Diaz- Noci, J., "Authors' Rights and the Media," in *Interaction in Digital News Media. From Principles to Practice*, ed. M. Pérez-Montoro, (Palgrave Macmillan, 2018).

Dormont, S., "L'élaboration de la norme en droit d'auteur : les discours sur la légitimité," *Légipresse,* no. 62, (2019).

Dreier,T., B. Hugenholtz (ed.), *Concise European Copyright Law*, (Kluwer Law International, 2006).

Dreyer, E., *Droit de la communication,* 2ème édition, (LexisNexis, 2022).

Drzewicki, A., "Komentarz do art. 79 Ustawy o prawie autorskim i prawach pokrewnych," in *Ustawa o prawie autorskim i prawach pokrewnych. Komentarz,* ed. E. Ferenc-Szydełko, (Wydawnictwo C.H. BECK, 2021, LEGALIS).

Ducoulombier, P., "Interaction Between Human Rights: Are All Human Rights Equal?," in *Research Handbook on Human Rights and Intellectual Property,* ed. Ch. Geiger (Edward Elgar Publishing, 2016).

Dussolier S., et al., *Contractual Arrangements Applicable to Creators: Law and Practice of Selected Member States, Study, European Parliament,* (2014), 36, https://www.europarl.europa.eu/meetdocs/2009_2014/documents/juri/dv/contractualarangements_/contractualarangements_en.pdf, accessed: 24.101.2024.

Dusollier, S., *Scoping Study on Copyright and Related Rights and the Public Domain,* (WIPO, 2010).

Dusollier, S., "The 2019 Directive on Copyright in the Digital Single Market: Some Progress, a Few Bad Choices, and an Overall Failed Ambition," *Common Market Law Review* 57, no. 4 (2020).

Dusollier, S., Ch. Geiger, P. B. Hugenholtz, M. Kretschmer, "The European Commission's Public Consultation on the Role of Publishers in the Copyright Value Chain: A Response by the European Copyright Society," CREATe Working Paper, (2016).

Dusollier, S., Ch. Geiger, P. B. Hugenholtz, M. Kretschmer, "The European Commission's Public Consultation on the Role of Publishers in the Copyright Value Chain: A Response by the European Copyright Society," *European Intellectual Property Review* 38, no. 10 (2016).

Dworschak, S., Ch. Kersting, "Leistungsschutzrecht für Presseverlage: Müsste Google wirklich zahlen? – eine kartellrechtliche Analyse," *NZKart - Neue Zeitschrift für Kartellrecht* 46 (2013).

ECtHR, *Guide on Article 10 of the European Convention on Human Rights*, (2022), 16, https://rm.coe.int/guide-on-article-10-freedom-of-expression-eng/native/1680ad61d6, accessed: 26.12.2024.

Emanuilov, I., T. Margoni, "Memorisation in Generative Models and EU Copyright Law: An Interdisciplinary View," *Kluwer Copyright Blog*, March 26, 2024, https://copyrightblog.kluweriplaw.com/2024/03/26/memorisation-in-generative-models-and-eu-copyright-law-an-interdisciplinary-view/, accessed: 03.01.2025.

Engelmann, I., S. H. Kessler, "Why Do We Click? Investigating Reasons for User Selection on a News Aggregator Website," *Communications* 44 (2019).

Engelmann, S., S. H. Kessler, S. M. Luebke, "Effects of News Factors on Users' News Attention and Selective Exposure on a News Aggregator Website," *Journalism Studies* 22, no. 6 (2011).

Eskens, S., N. Helberger, J. Moeller, "Challenged by News Personalisation: Five Perspectives on the Right to Receive Information," *Journal of Media Law* 9, no. 2 (2017).

Ferenc-Szydełko, E., *Prawo prasowe. Komentarz, art.8*, (Wolters Kluwer, LEX, 2013).

Ficsor, M., "Collective Rights Management From the Viewpoint of International Treaties, With Special Attention to the EU 'Acquis'," in *Collective Management of Copyright and Related Rights*, ed. D. Gervais, (Wolters Kluwer, 2016).

Fletcher, R., R. K. Nielsen, "Automated Serendipity. The Effect of Using Search Engines on News Repertoire Balance and Diversity," *Digital Journalism* 6, no. 8 (2018).

Fletcher, R., A. Kalogeropoulos, R. K. Nielsen, "More Diverse, More Politically Varied: How Social Media, Search Engines and Aggregators Shape News Repertoires in the United Kingdom," *New Media & Society* 25 (2021).

Fletcher, R., N. Newman, "Platform Reliance, Information Intermediaries, and News Diversity. A Look at the Evidence," in *The Power of Google, Amazon, Facebook and People,* ed. M. Moore, D. Tambini, (Oxford University Press, 2018).

Fletcher, R., S. Schifferes, N. Thurman, "Building the 'Truthmeter': Training Algorithms to Help Journalists Assess the Credibility of Social Media Sources," *Convergence* 26, no. 1 (2020): 19–34, https://journals.sagepub.com/doi/epub/10.1177/1354856517714955, accessed: 20.01.2023.

Frantziou, E., "The Horizontal Effect of the Charter of Fundamental Rights of the EU: Rediscovering the Reasons for Horizontality," *European Law Journal* 21, no. 5 (2015).

Fray, P., E. McKewon, S. Molitorisz, D. Wilding, *The Impact of Digital Platforms on News and Journalistic Content*, (University of Technology Sydney, 2018).

Furgał, U., "The Emperor Has No Clothes: How the Press Publishers' Right Implementation Exposes Its Shortcomings," *GRUR International* 72, no. 7, (2023).

Furgał, U., "The EU Press Publishers' Right: Where Do Member States Stand?," *Journal of Intellectual Property Law & Practice* 16, no. 8 (2021).

Gajlewicz- Korab, K."Wpływ preferencji czytelników na rozwój francuskiego rynku współczesnej prasy codziennej," *Studia Medioznawcze* 3, no. 66 (2016).

Ganter, S. A., R. K. Nielsen, "Dealing with Digital Intermediaries: A Case Study of the Relations Between Publishers and Platforms," *New Media and Society* 20, no. 4 (2018).

Geiger, Ch., "The Constitutional Dimension of Intellectual Property," in *Intellectual Property and Human Rights. Enhanced Edition pf Copyright and Human Rights*, ed. P. L. C. Torremans (Information Law Series, Kluwer Law International, 2008).

Geiger, Ch., "Constitutionalising Intellectual Property Law? The Influence of Fundamental Rights on Intellectual Property in the European Union," *II-C International Review of Intellectual Property in the European Union* 37, no. 4 (2006).

Geiger, Ch., E. Izyumenko, "Shaping Intellectual Property Rights through Human Rights Adjudication: The Example of the European Court of Human Rights," *Mitchell Hamline Law Review* 46, no. 3 (2020).

George, L. M., Ch. Hogendorn, "Local News Online: Aggregators, Geo-Targeting and the Market for Local News," *The Journal of Industrial Economics* 68, no. 4 (2020).

Geradin, D., "Complements or Substitutes, The Competitive Dynamics Between News Publishers and Digital Platforms and What it Means for Competition Policy," *Antitrust & Public Policies*, (2019).

Gerards, J., "How to Improve the Necessity Test of the European Court of Human Rights," *I•CON* 11, no. 2 (2013).

Gervais, D., *Collective Management of Copyright and Related Rights*, (Wolters Kluwer, 2016).

Gervais, D., "Humans as a Matter of Law. How Courts Can Define Humanness in the Age of AI.," *Vanderbilt Law Research Paper, No. 22-3*, (2022), https://papers.ssrn.com/sol3/papers.cfm?abstract_id=4213543, accessed: 14.09.2022.

Gervais, D., "Intellectual Property and Human Rights: Learning to Live Together," in *Intellectaul Property and Human Rights,* Enhanced Edition of *Copyright and Human Rights,* ed. P. L. C. Torremans, (Kluwer Law International, 2008).

Ghazal, N., *Prawo do fonogramu w świetle ustawy o prawie autorskim i prawach pokrewnych*, (Wolters Kluwer Polska, 2016).

Ginsburg, J. C., "Floors and Ceilings in International Copyright Treaties Berne, TRIPS, WCT Minima and Maxima," in *Intellectual Property Ordering beyond Borders*, ed. H. G. Ruse-Khan, A. Metzger, (Oxford University Press, 2022).

Ginsburg, J. C., S. Ricketson, *International Copyright and Neighbouring Rights. The Berne Convention and Beyond*, vol. 2 (Oxford University Press, 2022).

Ginsburg, J. C., S. Ricketson, *International Copyright and Neighbouring Rights. The Berne Convention and Beyond*, vol. 2 (Oxford University Press, 2006).

Grabenwarter, Ch., *Article 10: Freedom of Expression. European Convention on Human Rights: Commentary*, (Bloomsbury Academic, 2013).

Grubow, J. V. , "O.K. Computer: The Devolution of Human Creativity and Granting Musical Copyrights to Artificially Intelligent Joint Authors," *Cardozo Law Review* 40, no. 1 (2018).

Grzybczyk, K., "Komentarz do art. 94," in *Ustawa o prawie autorskim i prawach pokrewnych,* ed. Komentarz, P. Ślęzak, (C.H. BECK, 2017).

Guibault, L., "Extended Collective Licensing for the Use of Out-of-Commerce Works in Europe: A Matter of Legitimacy Vis-à-Vis Rights Holders," *International Review of Intellectual Property and Competition Law (IIC)* 49 (2018).

Guibault L., et al., *Study on the Implementation and Effect in Member States' Laws of Directive 2001/29/EC on the Harmonisation of Certain Aspects of Copyright and Related Rights in the Information Society*, Institute for Information Law (2012).

Hancox, E., "The Relationship Between the Charter and General Principles: Looking Back and Looking Forward," in *Cambridge Yearbook of European Legal Studies*, (2020), https://www.cambridge.org/core/journals/cambridge-yearbook-of-european-legal-studies/article/relationship-between-the-charter-and-general-principles-looking-back-and-looking-forward/A211AA0828910B38002F4B4805410223.

Heilmann S., W. Schulz, *Editorial Responsibility*, (IRIS Special, European Audiovisual Observatory, 2008), 16, https://rm.coe.int/1680783c0e, accessed: 24.01.2024.

Helberger, N., "Diversity Label: Exploring the Potential and Limits of a Transparency Approach to Media Diversity," *Journal of Information Policy*, 1 (2011).

Helberger, N., "Merely Facilitating or Actively Stimulating Diverse Media Choices? Public Service Media at the Crossroad," *International Journal of Communication* 9 (2015).

Helberger, N., J. Moeller, "Beyond the Filter Bubble: Concepts, Myths, Evidence and Issues for Future Debates," *University of Amsterdam*, (2018), https://www.ivir.nl/publicaties/download/Beyond_the_filter_bubble__concepts_myths_evidence_and_issues_for_future_debates.pdf, accessed: 06.02.2023.

Helberger, N., K. Karpinen, L. d'Acunto, "Exposure Diversity as a Design Principle for Recommender Systems," *Information, Communication & Society* 21, no. 2 (2018).

Hilty, R. M., V. Moscon, *Modernisation of the EU Copyright Rules Position Statement of the Max Planck Institute for Innovation and Competition*, (Max Planck Institute for Innovation and Competition, 2017).

Höppner, T., *The Proposed Directive on Copyright in the Digital Single Market (Articles 11, 14 and 16). Strengthening the Press Through Copyright*, (European Parliament, 2017), https://www.europarl.europa.eu/RegData/etudes/BRIE/2017/596835/IPOL_BRI(2017)596835_EN.pdf, accessed: 22.10.2024.

Höppner,T., M. Kretschmer, R. Xalabarder, "CREATe Public Lectures on the Proposed EU Right for Press Publishers," *European Intellectual Property Review* 39, no. 10 (2015).

Hugenholtz, P. B., *Copyright, Related Rights and the News in the EU: Assessing Potential New Laws, Transcript of Conference*, (University of Amsterdam, 2016), 80, https://resources.law.cam.ac.uk/cipil/documents/potential_legal_responses_complete_transcript.pdf, accessed: 12.11.2022.

Hugenholtz, P. B., "Data Property: Unwelcome Guest in the House of IP in: Better Regulation for Copyright. Academics Meet Policy Makers," (2017), 59–63, https://felixreda.eu/wp-content/uploads/2017/09/2017-09-06_Better-Regulation-for-Copyright-Academics-meet-Policy-Makers_Proceedings.pdf, accessed: 08.11.2022.

Hugenholtz, P. B., "Neighbouring Rights Are Obsolete," *International Review of Intellectual Property and Competition Law (IIC)* 50, no. 8, 1009, https://link.springer.com/article/10.1007/s40319-019-00864-3, accessed: 18.10.2022.

Hugenholtz, P. B., et al., *Trends and Developments in Artificial Intelligence. Challenges to the Intellectual Property Rights Framework, Final Report*, (2020), https://www.ivir.nl/publicaties/download/Trends_and_Developments_in_Artificial_Intelligence-1.pdf, accessed: 22.05.2023.

Hugenholtz, P. B., J. P. Quintais, "Copyright and Artificial Creation: Does EU Copyright Law Protect AI-Assisted Output?," *International Review of Intellectual Property and Competition Law (IIC)* 52 (2021).

Husovec, M., "Intellectual Property Rights and Integration by Conflict: The Past, Present and Future," in *Cambridge Yearbook of European Legal Studies*, (Cambridge University Press, 2016).

Irion, K., P. Valcke, "Cultural Diversity in the Digital Age: EU Competences, Policies and Regulations for Diverse Audiovisual and Online Content," in *Cultural Governance and the European Union*, ed. E. Psychogiopoulou, (Palgrave Macmillan, 2014).

Isbell, K. A., "The Rise of the News Aggregator: Legal Implications and Best Practices," *Berkman Center Research Publication*, no. 10, (2010).

IViR, *Information Law: Expanding Horizons' IViR Research Program 2012-2016*, (2012), 2–3, https://www.ivir.nl/syscontent/pdfs/80.pdf, accessed: 06.11.2023.

Jakubowicz, K., "New Media Ecology: Reconceptualizing Media Pluralism," in *Media Pluralism and Diversity. Concepts, Risks and Global Trends*, ed. P. Valcke, M. Sükösd, R. G. Picard, (Palgrave Global Media Policy and Business Series, 2015).

Jeanneney, J. N., A. Strowel, *Quand Google défie le droit*, (De Boeck & Larcier, 2011).

Jehoram, H. C., "Freedom of Expression in Copyright and Media Law," *GRUR International* (1983).

Jeon, D. S., "News Aggregators and Competition among Newspapers on the Internet," *American Economic Journal: Microeconomics* 8, no. 4, (2016): 107.

Jougleux, P., "Access to Works Protected by Copyright Law," in *Pluralism or Universalism in International Copyright Law*, ed. T. E. Synodinou, (Wolters Kluwer, 2019).

Jütte, B. J., "The Beginning of a (Happy?) Relationship: Copyright and Freedom of Expression in Europe," *European Intellectual Property Review* 38, no. 1 (2016).

Karapapa, S., "The Press Publication Right in the European Union: An Overreaching Proposal and the Future of News Online," in *Non-Conventional Copyright: Do New and Non-Traditional Works Deserve Protection?*, ed. E. Bonadio and N. Lucchi, (Edward Elgar, 2018).

Karppinen, K,. "Rethinking Media Pluralism and Communicative Abundance," *McGannon Center Research Resources*, 5 (2009).

Keller, P., "The Press Publishers Right Will Fail – To Support the Media We Should Tax Information Aggregators Instead," Shared Digital Europe, April 30, 2020, https://shared-digital.eu/as-predicted-the-new-press-publishers-right-is-a-failure-lets-make-information-aggregators-pay-news-media-producers-for-real/, accessed: 04.11.2023.

Kerever, A., "Est-ce qu'il est nécessaire de réviser la Convention de Rome et, dans l'affirmative, est-ce le moment opportun pour le faire?," *Bulletin du droit d'auteur* 25, no. 4 (1991).

Klafkowska-Waśniowska K., "Nowe formy usług medialnych a przesłanka odpowiedzialności redakcyjnej w dyrektywie o audiowizualnych usługach medialnych," *Zeszyty Naukowe. Prace z Prawa Własności Intelektualnej*, no. 124 (2014).

Klimkiewicz, B. "Is the Clash of Rationalities Leading Nowhere? Media Pluralism in European Regulatory Policies," in *Press Freedom and Pluralism in Europe. Concepts and Conditions*, ed. A. Czepek, M. Hellwig, (Intellect Books, 2009).

Klimkiewicz, B., "Krajobraz medialny w Polsce: Struktura własności i pluralizm mediów," in *Własność medialna i jej wpływ na pluralizm oraz niezleżność mediów,* ed. B. Klimkiewicz, (Wydawnictwo Uniwersytetu Jagiellońskiego, 2005).

Komorek, E., *Media Pluralism and European Law*, (Wolters Kluwer Law & Business, 2013)

Koo, J., *The Right of Communication to the Public in EU Copyright Law*, (Hart Publishing, 2019).
Kopff, A., "Prawa pokrewne i sąsiednie," *Zeszyty Naukowe Uniwersytetu Jagiellońskiego, Prace z Wynalazczości i Ochrony Własności Intelektualnej* 61 (1993).
Kowala, M., "Algorytmiczne dziennikarstwo w świetle prawa autorskiego," *Zeszyt Studencki Kół Naukowych Wydziału Prawa i Administracji UAM*, no. 10 (2020).
Kowala, M., *Media kontra platformy internetowe. Zasady wynagradzania i ich egzekwowanie, Raport dla Fundacji im. Stefana Batorego,* (2024), media-kontra-platformy-internetowe-zasady-wynagradzania-i-ich-egzekwowanie, accessed: 08.01.2025.
Kowala, M., "Protection of Press Publishers in the Age of Generative AI – In Search of Legal Remedies to Adapt to the Pace of Technology," *International Review of Intellectual Property and Competition Law (IIC)*, 55, no. 10 (2024).
Kowala, M., M. Malaga, "Press Publishers' Right and Competition Law. Case Comment on the French Competition Authority's Decisions Against Google," *Yearbook of Antitrust and Regulatory Studies* 17, no. 30 (2024).
Kuczerawy, A., *Private Enforcement of Public Policy: Freedom of Expression in the Era of Online Gatekeeping*, (KU Leuven, 2018), https://www.kuleuven.be/doctoraatsverdediging/fiches/3H13/3H130125.htm, accessed: 31.03.2023.
Kunert, J., S. C. Lewis, N. Thurman, "Algorithms, Automation, and News," *Digital Journalism* 7, no. 8 (2019).
Kurosz, K., *Artystyczne wykonanie utworu. Prawa osobiste i majątkowe aktorów, muzyków i innych wykonawców*, (Wolters Kluwer Polska, 2014).
Laskowska-Litak, E., "Sprawa upadłej dyrektywy prawnoautorskiej i (nie)jednolitego rynku cyfrowego," *Europejski Przegląd Sądowy*, no. 9 (2018).
Laskowska-Litak, E., J. Marcinkowska, J. Preussner-Zamorska, "Dozwolony użytek chronionych utworów," in *System Prawa Prywatnego,* ed. J. Barta, (C.H. Beck, Legalis, 2017).
Lazarova, A., "Re-Use the News: Between the EU Press Publishers' Right's Addressees and the Informatory Exceptions' Beneficiaries," *Journal of Intellectual Property Law & Practice* 16, no. 3 (2021).
Lebois A., "Google et le droit voisin des éditeurs de presse," *Recueil Dalloz*, no. 37 (2019).
Lebois A., "Droit voisin des éditeurs de presse : fin du contentieux avec Google," *L'essentiel Droit de la propriété intellectuelle* 8 (2022), no. DPI200z9.
Lebois, A., "La légitimité du nouveau droit voisin de l'éditeur et de l'agence de presse." *Légipresse,* (2019).
Lebois, A., "Oeuvre de presse - Quelle protection juridique pour les créations des robots journalistes?," *Communication Commerce électronique*, no. 1 (2015).
Leistner, M., "Copyright Law on the Internet in Need of Reform: Hyperlinks, Online Platforms and Aggregators," *Journal of Intellectual Property Law & Practice* 12, no. 2 (2017).
Lenaerts, K., "Exploring the Limits of the EU Charter of Fundamental Rights," *European Constitutional Law Review* 8, no. 3 (2012).
Leurdijk, A., M. Slot, O. Nieuwenhuis, "Statistical, Ecosystems and Competitiveness Analysis of the Media and Content Industries: The Newspaper Publishing Industry," *JRC Technical Reports,* (2012).
Lewis, S. C., E. Nechushtai, "What Kind of News Gatekeepers Do We Want Machines to Be? Filter Bubbles, Fragmentation, and the Normative Dimensions of Algorithmic Recommendations," *Computers in Human Behavior* 90 (2019).
Lucas-Schloetter, A., "European Copyright Contract Law: A Plea for Harmonisation," *International Review of Intellectual Property and Competition Law (IIC)* 48, (2017).
Luigi Parcu, P., E. Brogi, *Research Handbook on EU Media Law and Policy*, (Edward Elgar Publishing, 2021).

Machlis, S., "Inside the Google News Algorithm, Computer World," October 5, 2009, https://www.computerworld.com/article/2467854/inside-the-google-news-algorithm.html, accessed: 02.02.2023.

Markiewicz, R., *Ilustrowane prawo autorskie*, (Wolters Kluwer Polska, LEX, 2018).

Markiewicz, R., *Prawo autorskie na jednolitym rynku cyfrowym. Dyrektywa Parlamentu Europejskiego i Rady (UE) 2019/790*, (Wolters Kluwer, 2021).

Markiewicz, R., "Prawo pokrewne wydawców prasy," *Zeszyty Naukowe Uniwersytetu Jagiellońskiego*, no. 4 (2019).

Markiewicz, R., *Zasada proporcjonalności w prawie autorskim Unii Europejskiej*, (Wolters Kluwer Polska, 2023).

Martens, B., et al., *The Digital Transformation of News Media and the Rise of Disinformation and Fake News*, JRC Digital Economy Working Paper 2018-02 (2018).

Maślanka, J., *Encyklopedia wiedzy o prasie*, (Ossolineum, 1976), 200–201.

Masouyé, C., *Guide to the Rome Convention and to the Phonograms Convention*, WIPO, no. 617 (E), (1981).

Mela, C. F., J. M. T. Roos, R. Shachar, "The Effect of Links and Excerpts on Internet News Consumption," *Journal of Marketing Research* 57, no. 3 (2020).

Mendoza- Caminade, A., "Le droit voisin des éditeurs de presse et des agences de presse à l'épreuve de la puissance des plateformes en ligne : la longue marche vers l'effectivité du droit," *Revue Lamy de la concurrence*, no. 106 (2021).

Mezei, P., A. Trapova, "*Robojournalism* – A Copyright Study on the Use of Artificial Intelligence in the European News Industry," *GRUR International* 71, no. 7 (2022).

Monzer, C., et al., "User Perspectives on the News Personalisation Process: Agency, Trust and Utility as Building Blocks," *Digital Journalism* 8, no. 9 (2020).

Moscon, V., "Neighbouring Rights: In Search of a Dogmatic Foundation. The Press Publishers' Case," *Max Planck Institute for Innovation and Competition Research Paper*, no. 18-17, (2018), https://papers.ssrn.com/sol3/papers.cfm?abstract_id=3208601, accessed: 22.01.2024.

Moscon, V., "Use and Abuse of Neighbouring Rights and the Growing Need for a Sound Understanding: The Case of Online News Protection in Europe," in *The Object and Purpose of Intellectual Property,* ed. S. Frankel, (Edward Elgar Publishing, 2019).

Mouron, P., "L'Autorité de la concurrence au secours du droit voisin des éditeurs et agences de presse." *Revue européenne des médias et du numérique*, no. 54 (2020): 10–14, https://amu.hal.science/hal-02885794/document, accessed: 05.08.2023.

Mylly, T., "Regulating with Rights Proportionality? Copyright, Fundamental Rights, and Internet in the Case Law of the CJEU," in: *Copyright versus (other) Fundamental Rights in the Digital Age. A Comparative Analysis in Search of a Common Constitutional Ground*, ed. O. Pollicino, G. M. Riccio, and M. Bassini (Edward Elgar Publishing, 2020).

Napoli, P., *Social Media and the Public Interest: Media Regulation in the Disinformation Age, New York Chichester*, (West Sussex: Columbia University Press, 2019).

Napoli, P. M., "Deconstructing the Diversity Principle," *Journal of Communication* 49, no. 4 (1999).

Niewęgłowski, A., "Komentarz do art.4," in *Prawo autorskie, Komentarz*, ed. A. Niewęgłowski (Wolters Kluwer, LEX, 2021).

Niewęgłowski, A., "Komentarz do art.11," in *Prawo autorskie. Komentarz*, ed. A. Niewęgłowski (Wolters Kluwer Polska, LEX, 2021).

Nowicka, A., "Podmiot prawa autorskiego, Utwory zbiorowe," in *System Prawa Prywatnego Prawo autorskie,* ed. J. Barta, vol. 13, (C.H.Beck, 2017).

Ohly, A., "European Fundamental Rights and Intellectual Property," in *The Europeanization of Intellectual Property Law*, ed. A. Ohly, J. Pila, (Oxford University Press, 2013).

Olejniczak, A., Z. Radwański, *Prawo cywilne – część ogólna*, (C.H. Beck, 2015).

Oster, J., *European and International Media Law*, (Cambridge University Press, 2017).

Oster, J., *Media Freedom as Fundamental Rigths,* (Cambridge University Press, 2015).

Panagiotidis, K., A. Veglis, "Transitions in Journalism—Toward a Semantic-Oriented Technological Framework," *Journal.Media* 1, no. 1 (2020), https://www.mdpi.com/2673-5172/1/1/1, accessed: 06.09.2023.

Papaevangelou, Ch., N. Smyrnaios, "Regulating Dependency: The Political Stakes of Online Platforms' Deals with French Publishers," *Anàlisi: Quaderns de Comunicació i Cultura*, no. 68 (2023), https://shs.hal.science/halshs-03747847/document, accessed: 08.08.2023.

Papp, P., "The Promotion of European Works: An Analysis on Quotas for European Audiovisual Works and their Effect on Culture and Industry," *European Union Law Working Papers*, no. 50, (2020), https://law.stanford.edu/wp-content/uploads/2020/10/papp_eulawwp50.pdf, accessed: 01.09.2023.

Parcu, P. L., "New Digital Threats to Media Pluralism in the Information Age," *Robert Schuman Centre for Advanced Studies Centre for Media Pluralism and Media Freedom*, no. 19 (2019).

Parkin, J., "The Copyright Quotation Exception: Not Fair Use by Another Name," *Oxford University Commonwealth Law Journal* 19, no. 1 (2019).

Pasquale, F., *The Black Box Society: The Secret Algorithms That Control Money and Information*, (Harvard University Press, 2015).

Peukert, A., "Intellectual Property as an End in Itself?," *European Intellectual Property Review* 33 (2011).

Peukert, A., "An EU Related Right for Press Publishers Concerning Digital Uses. A Legal Analysis," Research Paper, no. 22, (Goethe Universitat, 2016).

Peukert, A., "Related Rights," in *Encyclopaedia of European Private Law,* ed. J. Basedow, K. J. Hopt, R. Zimmermann, (Oxford University Press, 2011), https://papers.ssrn.com/sol3/papers.cfm?abstract_id=1550103, accessed: 15.10.2022.

Picard, R. G., *Mapping Digital Media. Digitalisation and Media Business Models*, (Open Society Foundations, no. 5, 2011).

Pihlajarinne, T., et al., "European Copyright System as a Suitable Incentive for AI Based Journalism?," *Legal Studies Research Paper Series*, no. 67, (2021).

Pihlajarinne, T., J. Vesala, "Proposed Right of Press Publishers: A Workable Solution?," (2018), 1, https://helda.helsinki.fi/bitstream/handle/10138/312548/Pihlajarinne_Vesala_2018_proposed_right_of_press_publishers.pdf?sequence=1, accessed: 27.10.2022.

Pollaud-Dulian, F., "Droit d'auteur et droit voisins dans le marché numérique," *Revue trimestrielle de droit commercial et de droit économique*, no. 3 (2019).

Pollaud-Dulian, F., *Propriété intellectuelle. Le droit d'auteur*, (Economica, 2014).

Princen, S., H. Smekal, R. Zbíral, "Mapping the Legal Scope for Flexible Implementation in EU Directives," RSC 2022/46 Robert Schuman Centre for Advanced Studies Integrating Diversity in the European Union (InDivEU), (2022).

Pyziak-Szafnicka, M., "Prawo cywilne– część ogólna," in *System prawa prywatnego,* ed. M. Safjan, vol. 1 (Warszawa 2012).

Quintais, J. P., J. Poort, "A Brief History of Value Gaps: Pre-Internet Copyright Protection and Exploitation Models, Copyright Reconstructed Rethinking Copyright's Economic Rights," in *Time of Highly Dynamic Technological and Economic Change,* ed. P. B. Hugenholtz, (Wolters Kluwer, 2018).

Quintais, J. P., *Copyright in the Age of Online Access: Alternative Compensation Systems in EU Law*, (Kluwer Law International, 2017).

Quintais, J. P., "Generative AI, Copyright and the AI Act," *Kluwer Copyright Blog*, May 09, 2023, https://copyrightblog.kluweriplaw.com/2023/05/09/generative-ai-copyright-and-the-ai-act/, accessed: 03.01.2025.

Rebillard, F., N. Smyrnaios, "L'actualité selon Google. L'emprise du principal moteur de recherche sur l'information en ligne," *Communication & Langages*, no. 16 (2009).

Rendas, T., *Exceptions in EU Copyright Law. In Search of a Balance Between Flexibility and Legal Certainty*, (Wolters Kluwers Law International, 2021).

Ricketson, S., "Rights on the Border: The Berne Convention and Neighbouring Rights," in *Copyright Law in an Age of Limitations and Exceptions*, ed. R. L. Okediji, (Cambridge University Press, 2017).

Rosati, E., *Copyright in the Digital Single Market: Article-by-Article Commentary to the Provisions of Directive 2019/790* (Oxford University Press, 2021).

Rubio, M., "Mediapart : les clés du succès d'un média d'enquête indépendant," *Global Investigate Journalism Network*, March 16, 2022, https://gijn.org/2022/03/16/francais-mediapart-independance/, accessed: 20.01.2023.

Ruse-Khan, H. G., "Overlaps and Conflict Norms in Human Rights Law: Approaches of European Courts to Address Intersections With Intellectual Property Rights," in *Research Handbook on Human Rights and Intellectual Property,* ed. Ch. Geiger (Edward Elgar Publishing, 2016).

Rutt, J., *Aggregators and the News Industry: Charging for Access to Content*, NET Institute, Working Paper 11-19, (2011).

Sartor, G., "Fundamental Legal Concepts: A Formal and Teleological Characterisation," *Artificial Intelligence and Law* 14, (2006).

Sax, M., "Algorithmic News Diversity and Democratic Theory: Adding Agonism to the Mix," *Digital Journalism*, (2022).

Scalzini, S., "The New Related Right for Press Publishers: What Way Forward?," in *Routledge Handbook of EU Copyright Law*, ed. E. Rosati, (2021).

Sganga, C., "EU Copyright Law Between Property and Fundamental Rights: A Proposal to Connect the Dots," in *Balancing Copyright Law in the Digital Age. Comparative Perspectives*, ed. R. Caso, F. Giovanella (Springer, 2015).

Sganga, C., *Propertizing European Copyright. History, Challenges and Opportunities*, (Edward Elgar Publishing, 2018).

Simpson, J., "Google Faces US Government Attempt to Break it Up," *The Guardian*, October 9, 2024, https://www.theguardian.com/technology/2024/oct/09/google-us-government-attempt-break-up-business-court-filing, accessed: 06.01.2025.

Skrzypczak, J., "Media Ownership Regulation in Europe – A Threat or Opportunity for Freedom of Speech?" *Przegląd Polityczny*, no. 4 (2017).

Sobczak, J., *Prawo prasowe. Komentarz, art. 8*, (Wolters Kluwer, LEX, 2008).

Sokołowska D., *Utwory zbiorowe w prawie autorskim ze szczególnym uwzględnieniem encyklopedii i słowników*, (Uniwersytet Jagielloński, 2001).

Spina, G. A., "Intellectual Property and Human Rights: A Taxonomy of Their Interactions," *International Review of Intellectual Property and Competition Law (IIC)* 51, no. 4 (2020).

Strowel, A., F. Tulkens, "Freedom of Expression and Copyright Under Civil Law: Of Balance, Adaptation, and Access," in *Copyright and Free Speech*, ed. J.Griffiths, U. Suthersanen, (Oxford University Press, 2005).

Strowel, A., "Copyright Strengthened by the Court of Justice Interpretation of Art. 17 (2) of the EU Charter of Fundamental Rights," in *Copyright versus (Other) Fundamental Rights in the Digital Age. A Comparative Analysis in Search of a Common Constitutional Ground*, ed. O. Pollicino, G. M. Riccio and M. Bassini, (Edward Elgar Publishing, 2020).

Szynol, A., "Czy paywall to być albo nie być wydawców prasy codziennej?" *Zeszyty prasoznawcze* 64, no. 4 (2019).

Ślęzak,P., "Umowy w zakresie współczesnych sztuk wizualnych," (Wolters Kluwer Polska, 2012).

Święcka, K., J. S. Święcki, "Dyferencjacje prawne pojęcia "Media"," *Roczniki Nauk Prawnych* 16 (2006).

Tambini, D., "A Theory of Media Freedom," *Journal of Media Law* 13, no. 2 (2021).

Thurman, N., et al., "Giving Computers a Nose for News: Exploring the Limits of Story Detection and Verification," *Digital Journalism* 4, no. 7 (2016): 838–848, https://eprints

.qut.edu.au/221748/1/cardiff-2015-v26%2Bfor%2Bopen%2Baccess%2Bcity.pdf, accessed: 19.01.2023

Tomczyk, S., "Komentarz do art. 94," in *Ustawa o prawie autorskim i prawach pokrewnych. Komentarz*, ed. E. Ferenc – Szydełko, (C.H. Beck, 2016).

Torremans, P. L. C., "Copyright as a Human Right," in *Intellectual Property Law and Human Rights*, ed. P. L. C. Torremans, (Kluwer Law International, 2015).

Traple E., *Dzieło zależne jako przedmiot prawa autorskiego*, (Wydawnictwo Prawnicze, 1979).

Trapova, A., "Copyright for AI-Generated Works: A Task for the Internal Market?," *Kluwer Copyright Blog*, February 8, 2023, https://copyrightblog.kluweriplaw.com/2023/02/08/copyright-for-ai-generated-works-a-task-for-the-internal-market/, accessed: 02.12.2023.

van Eechoud, M., "A Publisher's Intellectual Property Right. Implications for Freedom of Expression, Authors and Open Content Policies," (University of Amsterdam, 2017), 14, https://www.openforumeurope.org/wp-content/uploads/2017/01/OFE-Academic-Paper-Implications-of-publishers-right_FINAL.pdf, accessed: 27.10.2022.

van Eechoud, M., *Choice of Law in Copyright and Related Rights. Alternatives to the Lex Protectionis*, (Kluwer Law International, 2003).

van Eechoud, M., S. van Gompel, P. B. Hugenholtz, et al., *Harmonizing European Copyright Law. The Challenges of Better Lawmaking*, (Kluwer Law International, 2009).

van Hoboken, J., "Search Engines, Pluralism and Diversity: What is at Stake and How to Move Policy Forward," in *Media Pluralism and Diversity. Concepts, Risks and Global Trends*, ed. P. Valcke, M. Sükösd, R. G. Picard, (Palgrave Global Media Policy and Business Series, 2015).

Varoufakis, Y., *Technofeudalism. What Killed Capitalism*, (Vintage 2024).

Valcke, P., "Looking for the User in Media Pluralism Regulation: Unraveling the Traditional Diversity Chain and Recent Trends of User Empowerement in European Media Regulation," *Journal of Information Policy* 1 (2011).

Valcke, P., et al., *Independent Study on Indicators for Media Pluralism in the Member States – Towards a Risk-Based Approach* (KU Leuven ICRI, 2009).

Voorhoof, D., *Critical Perspectives on the Scope and Interpretation of Art. 10 of the European Convention on Human Rights*, (Strasbourg: Council of Europe Press, 1995).

Walters, P., "A Public Good: Can Government *Really* Save the Press?," *Sage Journals* 23, no. 8 (2020), https://journals.sagepub.com/doi/full/10.1177/1464884920982404, accessed: 09.10.2023.

Wang, Q., "Normalization and Differentiation in Google News: A Multi-Method Analysis of the World's Largest News Aggregator," Rutgers University, (2020), https://rucore.libraries.rutgers.edu/rutgers-lib/62647/, accessed: 31.01.2023.

Wasilewski P., "Dopuszczalność embedowania w świetle ewolucji orzecznictwa Trybunału Sprawiedliwości Unii Europejskiej w zakresie linkowania," in *Experientia docet. Księga jubileuszowa ofiarowana Pani Profesor Elżbiecie Traple*, ed. P. Podrecki, T. Targosz, (Wolters Kluwer Polska, 2017, LEX).

Xalabarder, R., "Google News and Copyright," in *Empirical Approaches to Legal Aspects of Knowledge-Economy Business Models,* ed. A. Lopez - Taruella, (Springer, 2012).

Xalabarder, R., "The Principle of Appropriate and Proportionate Remuneration for Authors and Performers in Art.18 Copyright in the Digital Single Market Directive," *InDret* 4 (2020), https://indret.com/wp-content/uploads/2020/10/1591.pdf, accessed: 24.01.2024.

Xalabarder, R., "The Remunerated Statutory Limitations for News Aggregation and Search Engines Proposed by the Spanish Governement- Its Compliance With International and EU Law," IN3 Working Paper Series, (2014), https://papers.ssrn.com/sol3/papers.cfm?abstract_id=2504596, accessed: 01.11.2022.

Yanisky-Ravid, S., L. A. Velez-Hernandez, "Copyrightability of Artworks Produced by Creative Robots and Originality: The Formality-Objective Model," *The Minnesota Journal of Law, Science & Technology* 19, no. 1 (2018).

Yu, P., "Challenges to the Development of a Human- Rights Framework for Intellectual Property," in *Intellectual Property and Human Rights. Enhanced Edition of Copyright and Human Rights,* ed. P. L. C. Torremans, (Kluwer Law International, 2008).
Yu, P., "Ten Common Questions about Intellectual Property and Human Rights," *Texas A&M University School of Law* 23, no. 7 (2007): 713–714, https://scholarship.law.tamu.edu/cgi/viewcontent.cgi?article=1385&context=facscholar, accessed: 24.03.2023.
Zawadzka, Z., "Sui Generis Ochrona Baz Danych," in *Prawo własności intelektualnej. Teoria i praktyka,* ed. J. Sieńczyło – Chlabicz, (Wolters Kluwer Polska, 2021, LEX).
Zuiderveen Borgesius, F. J., et al., "Should We Worry About Filter Bubbles?," *Internet Policy Review* 5, no. 1 (2016).
Zwaak, L., "General Survey of the European Convention," in *Theory and Practice of the European Convention on Human Rights,* ed. P. van Dijk, F. van Hoof, A. van Rijn, L. Zwaak, (Intersentia, 2018).

Studies and reports

Cornia, A., A. Karogelopulos, R. K. Nielsen, *Challenges and Opportunities for News Media and Journalism in Increasingly Digital, Mobile, and Social Media Environment*, (Council of Europe Report, DGI 2016, 18, Reuters Institute for the Study of Journalism, 2016).
Cour des comptes, *Les aides à la presse écrite : des choix nécessaires, Rapport public annuel,* (2018), https://www.ccomptes.fr/sites/default/files/2018-01/12-aides-presse-ecrite-Tome-2.pdf, accessed: 12.02.2023.
Deloitte, *The Impact of Web Traffic on Revenues of Traditional Newspaper Publishers. A Study for France, Germany, Spain, and the UK*, (2016), 9, https://www2.deloitte.com/content/dam/Deloitte/uk/Documents/technology-media-telecommunications/deloitte-uk-impact-of-web-traffic-on-newspaper-revenues-2016.pdf, accessed: 18.01.2023.
Duby–Muller, V., L. Garcia, *Rapport d'information sur l'application du droit voisin au bénéfice des agences, des éditeurs et professionnels du secteur de la presse*, (Assemblée Nationale, 2022), https://www.assemblee-nationale.fr/dyn/15/rapports/dv/l15b4902_rapport-information.pdf, accessed: 18.07.2023.
Estivalèzes, M., L. Franceschini, *Rapport sur l'objet et le champ d'application du droit voisin des éditeurs de publication de presse*, Ministère de la Culture, Conseil Supérieur de la propriété littéraire et artistique, (2018), https://www.culture.gouv.fr/content/download/182559/file/Rapport%20droit%20voisin%20des%20éditeurs%20de%20presse%20vdef.pdf?inLanguage=fre-FR&version=1, accessed: 30.12.2024.
European Commission, *Flash Eurobarometer 437: Report, Internet Users' Preferences for Accessing Content Online*, (September 14, 2016), 437, https://digital-strategy.ec.europa.eu/en/library/eurobarometer-internet-users-preferences-accessing-content-online, accessed: 30.12.2024.
European Publishers Council, *Online Platforms and Digital Advertising Market Study Observations of the European Publishers Council (EPC) on the Statement of Scope*, (2019), https://assets.publishing.service.gov.uk/media/5d6906e9e5274a17125628c2/European_Publishers_Council__-_Response_to_SoS.pdf, accessed: 30.12.2024.
European Union, *Flash Eurobarometer: News & Media Survey 2022*, (July 2022), https://europa.eu/eurobarometer/surveys/detail/2832, accessed: 18.01.2023.
Ministère de la Culture, *Droit voisin au profit des agences de presse et des éditeurs de presse. Recueil des travaux préparatoires de la loi n° 2019-775 du 24 juillet 2019 tendant à créer un droit voisin au profit des agences de presse et des éditeurs de presse,* Service de la coordination des politiques culturelles et de l'innovation Mission de la politique documentaire, (2019), 105, https://www.culture.gouv.fr/fr/content/download/219602/pdf_file/Droit_voisin_agences_editeurs_presse.pdf?inLanguage=fre-FR&version=4, accessed: 07.01.2025.

Navarro, J. G., "Newspaper Advertising Expenditure in the European Union (EU 28) from 2009 to 2018," *Statista*, November 9, 2024, https://www.statista.com/statistics/434708/newspaper-advertising-expenditure-in-the-eu/, accessed: 23.01.2025.

Newman N., *et al.*, *Journalism, Media and Technology Trends and Predictions 2022*, (Digital News Project, Reuters Institute for the Study of Journalism, University of Oxford, 2022), 8, https://reutersinstitute.politics.ox.ac.uk/sites/default/files/2022-01/Newman%20-%20Trends%20and%20Predictions%202022%20FINAL.pdf, accessed: 18.01.2023.

Newman N., et al., *Reuters Institute Digital News Report 2018*, (Reuters Institute for the Study of Journalism, University of Oxford, 2018).

Newman N., et al., *Reuters Institute Digital News Report 2019*, (Reuters Institute for the Study of Journalism, University of Oxford, 2019).

Newman N., et al., *Reuters Institute Digital News Report 2022*, (Reuters Institute, University of Oxford, 2022).

Ofcom, *Measuring Media Plurality Ofcom's Advice to the Secretary of State for Culture, Olympics, Media and Sport,* https://www.ofcom.org.uk/__data/assets/pdf_file/0031/57694/measuring-media-plurality.pdf, 8, accessed: 01.04.2023.

Posada P. de la Concha, A. Gutiérrez García, H. Hernández Cobos, *Impacto del Nuevo Artículo 32.2 de la Ley de Propiedad Intelectual Informe para la Asociación Española de Editoriales de Publicaciones Periódicas (AEEPP)*, (2015), 6, https://clabe.org/pdf/InformeNera.pdf, accessed: 04.02.2023.

Standard Eurobarometer 96, "Public Opinion in the European Union," January–February 2022, T196, https://europa.eu/eurobarometer/api/deliverable/download/file?deliverableId=81059, accessed: 18.01.2023.

Statista, "Advertising rRevenue Generated by Google from 2017 to 2026," August 2023, https://www.statista.com/statistics/539447/google-global-net-advertising-revenues/, accessed: 03.02.2023.

Statista, "Share of Respondents Who Read tThe Written Press Every Day or Almost Every Day in the European Union From 2011 to 2022," April 2022, https://www.statista.com/statistics/452430/europe-daily-newspaper-consumption/, accessed: 18.01.2023.

Other sources

ACPM, "Classement Diffusion Presse Quotidienne Nationale 2023-2024," https://www.acpm.fr/Les-chiffres/Diffusion-Presse/Presse-Payante/Presse-Quotidienne-Nationale, accessed: 10.01.2023.

Adami, M., "Is ChatGPT a Threat or an Opportunity for Journalism? Five AI Experts Weigh in," March 23, 2023, https://reutersinstitute.politics.ox.ac.uk/news/chatgpt-threat-or-opportunity-journalism-five-ai-experts-weigh, accessed: 23.11.2023.

Adjust, "What is Deep Linking," https://www.adjust.com/glossary/deep-linking/, accessed: 11.11.2022.

Alcaraz, M., "OpenAI signe un accord avec le groupe de presse Condé Nast," *LesEchos*, August 21, 2024, https://www.lesechos.fr/tech-medias/intelligence-artificielle/openai-signe-un-accord-avec-le-groupe-de-presse-conde-nast-2114539, accessed: 23.12.2024.

AP, "Canadian News Publishers Sue OpenAI Over Alleged Copyright Infringement," November 29, 2024, https://apnews.com/article/canada-news-publishers-lawsuit-chatgpt-3e1790fcf4c9f001f1d32609c4d547af, accessed: 23.12.2024.

APIG, "Les éditeurs de presse d'information engagent des actions judiciaires contre Microsoft pour faire respecter la loi sur le droit voisin," November 08, 2024, https://www.alliancepresse.fr/actualite/les-editeurs-de-presse-dinformation-engagent-des-actions-judiciaires-contre-microsoft-pour-faire-respecter-la-loi-sur-le-droit-voisin/, accessed: 08.12.2024.

Baekkeskov, E., "Market Failure," Britannica, https://www.britannica.com/money/topic/market-failure, accessed: 09.10.2023.

Bender, B., O. Ma, "Read All About It: A New Look for Google News," June 22, 2022, https://blog.google/products/news/google-news-anniversary-local-reporting-funding/, accessed: 31.01.2023.

Borger, M., "Journalism Funding in Europe. Reflections and Key Lessons from the Journalism Funders Forum," Philantropy Europe Assosiation, June 26, 2019, https://philea.eu/journalism-funding-in-europe/, accessed: 23.01.2023.

Bourgin, Y., "Droits voisins : un accord conclu au Monde, 25% seront reversés aux journalistes," *L'UsineDigitale*, June 10, 2024, https://www.usine-digitale.fr/article/droits-voisins-un-accord-conclu-au-monde-25-seront-reverses-aux-journalistes.N2214416, accessed: 23.12.2024.

Breczko, B., "Czy dziennikarze są jeszcze potrzebni? Mój ostatni artykuł napisał ChatGPT," *Gazeta Wyborcza*, April 17, 2023, https://wyborcza.biz/biznes/7,177150,29639137,czy-dziennikarze-sa-jeszcze-potrzebni-moj-ostatni-artykul-napisal.html, accessed: 22.05.2023.

Brevo, "Le Microblogging, qu'est-ce que c'est et comment en faire profiter votre entreprise," August 31, 2021, https://www.brevo.com/fr/blog/microblogging/, accessed: 31.08.2023.

Bundeskartellamnt, "Improvements for Publishers Using Google News Showcase," December 21, 2022, https://www.bundeskartellamt.de/SharedDocs/Meldung/EN/Pressemitteilungen/2022/21_12_2022_Google_News_Showcase.html?nn=3591568, accessed: 08.11.2023.

Cambridge Dictionary, "Collection," https://dictionary.cambridge.org/dictionary/english/collection, accessed: 14.06.2023.

Cambridge Dictionary, "Effectiveness," https://dictionary.cambridge.org/dictionary/english/effectiveness, accessed: 06.10.2023.

Cambridge Dictionary, "Safeguard," https://dictionary.cambridge.org/dictionary/english/safeguard, accessed: 10.01.2024.

Cambridge Dictionary, "Snippet," https://dictionary.cambridge.org/dictionary/english/snippet, accessed: 09.11.2022.

Chrisafis, A., "French News Titles Sue X Over Allegedly Running Their Content Without Payment," *The Guardian*, November 12, 2024, https://www.theguardian.com/world/2024/nov/12/french-news-titles-sue-x-over-allegedly-running-their-content-without-payment, accessed: 21.12.2024.

Cohen, C., "Droits voisins : Google signe avec la presse d'information," Le Figaro, no. 24114, Europresse, 2022.

Cohen, J., "Same Protocol, More Options for News Publishers," *Google News Blog*, December 2, 2009, https://news.googleblog.com/2009/12/same-protocol-more-options-for-news.html, accessed: 31.01.2023.

Connal, S., "Un accord afin de régler un différend qui dure depuis trop longtemps," *Google Blog France*, March 20, 2024, https://blog.google/intl/fr-fr/nouvelles-de-lentreprise/chez-google/accord-regler-differend-qui-dure-depuis-trop-longtemps/, accessed: 08.12.2024.

Corint Media, "First Decision on Ancillary Copyrights for Press Publishers," September 24, 2015, https://www.corint-media.com/en/first-decision-on-ancillary-copyright-for-press-publishers-google-is-obliged-to-pay/, accessed: 31.10.2022.

Coster, H., "As Google Pushes Deeper into AI, Publishers See Fresh Challenges," *Reuters*, October 19, 2023, https://www.reuters.com/technology/google-pushes-deeper-into-ai-publishers-see-fresh-challenges-2023-10-19/, accessed: 23.10.2023.

CPPAP, "Critères d'admission," http://www.cppap.fr/criteres-dadmission/, http://www.cppap.fr/linscription-sur-les-registres-de-la-cppap-est-elle-une-obligation-pour-faire-paraitre-une-publication-de-presse/, accessed: 12.01.2023.

CPPAP, http://www.cppap.fr/publications/, accessed: 12.01.2023.

Danbury, R., "The DSM Copyright Directive: Article 15: What? – Part II, 2021," *Kluwer Copyright Blog*, April 9, 2021, https://copyrightblog.kluweriplaw.com/2021/04/29/the-dsm-copyright-directive-article-15-what-part-ii/, accessed: 02.01.2025.

Depreeuw, S., "Mandatory Collective Management of Copyright: When the Road to Deadlock is Saved with Good Intentions," *Kluwer Copyright Blog*, February 09, 2022, https://copyrightblog.kluweriplaw.com/2022/02/09/mandatory-collective-management-of-copyright-when-the-road-to-deadlock-is-paved-with-good-intentions/, accessed: 02.10.2023.

DVP, "La Société des Droits Voisins de la Presse (DVP) annonce la signature d'un premier accord avec Google," October 17, 2023, https://www.dvpresse.fr/la-societe-des-droits-voisins-de-la-presse-dvp-annonce-la-signature-dun-premier-accord-avec-google/, accessed: 02.12.2024.

DVP, "La Société des Droits Voisins de la Presse signe un accord avec Meta," June 25, 2024, https://www.dvpresse.fr/signature-avec-meta/, accessed: 02.12.2024.

EDRi, "Join the Coordinated Calls against EU's Censorship Machine," May 30, 2018, https://edri.org/our-work/coordinated-action-censorship-machine-call/, accessed: 27.06.2023.

European Commission, "General-Purpose AI Code of Practice," https://digital-strategy.ec.europa.eu/en/policies/ai-code-practice, accessed: 23.12.2024.

European Parliament, "Parliamentary question – E-004603//2020(ASW)," November 09, 2020, https://www.europarl.europa.eu/doceo/document/E-9-2020-004603-ASW_EN.html, accessed: 22.11.2022.

Farhi, P., "A News Site Used AI to Write Articles. It Was a Journalistic Disaster," *The Washington Post*, January 17, 2023, https://www.washingtonpost.com/media/2023/01/17/cnet-ai-articles-journalism-corrections/, accessed: 19.01.2023.

FCA, "Dans le cadre de l'instruction au fond du dossier sur les droits voisins, Google propose des engagements. L'Autorité les soumet à consultation publique," December 15, 2021, https://www.autoritedelaconcurrence.fr/fr/communiques-de-presse/dans-le-cadre-de-linstruction-au-fond-du-dossier-sur-les-droits-voisins, accessed: 24.07.2023.

FCA, "Related Rights: The Autorité Accepts Google's Commitments," June 21, 2022, https://www.autoritedelaconcurrence.fr/en/press-release/related-rights-autorite-accepts-googles-commitments, accessed: 24.07.2023.

FCA, "Related Rights: The Autorité Fines Google €250 Million," March 20, 2024, https://www.autoritedelaconcurrence.fr/en/article/related-rights-autorite-fines-google-eu250-million, accessed: 08.12.2024.

Franque, A., "Droits voisins : Google signe un accord-cadre avec les éditeurs de presse," *Libération*, January 21, 2021, https://www.liberation.fr/france/2021/01/21/droits-voisins-google-signe-un-accord-cadre-avec-les-editeurs-de-presse_1818139/, accessed: 24.01.2024.

Fundacja Panoptykon, "Co to jest Panoptykon," https://panoptykon.org/organizacja, accessed: 22.06.2023.

Gani A., L. Haddou, "Could Robots be the Journalists of the Future?," *The Guardian*, March 16, 2014, https://www.theguardian.com/media/shortcuts/2014/mar/16/could-robots-be-journalist-of-future, accessed: 22.05.2023.

Gaudiaut, T., "Les GAFA dans le viseur de l'Autorité de la concurrence," Statista, July 23, 2021, https://fr.statista.com/infographie/25325/plus-grosses-amendes-antitrust-infligees-a-une-entreprise-en-france/, accessed: 24.07.2023.

Google, "Digital News Innovation Fund Impact Report," 2021, https://newsinitiative.withgoogle.com/impact/, accessed: 23.01.2023.

Google, "How Google Supports Journalism and the News Industry," https://blog.google/supportingnews/#overview, accessed: 04.02.2023.

Google, "L'Agence France-Presse et Google signent un accord sur les droits voisins," November 17, 2021, https://blog.google/intl/fr-fr/nouvelles-de-lentreprise/chez-google/afp-google/, accessed: 08.01.2025.

Google, Publisher Center Help, "Show Up in Google News," https://support.google.com/news/publisher-center/answer/9607025?hl=en, accessed: 04.02.2023.

Google Ads Help, "About Accelerated Mobile Pages (AMP)," https://support.google.com/google-ads/answer/7496737?hl=en, accessed: 01.02.2023.

Google Search Central, "Updates to Google's Services in Czechia in Light of the Czech Transposition of the European Copyright Directive," December 12, 2022, https://developers.google.com/search/blog/2022/12/google-services-in-czechia, accessed: 09.12.2024.

Goujard, C., "We're Fine as We Are, Press Tells EU as Brussels Plans Media Freedom Law," Politico, 2022, https://www.politico.eu/article/eu-law-to-protect-media-freedom-scares-off-press-publishers/, accessed: 03.03.2023.

Grupa Kapitałowa Agora S.A., *Sprawozdanie niezależnego biegłego rewidenta z badania roku obrotowego kończącego się 31 grudnia 2017r.* (2017).

Grupa Kapitałowa Agora S.A., *Sprawozdanie niezależnego biegłego rewidenta z badania roku obrotowego kończącego się 31 grudnia 2021r.* (2021).

Henriksson, T., "World Press Trends Preview: Publishers Brace for a Period Marked by Uncertainty," World Association of News Publishers, September 29, 2022, https://wan-ifra.org/2022/09/world-press-trends-preview-publishers-brace-for-a-period-marked-by-uncertainty/, accessed: 23.01.2023.

Höppner, T., Post on Linkedin, (2022), https://www.linkedin.com/posts/thomas-höppner-7ba59a70_related-rights-the-autorité-accepts-googles-activity-6944995588136435712-zfaV, accessed: 10.08.2023.

Izba Wydawców Prasy, "Rynek wydawców," https://www.iwp.pl/rynek-wydawcow/, accessed: 09.01.2023.

James Breiner: Entrepreneurial Journalism, "How AI and Data Boost Journalism Sustainability," https://jamesbreiner.com/how-ai-and-data-boost-journalism-sustainability/, accessed: 25.12.2024.

Kancelaria Prezesa Rady Ministrów, "Projekt ustawy o zmianie ustawy o prawie autorskim i prawach pokrewnych oraz niektórych innych ustaw," (2024), https://www.gov.pl/web/premier/projekt-ustawy-o-zmianie-ustawy-o-prawie-autorskim-i-prawach-pokrewnych-oraz-niektorych-innych-ustaw3, accessed:05.02.2024.

Kurdupski, M., "Sprzedaż "Faktu" spadła do 138 tys. egz. w 2022 roku. "Perspektywa rezygnacji z papieru nieunikniona", Wirtualne Media, February 07, 2023, https://www.wirtualnemedia.pl/artykul/wyniki-sprzedazy-dzienniki-2022-rok-koniec-pracy-gazeta-wyborcza-fakt-rzeczpospolita, accessed: 01.04.2023.

La Correspondance de la Presse, "Droits voisins : sur la base de l'accord conclu entre l'Agence France-Presse (AFP) et Google, le SNJ de l'AFP a signé un accord collectif relatif à la réversion de la "part appropriée et équitable" des journalistes de l'agence de presse," May 04, 2022, https://www.lacorrespondancedelapresse.fr/2022-05-04, accessed: 13.07.2023.

La Correspondance de la Presse, "Droits voisins / Belgique : Meta et Google conteste la loi belge qui selon eux porte atteinte à leur liberté de commerce et d'industrie; le législateur belge a "placé toute une industrie dans une insécurité juridique majeure,"" Europresse, March 13, 2023, https://www.lacorrespondancedelapresse.fr/2023-03-13, accessed: 08.01.2025.

La Croix, "Droits voisins : le réseau X attaqué en justice par plusieurs groupes de presse," November 12, 2024, https://www.la-croix.com/droits-voisins-le-figaro-le-monde-et-d-autres-journaux-trainent-x-au-tribunal-20241112, accessed: 08.12.2024.

Lazarova, A., "The Last in Line: Bulgaria Implements the CDSM Directive," *Kluwer Copyright Blog*, December 27, 2023, https://copyrightblog.kluweriplaw.com/2023/12/27/the-last-in-line-bulgaria-implements-the-cdsm-directive/, accessed: 20.12.2024.

Le Monde, "Les revenus du "Monde", des sources diversifiées," January 26, 2022, https://www.lemonde.fr/le-monde-et-vous/article/2021/01/26/les-revenus-du-monde-des-sources-diversifiees_6067680_6065879.html, accessed: 21.01.2023.

Le Monde, "Microsoft : une cinquantaine d'éditeurs de presse assignent le géant américain en justice concernant les droits voisins," November 08, 2024, https://www.lemonde.fr/economie/article/2024/11/08/droits-voisins-une-cinquantaine-d-editeurs-de-presse-assignent-en-justice-microsoft_6383770_3234.html, accessed: 08.12.2024.

Majid, A., "Publishers Square Up for New Battle with Google in Spain," Presse Gazette. Future of Media, (2023), https://pressgazette.co.uk/platforms/google-news-spain-facebook-challenge/, accessed: 12.08.2023.

Martin, N., "Did A Robot Write This? How AI Is Impacting Journalism," *Forbes*, February 8, 2019, https://www.forbes.com/sites/nicolemartin1/2019/02/08/did-a-robot-write-this-how-ai-is-impacting-journalism/?sh=f6ff72a77957, accessed: 22.05.2023.

Max-Planck-Institut für Immaterialgüter- und Wettbewerbsrecht, "Stellungnahme zum Gesetzesentwurf für eine Ergänzung des Urheberrechtsgesetzes durch ein Leistungsschutzrecht für Verleger, Max-Planck-Institut für Immaterialgüter- und Wettbewerbsrecht," https://www.ip.mpg.de/fileadmin/ipmpg/content/stellungnahmen/leistungsschutzrecht_fuer_verleger_01.pdf, accessed: 31.10.2022.

Ministère de la culture, "Commission droits d'auteur et droits voisins (CDADV)," December 05, 2024, https://www.culture.gouv.fr/Thematiques/Presse-ecrite/Commissions/Commission-droits-d-auteur-et-droits-voisins-CDADV, accessed: 03.01.2025.

Ministerstwo Kultury i Dziedzictwa Narodowego, "Czasopisma," https://www.gov.pl/web/kultura/czasopisma4, accessed: 21.01.2023.

Ministry of Industry and Trade of Czech Republic, *Report on the Improvements of the IPR Protection and Enforcement in the Czech Republic in 2022: 2023 Special 301 Review*, https://downloads.regulations.gov/USTR-2022-0016-0073/attachment_1.pdf, accessed: 09.12.2024.

Missoffe, S., "Google a signé plus de 150 contrats portant sur les droits voisins, tandis que l'Autorité de la Concurrence accepte ses engagements," *Google Blog France*, July 22, 2022, https://blog.google/intl/fr-fr/nouvelles-de-lentreprise/chez-google/google-a-signe-plus-de-150-contrats-portant-sur-les-droits-voisins-tandis-que-lautorite-de-la-concurrence-accepte-ses-engagements/, accessed: 08.08.2023.

Media Specs, ""Apig" : l'Alliance de la presse française contre les GAFA," September 20, 2018, https://www.mediaspecs.fr/apig-lalliance-de-la-presse-francaise-contre-les-gafa/, accessed: 18.07.2023.

Meta, "European News Publishers Build Big Business Through Meta Accelerators," October 03, 2022, https://www.facebook.com/formedia/blog/european-publishers-accelerator-program, accessed: 23.01.2023.

Meta, "Facebook Helps Local News Publishers Build Digital Subscriptions," February 27, 2018, https://www.facebook.com/formedia/blog/facebook-local-news-digital-subscriptions, accessed: 21.01.2023.

Nowe Media, "Embeding," February 13, 2019, https://www.nowemedia.org.pl/glossary/embedding/, accessed: 10.11.2022.

Ofcom, *Scrolling News: The Changing Face of Online News Consumption*, A Report for Ofcom, (2018), 20, https://www.ofcom.org.uk/__data/assets/pdf_file/0022/115915/Scrolling-News.pdf, accessed: 06.02.2023.

oko.press, "Minister Gliński i czasopisma. Dotacje tylko dla swoich. Dostała nawet kościelna gazetka dla dzieci," February 13, 2020, https://oko.press/minister-glinski-i-czasopisma-dotacje-tylko-dla-swoich, accessed: 21.01.2023.

Orlen, "Organy i struktura spółki," https://www.orlen.pl/pl/o-firmie/o-spolce/organy-i-struktura-spolki/struktura-akcjonariatu, accessed: 09.01.2022.

Poiares Maduro, M. F. de Abreu Duarte, "Regulating Big Tech Will Take Pluralism and Institutions," *Euronews*, October 7, 2021, https://www.euronews.com/2021/10/07/regulating-big-tech-will-take-pluralism-and-institutions-view, accessed: 06.01.2023.

Polityka, "Wprost już tylko online," March 31, 2020, https://www.polityka.pl/opolityce/1950926,1,wprost-juz-tylko-online.read, accessed: 18.01.2023.

Press, "Polskie media reagują na złośliwe działania Facebooka. "Meta gra ostro"," September 23, 2024, https://www.press.pl/tresc/83710,polskie-media-reaguja-na-zlosliwe-dzialania-facebooka_-_meta-gra-ostro_, accessed: 22.12.2024.

Press, "Projekt Media Freedom Act w obecnej postaci jest dla wydawców nie do przyjęcia," 2022, https://www.press.pl/tresc/74375,projekt-media-freedom-act-w-obecnej-postaci-jest-dla-wydawcow-nie-do-przyjecia, accessed: 03.03.2023.

Press Gazette, "Future of Media, Top 50 News Websites in the World: Half Grow Traffic Year on Year," December 19, 2024, https://pressgazette.co.uk/media-audience-and-business-data/media_metrics/most-popular-websites-news-world-monthly-2/, accessed: 26.12.2024.

Press Gazette, "Next Challenge for Publishers iIs Restoring Revenue Back tTo Print Levels," December 12, 2022, https://pressgazette.co.uk/publishing-services-content/next-challenge-for-publishers-is-restoring-revenue-back-to-print-levels/, accessed: 23.01.2023.

Priora, G., "News Aggregation and the Reform of EU Copyright Law," CEU Democracy Institute, Center for Media, Data and Society, (2018), https://cmds.ceu.edu/article/2018-07-03/news-aggregation-and-reform-eu-copyright-law, accessed: 31.01.2023.

Rashidian, N., et al., *Friend & Foe: The Platform Press at the Heart of Journalism*, (Tow Center for Digital Journalism A Tow/Knight Report, 2018).

Ray, S., "Twitter Sued For Allegedly Ignoring French Law That Requires It To Pay News Publishers," *Forbes*, August 03, 2023, https://www.forbes.com/sites/siladityaray/2023/08/03/twitter-gets-sued-for-allegedly-not-complying-with-french-law-that-requires-it-to-pay-news-publishers/?sh=28dcfc8f320c, accessed: 15.08.2023.

Renault, E., "Le groupe Figaro a terminé l'année 2017 sur de bons résultats," Le Figaro, February 15, 2018, https://www.lefigaro.fr/medias/2018/02/15/20004-20180215ARTFIG00017-le-groupe-figaro-a-termine-l-annee-2017-sur-de-bons-resultats.php, accessed: 12.01.2023.

Reda, F., "Last-Minute Attempt to Sneak "Snippet Tax" iInto Copyright Report," July 06, 2015, https://felixreda.eu/2015/07/last-minute-snippet-tax/, accessed: 10.11.2022.

Repropol, "Repropol uzyskał rozszerzenie zezwolenia i może reprezentować Wydawców w negocjacjach z Big Techami," November 23, 2024, https://repropol.pl/aktualnosci/repropol-na-podstawie-rozszerzonego-zezwolenia-na-prawa-pokrewne-wydanego-przez-ministerstwo-kultury-i-dziedzictwa-narodowego-moze-reprezentowac-wydawcow-w-negocjacjach-z-big-techami/, accessed: 08.01.2025.

Robles, S., "What is an RSS Feed: Beginners Guide on How RSS Feeds Work," *Riverside*, December 28, 2023, https://riverside.fm/blog/what-is-an-rss-feed, accessed: 31.01.2023.

Rouse, M., "Hyperlink," Technopedia, September 20, 2023, https://www.techopedia.com/definition/5175/hyperlink, accessed: 10.11.2022.

Savage, R., "Macron Swears Amid Furious Exchange With Cyclone-Hit Mayotte Islanders," *The Guardian*, December 20, 2024, https://www.theguardian.com/world/2024/dec/20/emmanuel-macron-swears-amid-furious-exchange-with-cyclone-hit-mayotte-islanders, accessed: 20.12.2024.

Schiffrin, A., "Platforms Push Back against Laws Like Australia's Media Bargaining Code," *CEPR*, July 20, 2022, https://cepr.org/platforms-push-back-against-laws-australias-media-bargaining-code, accessed: 26.07.2023.

Schuetze, B., "Bestwater: CJEU Embeds Decision on Framed Content in Order," *Kluwer Copyright Blog*, November 3, 2014, http://copyrightblog.kluweriplaw.com/2014/11/03/bestwater-cjeu-embeds-decision-on-framed-content-in-order/, accessed: 10.11.2022.

Shapiro, M., "The False Promise of Paywalls for Local News," *E&P*, Apirl 3, 2020, https://www.editorandpublisher.com/stories/shoptalk-the-false-promise-of-paywalls-for-local-news, 1303, accessed: 21.01.2023.

Sims, R., "Instruments and Objectives; Explaining the News Media Bargaining Code," Judith Neilson Institute for Journalism and Ideas, (2022), 3, https://jninstitute.org/wp

-content/uploads/2022/05/Rod-Sims_News-Bargaining-Code_2022.pdf, accessed: 26.07.2023.

SNJ, "Droits voisins dans le groupe Ebra : chronique d'un échec annoncé," July 08, 2022, https://www.snj.fr/droits-voisins-dans-le-groupe-ebra-chronique-dun-echec-annonce/1589, accessed: 03.01.2025.

SP, "How the Bundesliga is Using AI to Increase Brand Reach," March 03, 2020, https://www.sportspromedia.com/opinions/bundesliga-ai-dfl-deltatre/?zephr_sso_ott=exInKO, accessed: 22.05.2023.

SudOuest, "Bataille entre Google et la presse française : qu'est-ce que "le droit voisin" et quels sont les enjeux ?," SudOuest, October 5, 2020, https://www.sudouest.fr/international/europe/bataille-entre-google-et-la-presse-francaise-qu-est-ce-que-le-droit-voisin-et-quels-sont-les-enjeux-1716961.php, accessed: 07.02.2023.

Susarla, A., "Generative AI Could Leave Users Holding the Bag for Copyright Violations," *The Conversation*, March 22, 2024, https://theconversation.com/generative-ai-could-leave-users-holding-the-bag-forcopyright-violations-225760, accessed: 03.01.2025.

The Cairncross Review, *A Sustainable Future for Journalism*, (2019), 28, https://assets.publishing.service.gov.uk/media/5c6bfcd4e5274a72b933311d/021919_DCMS_Cairncross_Review_.pdf, accessed: 30.12.2024.

The Economic Times, "Google Agrees to Pay Italian Publishers for News," March 25, 2021, https://economictimes.indiatimes.com/tech/technology/google-agrees-to-pay-italian-publishers-for-news/articleshow/81683034.cms?utm_source=contentofinterest&utm_medium=text&utm_campaign=cppst, accessed: 07.01.2025.

UOKiK, "Meta – postępowanie wyjaśniające," October 22, 2024, https://uokik.gov.pl/meta-postepowanie-wyjasniajace, accessed: 22.12.2024.

UPP, "Accord entre Google et la presse magazine sur les droits voisins," April 21, 2022, https://www.upp.photo/fr/news/accord-entre-google-et-la-presse-magazine-sur-les-droits-voisins-3022, accessed: 08.12.2024.

Wang, O., "Droit voisin des éditeurs de presse et concurrence : quelles perspectives après l'affaire *Google* ?," Dalloz, September 27, 2022, https://www.dalloz-actualite.fr/node/droit-voisin-des-editeurs-de-presse-et-concurrence-quelles-perspectives-apres-l-affaire-google, accessed: 05.08.2023.

Walker, K., "An Update on Canada's Bill C-18 and Our Search and News Products, Google Canada Blog," November 29, 2023, https://blog.google/intl/en-ca/company-news/outreach-initiatives/an-update-on-canadas-bill-c-18-and-our-search-and-news-products/, accessed: 26.07.2023.

Washington Post, "The Washington Post to Debut AI-Powered Audio Updates for 2020 Election Results," October 13, 2020, https://www.washingtonpost.com/pr/2020/10/13/washington-post-debut-ai-powered-audio-updates-2020-election-results/, accessed: 22.05.2023.

Williams, O., "Google News Spain to be Shut Down: What Does It Mean?," *The Guardian*, December 12, 2014, https://www.theguardian.com/media-network/2014/dec/12/google-news-spain-tax-withdraws, accessed: 01.11.2022.

WirtualneMedia.pl, "64 projekty wspierające czasopisma kulturalne otrzymają dotację MKiDN," February 12, 2021, https://www.wirtualnemedia.pl/artykul/64-projekty-wspierajace-czasopisma-kulturalne-otrzymaja-dotacje-mkidn, accessed: 21.01.2023.

Wirtualnemedia.pl, "Subskrypcje "Gazety Radomszczańskiej": 90 proc. czytelników odnawia abonament," January 21, 2022, https://www.wirtualnemedia.pl/artykul/subskrypcje-gazety-radomszczanskiej-przekroczyly-polowe-papierowego-nakladu-90-procent-czytelnikow-odnawia-abonament, accessed: 24.01.2023.

Wirtualne Media, "Sztuczna inteligencja napisała artykuł w "Gazecie Wyborczej". "Nikt się nie zorientował, tekst był słaby"," April 18, 2023, https://www.wirtualnemedia.pl/artykul/sztuczna-inteligencja-tekst-gazeta-wyborcza-boleslaw-breczko, accessed: 22.05.2023.

World Association of News Publishers, "World Press Trends Preview: Publishers Brace for a Period Marked by Uncertainty," September 29, 2022, https://wan-ifra.org/2022/09/world-press-trends-preview-publishers-brace-for-a-period-marked-by-uncertainty/, accessed: 20.01.2023.

Zdzieborska, M., "Rząd milczy w sprawie dotacji dla prasy lokalnej," Press, June 24, 2022, https://www.press.pl/tresc/71406,rzad-milczy-w-sprawie-dotacji-dla-prasy-lokalnej, accessed: 11.01.2023.

Index

MIX
Papier | Fördert gute Waldnutzung
FSC® C083411

Kolibri 360 GmbH
Ferdinand-Jühlke-Straße 7
99095 Erfurt, Deutschland
produktsicherheit@kolibri360.de